Dedicated to the wonderful women in my life:
Deb and Kate.

-Robert Greenberger

Thanks to the following DC Comics writers and artists for their contributions to this book:

Dan Adkins, Marlo Alquiza, Murphy Anderson, Ross Andru, Jim Aparo, Shawn Atkinson, Michael Bair, Jon L. Blummer, Brian Bolland, John Byrne, Robert Campanella, Bernard Chang, Vince Colletta, Paris Cullins, Mike Deodato, Jr., Rachel Dodson, Terry Dodson, Mike Esposito, Gary Frank, Jose Luis García-López, Frank Giacoia, Dick Giordano, Wade von Grawbadger, Irwin Hasen, Don Heck, Everett E. Hibbard, Adam Hughes, Phil Jimenez, Drew Johnson, J. G. Jones, Gil Kane, Robert Kanigher, Andy Kubert, Andy Lanning, Jim Lee, Livesay, Aaron Lopresti, Aaron McClellan, William Messner-Loebs, Ted McKeever, Lee Moder, Chris Moeller, William Moulton Marston, Bob McLeod, Jesús Merino, Frank Miller, Rags Morales, Michael Nasser, Irv Novick, Bob Oksner, Denny O'Neil, Carlos Pacheco, Yanick Paquette, Ande Parks, Bruce Patterson, Gabriel Pearce, George Pérez, Harry G. Peter, Sean Phillips, Howard Porter, Greg Potter, Jesus Raiz, Cliff Richards, Eduardo Risso, Alex Ross, Greg Rucka, Matt Ryan, Salgood Sam, Mike Sekowsky, Jon Sibal, Ray Snyder, Curt Swan, Romeo Tanghal, Michael Turner, Matt Wagner, Scott Williams, Phil Winslade, and Pete Woods

Special thanks to Matthew Manning for additional historical material

The author thanks John Wells for his research assistance

First published in the United States of America in 2010
by Universe Publishing
A Division of Rizzoli International Publications, Inc.
300 Park Avenue South
New York, NY 10010
www.rizzoliusa.com

2010 2011 2012 2013 2014 / 10 9 8 7 6 5 4 3 2 1

ISBN-13: 978-0-7893-2035-3

Library of Congress Control Number: 2009938118

Printed in China

WONDER WOMAN

AMAZON ★ HERO ★ ICON

BY ROBERT GREENBERGER
FOREWORD BY GEORGE PÉREZ

WONDER WOMAN CREATED BY WILLIAM MOULTON MARSTON

ART DIRECTION & DESIGN BY CHRIS MCDONNELL

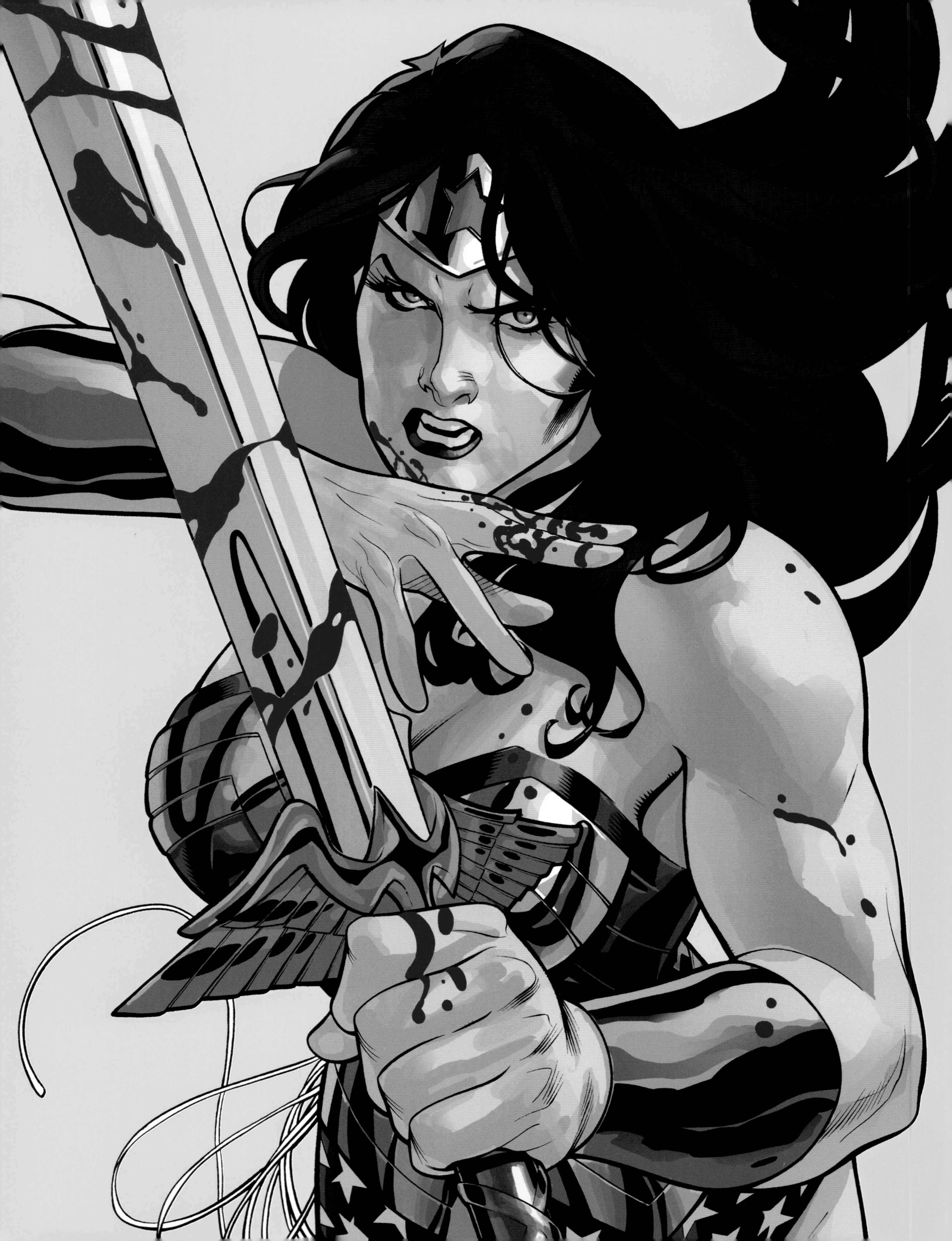

★ CONTENTS ★

FOREWORD - 6

THE CREATOR - 12

THE AMAZONS - 26

THE CONTEST - 56

THE OLYMPIANS - 68

TOOLS OF THE TRADE - 82

COMING TO MAN'S WORLD - 96

THE OPPONENTS - 110

THE LOVERS - 132

FRIENDS AND ALLIES - 146

THE MOD - 168

THE DIPLOMAT - 182

THE OTHER REALITIES - 194

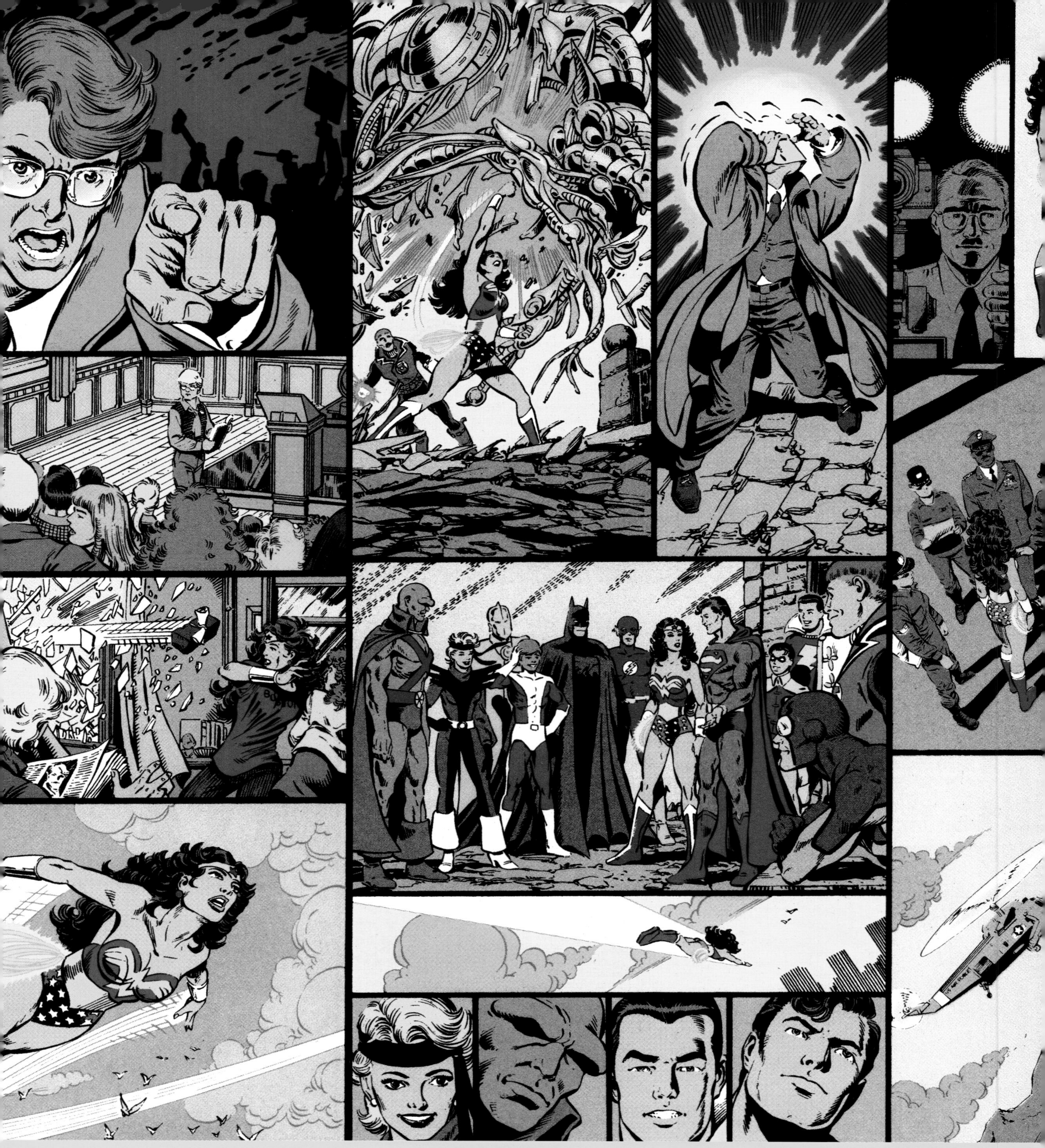

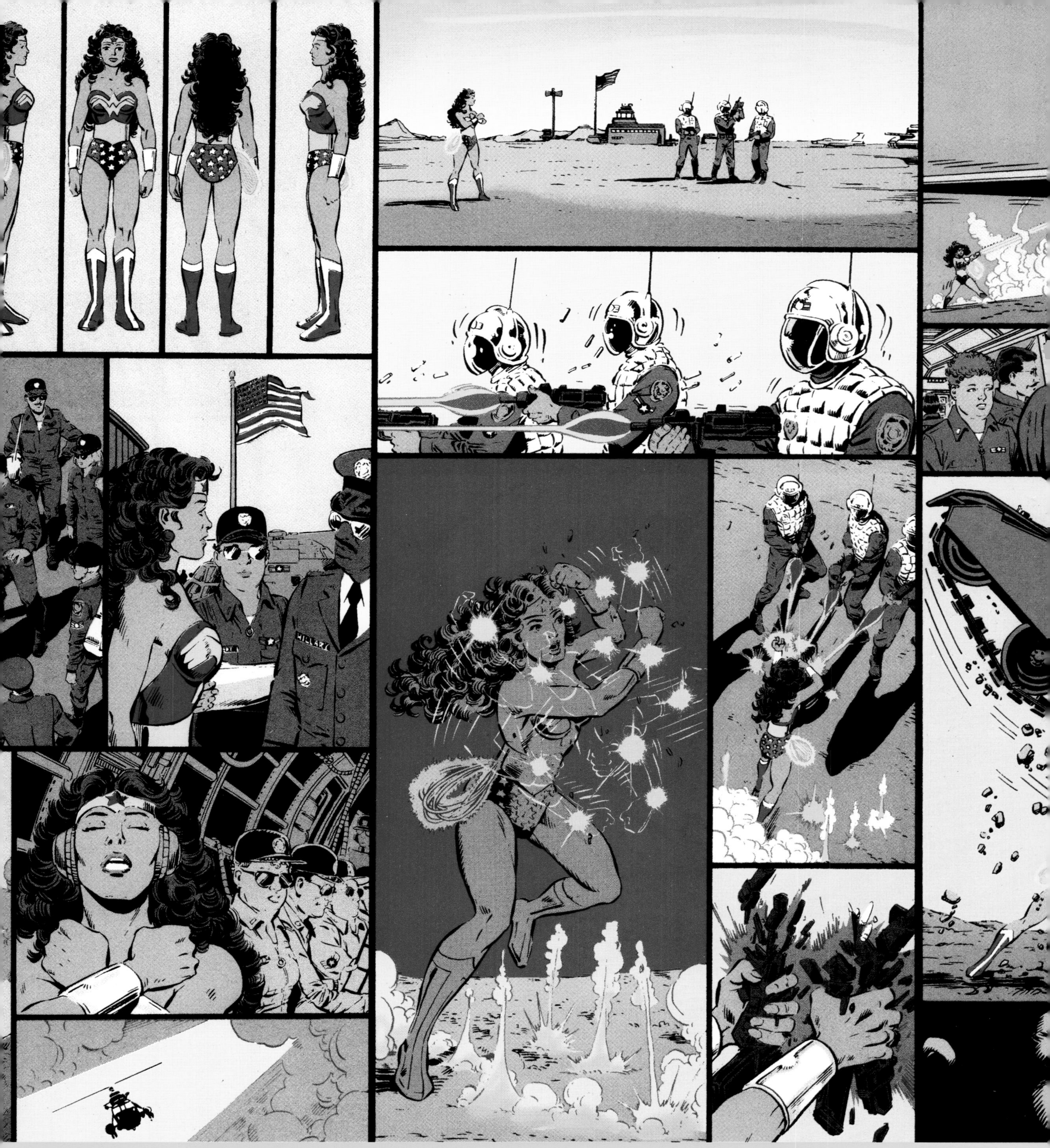
HILLARY

★ Foreword

BY GEORGE PÉREZ

ANNUAL
1
1988
U.S. $1.50
WONDER WOMAN
by GEORGE PÉREZ · ART ADAMS · ROSS ANDRU · BRIAN BOLLAND
JOHN BOLTON · JOSÉ LUÍS GARCÍA-LÓPEZ · CURT SWAN
EXTRA FEATURE!
"PRIVATE LIVES"

6
75¢
JULY 87
WONDER WOMAN
PEREZ • WEIN
PATTERSON
THE Ares ONSLAUGHT!
WHO watches the WATCHMEN?

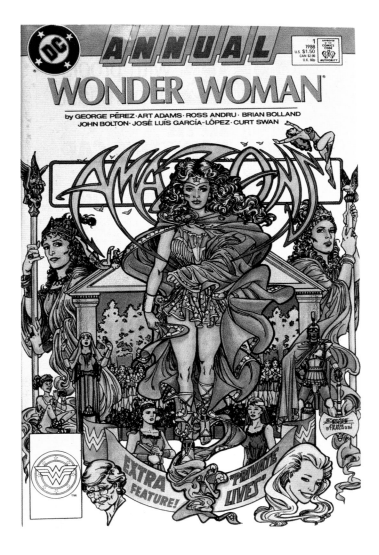

She was born of clay in an island paradise. To her queen mother she was, quite literally, a godsend. Among the Amazons of Themyscira she would be known as Princess Diana.

But to the world beyond, she would be known as Wonder Woman.

When William Moulton Marston—working under the pen name Charles Moulton—and artist H. G. Peter first introduced Wonder Woman in the pages of *Sensation Comics* in 1941, he could hardly have foretold that a book like the one you're holding right now would ever exist. Could he have even imagined that his unique creation, the first comic book super heroine—a star-spangled amalgam of fantasy, American patriotism, ancient myth, science fiction, and even a not-so-subtle hint of kinkiness—would still be around today, let alone command such attention, affection and, dare I say, reverence?

Yeah, I said reverence. In the decades since I first worked as the chronicler of the Amazon Princess' adventures, I've discovered how fervently loyal her fans are, how inspirational the character has been to their lives. This, of course, might come as a bit of a surprise to those who don't read comic books. To those outsiders Wonder Woman is probably perceived as little more than a female version of Superman. However, to the true Wonder Woman fan, she has always been so much more. With as long and varied a history as Diana has, it's no wonder (no pun intended) that she has become so many things to so many people.

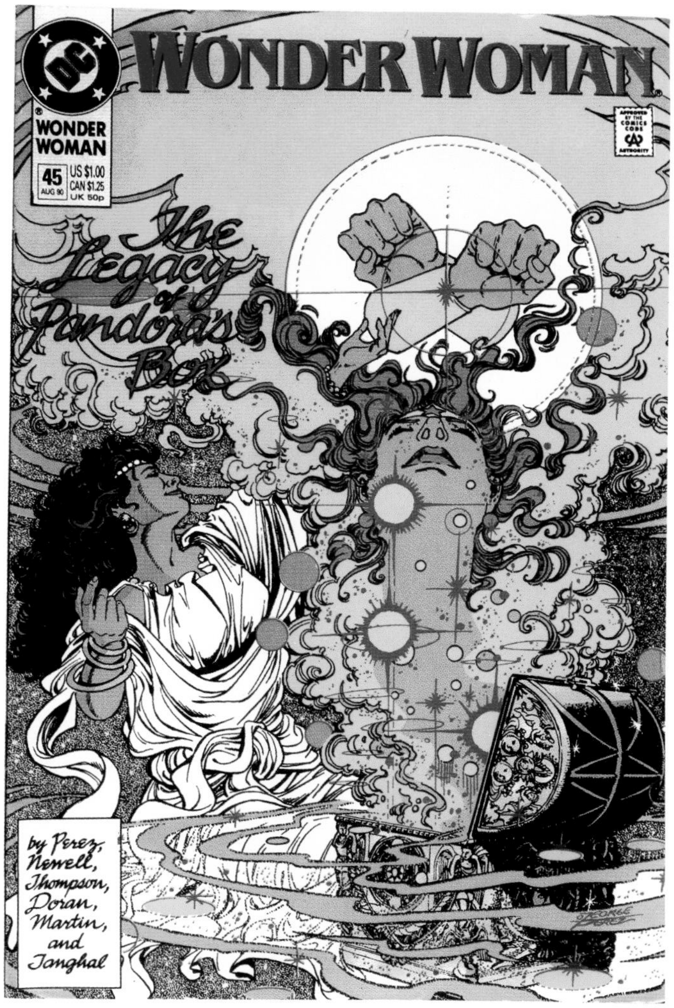
WONDER WOMAN
WONDER WOMAN
45
AUG 90
US $1.00
CAN $1.25
UK 50p
The Legacy of Pandora's Box
by Perez, Newell, Thompson, Doran, Martin, and Tanghal

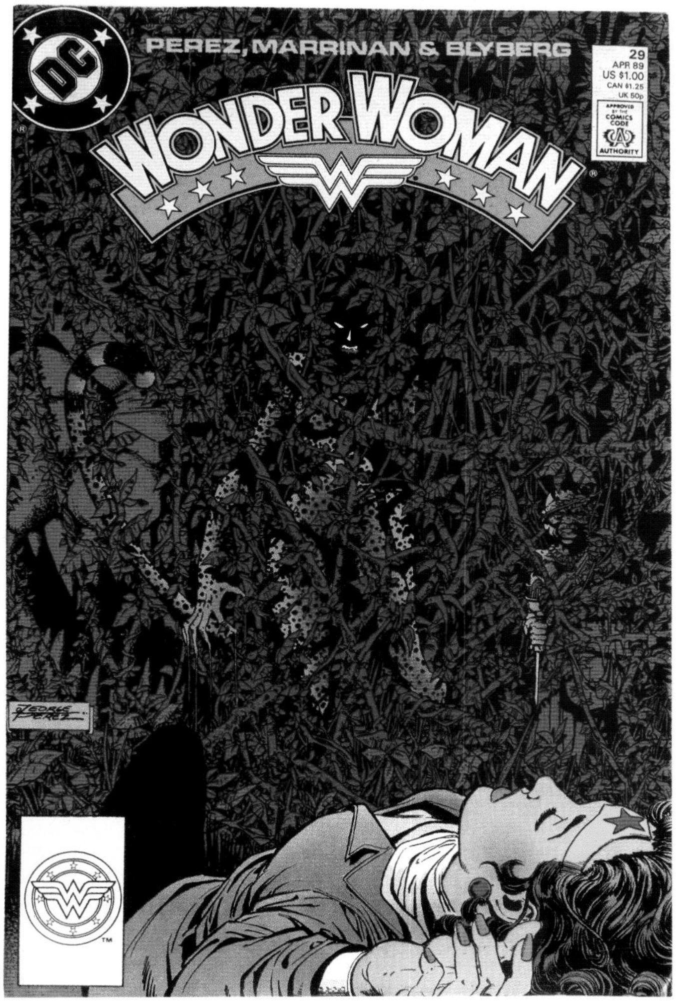
PEREZ, MARRINAN & BLYBERG
29
APR 89
US $1.00
CAN $1.25
UK 50p
WONDER WOMAN

Peter's stylized drawings suited Moulton's unique storytelling visions well. Their combined creative efforts produced all the elements that would forever define Diana's world: the Amazons, Steve Trevor, Etta Candy, the Robot Plane, the magic lasso, bullets and bracelets, her secret identity as Diana Prince (along with Clark Kent–style glasses). She fought some pretty colorful and often bizarre villains; she even fought the Nazis, reflecting the times in which her earliest adventures occurred. This was the Golden Age of Wonder Woman, the version fondly embraced by those old enough to have read them firsthand or historians who discovered these adventures years later.

After the departure of Marston and Peter, Wonder Woman continued under the guidance of writer Robert Kanigher and artist Ross Andru. Signature elements of Diana's world were redefined and new elements were added. In time, this version, later referred to as the Silver Age Wonder Woman, became the definitive Wonder Woman for a whole generation. This was their Wonder Woman—and mine.

Other landmark periods followed, with many new creators coming in and putting their own unique and diverse spins on the character, including stripping Wonder Woman of her powers and converting her into an Emma Peel–like adventuress. Yet despite the extreme nature of this change, the character was still essentially Wonder Woman, with the same history, even if that history was not used as a storytelling device. I myself loved these stories, quite a bit. This was my Wonder Woman, too—although I really did miss that earlier star-spangled costume.

In the 1970s, a version of Wonder Woman appeared that truly brought the character to life as no other interpretation ever had. For many it would be their first exposure to the Amazon Princess. When the beautiful Lynda Carter first appeared on television in 1975 wearing that iconic costume, she turned Wonder Woman into a household name. Most of the character's defining elements were there, from Paradise Island to

the Robot Plane, and from the Amazons to Steve Trevor. The series even introduced a new bit, the "Wonder Woman spin," during which Diana Prince transformed into Wonder Woman. To a new generation of fans—yes, including me again—this was their Wonder Woman: loving, loyal, powerful, courageous, and inspiring.

In the comics, Wonder Woman would regain her costume and undergo many more revisions and redirections until, in 1987, I was given the opportunity to do what no other comics creator had ever been allowed to do with Wonder Woman. I was allowed to start from scratch, unfettered by any of the often-conflicting continuities in the Princess's long printed history. I eliminated what I thought didn't work and reworked some of the more iconic touchstones, which, if I excised, would dilute some of the elements that made the character definable. I also gave her a new purpose. She would be an ambassador of peace, sworn to bring enlightenment and inspiration to Man's World. I am grateful that this version was quite successful and it would be regarded, this time literally, as my Wonder Woman—and, for yet another generation of fans, their Wonder Woman.

However, Wonder Woman's mythos runs deep. Eventually, long after I had left the series, many of the past story and character elements that I removed would be reinstated and reinterpreted. History and legacy continue to intermingle as each new generation lays claim to its own Wonder Woman. Wonder Woman's challenges have become more intense, both physically and spiritually, in ways William Marston likely never dreamed of. And through it all, she survives—and thrives.

To her fans, Wonder Woman has become more than a character. She is the sum of many parts.

She is an Amazon, a superheroine, an ambassador, a spy, and a warrior.

An avatar of truth, champion of the gods, and an emissary of peace.

A loving daughter, trusted friend, steadfast protector, and formidable foe.

She is Diana, Princess of Themyscira.

Wonder Woman.

Icon.

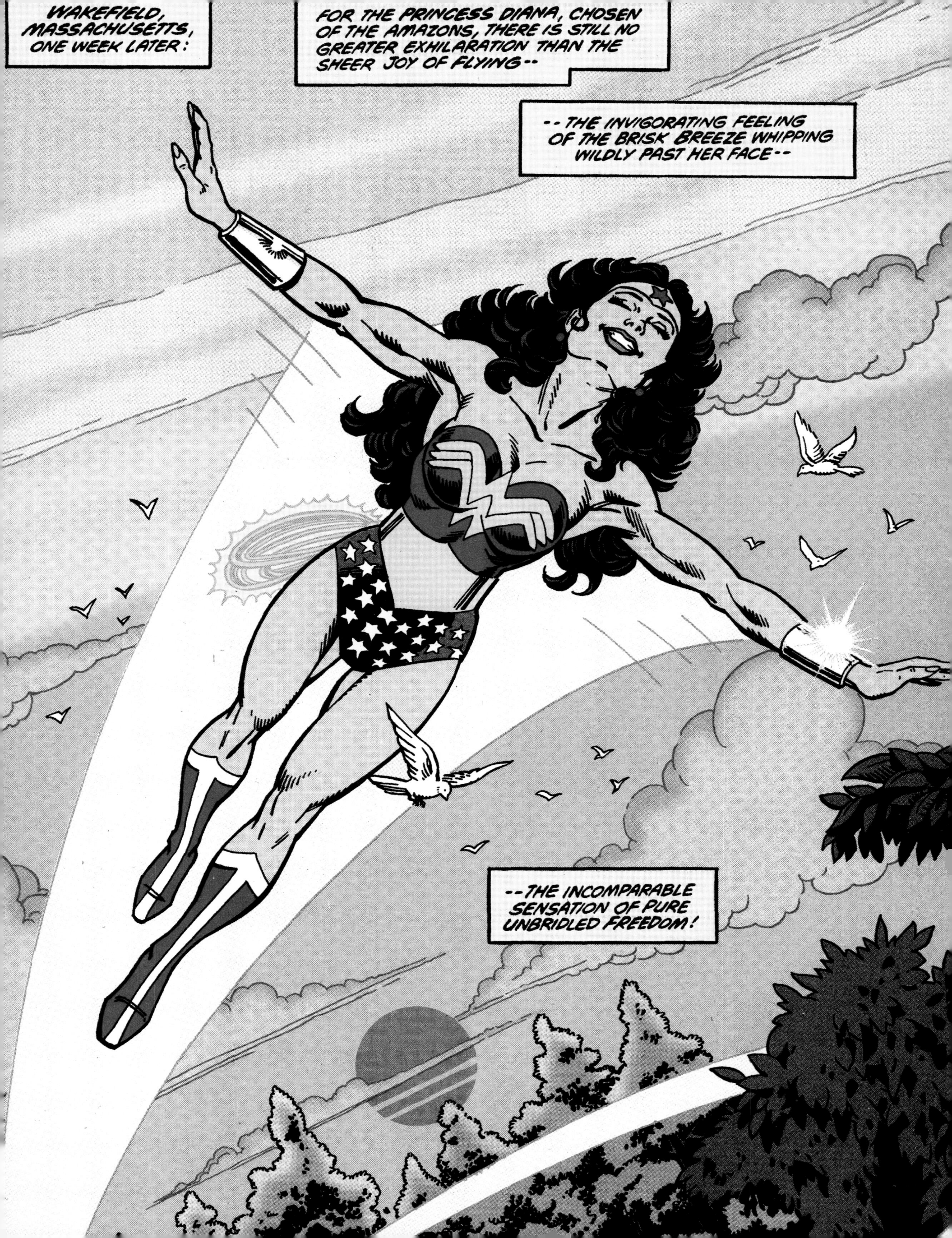
WAKEFIELD, MASSACHUSETTS, ONE WEEK LATER:
FOR THE PRINCESS DIANA, CHOSEN OF THE AMAZONS, THERE IS STILL NO GREATER EXHILARATION THAN THE SHEER JOY OF FLYING--
--THE INVIGORATING FEELING OF THE BRISK BREEZE WHIPPING WILDLY PAST HER FACE--
--THE INCOMPARABLE SENSATION OF PURE UNBRIDLED FREEDOM!

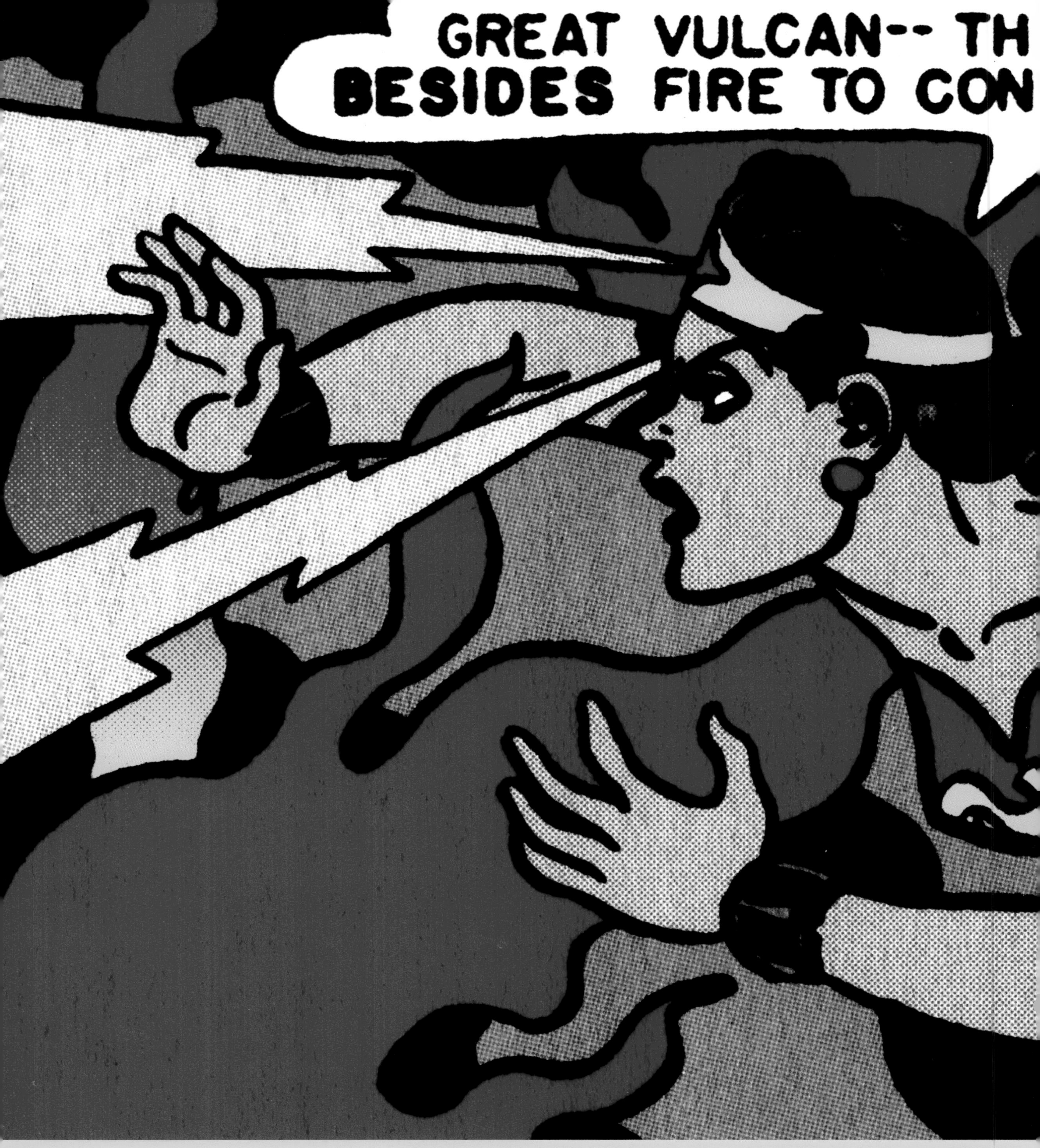
GREAT VULCAN-- TH
BESIDES FIRE TO CON

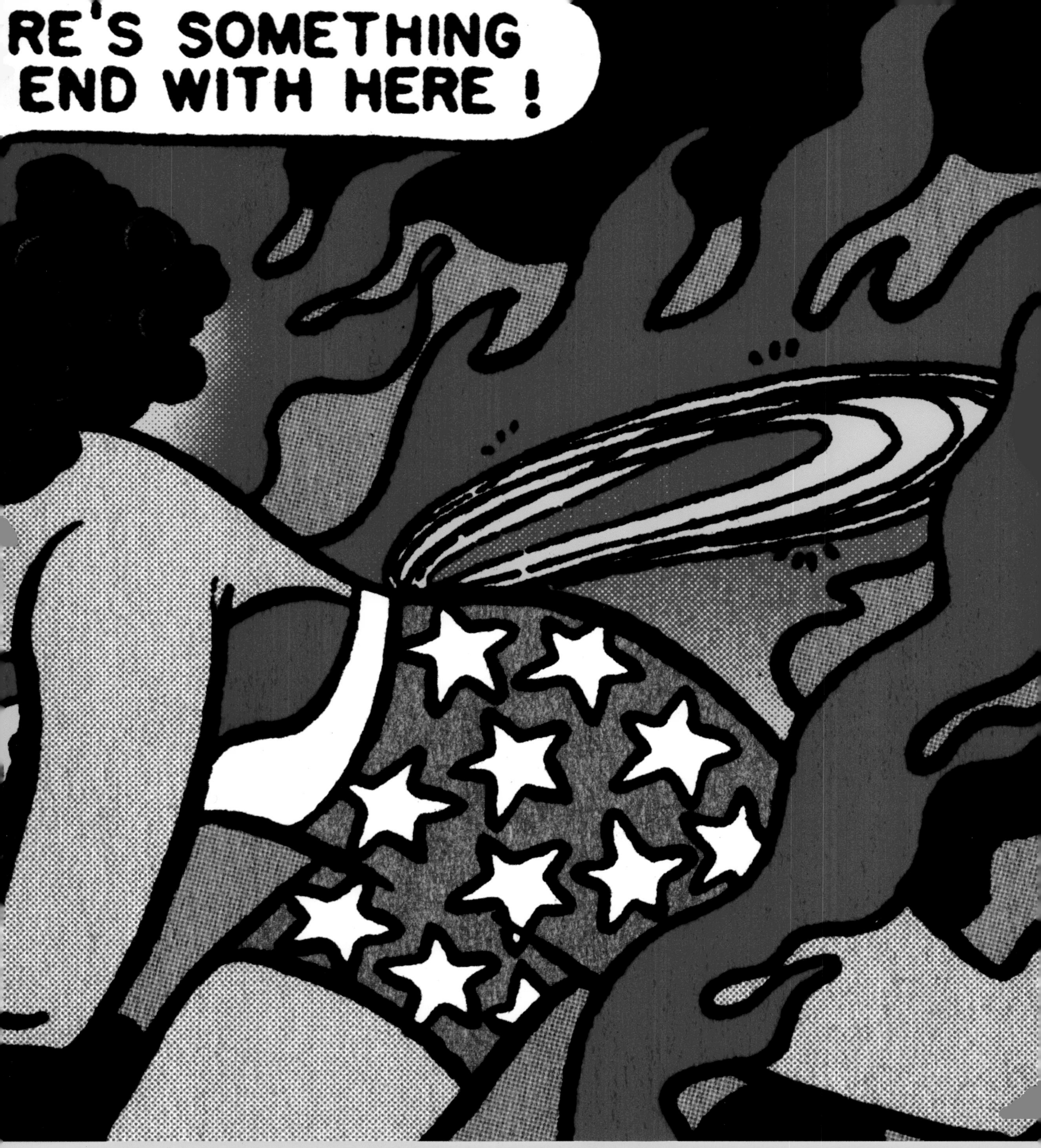
RE'S SOMETHING
END WITH HERE !

★ The Creator

The Newest of the DC magazines
NO.1 JANUARY
SENSATION COMICS
A SUPERMAN DC PUBLICATION
10¢
Featuring
THE SENSATIONAL
NEW ADVENTURE
STRIP CHARACTER-
Wonder Woman!

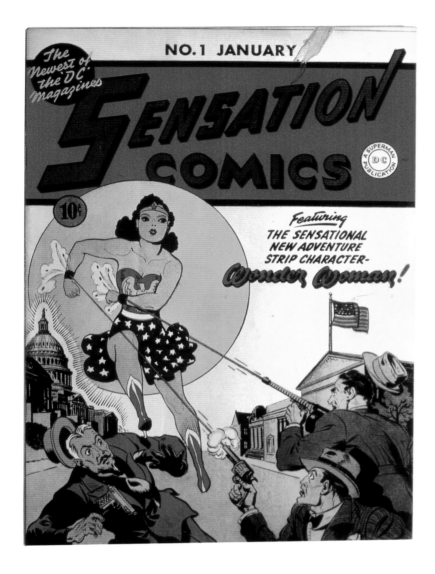

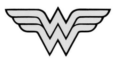

Left: Two weeks after her first appearance in comics, she headlined All American Comics' newest title. Other features included Wildcat, Mr. Terrific, the Gay Ghost, Little Boy Blue, and the Black Pirate. Wonder Woman remained the cover feature until issue #106 when it became clear super heroes were no longer as popular as they used to be. Recast as a mystery title, *Sensation Comics* stopped publishing in 1953 with issue #116.

Right: A family portrait from 1947. Standing left to right: Byrne Marston, Moulton (Pete) Marston, Olive Byrne Richard. Seated left to right: Marjorie Wilkes, Olive Ann Marston, William Moulton Marston, Donn Marston, Elizabeth Holloway Marston.

Below right: In the late 1940s, Wonder Woman was given an active role as a member of the Justice Society of America.

She was unconventional from the start. Emerging from the conservative world of 1940s America, Wonder Woman was the lone female figure against a backdrop of male-dominated comic books. But she wouldn't be content to play the role of girlfriend or supporting character as her four-color female predecessors had done. She was destined for a lead role, and more than that—the role of a hero. An unorthodox idea in an era of homemakers and housewives, Wonder Woman was a trailblazer years before her time. So it was only fitting that the man who created her would live a life just as unique as the amazing Amazon herself.

William Moulton Marston was born in Massachusetts in 1893. Described as flamboyant by his peers and family, Marston was a natural showman with an interest in psychology and the dynamics between men and women. He attended college at Harvard University and graduated in 1915, achieving his law degree in 1918, although he hardly practiced that particular profession. Instead, after a brief service in the Army's psychological division, where he was promoted to second lieutenant, he achieved his Ph.D. in 1921, and continued his investigation into the realm of human behavior. Chief among his interests was the concept of the detection of deception.

As early as 1915, Marston had begun to study the key traits that emerged when a human being was untruthful. In a paper published in *The Journal of Experimental Psychology* in 1917, he concluded that a subject's blood pressure level would rise when he or she was telling a lie. His subsequent experiments and research into this phenomenon led to his claim of creating the first prototype of the original lie detector test. Still used by the police

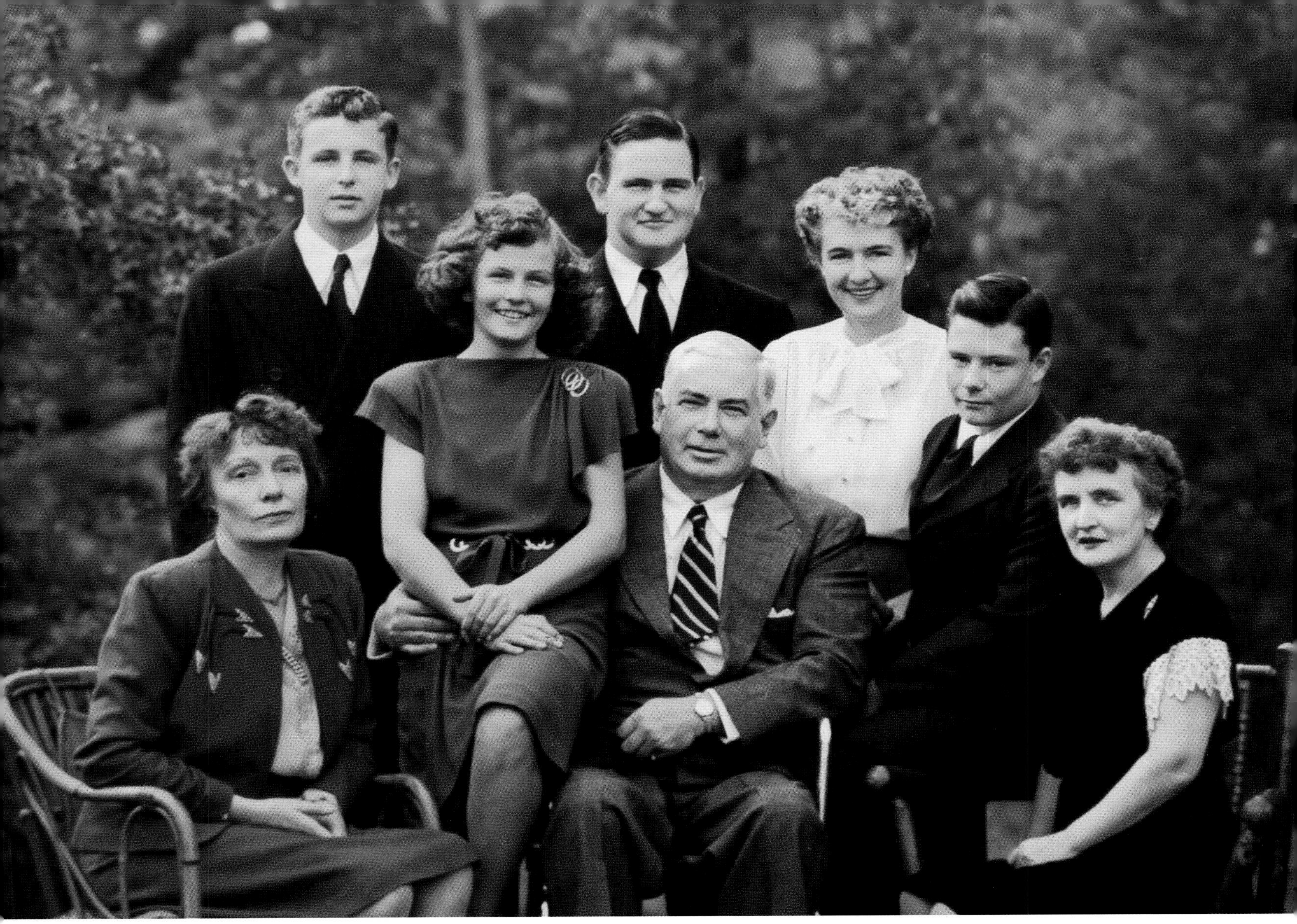

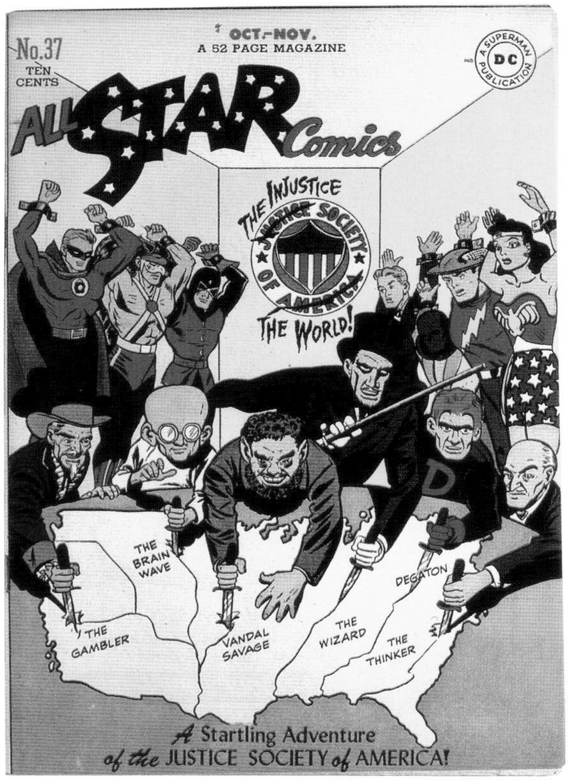
OCT.-NOV.
A 52 PAGE MAGAZINE
No.37
TEN CENTS
A SUPERMAN PUBLICATION
DC
ALL STAR Comics
THE INJUSTICE
JUSTICE SOCIETY
OF AMERICA
THE WORLD!
THE BRAIN WAVE
DEGATON
THE GAMBLER
VANDAL SAVAGE
THE WIZARD
THE THINKER
A Startling Adventure
of the JUSTICE SOCIETY of AMERICA!

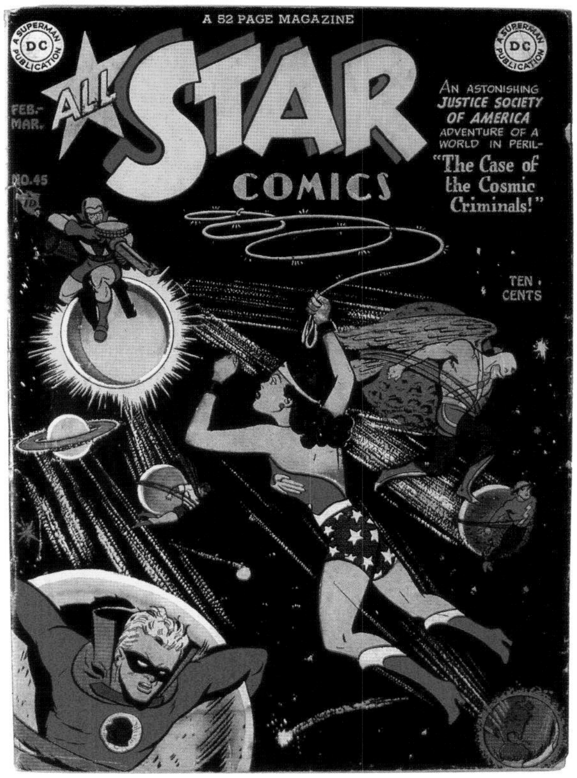
A 52 PAGE MAGAZINE
A SUPERMAN PUBLICATION
DC
ALL STAR
COMICS
FEB.-MAR.
NO.45
AN ASTONISHING JUSTICE SOCIETY OF AMERICA ADVENTURE OF A WORLD IN PERIL–
"The Case of the Cosmic Criminals!"
TEN CENTS

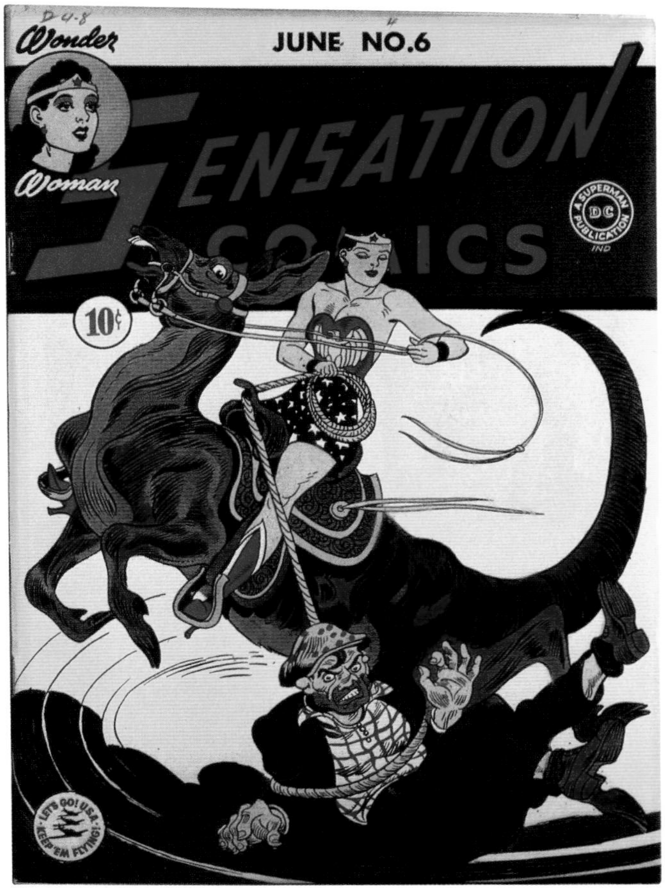
Wonder Woman
JUNE NO.6
SENSATION COMICS
A SUPERMAN DC PUBLICATION
10¢
LET'S GO! U.S.A. KEEP 'EM FLYING!

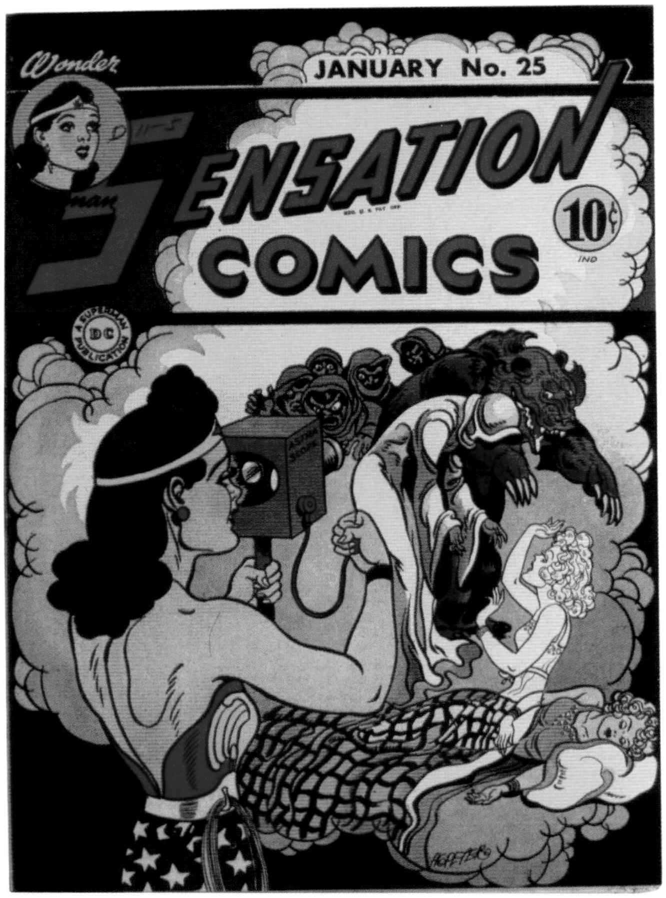
Wonder Woman
JANUARY No. 25
SENSATION COMICS
10¢
A SUPERMAN DC PUBLICATION

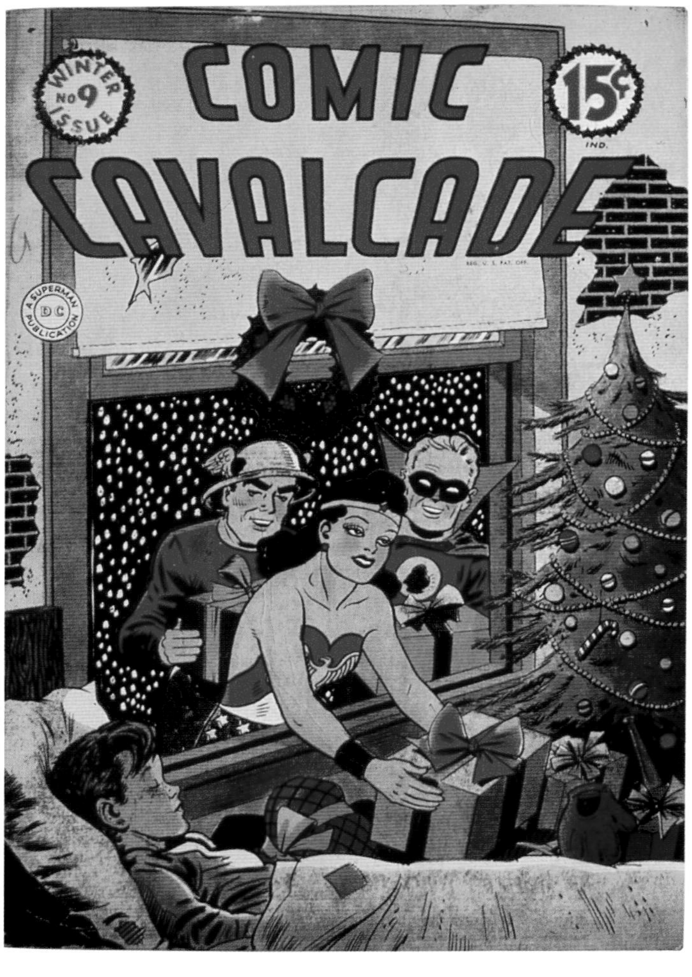
WINTER No 9 ISSUE
COMIC CAVALCADE
15¢
A SUPERMAN DC PUBLICATION

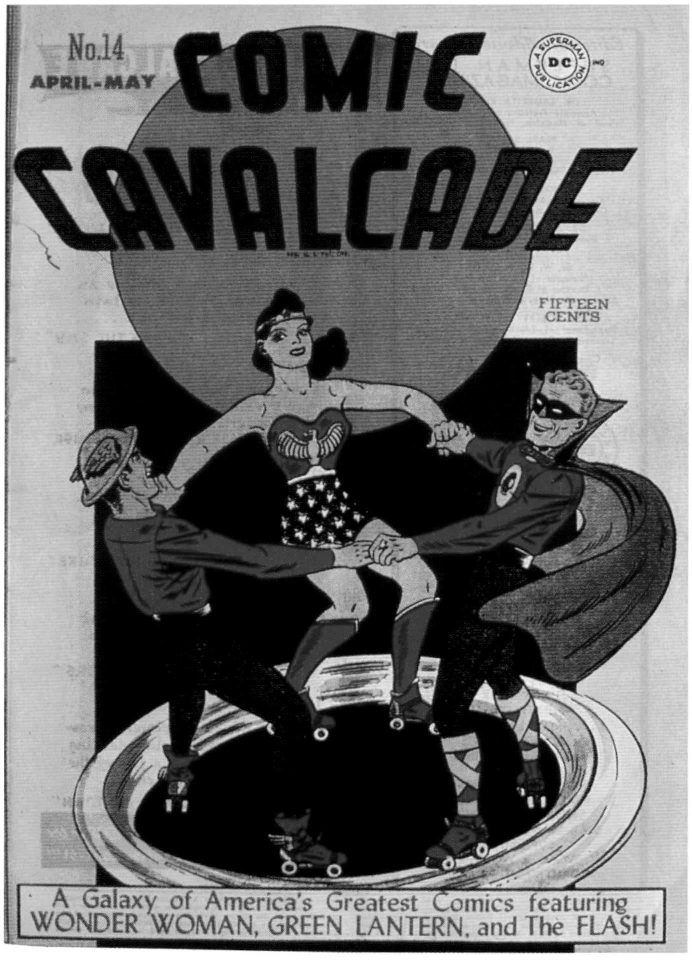
No.14
APRIL-MAY
COMIC CAVALCADE
A SUPERMAN DC PUBLICATION
FIFTEEN CENTS
A Galaxy of America's Greatest Comics featuring
WONDER WOMAN, GREEN LANTERN, and The FLASH!

Above: All American's Associate Editor Alice Marble reviews what appears to be a production dummy of *Wonder Woman* #1 (Summer 1942). The promotional photo appeared in *Sensation Comics* #9 (September 1942).

Top left: Harry G. Peter designed visually interesting covers that also displayed Wonder Woman's variety of stories, making her adventures unique among super heroes. Peter's evolution as a heroic artist took time, but it was evident that even in his sixties he employed new visual techniques.

Bottom left: In late 1942, All American Comics launched *Comics Cavalcade*, an oversized quarterly that featured new stories with the company's top stars: Wonder Woman, The Flash, and Green Lantern. Each cover featured the trio having fun as seen in these two by Flash artist Everett E. Hibbard.

force to this day, the lie detector captured the interest of many Americans of the time, and Marston's popularity grew as a result. He became the device's greatest advocate, and despite courts deeming its output unreliable and inadmissible as evidence, Marston continued to campaign for his invention for years. He used it in a publicity stunt to determine the differences between blondes, brunettes, and redheads for the *New York Times* in 1928, and attempted to display its potential usages for romantic disputes in an article for *Look Magazine* in 1938. That same year, he would even go so far as to use his machine to hawk razor blades in a Gillette advertisement in the pages of *Life Magazine*.

Although lie detection brought him limited fame, it wasn't Marston's greatest fascination. Throughout his psychology career, he was intrigued by the idea of dominance in the relationship between the sexes. He had the unconventional notion that women should govern over men, and that only by submitting to loving domination could men truly be happy. Marston stated, "Woman's body contains twice as many love-generating organs and endocrine mechanisms as the male. What woman lacks is the dominance or self-assertive power to put over and enforce her love desires."

Perhaps it was this unusual approach to personal relationships that led to fewer employment opportunities for Marston in the mid-1930s. Despite his various stints at fame, and a brief stint gauging audience reaction as a consultant to Universal Pictures, Marston had relied on teaching as his main source of income. Over the years he'd taught at Columbia, New York University, Radcliffe, Tufts, and the University of Southern California, but lacking tenure at any of these positions, he found that in the difficult economy of the time, his job options were few and far between. And although he was an avid writer with many self-help and academic tomes under his belt and a torrid pseudo-historical novel about the personal life of Julius Caesar entitled *Venus With Us*, Marston and his family were struggling. They even lived with his parents for a time due to economic restrictions.

In 1915, Marston had married Elizabeth Holloway, a graduate of Mount Holyoke. A well-educated woman who achieved a law and masters degree, Elizabeth was a forward thinker, with feminist views uncommon for her era. She and Marston had two children, Moulton "Pete" and Olive Ann, but that wasn't the extent of the Marston family. Besides having another daughter, Fredericka, who died at birth, William Marston sired two more children, Donn and Byrne Marston. It was his relationship with their mother, Olive Byrne, which defied the conventions of the time.

William Moulton Marston had met Olive Byrne in the late 1920s, when Olive was a student at Tufts University. The two became friends, and, with the blessing of Marston's wife Elizabeth, she moved in with the young couple. According to their children, Olive and Elizabeth got along quite well, a fact made apparent when Elizabeth named her daughter after her husband's mistress. In fact, years after Marston's death, the two women continued their living arrangement. "They really, really thought he was a great man, and they admired him," Byrne Marston said of his mother and Elizabeth. "It's kind of crazy, but it worked out, and they got along quite well. They were a pair from then on until their deaths."

But if Marston's avant-garde relationship with Olive Byrne cast a shadow on his academic career, that same relationship would also escort him into a brighter spotlight in the popular arena. Around the mid-1930s, Marston had once again reinvented himself. This time he became a consulting psychologist for a magazine entitled *The Family Circle*. Appearing in a series of articles, Marston was interviewed by Olive Richard, the penname of none other than Olive Byrne. Offering expert advice on a variety of subjects intended to appeal to a mostly adult female audience, Marston soon used this new forum as a spring-board into the world of what he considered a rich, untapped medium: the comic book.

In an issue of *The Family Circle* dated October 25, 1940, Olive Richard interviewed Dr. William Moulton Marston about the fledgling industry of comic books, and its effects on American children. Armed with a myriad of statistics and ready examples, Marston touted comics as being a healthy way for children to experience wish fulfillment fantasies and teach them the basics of good American citizenship. And while he condemned the gritty storytelling techniques of comic strips like "Dick Tracy," Marston went out of his way to praise the popular comic book character Superman, and the publisher, M. C. Gaines, whom Marston said possessed "the insight into fundamental emotional

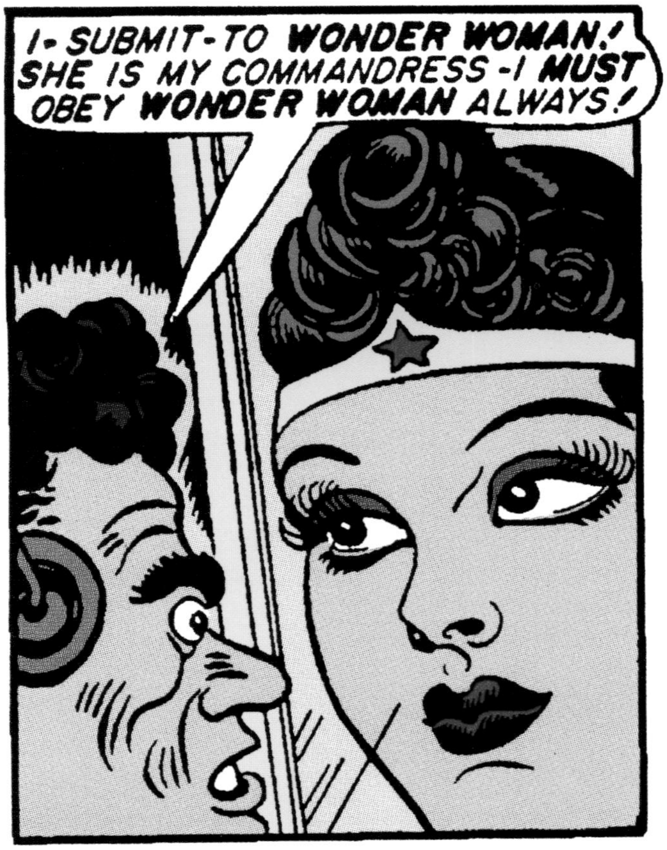
I- SUBMIT- TO WONDER WOMAN! SHE IS MY COMMANDRESS -I MUST OBEY WONDER WOMAN ALWAYS!

appeals which other publishers had lacked." Perhaps it was this bit of blatant flattery, or merely Marston's display of comic book expertise that caught Gaines's eye, but either way, Marston soon found himself working in an advisory capacity at the company that would later be known as DC Comics.

It wasn't long before Marston used his new position to launch the adventures of a comic character of his own. In an attempt to spread "psychological propaganda for the new type of woman who should, I believe, rule the world," Marston decided to create a strong female lead, perhaps basing her attributes on the two women closest to him in his life. His heroine would have dark hair and wear thick metal bands upon her wrists, traits familiar to Olive Byrne, who for years wore a pair of Indian bracelets. The setting for his new character would be the world of Greek mythology, a personal passion of Elizabeth Marston. And for a final touch, Marston's heroine would be armed with a magic lasso that forced anyone caught in its grasp to tell the truth: a nod to his other proud innovation, the lie detector. With the aid of artist Harry G. Peter, Marston soon delivered the first story of his creation, Suprema, the Wonder Woman, to the desk of his editor, Sheldon Mayer. After undergoing a slight name adjustment, Wonder Woman made her dramatic debut in the pages of December 1941's *All Star Comics* #8, a teaser meant to whet the appetites of its audience, and help launch the heroine's first cover appearance just one month later in *Sensation Comics* #1.

Just as he anticipated, Marston had created a cultural juggernaut, an unbridled success that would keep him occupied until his final days. Marston continued to script Wonder Woman stories until his death on May 2, 1947. Despite suffering from lung cancer and being treated with morphine, Marston wrote his final script for *Wonder Woman* #28, the week before he died, even going so far as to edit pencil artwork two days before his passing. With a life as unusual as anything he concocted on his typewriter, William Moulton Marston attempted to change the world and did just that, in the unlikeliest of ways. Through a simple four-color creation, Marston's unique outlook on the world continues to live on after him, his philosophies and theories on the human condition reaching a far greater audience than any academic textbook could ever hope to. What's more, he created an innovative icon that, for decades, has successfully inspired millions to follow in her heroic example.

Left: In this panel from *Wonder Woman* #8, Diana has once again convinced an evil-doer of women's superiority, a less than subtle message found in Marston's stories during his tenure from 1941 through his death in 1947.

Right: A feature about the gods of myth from *Wonder Woman* #3.

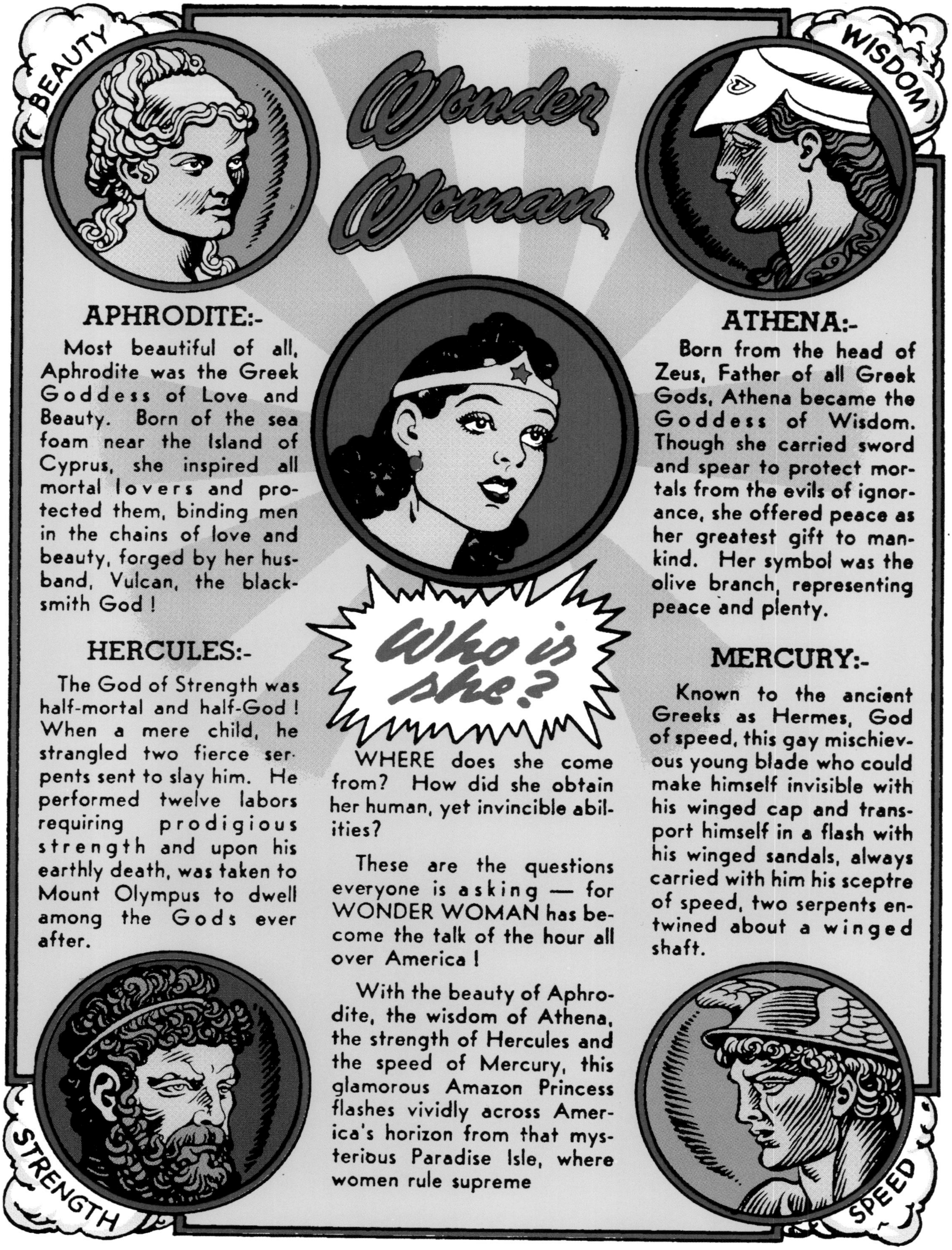
BEAUTY
WISDOM
Wonder Woman
APHRODITE:-
Most beautiful of all, Aphrodite was the Greek Goddess of Love and Beauty. Born of the sea foam near the Island of Cyprus, she inspired all mortal lovers and protected them, binding men in the chains of love and beauty, forged by her husband, Vulcan, the blacksmith God!
ATHENA:-
Born from the head of Zeus, Father of all Greek Gods, Athena became the Goddess of Wisdom. Though she carried sword and spear to protect mortals from the evils of ignorance, she offered peace as her greatest gift to mankind. Her symbol was the olive branch, representing peace and plenty.
Who is she?
HERCULES:-
The God of Strength was half-mortal and half-God! When a mere child, he strangled two fierce serpents sent to slay him. He performed twelve labors requiring prodigious strength and upon his earthly death, was taken to Mount Olympus to dwell among the Gods ever after.
WHERE does she come from? How did she obtain her human, yet invincible abilities?
These are the questions everyone is asking — for WONDER WOMAN has become the talk of the hour all over America!
With the beauty of Aphrodite, the wisdom of Athena, the strength of Hercules and the speed of Mercury, this glamorous Amazon Princess flashes vividly across America's horizon from that mysterious Paradise Isle, where women rule supreme
MERCURY:-
Known to the ancient Greeks as Hermes, God of speed, this gay mischievous young blade who could make himself invisible with his winged cap and transport himself in a flash with his winged sandals, always carried with him his sceptre of speed, two serpents entwined about a winged shaft.
STRENGTH
SPEED

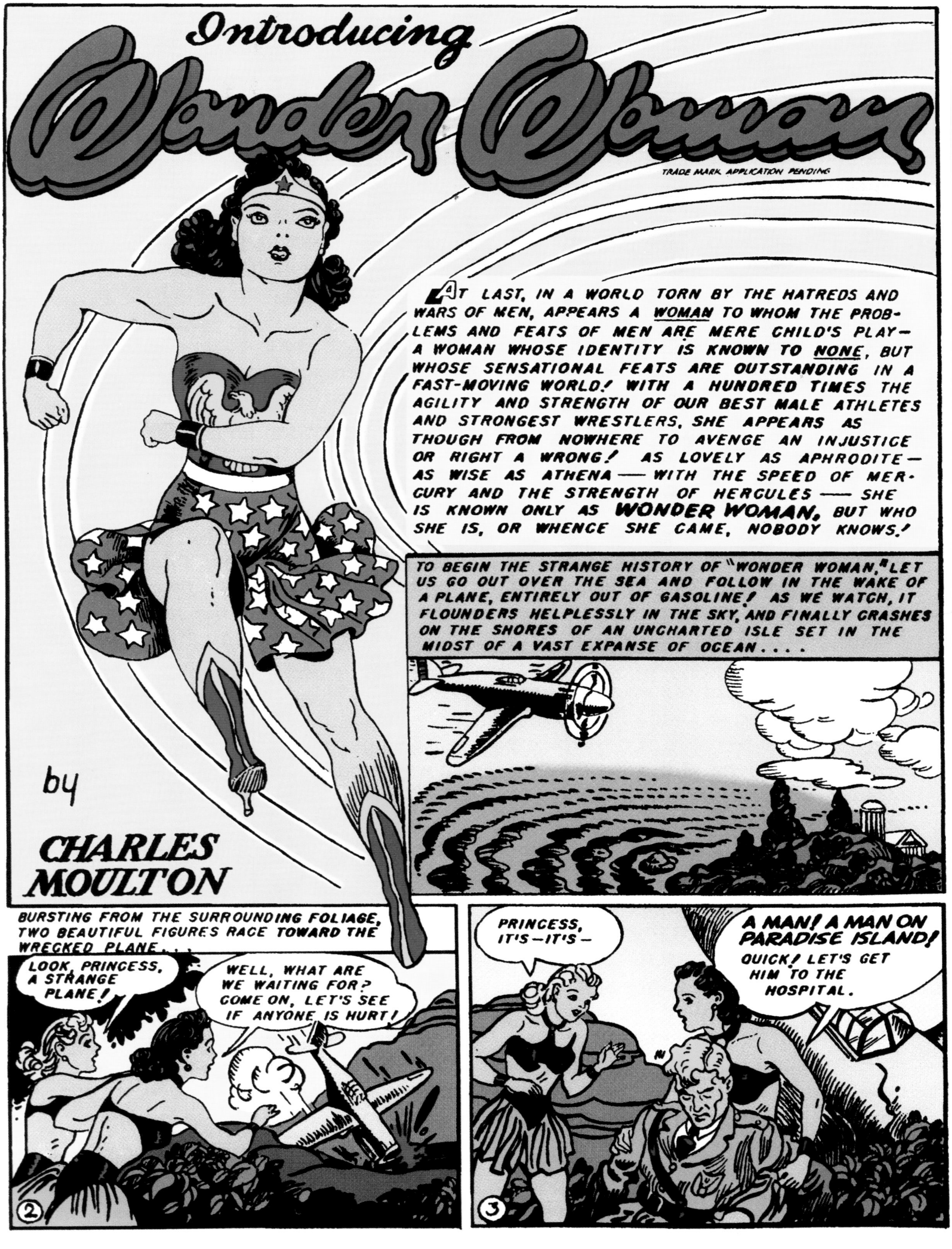

Introducing
Wonder Woman
TRADE MARK APPLICATION PENDING
AT LAST, IN A WORLD TORN BY THE HATREDS AND WARS OF MEN, APPEARS A WOMAN TO WHOM THE PROBLEMS AND FEATS OF MEN ARE MERE CHILD'S PLAY— A WOMAN WHOSE IDENTITY IS KNOWN TO NONE, BUT WHOSE SENSATIONAL FEATS ARE OUTSTANDING IN A FAST-MOVING WORLD! WITH A HUNDRED TIMES THE AGILITY AND STRENGTH OF OUR BEST MALE ATHLETES AND STRONGEST WRESTLERS, SHE APPEARS AS THOUGH FROM NOWHERE TO AVENGE AN INJUSTICE OR RIGHT A WRONG! AS LOVELY AS APHRODITE— AS WISE AS ATHENA — WITH THE SPEED OF MERCURY AND THE STRENGTH OF HERCULES — SHE IS KNOWN ONLY AS WONDER WOMAN, BUT WHO SHE IS, OR WHENCE SHE CAME, NOBODY KNOWS!
TO BEGIN THE STRANGE HISTORY OF "WONDER WOMAN," LET US GO OUT OVER THE SEA AND FOLLOW IN THE WAKE OF A PLANE, ENTIRELY OUT OF GASOLINE! AS WE WATCH, IT FLOUNDERS HELPLESSLY IN THE SKY, AND FINALLY CRASHES ON THE SHORES OF AN UNCHARTED ISLE SET IN THE MIDST OF A VAST EXPANSE OF OCEAN....
by
CHARLES MOULTON
BURSTING FROM THE SURROUNDING FOLIAGE, TWO BEAUTIFUL FIGURES RACE TOWARD THE WRECKED PLANE...
LOOK, PRINCESS, A STRANGE PLANE!
WELL, WHAT ARE WE WAITING FOR? COME ON, LET'S SEE IF ANYONE IS HURT!
2
PRINCESS, IT'S—IT'S—
A MAN! A MAN ON PARADISE ISLAND!
QUICK! LET'S GET HIM TO THE HOSPITAL.
3

CARRYING THE FULL GROWN MAN AS IF HE WERE A CHILD, THE YOUNG WOMAN STEPS THROUGH THE FOLIAGE AND ENTERS THE STREETS OF A CITY THAT FOR ALL THE WORLD SEEMS TO BE BORN OF ANCIENT GREECE!

A MAN!

HOW DID HE GET HERE?

SOMEONE TELL THE QUEEN THERE'S A **MAN** ON PARADISE ISLAND!

AT THE HOSPITAL —

IS HE ALL RIGHT? WILL HE LIVE?

I DON'T KNOW. HE'S HAD A CONCUSSION. WE WON'T KNOW ANYTHING FOR DAYS. I WONDER WHAT THE QUEEN WILL DO WITH HIM. HE CAN'T BE MOVED.

SUDDENLY, HIPPOLYTE, THE QUEEN, ENTERS THE HOSPITAL ROOM...

MOTHER!

THE QUEEN!

I HEARD THAT THERE WAS A MAN HERE, BUT I COULDN'T BELIEVE IT. WHO IS HE?

HIS PLANE CRASHED ON THE BEACH OF THE ISLAND THIS MORNING. THE PRINCESS AND MALA BROUGHT HIM HERE. I FOUND THESE PAPERS IN HIS POCKET.

" CAPT. STEVEN TREVOR, U.S. ARMY INTELLIGENCE SERVICE." HMM. WE CAN'T LET HIM DIE. SEE THAT HE GETS THE BEST OF ATTENTION. KEEP HIS EYES COVERED SO THAT, IF HE SHOULD AWAKE, HE WILL SEE NOTHING! HAVE HIS PLANE REPAIRED, FOR HE MUST LEAVE AS SOON AS HE IS WELL! KEEP ME INFORMED OF HIS PROGRESS!

IN THE ENSUING DAYS, THE PRINCESS, THE QUEEN'S ONLY DAUGHTER, IS CONSTANTLY AT THE BEDSIDE OF THE UNCONSCIOUS MAN, HELPING — WATCHING —

YOU OUGHT TO GET SOME SLEEP, PRINCESS. YOU HAVE BEEN ON THE JOB NOW FOR FOUR-TEEN HOURS.

NEVER MIND ME. WE - WE MUST MAKE HIM WELL.

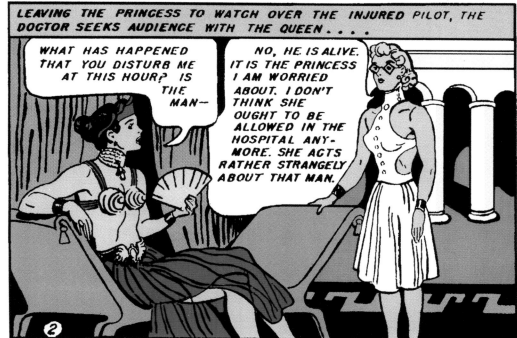

LEAVING THE PRINCESS TO WATCH OVER THE INJURED PILOT, THE DOCTOR SEEKS AUDIENCE WITH THE QUEEN....

WHAT HAS HAPPENED THAT YOU DISTURB ME AT THIS HOUR? IS THE MAN—

NO, HE IS ALIVE. IT IS THE PRINCESS I AM WORRIED ABOUT. I DON'T THINK SHE OUGHT TO BE ALLOWED IN THE HOSPITAL ANY-MORE. SHE ACTS RATHER STRANGELY ABOUT THAT MAN.

②

SO SHE IS IN LOVE! I WAS AFRAID OF THAT! YOU ARE QUITE RIGHT, DOCTOR. I SHALL TAKE STEPS IMMEDIATELY.

THAT WOULD BE WISE. IT'S FOR THE CHILD'S OWN GOOD.

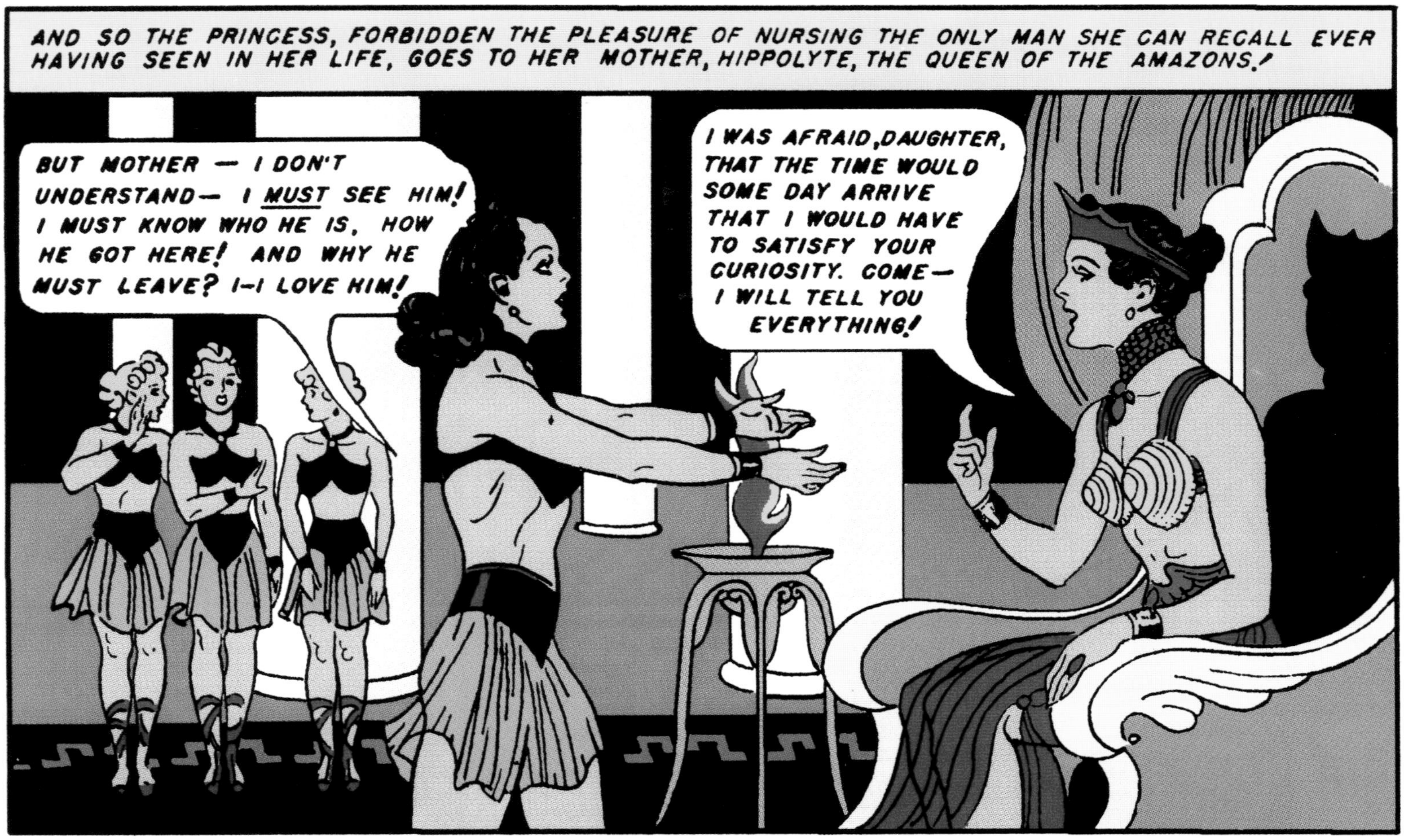
AND SO THE PRINCESS, FORBIDDEN THE PLEASURE OF NURSING THE ONLY MAN SHE CAN RECALL EVER HAVING SEEN IN HER LIFE, GOES TO HER MOTHER, HIPPOLYTE, THE QUEEN OF THE AMAZONS.!
BUT MOTHER — I DON'T UNDERSTAND— I MUST SEE HIM! I MUST KNOW WHO HE IS, HOW HE GOT HERE! AND WHY HE MUST LEAVE? I-I LOVE HIM!
I WAS AFRAID, DAUGHTER, THAT THE TIME WOULD SOME DAY ARRIVE THAT I WOULD HAVE TO SATISFY YOUR CURIOSITY. COME— I WILL TELL YOU EVERYTHING!

AND THIS IS THE STARTLING STORY UNFOLDED BY HIPPOLYTE, QUEEN OF THE AMAZONS, TO THE PRINCESS, HER DAUGHTER !

In the days of Ancient Greece, many centuries ago, we Amazons were the foremost nation in the world. In Amazonia, women ruled and all was well. Then one day, Hercules, the strongest man in the world, stung by taunts that he couldn't conquer the Amazon women, selected his strongest and fiercest warriors and landed on our shores. I challenged him to personal combat—because I knew that with my MAGIC GIRDLE, given me by Aphrodite, Goddess of Love, I could not lose.

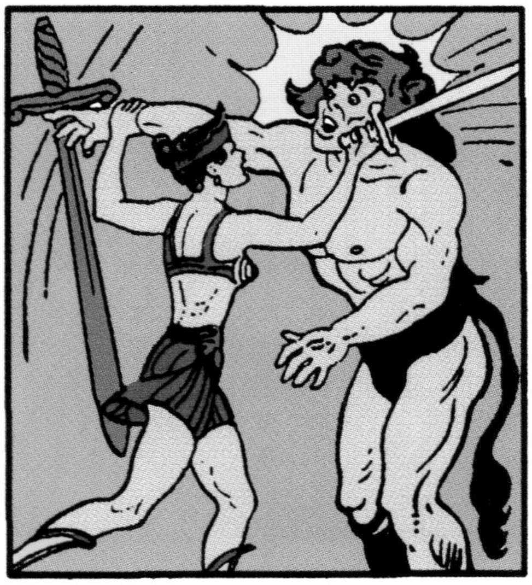

And win I did! But Hercules, by deceit and trickery, managed to secure my MAGIC GIRDLE—and soon we Amazons were taken into slavery. And Aphrodite, angry at me for having succumbed to the wiles of men, would do naught to help us!

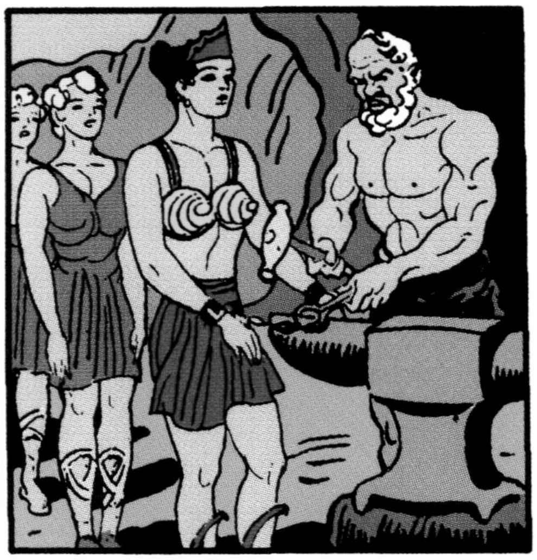

Finally our submission to men became unbearable—we could stand it no longer—and I appealed to the Goddess Aphrodite again. This time not in vain, for she relented and with her help, I secured the MAGIC GIRDLE from Hercules.

With the MAGIC GIRDLE in my possession, it didn't take us long to overcome our masters, the MEN—and taking from them their entire fleet, we set sail for another shore, for it was Aphrodite's condition that we leave the man-made world and establish a new world of our own! Aphrodite also decreed that we must always wear these bracelets fashioned by our captors, as a reminder that we must always keep aloof from men.

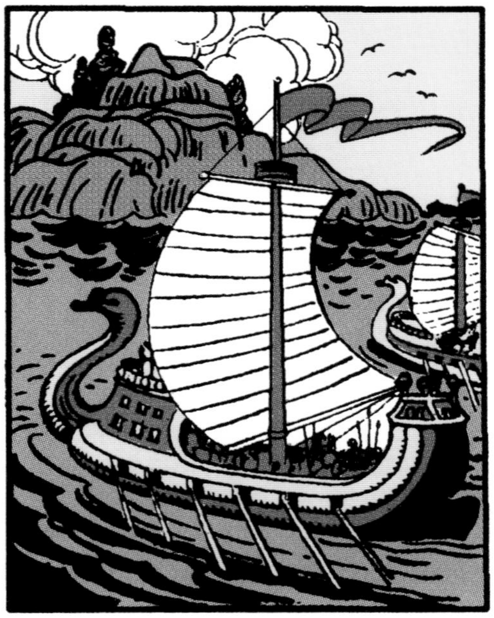

And so, after sailing the seas many days and many nights, we found Paradise Island and settled here to build a new World! With its fertile soil, its marvelous vegetation—its varied natural resources—here is no want, no illness, no hatreds, no wars, and as long as we remain on Paradise Island and I retain the MAGIC GIRDLE, we have the power of Eternal Life—so long as we do not permit ourselves to be again beguiled by men! We are indeed a race of Wonder Women!

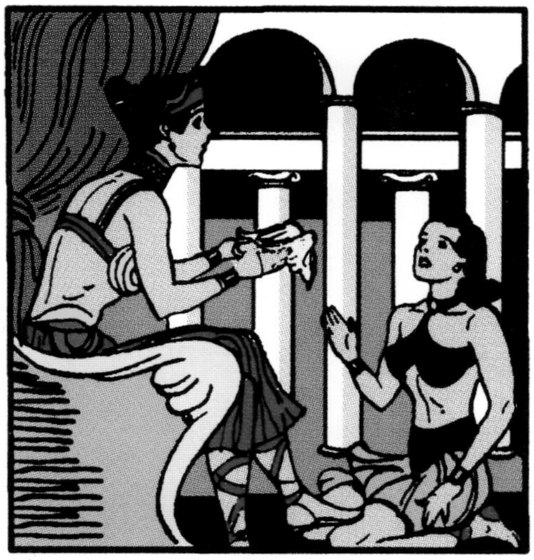

That was the promise of Aphrodite—and we must keep our promise to her if we are to remain here safe and in peace!

That is why this American must go and as soon as possible!

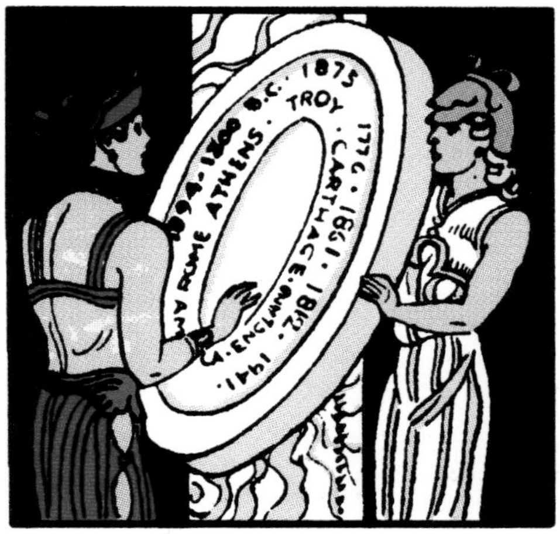

Come, let me show you the Magic Sphere you've heard me talk about. It was given to me by Athena, the Goddess of Wisdom, just after we conquered the Herculeans and set sail for Paradise Island! It is through this Magic Sphere that I have been able to know what has gone on and is going on in the other world, and even, at times, forecast the future!

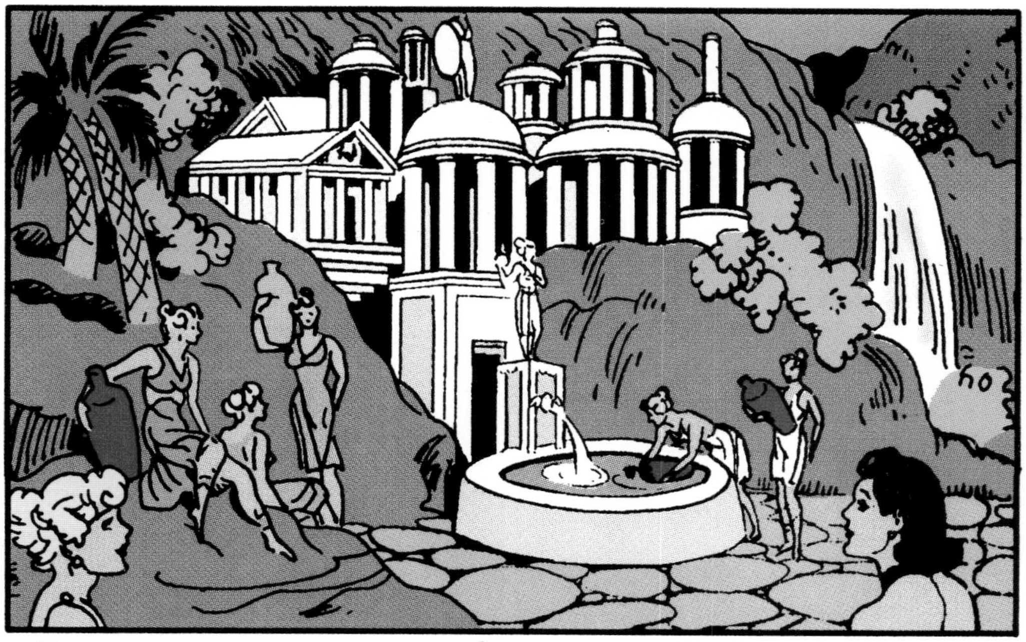

That is why we Amazons have been able to far surpass the inventions of the so-called man-made civilization! We are not only stronger and wiser than men—but our weapons are better—our flying machines are further advanced! And it is through the knowledge that I have gained from this Magic Sphere that I have taught you, my daughter, all the arts and sciences and languages of modern as well as ancient times!

But let us see where your American captain came from and how he got here. Watch closely—

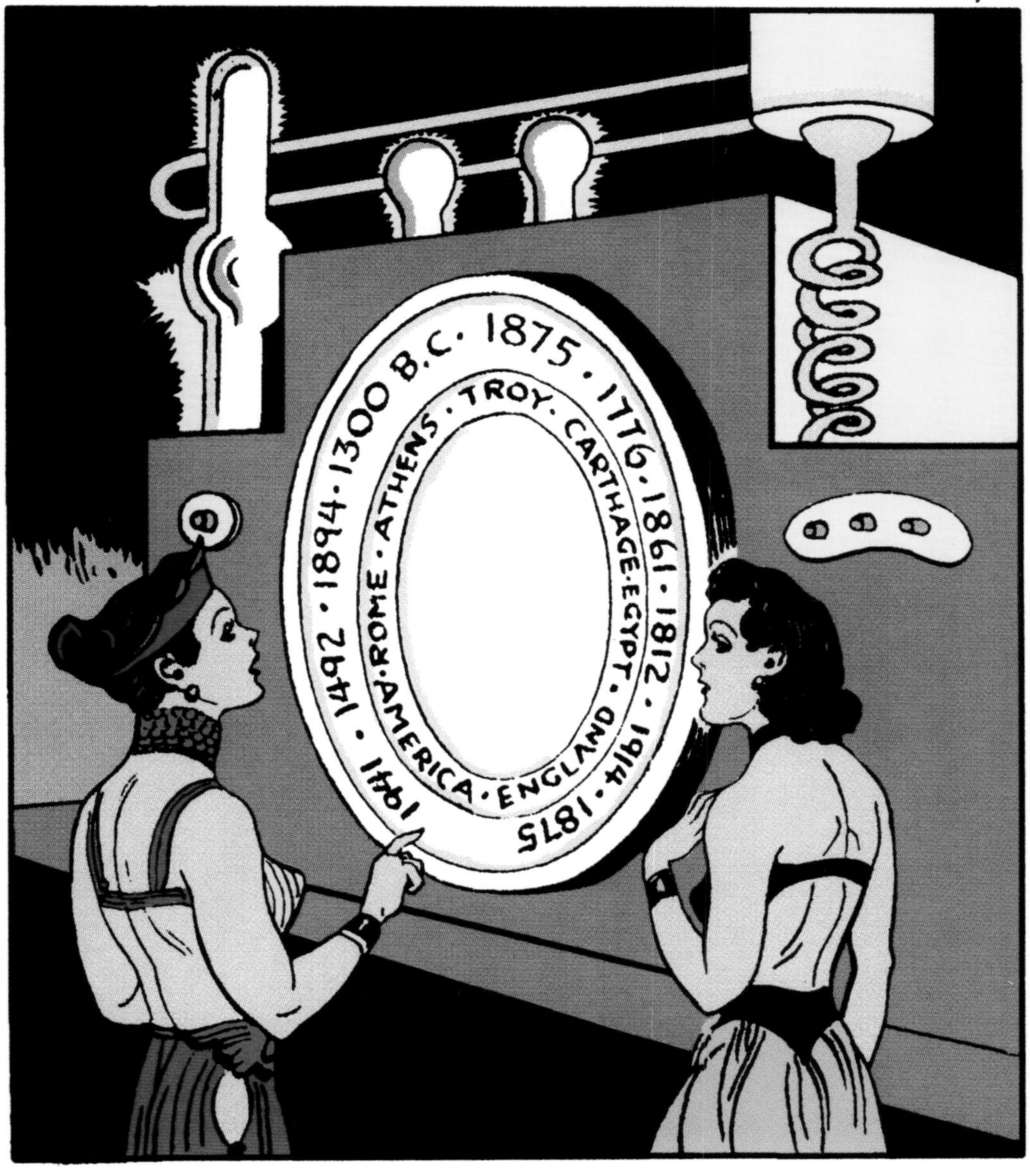
1941 · 1492 · 1894 · 1300 B.C. 1875 · 1776 · 1861 · 1812 · 1914 · 1875
ROME · ATHENS · TROY · CARTHAGE · EGYPT · ENGLAND · AMERICA

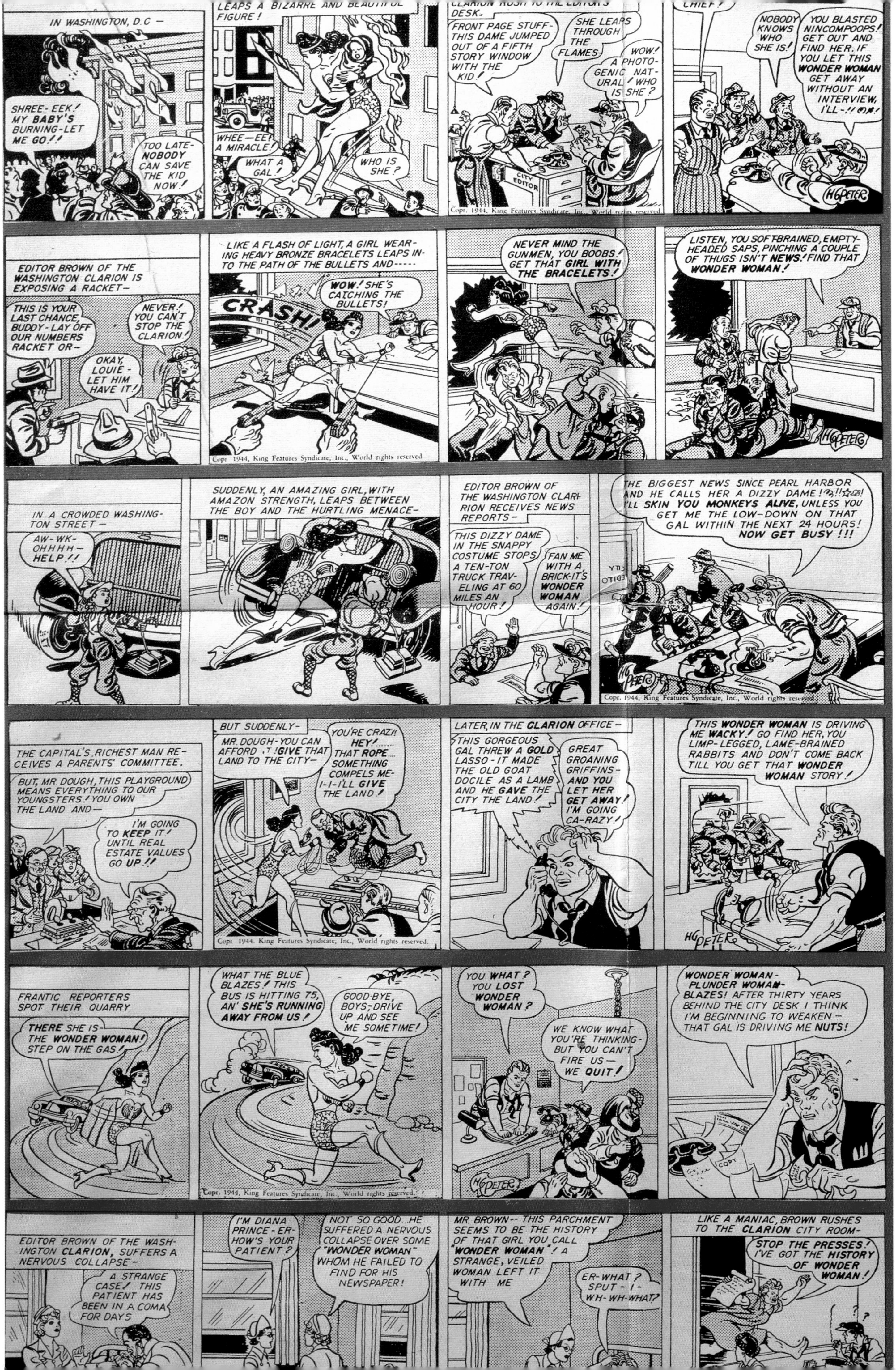
IN WASHINGTON, D.C —
SHREE-EEK! MY BABY'S BURNING-LET ME GO!!
TOO LATE-NOBODY CAN SAVE THE KID NOW!
LEAPS A BIZARRE AND BEAUTIFUL FIGURE!
WHEE—EE! A MIRACLE!
WHAT A GAL!
WHO IS SHE?
DESK.
FRONT PAGE STUFF-THIS DAME JUMPED OUT OF A FIFTH STORY WINDOW WITH THE KID!
SHE LEAPS THROUGH THE FLAMES
WOW! A PHOTO-GENIC NAT-URAL! WHO IS SHE?
CITY EDITOR
Copr. 1944, King Features Syndicate, Inc., World rights reserved
NOBODY KNOWS WHO SHE IS!
YOU BLASTED NINCOMPOOPS! GET OUT AND FIND HER. IF YOU LET THIS WONDER WOMAN GET AWAY WITHOUT AN INTERVIEW, I'LL-!!
HG PETER
EDITOR BROWN OF THE WASHINGTON CLARION IS EXPOSING A RACKET—
THIS IS YOUR LAST CHANCE, BUDDY-LAY OFF OUR NUMBERS RACKET OR—
NEVER! YOU CAN'T STOP THE CLARION!
OKAY, LOUIE-LET HIM HAVE IT!
LIKE A FLASH OF LIGHT, A GIRL WEARING HEAVY BRONZE BRACELETS LEAPS INTO THE PATH OF THE BULLETS AND-----
CRASH!
WOW! SHE'S CATCHING THE BULLETS!
Copr. 1944, King Features Syndicate, Inc., World rights reserved
NEVER MIND THE GUNMEN, YOU BOOBS! GET THAT GIRL WITH THE BRACELETS!
LISTEN, YOU SOFT-BRAINED, EMPTY-HEADED SAPS, PINCHING A COUPLE OF THUGS ISN'T NEWS! FIND THAT WONDER WOMAN!
HG PETER
IN A CROWDED WASHINGTON STREET—
AW-WK-OHHHH-HELP!!
SUDDENLY, AN AMAZING GIRL, WITH AMAZON STRENGTH, LEAPS BETWEEN THE BOY AND THE HURTLING MENACE—
EDITOR BROWN OF THE WASHINGTON CLARION RECEIVES NEWS REPORTS—
THIS DIZZY DAME IN THE SNAPPY COSTUME STOPS A TEN-TON TRUCK TRAVELING AT 60 MILES AN HOUR!
FAN ME WITH A BRICK-IT'S WONDER WOMAN AGAIN!
THE BIGGEST NEWS SINCE PEARL HARBOR AND HE CALLS HER A DIZZY DAME! I'LL SKIN YOU MONKEYS ALIVE, UNLESS YOU GET ME THE LOW-DOWN ON THAT GAL WITHIN THE NEXT 24 HOURS! NOW GET BUSY!!!
HG PETER
Copr. 1944, King Features Syndicate, Inc., World rights reserved
THE CAPITAL'S RICHEST MAN RECEIVES A PARENTS' COMMITTEE.
BUT, MR. DOUGH, THIS PLAYGROUND MEANS EVERYTHING TO OUR YOUNGSTERS! YOU OWN THE LAND AND—
I'M GOING TO KEEP IT! UNTIL REAL ESTATE VALUES GO UP!!
BUT SUDDENLY—
MR. DOUGH-YOU CAN AFFORD IT! GIVE THAT LAND TO THE CITY—
YOU'RE CRAZY! HEY!..... THAT ROPE-SOMETHING COMPELS ME-I-I-I'LL GIVE THE LAND!
Copr. 1944, King Features Syndicate, Inc., World rights reserved.
LATER, IN THE CLARION OFFICE—
THIS GORGEOUS GAL THREW A GOLD LASSO-IT MADE THE OLD GOAT DOCILE AS A LAMB AND HE GAVE THE CITY THE LAND!
GREAT GROANING GRIFFINS-AND YOU LET HER GET AWAY! I'M GOING CA-RAZY!
THIS WONDER WOMAN IS DRIVING ME WACKY! GO FIND HER, YOU LIMP-LEGGED, LAME-BRAINED RABBITS AND DON'T COME BACK TILL YOU GET THAT WONDER WOMAN STORY!
HG PETER
FRANTIC REPORTERS SPOT THEIR QUARRY
THERE SHE IS-THE WONDER WOMAN! STEP ON THE GAS!
WHAT THE BLUE BLAZES! THIS BUS IS HITTING 75, AN' SHE'S RUNNING AWAY FROM US!
GOOD-BYE, BOYS;-DRIVE UP AND SEE ME SOMETIME!
Copr. 1944, King Features Syndicate, Inc., World rights reserved
YOU WHAT? YOU LOST WONDER WOMAN?
WE KNOW WHAT YOU'RE THINKING-BUT YOU CAN'T FIRE US-WE QUIT!
HG PETER
WONDER WOMAN-PLUNDER WOMAN-BLAZES! AFTER THIRTY YEARS BEHIND THE CITY DESK I THINK I'M BEGINNING TO WEAKEN-THAT GAL IS DRIVING ME NUTS!
EDITOR BROWN OF THE WASHINGTON CLARION, SUFFERS A NERVOUS COLLAPSE—
A STRANGE CASE! THIS PATIENT HAS BEEN IN A COMA FOR DAYS
I'M DIANA PRINCE-ER-HOW'S YOUR PATIENT?
NOT SO GOOD...HE SUFFERED A NERVOUS COLLAPSE OVER SOME "WONDER WOMAN" WHOM HE FAILED TO FIND FOR HIS NEWSPAPER!
MR. BROWN-- THIS PARCHMENT SEEMS TO BE THE HISTORY OF THAT GIRL YOU CALL "WONDER WOMAN"! A STRANGE, VEILED WOMAN LEFT IT WITH ME
ER-WHAT? SPUT-I-WH-WH-WHAT?
LIKE A MANIAC, BROWN RUSHES TO THE CLARION CITY ROOM—
STOP THE PRESSES! I'VE GOT THE HISTORY OF WONDER WOMAN!
? ?

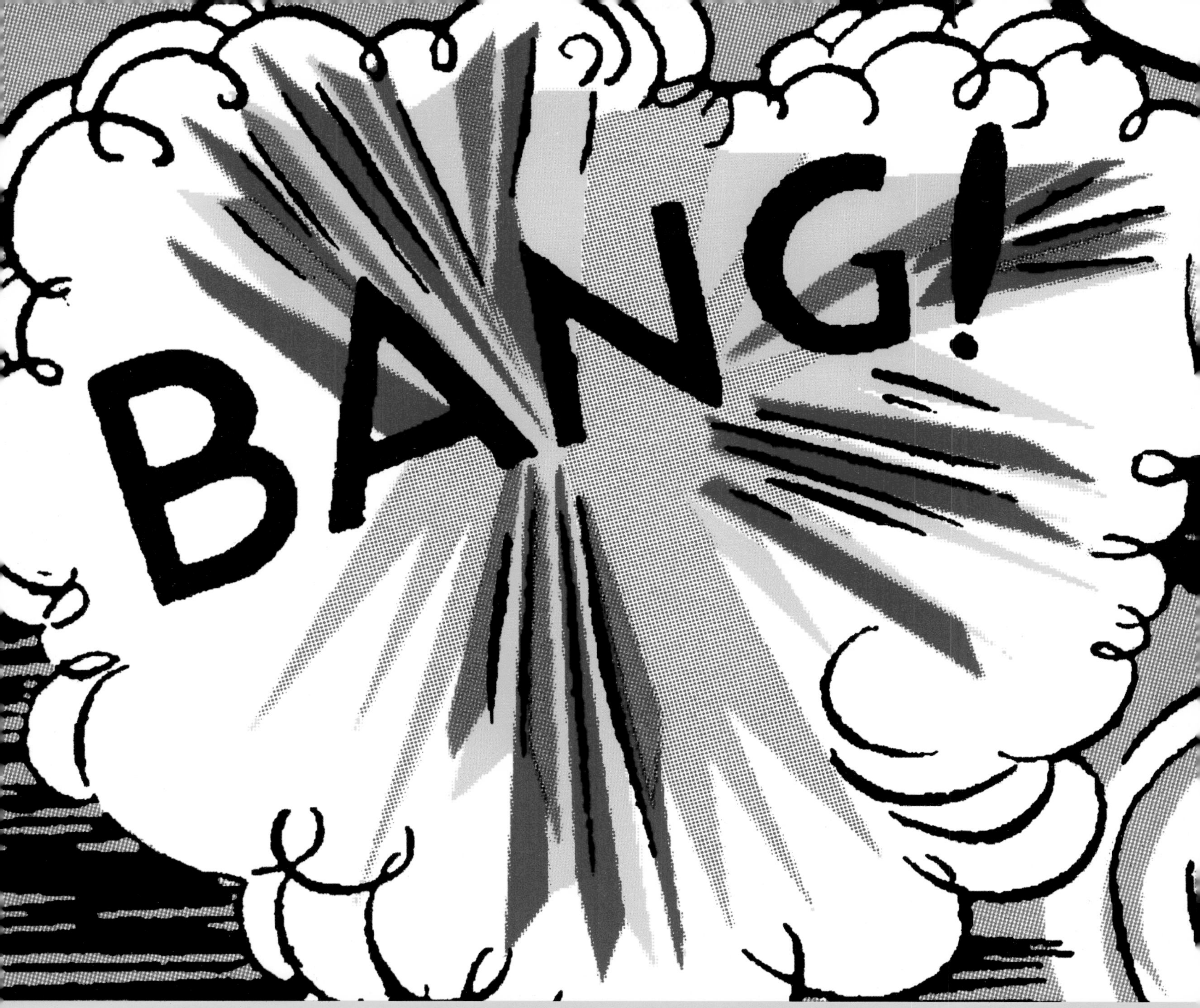
BANG!

Harry G. Peter

With a quiet personality, more subdued than his self-aggrandizing collaborator, the life of the artist of Wonder Woman, Harry G. Peter, isn't as well-publicized as that of William Moulton Marston. A cartoonist who according to Marston "knows what life's about," Peter worked as an illustrator for a variety of publications, including the *San Francisco Chronicle* and *Judge Magazine*, and reportedly lent his artistic abilities to the popular comic strip "Mutt and Jeff." Peter started work on the adventures of Wonder Woman despite conflicts with editor Sheldon Mayer, who disliked the artist's storytelling techniques, and considered some of his figures "grotesque." With a sense of humor remembered fondly by the Marston children, and the ability to win over the hardest critics, Peter eventually won over Mayer, and he continued to lend his classical style to Wonder Woman even after Marston's death.

Left: A rare look at a six-day sequence from the short-lived Wonder Woman comic strip, written by Marston and illustrated by Peter. Together, the two men produced about thirty-five pages per month of material for comic books and comic strips throughout the 1940s.

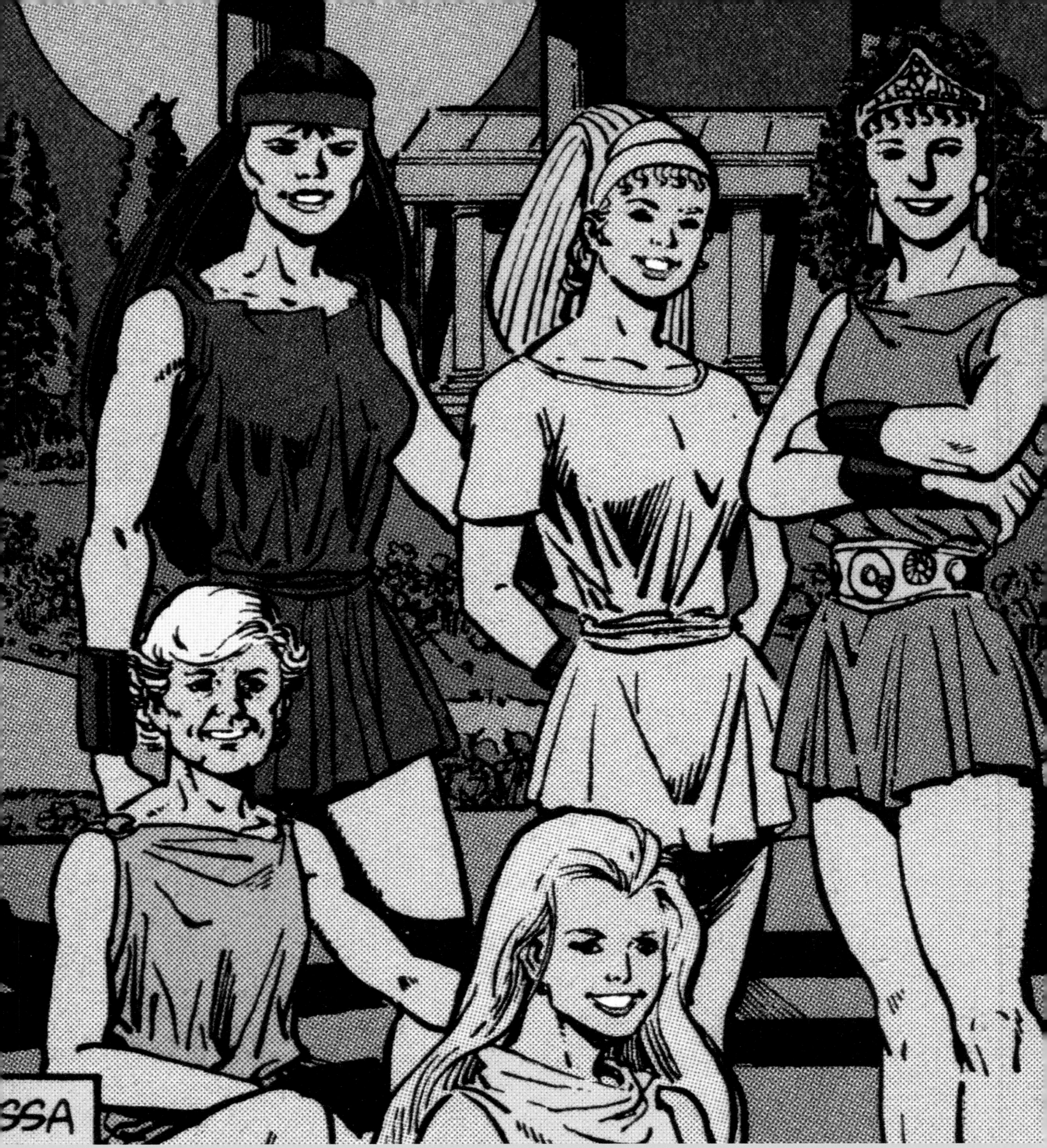

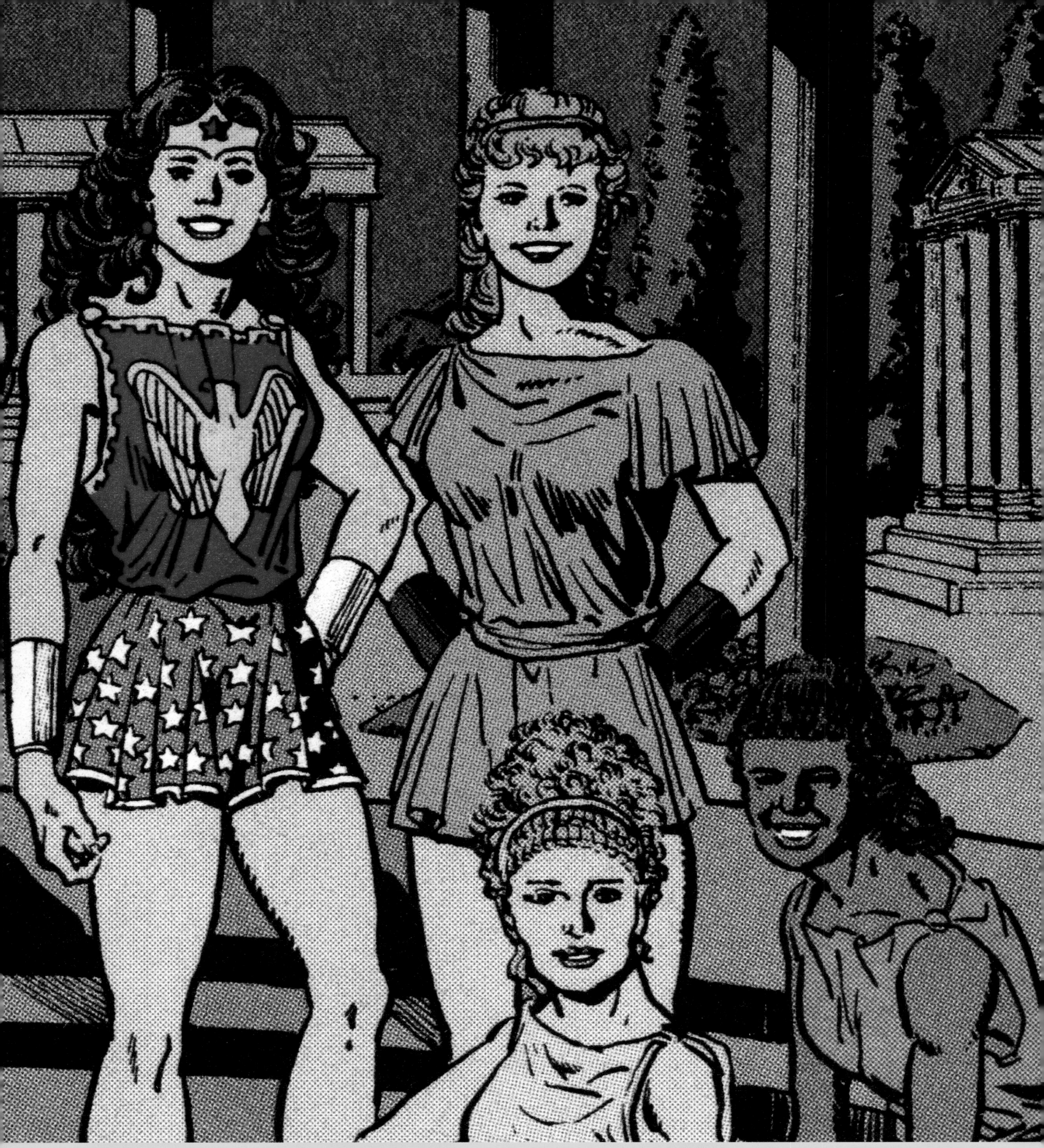

★ The Amazons

Marston borrowed heavily from the Greek myths when he created a race of immortal women who lived in self-imposed exile from "Man's World" on a tropical eden called Paradise Island.

Life was fairly quiet on the tranquil island, which was located on no known map. Based on clues in the stories, one can presume the island was somewhere near Greece and possibly located within the Aegean Sea. The band of women, called Amazons, lived in the fictitious land of Amazonia, and was undefeated warriors. Greek warriors taunted the demigod Hercules that he could not defeat the Amazons, and besting the female warriors and their queen, Hippolyta, in personal combat became a personal challenge to him. Hippolyta battled the arrogant Hercules, confident that her magic girdle—a gift from Aphrodite, goddess of love—would protect and sustain her. The Amazon queen bested Hercules, but the demigod took his revenge against Hippolyta that night by seducing her, removing her girdle, and enslaving her and her Amazon subjects. The Amazons suffered for years until the goddess Aphrodite finally responded to her subjects' pleadings. She agreed to help Hippolyta in exchange for the Amazons leaving Man's World forever to keep them safe.

Once Hercules and his men were beaten by the newly freed Amazons, the warrior women took his ships and set sail for a magical island, which the Amazons were told would grant them immortality. As the Amazons and their queen established their new home, Aphrodite demanded that the women never remove the metal bracelets Hercules and his men had placed on them, as a reminder of their days in subjugation.

Above: Queen Hippolyta crowns her daughter Diana as princess of the Amazons in the stirring last chapter of *Kingdom Come*, with art by comics icon Alex Ross. Ross always depicts Paradise Island as peaceful and tranquil.

Right: A look at the impressive Amazonian architecture on Themyscira as imagined by artists George Pérez and Romeo Tanghal.

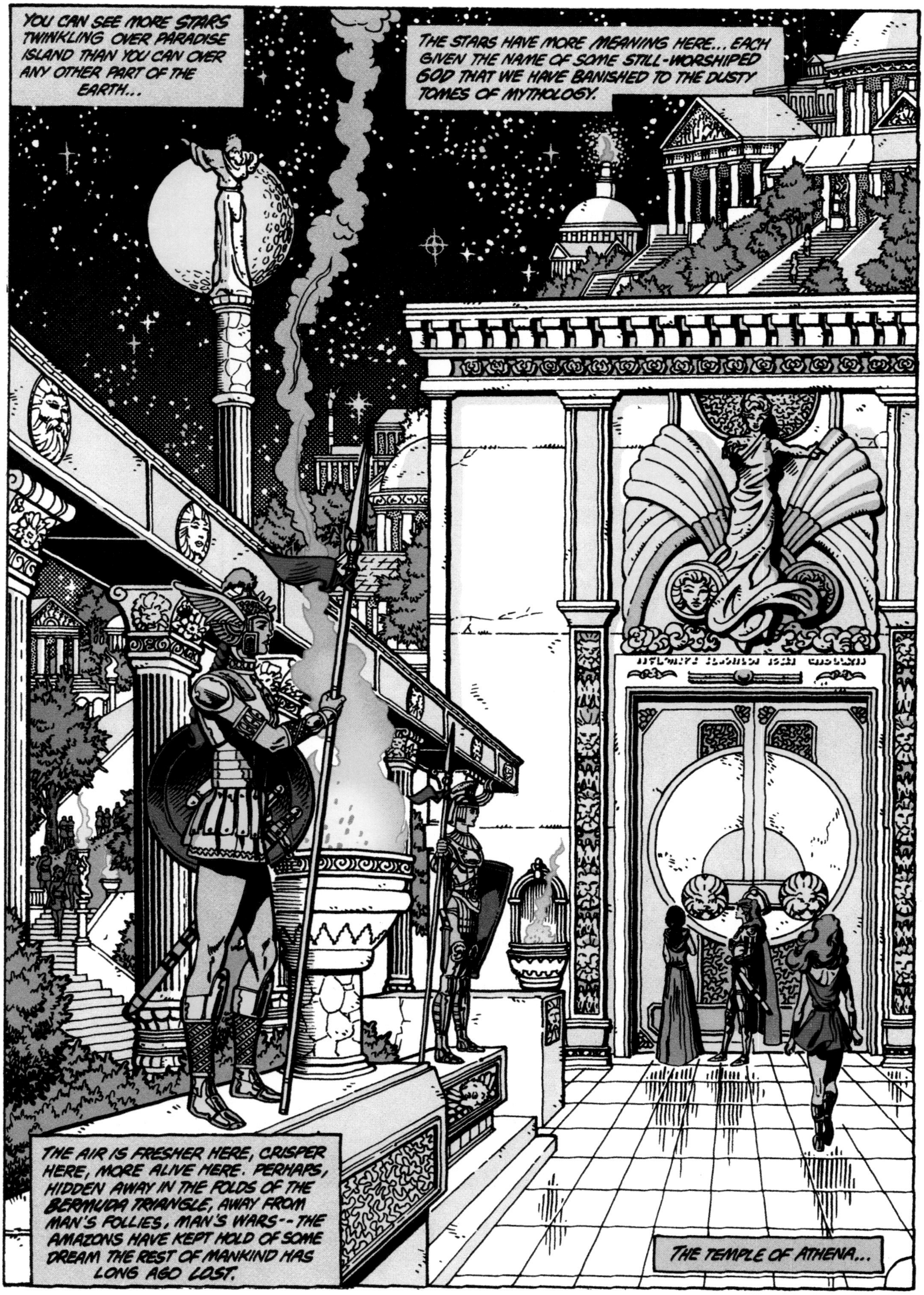
YOU CAN SEE MORE STARS TWINKLING OVER PARADISE ISLAND THAN YOU CAN OVER ANY OTHER PART OF THE EARTH...
THE STARS HAVE MORE MEANING HERE... EACH GIVEN THE NAME OF SOME STILL-WORSHIPED GOD THAT WE HAVE BANISHED TO THE DUSTY TOMES OF MYTHOLOGY.
THE AIR IS FRESHER HERE, CRISPER HERE, MORE ALIVE HERE. PERHAPS, HIDDEN AWAY IN THE FOLDS OF THE BERMUDA TRIANGLE, AWAY FROM MAN'S FOLLIES, MAN'S WARS--THE AMAZONS HAVE KEPT HOLD OF SOME DREAM THE REST OF MANKIND HAS LONG AGO LOST.
THE TEMPLE OF ATHENA...

As the centuries passed, the Amazons studied combat, arts and sciences, and other intellectual pursuits. The women were able to keep current on global events by using a magic sphere provided to Hippolyta by Athena, which allowed them to see the outside world. They watched as nations rose and fell, marveling at the technological advancements spreading across the globe. They also bested each modern innovation with creations such as the invisible plane and the Purple Healing Ray, the latter invention enabling the Amazons to cure almost any wound, sickness, or disease they encountered.

As for addressing human desire for affection, writers—beginning with the time George Pérez ran the scenes—implied that the women turned to one another for succor. For example, while it was clear Amazon Io secretly loved Diana, how the women satisfied their physical needs was alluded to with a wink and a nod.

It was centuries before loneliness and a desire to mother a child prompted Queen Hippolyta to beg the gods for a baby of her own. The gods agreed, and Hippolyta was instructed to mold a child's form from clay. The various gods and goddesses then breathed life into the baby, bestowing her with powerful gifts, and she was named Diana.

Marston used the denizens of Paradise Island as more than attractive window dressing, however. For example, Diana's friend Mala served as the overseer of nearby Transformation Island, who first appeared in *Wonder Woman* #4 (April/May 1942) and was where criminals were brought for reformation. Diana brought numerous foes there during her adventures.

After Marston's death from lung cancer on May 2, 1947, Robert Kanigher took over as both writer and editor from 1947 though 1968. He had Diana return to Paradise Island more often to visit her sisters, and minor recurring Amazons, such as Professor Alpha and Tara, made repeat appearances.

To reset the status quo, Kanigher chose to retell Diana's origin, this time identifying the Amazons as the widows of Greeks who died during countless wars, thereby dropping most of the previously established mythology. A once-brunette Queen Hippolyta was now mysteriously blond, and only the gods-blessed Diana had above-average physical and mental skills, making her the only choice to return the downed Steve Trevor to Man's World. The entire contest angle, where Diana bested her fellow Amazons to win the right to visit the outside world, was dropped from the origin story. Later, Kanigher disregarded his revised history and reverted to the initial Marston back-story.

With sagging sales, a dramatic overhaul on the *Wonder Woman* title was performed in 1968, resulting in Paradise Island and its inhabitants temporarily vanishing from the mortal plane. After their return a few years later, the Amazons played an increasing role in Wonder Woman's daily world. Kanigher—back behind the typewriter after a four-year break from mental exhaustion—for the first time integrated the women and introduced the first black-skinned Amazon, Nubia. She was presented to readers as Wonder Woman's sister, also derived of clay but raised by the malevolent god Mars who used her in his scheme to conquer the Amazons, until she was reunited with Diana and the plan fell apart. The two women battled each other until they learned the truth about their sisterhood, after which they quickly became close comrades in arms.

Kanigher essentially turned back the clock on the title, reliving the wild and wooly heyday, using the traditional *Wonder Woman* logo and a simplified art style in an attempt to appeal to a broader base of readers. Nubia was added for shock value, but it was quickly clear this approach was out of step with the early 1970s, and both writer/editor and Nubia were gone within one year.

Under a subsequent series of editors the Amazons' roles waxed and waned but they were never gone for long. In fact, the first series of *Wonder Woman* ended with Diana on Paradise Island, surrounded by her warrior comrades. The curtain came down on the series in late 1985 after 329 consecutive issues. Diana's final adventure dovetailed with a company-wide saga titled *Crisis on Infinite Earths*, in which Hades allied himself with the cosmic villain the Anti-Monitor. As a result, the deceased Amazons were returned to action as an undead army that assaulted Paradise Island. The living Amazons, as well as Diana, now reunited with Steve Trevor, face-off against the undead Amazons in a major battle orchestrated by the god Mars. When Trevor deduced that the gods of Olympus had been imprisoned, he freed Zeus, which turned the tide of the battle. A grateful Zeus presided over the long-awaited wedding between Diana and Steve, witnessed by the Amazons. She

Below: An action pose from a DC Style Guide.

THEMYSCIRA--
DOOM'S DOORWAY.

THERE SHOULD BE A *MARKER,* CASSIE. *GUIDE* ME TO IT, PLEASE.

Above: Wonder Woman was temporarily blinded for a storyline and she was therefore accompanied by Cassie Sandsmark, the second Wonder Girl, and Ferdinand, the Minotaur cook from the Themysciran Embassy, as they dared to enter Doom's Doorway, access to Hades and the Underworld. Art by Rags Morales and Michael Bair.

Pages 32–33: Amazons at war using ancient and modern weapons from *Wonder Woman* #169 as illustrated by Phil Jimenez and Andy Lanning.

then returned to the cosmic conflict, which returned her to a clay form, awaiting rebirth.

In February 1987, Greg Potter and George Pérez headlined a new *Wonder Woman* #1, re-envisioning Paradise Island as Themyscira, excising the Roman names, which had been blended with their Greek counterparts. The gods and goddesses played an increasing role in Wonder Woman's life. It was also revealed that Aphrodite created the Amazons with the souls of women who died as a result of man's aggressions, Queen Hippolyta being the first such victim. Aphrodite breathed life into the clay forms containing those souls, setting the stage for Diana's eventual creation.

The island itself was not only home to the Amazons, but readers learned it also included Doom's Doorway, a portal to Hades's Underworld realm called Tartarus. The doorway was placed there as the Amazons' penance for failing to help humanity achieve a higher plane of existence. Pérez's version of Nubia was Nu'bia, who served as guardian of the inner chamber. In time, Wonder Woman won a challenge from the gods, which removed the portal once and for all. To accomplish this, she had to complete tasks that were designed by Zeus, who was angered that Diana refused to surrender her virginity to him. These challenges included fending off the last of the Hecatoncheires: Cottus, a seven-headed Hydra, and, Echidna, a She-Serpent.

Later, Pérez introduced an offshoot of Amazons called the Bana-Mighdall. He postulated that the Amazons once had two queens: Hippolyta and Antiope. After achieving their freedom, the queens chose different paths: Hippolyta accepted immortality and agreed to guard Doom's Doorway on Themyscira; Antiope led her mortal faction across the globe until they settled in Egypt. As Antiope and her followers built their hidden city, they took the name Bana-Mighdall, which translates to The Temple of Women. Forsaking the gods of Olympus, they instead adopted beliefs based on other faiths popular throughout the world.

Their city was eventually discovered by Diana, which led to a series of adventures throughout the next several years and resulted in reconciliation between the Amazons and the Bana-Mighdall, who were now being led by Artemis. United to protect Themyscira from the witch Circe and later participated in a war against a cosmic conqueror named Imperiex, which devastated the island. Both immortal and mortal Amazons rebuilt a joint city on Themyscira's remains, sharing the governing chores.

The Bana-Mighdall were fiercer and less devoted to the arts and sciences than

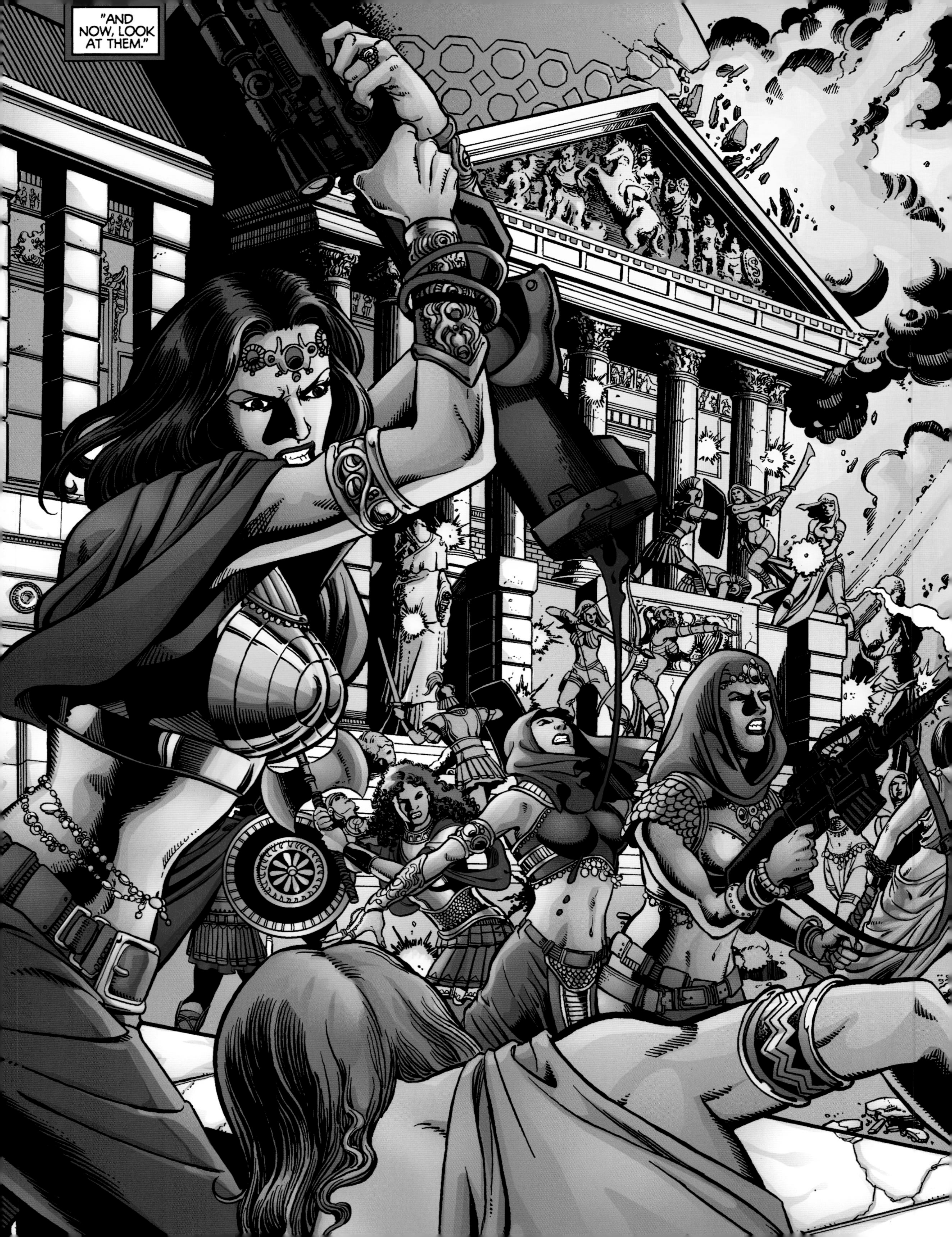
"AND NOW, LOOK AT THEM."

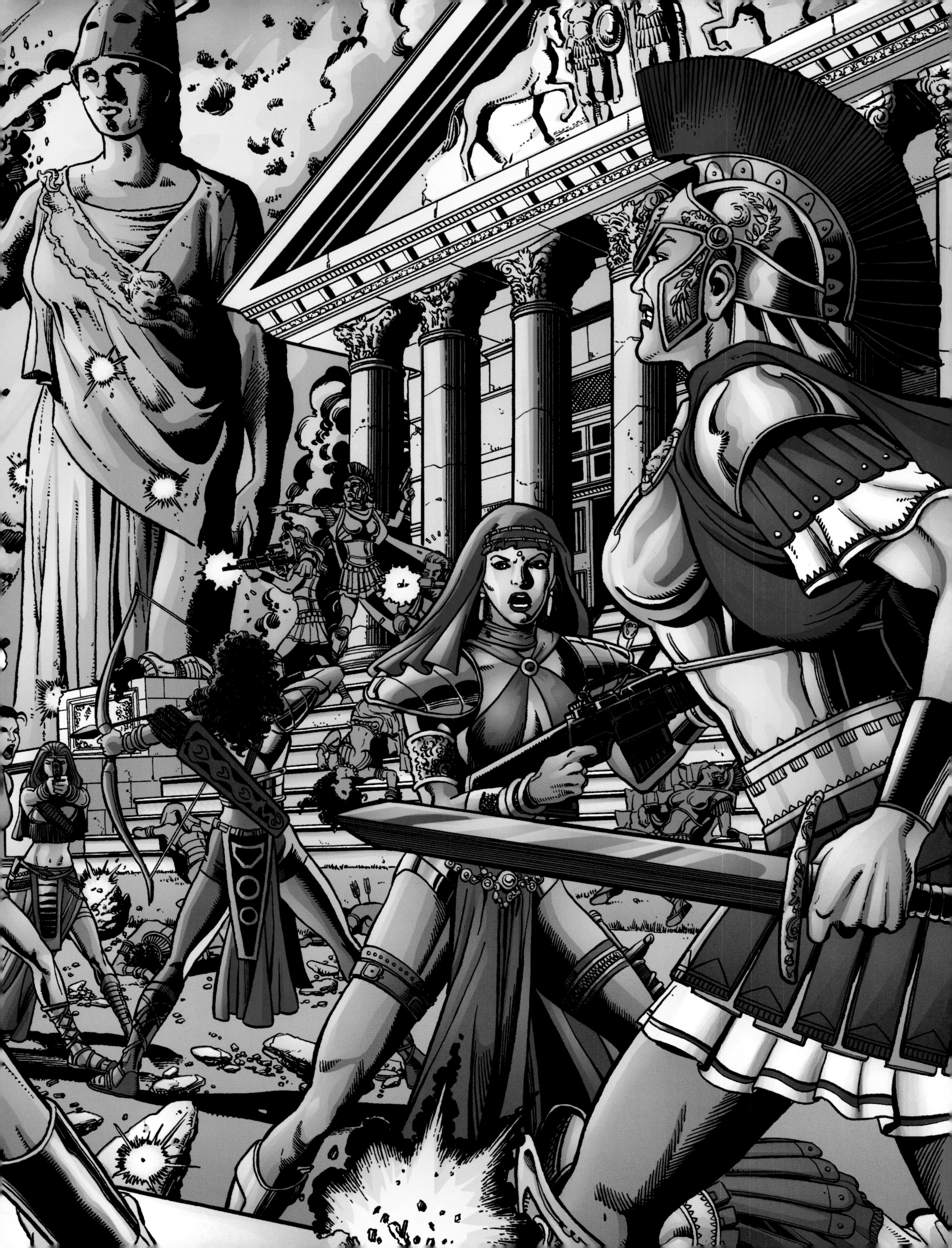

their Amazon sisters. Their current leader, the redheaded Artemis, bested Diana in a new Contest, called by Hippolyta. The queen had a vision foretelling Wonder Woman's death, and she feared for her daughter's life, and she no longer wanted Diana exposed to danger. After Artemis defeated Diana, she became Wonder Woman for two years, until she died in battle with Diana's archenemy, the powerful White Magician. Artemis's death confirmed Hippolyta's vision.

The number of Amazons have fluctuated through the years, but currently the population is small—approximately eleven hundred Amazons are still alive and living on Themyscira, down from a series-high of eight thousand.

In modern times the Amazons had specific responsibilities, such as defense or agriculture, and everyone had a specialty and contributed to the island's harmony. They feasted to honor the gods and treated all people with compassion, guided by the ideals on which their nation was founded.

But what would happen should a man step on the island? According to Wonder Woman's fellow heroine Black Canary, "Any Amazon seeing a man standing on our island will instantly fall hopelessly in love with him—so much so that they will fight over him ruthlessly . . . violently . . . until we, who base our society on love and respect, are reduced to barbarians over a man!" Of course, that statement from the 1970s was a product of the times. Under Marston and later Kanigher, a man stepping foot on the island could lead to the Amazons losing their immortality and power. However, male aliens, beasts, and other assorted threats to Paradise Island never seemed to risk the Amazons' gods-given life.

During George Pérez's tenure with writers Greg Potter and Len Wein, there was far less risk to the Amazons should a man arrive, but their strict customs kept them isolated.

Still, mere mortals did visit the island throughout the years. In the revamped series imagined by Pérez, pilot Diana Rockwell Trevor crashed near Paradise Island. The gods gently guided her unconscious form to Themyscira, where she awakened during a pitched battle between the Amazons and Cottus, a creature with one hundred arms that attempted to escape from the Underworld through Doom's Doorway. Diana and the Amazon Phillipus rushed the behemoth, and Diana aimed her pistol between the being's eyes and fired. Diana succeeded in killing it, but was crushed to death by Cottus's unyielding grip. Her sacrifice did not go unheralded; her life was remembered with a statue, and Diana's selfless actions prompted Hippolyta to name her infant daughter Diana in her honor.

The goddess Thetis also used Paradise Island as a place to harbor orphaned human children until they were healthy enough to be adopted. One of these children was Julia Kapatelis, a young girl who would later befriend Wonder Woman in adulthood.

Of course, the best-known citizen of Man's World was Steve Trevor, who in every retelling helped prompt Diana to journey from the safety and anonymity of Paradise Island to the vast and dangerous world of mortals as Wonder Woman.

Themyscira was kept a secret from the world until it was determined the Amazons were ready to reveal their existence, a story told in *Wonder Woman* #50 (January 1991). Diana, in her temporary role as Themyscira's ambassador, brought numerous United Nations officials and journalists, including Lois Lane of the *Daily Planet*, on official visits to the island.

Above: Cover sketches by Terry Dodson, exploring different ways to display the iconic image of the Amazon Princess as he prepared to become *Wonder Woman*'s newest illustrator.

Right: When humans trapped in cybernetic armor were forced to attack Themyscira, Wonder Woman led the defense, aided by Fury (in gold) and other Amazonian warriors. Illustrated by Phil Jimenez and Andy Lanning.

Pages 36–37: After Themyscira was largely destroyed during an attempted invasion of Earth by the cosmic conqueror Imperiex, the gods helped resurrect the land and a new era for the Amazons began.

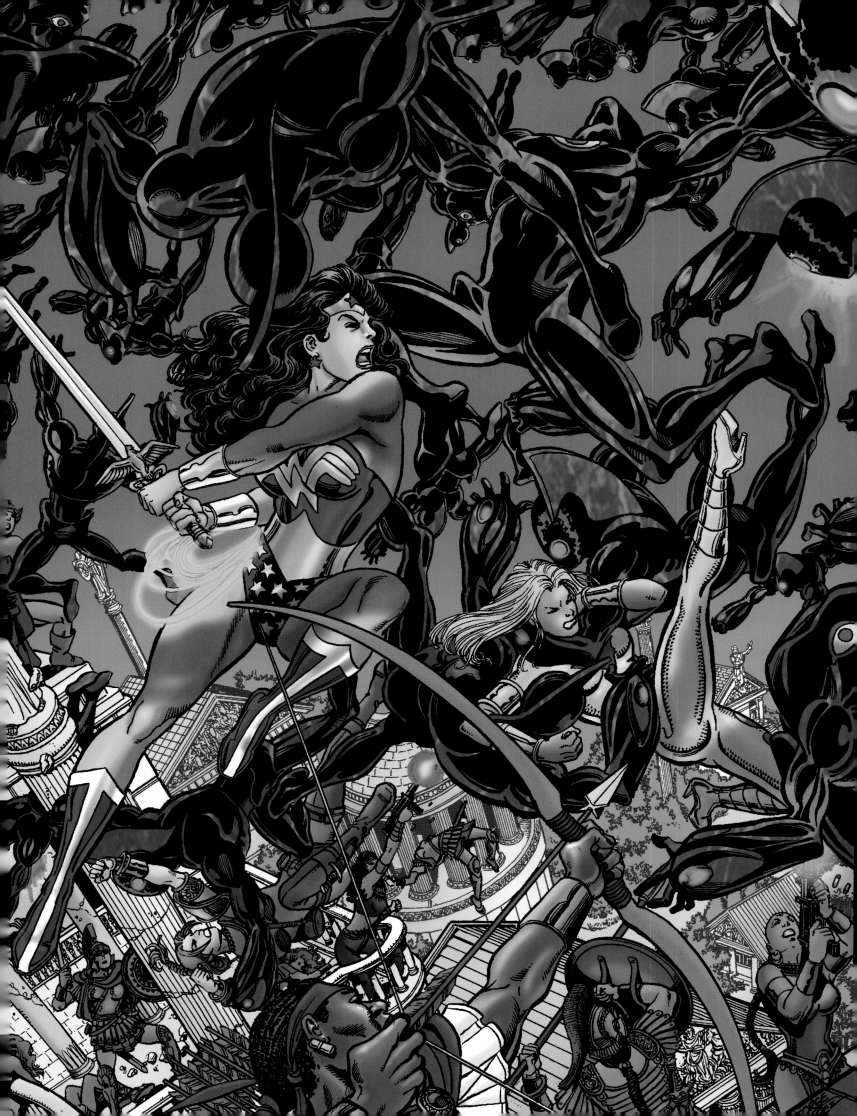

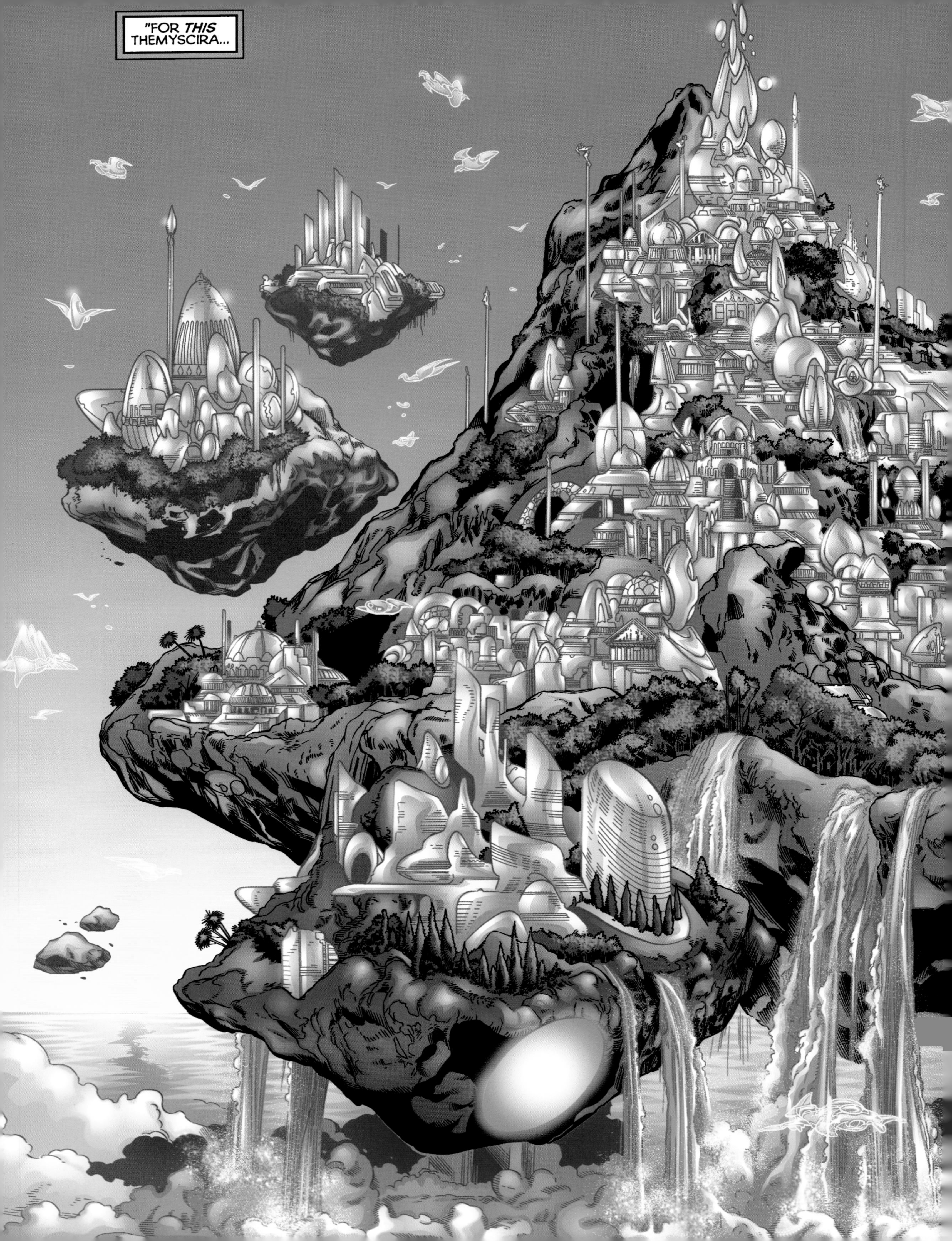
"FOR *THIS* THEMYSCIRA...

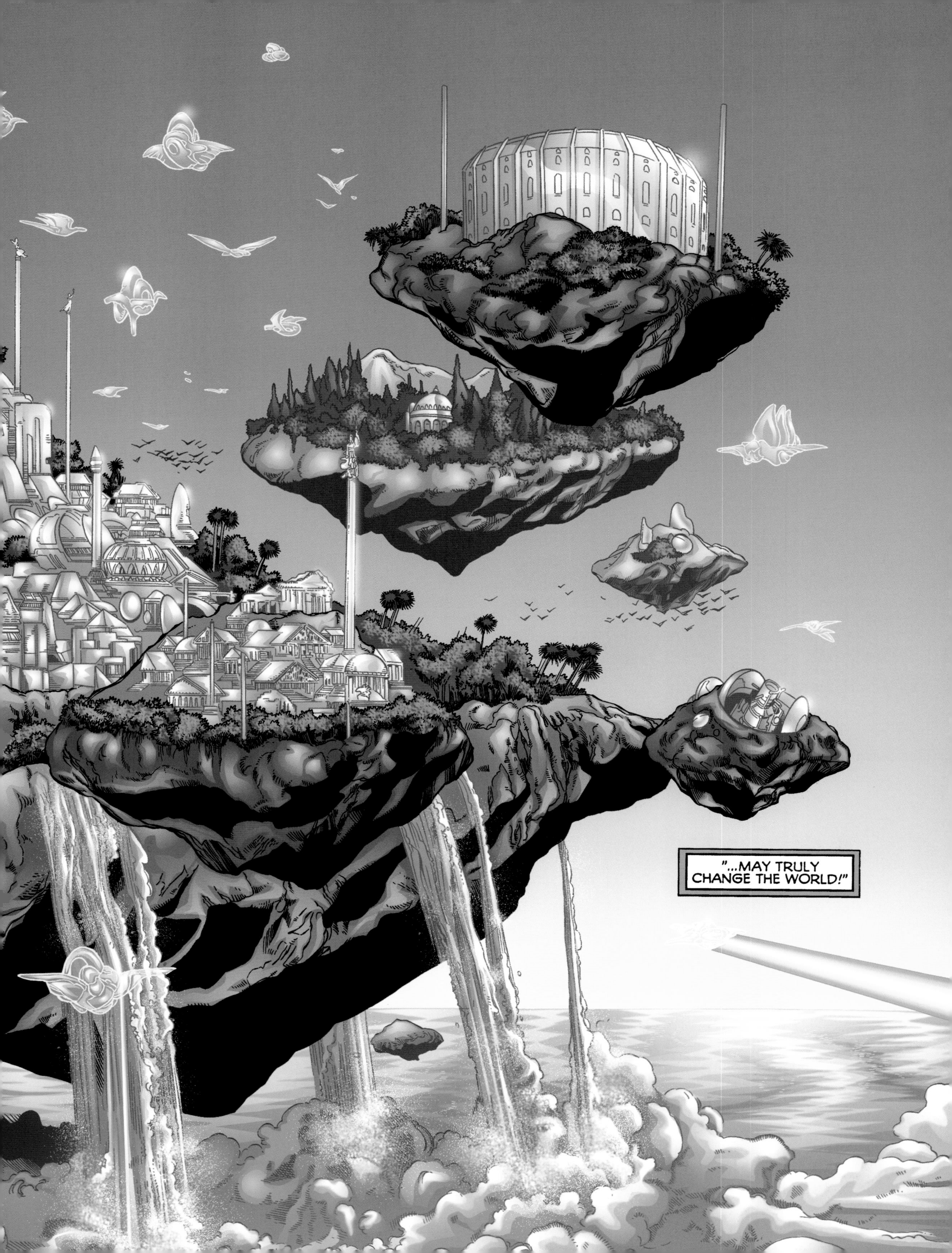
"...MAY TRULY CHANGE THE WORLD!"

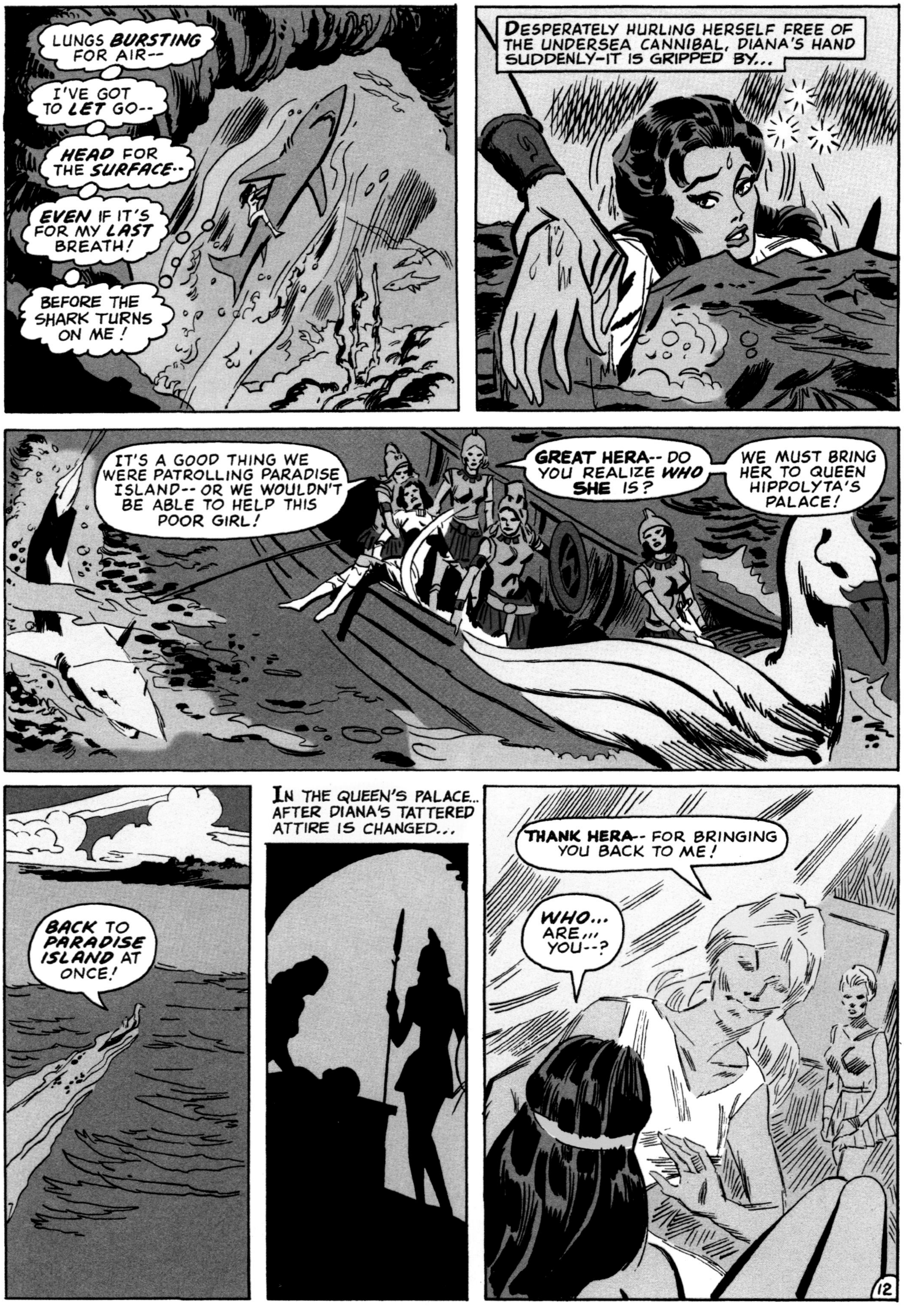
LUNGS BURSTING FOR AIR--
I'VE GOT TO LET GO--
HEAD FOR THE SURFACE--
EVEN IF IT'S FOR MY LAST BREATH!
BEFORE THE SHARK TURNS ON ME!
DESPERATELY HURLING HERSELF FREE OF THE UNDERSEA CANNIBAL, DIANA'S HAND SUDDENLY-IT IS GRIPPED BY...
IT'S A GOOD THING WE WERE PATROLLING PARADISE ISLAND-- OR WE WOULDN'T BE ABLE TO HELP THIS POOR GIRL!
GREAT HERA-- DO YOU REALIZE WHO SHE IS?
WE MUST BRING HER TO QUEEN HIPPOLYTA'S PALACE!
BACK TO PARADISE ISLAND AT ONCE!
IN THE QUEEN'S PALACE... AFTER DIANA'S TATTERED ATTIRE IS CHANGED...
THANK HERA-- FOR BRINGING YOU BACK TO ME!
WHO... ARE... YOU--?
12

Above and right: This two-page sequence illustrates Diana's reunion with Queen Hippolyta and Paradise Island after they returned from an extended stay in another dimension. Art by Don Heck and Dick Giordano.

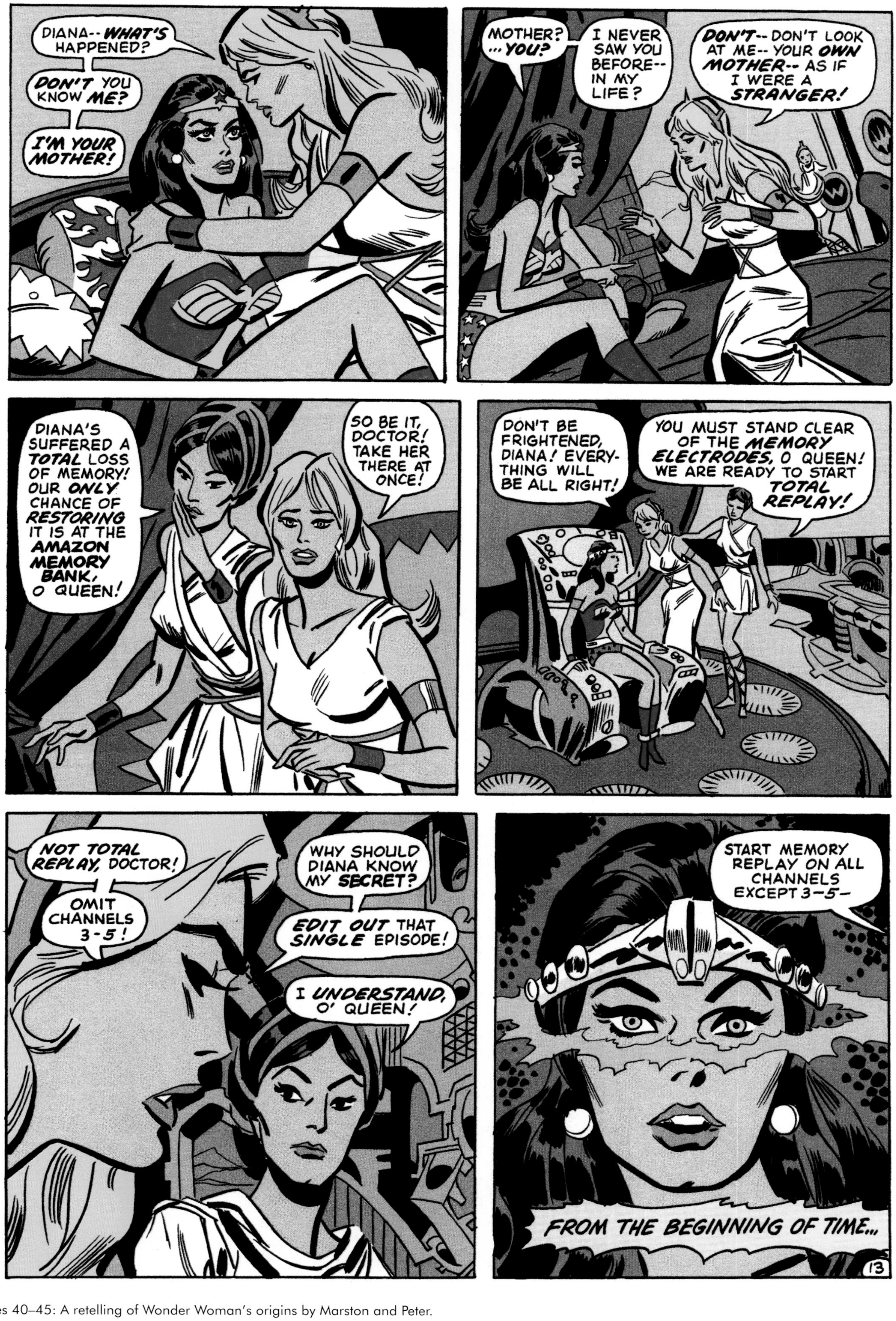
DIANA-- WHAT'S HAPPENED?
DON'T YOU KNOW ME?
I'M YOUR MOTHER!
MOTHER? ...YOU?
I NEVER SAW YOU BEFORE-- IN MY LIFE?
DON'T-- DON'T LOOK AT ME-- YOUR OWN MOTHER-- AS IF I WERE A STRANGER!
DIANA'S SUFFERED A TOTAL LOSS OF MEMORY! OUR ONLY CHANCE OF RESTORING IT IS AT THE AMAZON MEMORY BANK, O QUEEN!
SO BE IT, DOCTOR! TAKE HER THERE AT ONCE!
DON'T BE FRIGHTENED, DIANA! EVERY-THING WILL BE ALL RIGHT!
YOU MUST STAND CLEAR OF THE MEMORY ELECTRODES, O QUEEN! WE ARE READY TO START TOTAL REPLAY!
NOT TOTAL REPLAY, DOCTOR!
OMIT CHANNELS 3-5!
WHY SHOULD DIANA KNOW MY SECRET?
EDIT OUT THAT SINGLE EPISODE!
I UNDERSTAND, O' QUEEN!
START MEMORY REPLAY ON ALL CHANNELS EXCEPT 3-5-
FROM THE BEGINNING OF TIME...
13

Pages 40–45: A retelling of Wonder Woman's origins by Marston and Peter.

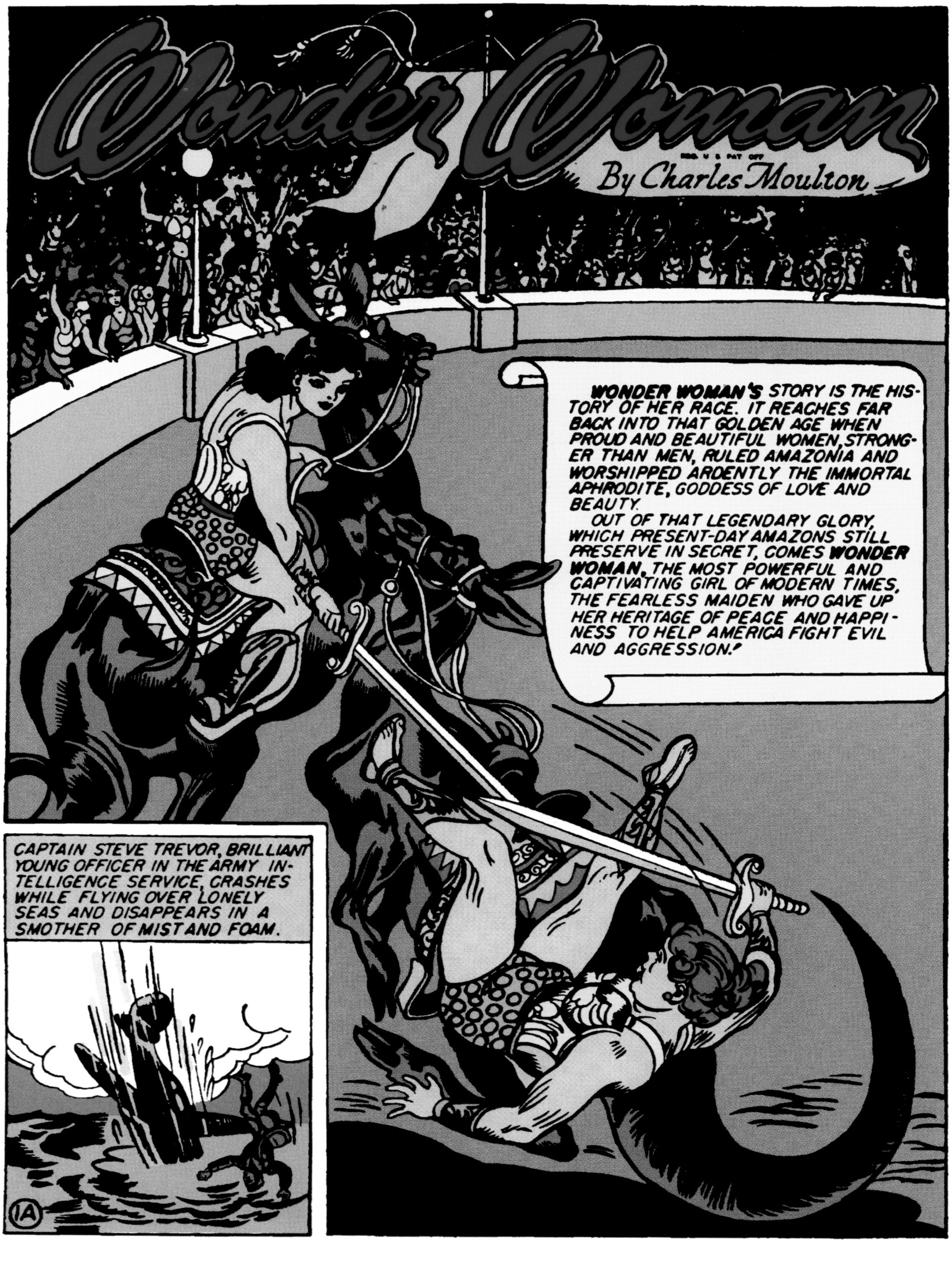
Wonder Woman
REG. U.S. PAT. OFF.
By Charles Moulton
WONDER WOMAN'S STORY IS THE HISTORY OF HER RACE. IT REACHES FAR BACK INTO THAT GOLDEN AGE WHEN PROUD AND BEAUTIFUL WOMEN, STRONGER THAN MEN, RULED AMAZONIA AND WORSHIPPED ARDENTLY THE IMMORTAL APHRODITE, GODDESS OF LOVE AND BEAUTY.
OUT OF THAT LEGENDARY GLORY, WHICH PRESENT-DAY AMAZONS STILL PRESERVE IN SECRET, COMES WONDER WOMAN, THE MOST POWERFUL AND CAPTIVATING GIRL OF MODERN TIMES, THE FEARLESS MAIDEN WHO GAVE UP HER HERITAGE OF PEACE AND HAPPINESS TO HELP AMERICA FIGHT EVIL AND AGGRESSION!
CAPTAIN STEVE TREVOR, BRILLIANT YOUNG OFFICER IN THE ARMY INTELLIGENCE SERVICE, CRASHES WHILE FLYING OVER LONELY SEAS AND DISAPPEARS IN A SMOTHER OF MIST AND FOAM.
1A

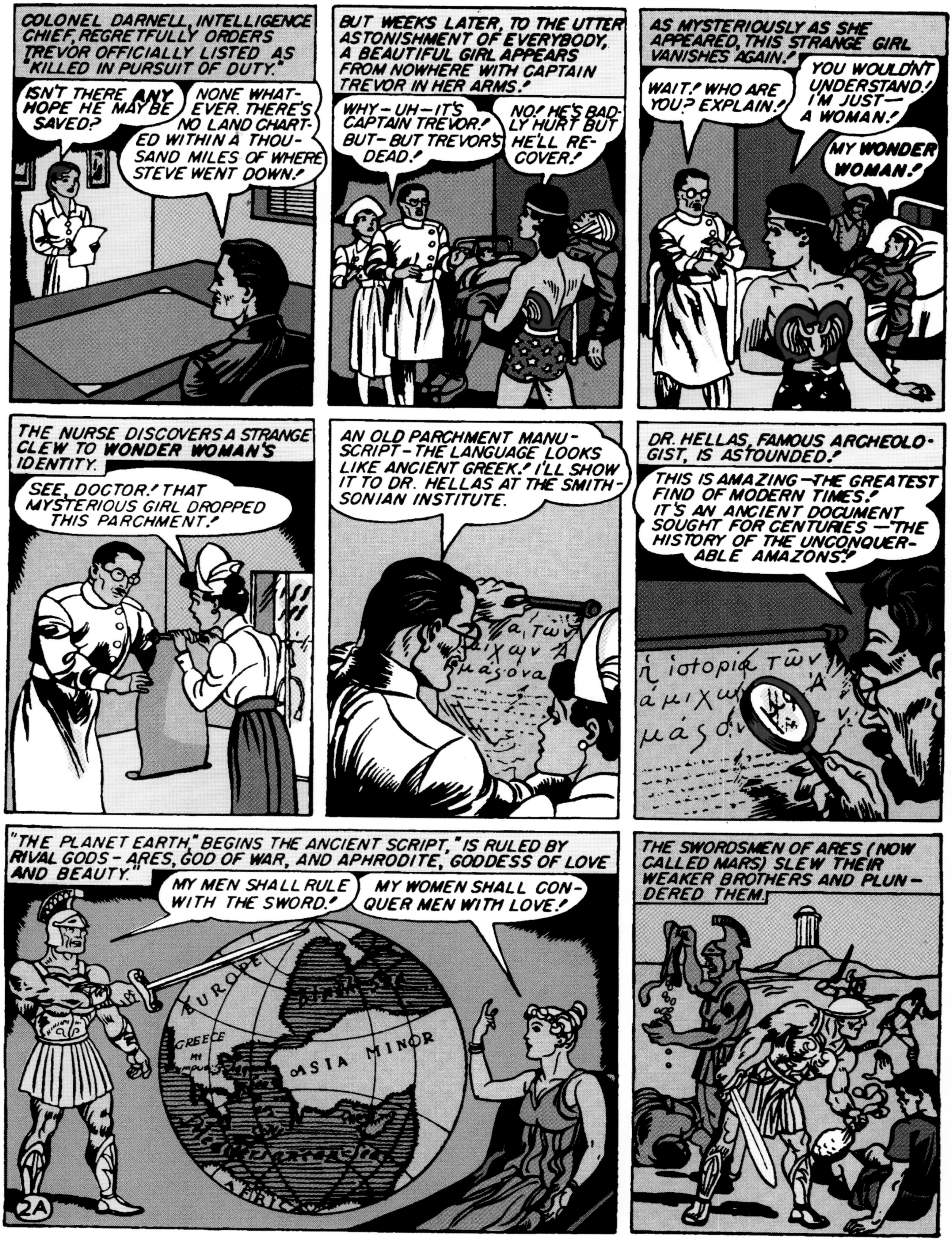

COLONEL DARNELL, INTELLIGENCE CHIEF, REGRETFULLY ORDERS TREVOR OFFICIALLY LISTED AS "KILLED IN PURSUIT OF DUTY."
ISN'T THERE ANY HOPE HE MAY BE SAVED?
NONE WHAT-EVER. THERE'S NO LAND CHART-ED WITHIN A THOU-SAND MILES OF WHERE STEVE WENT DOWN!
BUT WEEKS LATER, TO THE UTTER ASTONISHMENT OF EVERYBODY, A BEAUTIFUL GIRL APPEARS FROM NOWHERE WITH CAPTAIN TREVOR IN HER ARMS!
WHY-UH-IT'S CAPTAIN TREVOR! BUT-BUT TREVOR'S DEAD!
NO! HE'S BAD-LY HURT BUT HE'LL RE-COVER!
AS MYSTERIOUSLY AS SHE APPEARED, THIS STRANGE GIRL VANISHES AGAIN!
WAIT! WHO ARE YOU? EXPLAIN!
YOU WOULDN'T UNDERSTAND! I'M JUST—A WOMAN!
MY WONDER WOMAN!
THE NURSE DISCOVERS A STRANGE CLEW TO WONDER WOMAN'S IDENTITY.
SEE, DOCTOR! THAT MYSTERIOUS GIRL DROPPED THIS PARCHMENT!
AN OLD PARCHMENT MANU-SCRIPT—THE LANGUAGE LOOKS LIKE ANCIENT GREEK! I'LL SHOW IT TO DR. HELLAS AT THE SMITH-SONIAN INSTITUTE.
DR. HELLAS, FAMOUS ARCHEOLO-GIST, IS ASTOUNDED!
THIS IS AMAZING—THE GREATEST FIND OF MODERN TIMES! IT'S AN ANCIENT DOCUMENT SOUGHT FOR CENTURIES—"THE HISTORY OF THE UNCONQUER-ABLE AMAZONS"!
"THE PLANET EARTH," BEGINS THE ANCIENT SCRIPT, "IS RULED BY RIVAL GODS - ARES, GOD OF WAR, AND APHRODITE, GODDESS OF LOVE AND BEAUTY."
MY MEN SHALL RULE WITH THE SWORD!
MY WOMEN SHALL CON-QUER MEN WITH LOVE!
EUROPE
GREECE
ASIA MINOR
THE SWORDSMEN OF ARES (NOW CALLED MARS) SLEW THEIR WEAKER BROTHERS AND PLUN-DERED THEM.

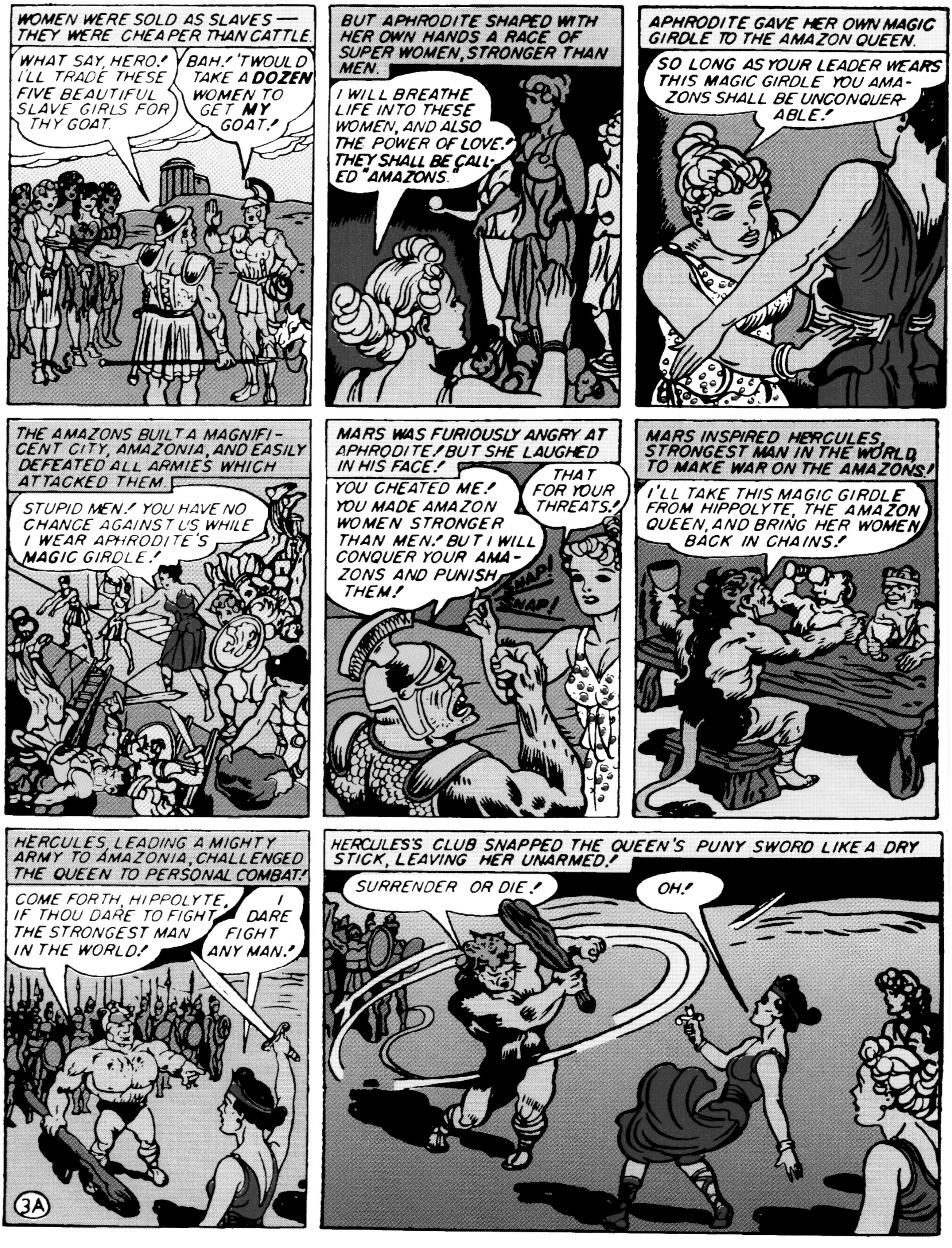
WOMEN WERE SOLD AS SLAVES — THEY WERE CHEAPER THAN CATTLE.
WHAT SAY, HERO! I'LL TRADE THESE FIVE BEAUTIFUL SLAVE GIRLS FOR THY GOAT.
BAH! 'TWOULD TAKE A DOZEN WOMEN TO GET MY GOAT!
BUT APHRODITE SHAPED WITH HER OWN HANDS A RACE OF SUPER WOMEN, STRONGER THAN MEN.
I WILL BREATHE LIFE INTO THESE WOMEN, AND ALSO THE POWER OF LOVE! THEY SHALL BE CALL-ED "AMAZONS."
APHRODITE GAVE HER OWN MAGIC GIRDLE TO THE AMAZON QUEEN.
SO LONG AS YOUR LEADER WEARS THIS MAGIC GIRDLE YOU AMA-ZONS SHALL BE UNCONQUER-ABLE!
THE AMAZONS BUILT A MAGNIFI-CENT CITY, AMAZONIA, AND EASILY DEFEATED ALL ARMIES WHICH ATTACKED THEM.
STUPID MEN! YOU HAVE NO CHANCE AGAINST US WHILE I WEAR APHRODITE'S MAGIC GIRDLE!
MARS WAS FURIOUSLY ANGRY AT APHRODITE! BUT SHE LAUGHED IN HIS FACE!
YOU CHEATED ME! YOU MADE AMAZON WOMEN STRONGER THAN MEN! BUT I WILL CONQUER YOUR AMA-ZONS AND PUNISH THEM!
THAT FOR YOUR THREATS!
SNAP! SNAP!
MARS INSPIRED HERCULES, STRONGEST MAN IN THE WORLD, TO MAKE WAR ON THE AMAZONS!
I'LL TAKE THIS MAGIC GIRDLE FROM HIPPOLYTE, THE AMAZON QUEEN, AND BRING HER WOMEN BACK IN CHAINS!
HERCULES, LEADING A MIGHTY ARMY TO AMAZONIA, CHALLENGED THE QUEEN TO PERSONAL COMBAT!
COME FORTH, HIPPOLYTE, IF THOU DARE TO FIGHT THE STRONGEST MAN IN THE WORLD!
I DARE FIGHT ANY MAN!
3A
HERCULES'S CLUB SNAPPED THE QUEEN'S PUNY SWORD LIKE A DRY STICK, LEAVING HER UNARMED!
SURRENDER OR DIE!
OH!

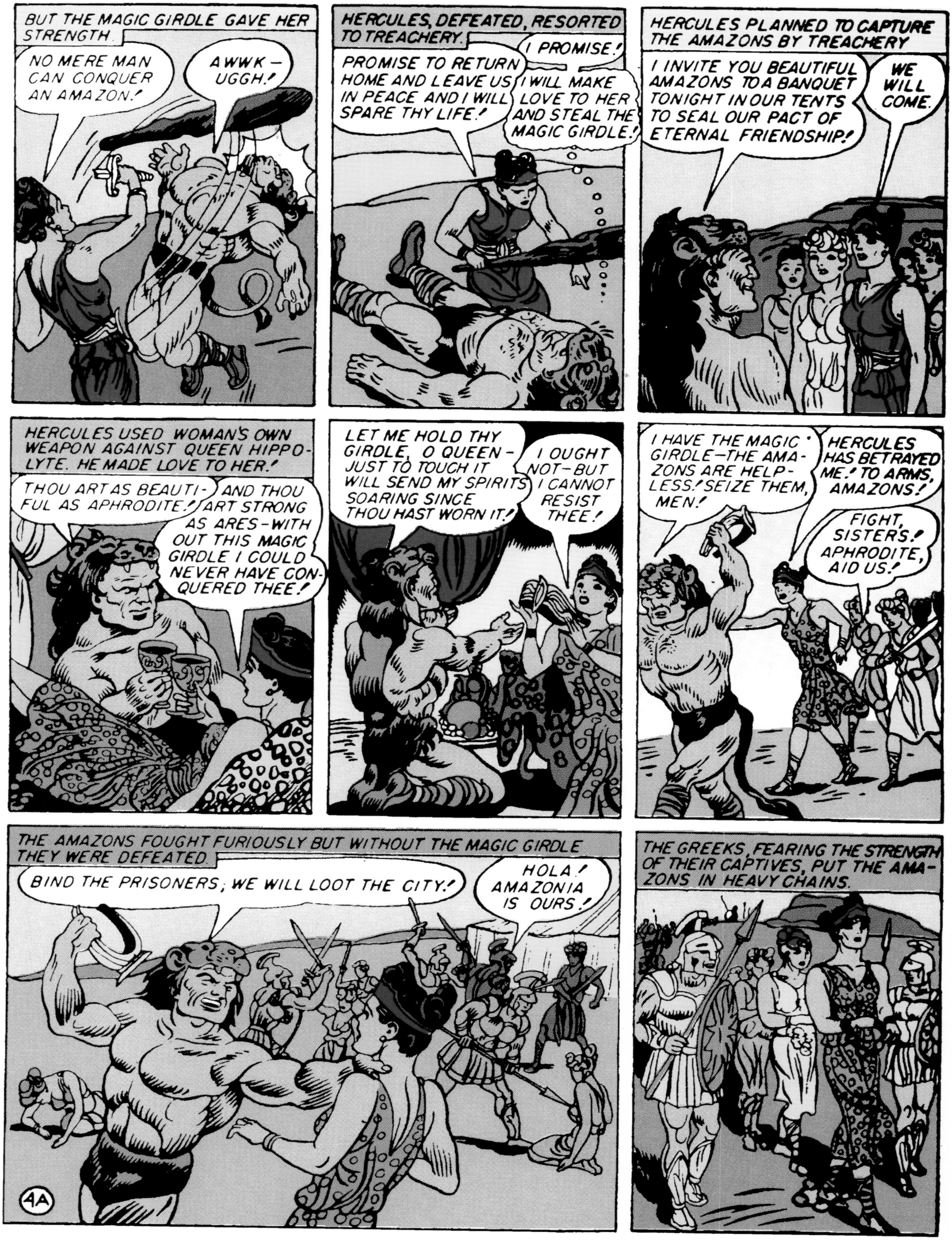
BUT THE MAGIC GIRDLE GAVE HER STRENGTH.
NO MERE MAN CAN CONQUER AN AMAZON!
AWWK — UGGH!
HERCULES, DEFEATED, RESORTED TO TREACHERY.
PROMISE TO RETURN HOME AND LEAVE US IN PEACE AND I WILL SPARE THY LIFE!
I PROMISE!
I WILL MAKE LOVE TO HER AND STEAL THE MAGIC GIRDLE!
HERCULES PLANNED TO CAPTURE THE AMAZONS BY TREACHERY
I INVITE YOU BEAUTIFUL AMAZONS TO A BANQUET TONIGHT IN OUR TENTS TO SEAL OUR PACT OF ETERNAL FRIENDSHIP!
WE WILL COME.
HERCULES USED WOMAN'S OWN WEAPON AGAINST QUEEN HIPPOLYTE. HE MADE LOVE TO HER!
THOU ART AS BEAUTIFUL AS APHRODITE!
AND THOU ART STRONG AS ARES — WITHOUT THIS MAGIC GIRDLE I COULD NEVER HAVE CONQUERED THEE!
LET ME HOLD THY GIRDLE, O QUEEN — JUST TO TOUCH IT WILL SEND MY SPIRITS SOARING SINCE THOU HAST WORN IT!
I OUGHT NOT — BUT I CANNOT RESIST THEE!
I HAVE THE MAGIC GIRDLE — THE AMAZONS ARE HELPLESS! SEIZE THEM, MEN!
HERCULES HAS BETRAYED ME! TO ARMS, AMAZONS!
FIGHT, SISTERS! APHRODITE, AID US!
THE AMAZONS FOUGHT FURIOUSLY BUT WITHOUT THE MAGIC GIRDLE THEY WERE DEFEATED.
BIND THE PRISONERS; WE WILL LOOT THE CITY!
HOLA! AMAZONIA IS OURS!
4A
THE GREEKS, FEARING THE STRENGTH OF THEIR CAPTIVES, PUT THE AMAZONS IN HEAVY CHAINS.

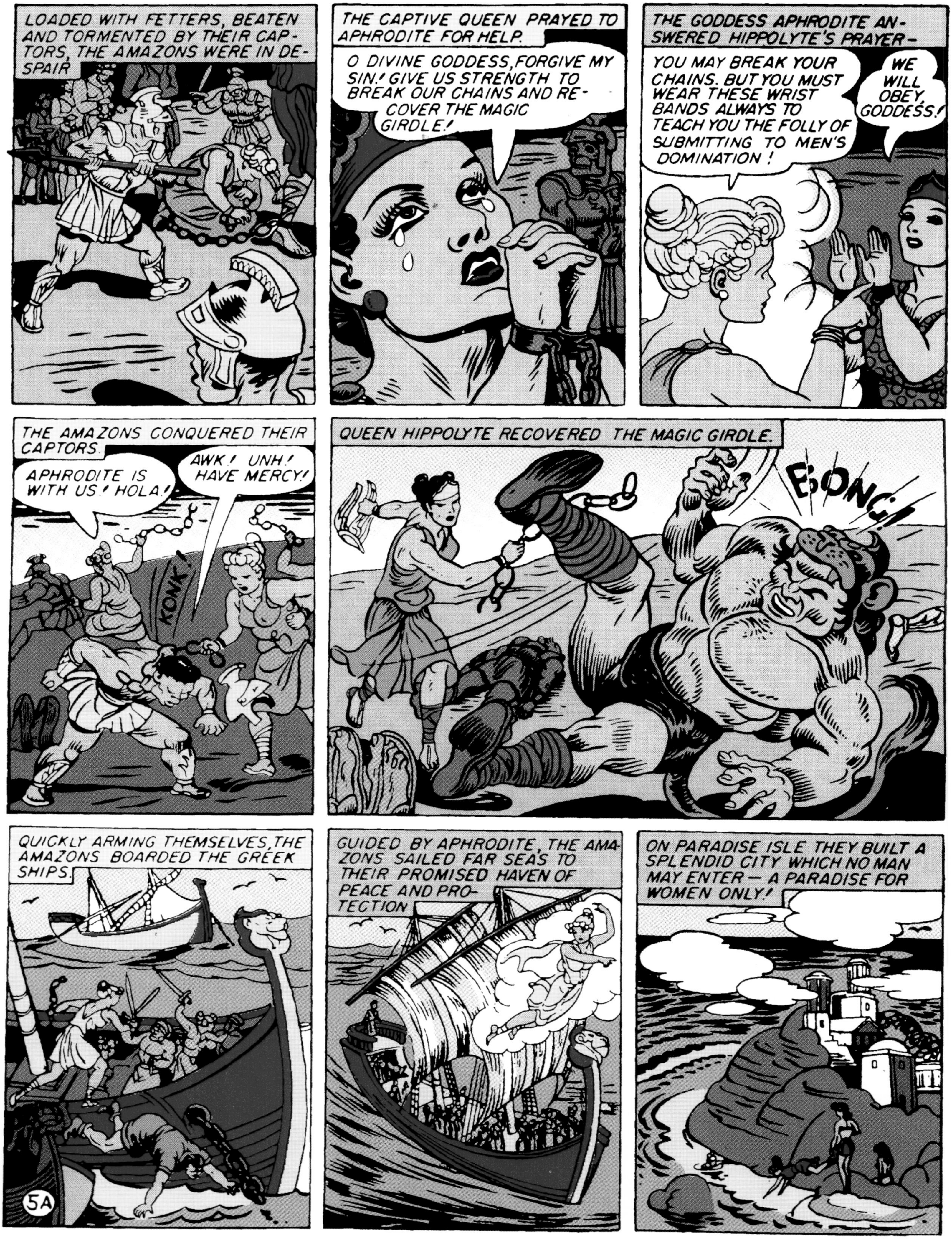
LOADED WITH FETTERS, BEATEN AND TORMENTED BY THEIR CAPTORS, THE AMAZONS WERE IN DESPAIR
THE CAPTIVE QUEEN PRAYED TO APHRODITE FOR HELP.
O DIVINE GODDESS, FORGIVE MY SIN! GIVE US STRENGTH TO BREAK OUR CHAINS AND RECOVER THE MAGIC GIRDLE!
THE GODDESS APHRODITE ANSWERED HIPPOLYTE'S PRAYER–
YOU MAY BREAK YOUR CHAINS. BUT YOU MUST WEAR THESE WRIST BANDS ALWAYS TO TEACH YOU THE FOLLY OF SUBMITTING TO MEN'S DOMINATION!
WE WILL OBEY, GODDESS!
THE AMAZONS CONQUERED THEIR CAPTORS.
APHRODITE IS WITH US! HOLA!
AWK! UNH! HAVE MERCY!
KONK!
QUEEN HIPPOLYTE RECOVERED THE MAGIC GIRDLE.
BONG!
QUICKLY ARMING THEMSELVES, THE AMAZONS BOARDED THE GREEK SHIPS.
5A
GUIDED BY APHRODITE, THE AMAZONS SAILED FAR SEAS TO THEIR PROMISED HAVEN OF PEACE AND PROTECTION
ON PARADISE ISLE THEY BUILT A SPLENDID CITY WHICH NO MAN MAY ENTER — A PARADISE FOR WOMEN ONLY!

HERE ENDS THE ANCIENT "HISTORY OF THE AMAZONS" AS TOLD IN THE PARCHMENT **WONDER WOMAN** LEFT! RELYING ON LATER SOURCES OF INFORMATION, WE SHALL CONTINUE THE STORY OF THE BEGINNINGS OF **WONDER WOMAN!**

THE QUEEN, UNDER DIRECTION OF ATHENA, GODDESS OF WISDOM, LEARNS THE SECRET ART OF MOULDING A HUMAN FORM!

HIPPOLYTE ADORES THE TINY STATUE SHE HAS MADE AS PYGMALION WORSHIPED GALATEA. APHRODITE, GRANTING THE QUEEN HER PRAYER, BESTOWS UPON IT THE DIVINE GIFT OF LIFE!

I NAME THEE DIANA, AFTER THE MOON GODDESS, MISTRESS OF THE CHASE!

BABY DIANA, TO HER MOTHER'S ASTONISHMENT, LEAPS HIGH INTO THE QUEEN'S ARMS!

HOW MARVELOUS — SHE IS MY LITTLE WONDER CHILD!

AT THREE, THE WONDER CHILD PULLS UP A FRUIT TREE BY ITS ROOTS.

GREAT THUNDERBOLTS OF ZEUS! SHE PULLS THAT TREE UP LIKE A WEED!

ALREADY OUR LITTLE PRINCESS HAS THE STRENGTH OF HERCULES!

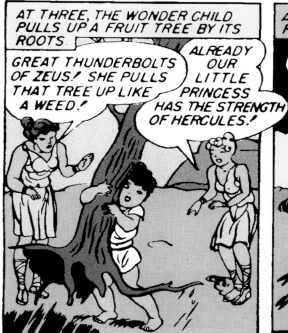

AT FIVE, DIANA LIKE HER NAMESAKE THE GODDESS OF THE CHASE, RACES DEER THROUGH THE FOREST.

THE QUEEN'S CHILD IS SWIFTER THAN MERCURY!

AT 15, THE YOUNG AMAZON GIRL RECEIVES HER BRACELETS OF SUBMISSION AT APHRODITE'S ALTAR.

I PLEDGE MYSELF FOREVER TO THY SERVICE, O GODDESS OF LOVE AND BEAUTY!

6A

DRINK, DIANA, FROM THE FOUNTAIN OF ETERNAL YOUTH! BEAUTY AND HAPPINESS ARE YOUR AMAZON BIRTHRIGHT SO LONG AS YOU REMAIN ON PARADISE ISLAND!

IT IS A WONDERFUL BIRTHRIGHT. I'LL NEVER GIVE IT UP!

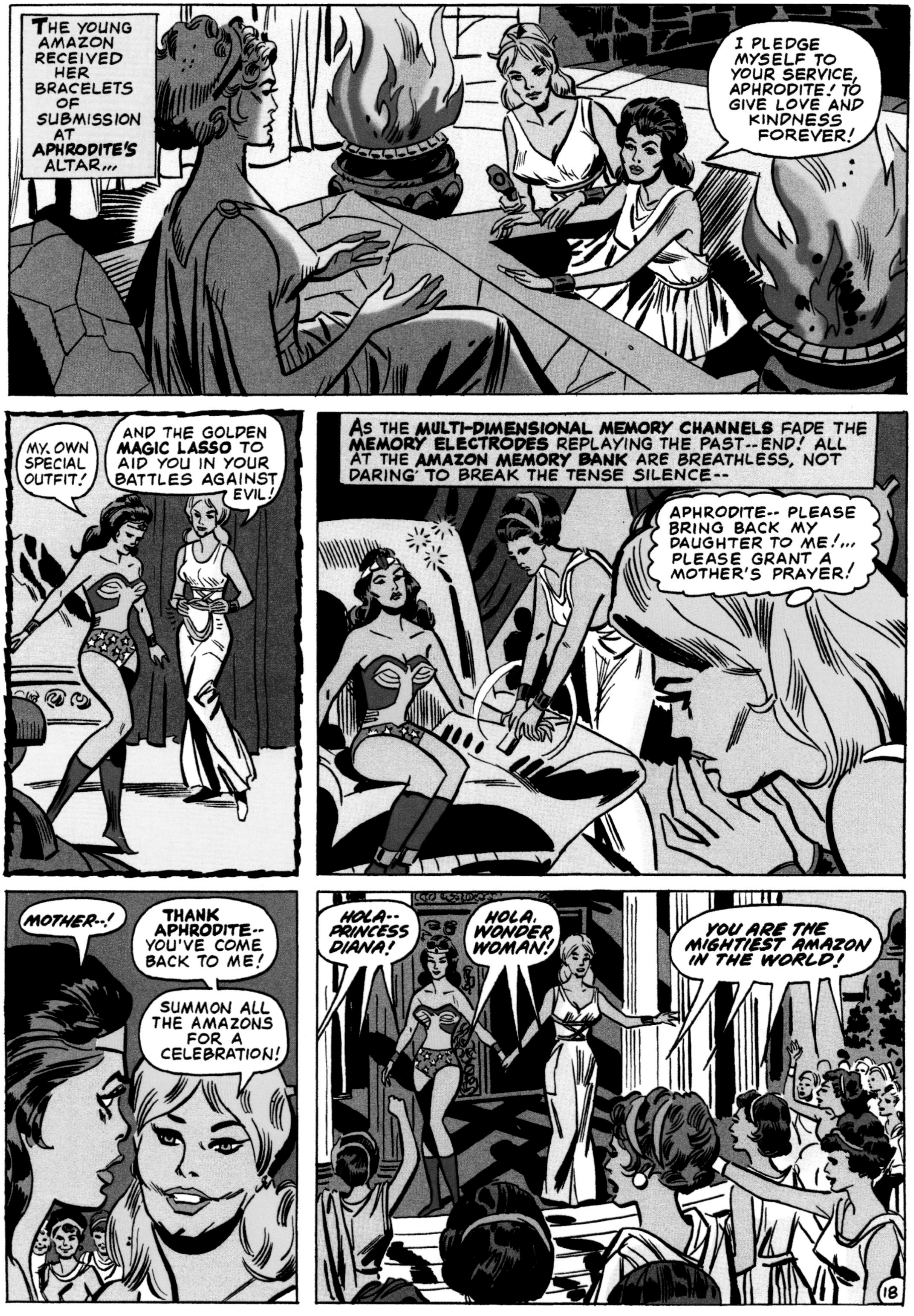
THE YOUNG AMAZON RECEIVED HER BRACELETS OF SUBMISSION AT APHRODITE'S ALTAR...
I PLEDGE MYSELF TO YOUR SERVICE, APHRODITE! TO GIVE LOVE AND KINDNESS FOREVER!
MY OWN SPECIAL OUTFIT!
AND THE GOLDEN MAGIC LASSO TO AID YOU IN YOUR BATTLES AGAINST EVIL!
AS THE MULTI-DIMENSIONAL MEMORY CHANNELS FADE THE MEMORY ELECTRODES REPLAYING THE PAST--END! ALL AT THE AMAZON MEMORY BANK ARE BREATHLESS, NOT DARING TO BREAK THE TENSE SILENCE--
APHRODITE-- PLEASE BRING BACK MY DAUGHTER TO ME!... PLEASE GRANT A MOTHER'S PRAYER!
MOTHER--!
THANK APHRODITE-- YOU'VE COME BACK TO ME!
SUMMON ALL THE AMAZONS FOR A CELEBRATION!
HOLA-- PRINCESS DIANA!
HOLA, WONDER WOMAN!
YOU ARE THE MIGHTIEST AMAZON IN THE WORLD!
18

Above: The reunion continues in this sequence from writer/editor Robert Kanigher and artists Don Heck and Dick Giordano.

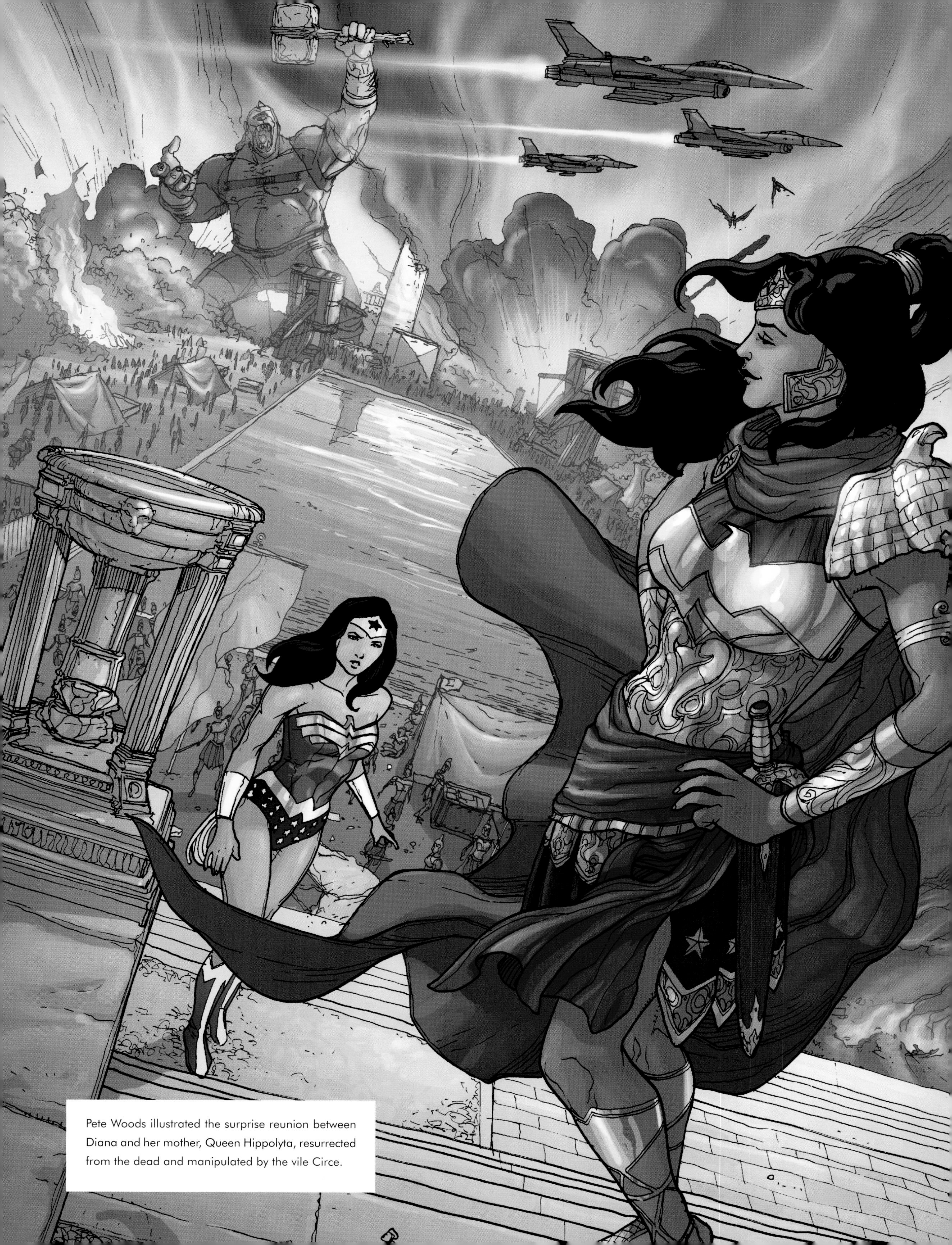

Pete Woods illustrated the surprise reunion between Diana and her mother, Queen Hippolyta, resurrected from the dead and manipulated by the vile Circe.

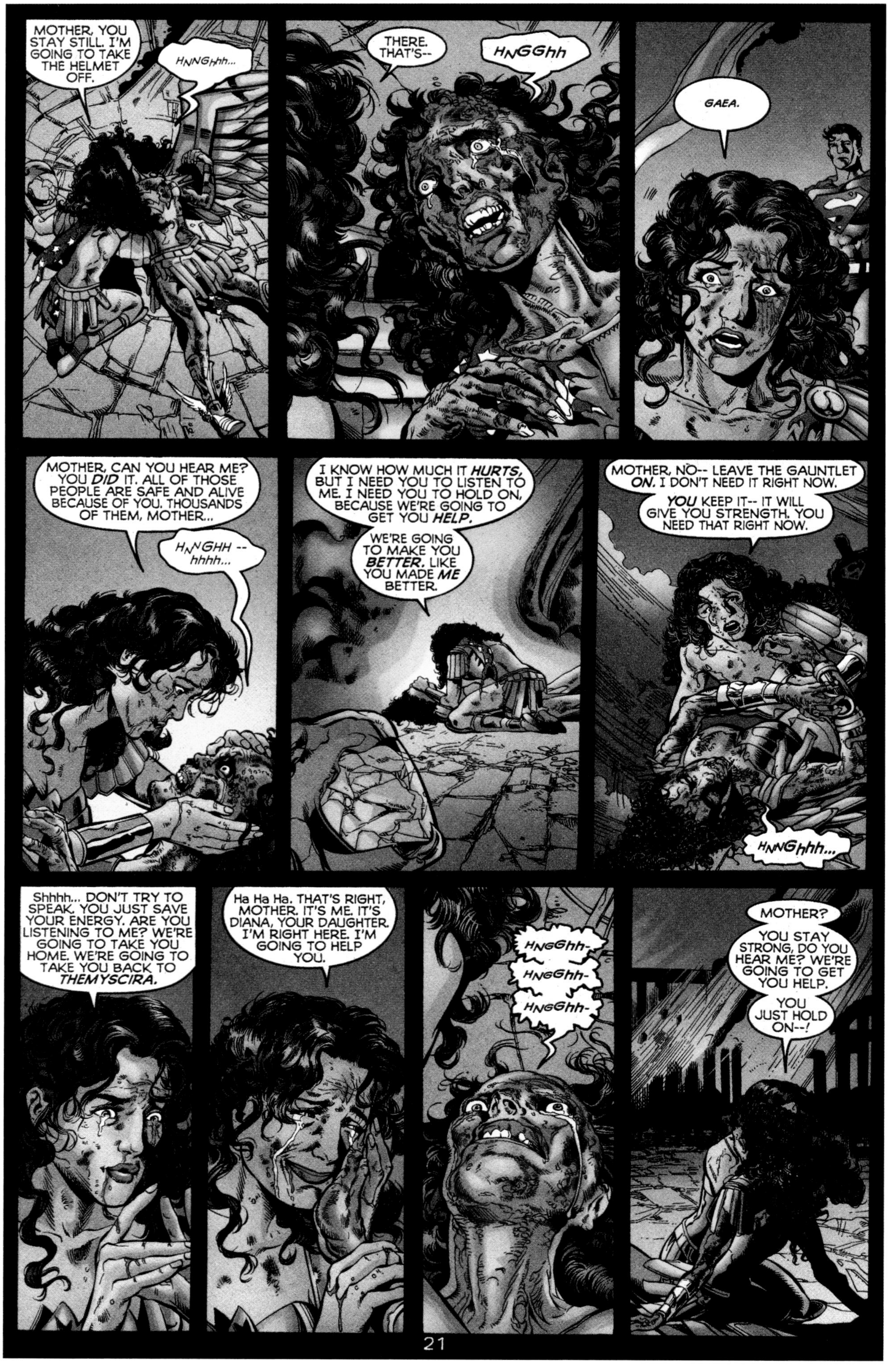
MOTHER, YOU STAY STILL. I'M GOING TO TAKE THE HELMET OFF.
HNNGhhh...
THERE. THAT'S--
HNGGhh
GAEA.
MOTHER, CAN YOU HEAR ME? YOU DID IT. ALL OF THOSE PEOPLE ARE SAFE AND ALIVE BECAUSE OF YOU. THOUSANDS OF THEM, MOTHER...
HNNGHH -- hhhh...
I KNOW HOW MUCH IT HURTS, BUT I NEED YOU TO LISTEN TO ME. I NEED YOU TO HOLD ON, BECAUSE WE'RE GOING TO GET YOU HELP.
WE'RE GOING TO MAKE YOU BETTER. LIKE YOU MADE ME BETTER.
MOTHER, NO-- LEAVE THE GAUNTLET ON. I DON'T NEED IT RIGHT NOW.
YOU KEEP IT-- IT WILL GIVE YOU STRENGTH. YOU NEED THAT RIGHT NOW.
HNNGhhh...
Shhhh... DON'T TRY TO SPEAK. YOU JUST SAVE YOUR ENERGY. ARE YOU LISTENING TO ME? WE'RE GOING TO TAKE YOU HOME. WE'RE GOING TO TAKE YOU BACK TO THEMYSCIRA.
Ha Ha Ha. THAT'S RIGHT, MOTHER. IT'S ME. IT'S DIANA, YOUR DAUGHTER. I'M RIGHT HERE. I'M GOING TO HELP YOU.
HNGGhh-
HNGGhh-
HNGGhh-
MOTHER?
YOU STAY STRONG, DO YOU HEAR ME? WE'RE GOING TO GET YOU HELP.
YOU JUST HOLD ON--!
21

Above and right: This two page sequence from *Wonder Woman* #172 shows the tearful farewell between mother and daughter. Queen Hippolyta led a charge against the invader Imperiex and won the day at a terrible cost. Story and pencils by Phil Jimenez, with inks by Andy Lanning.

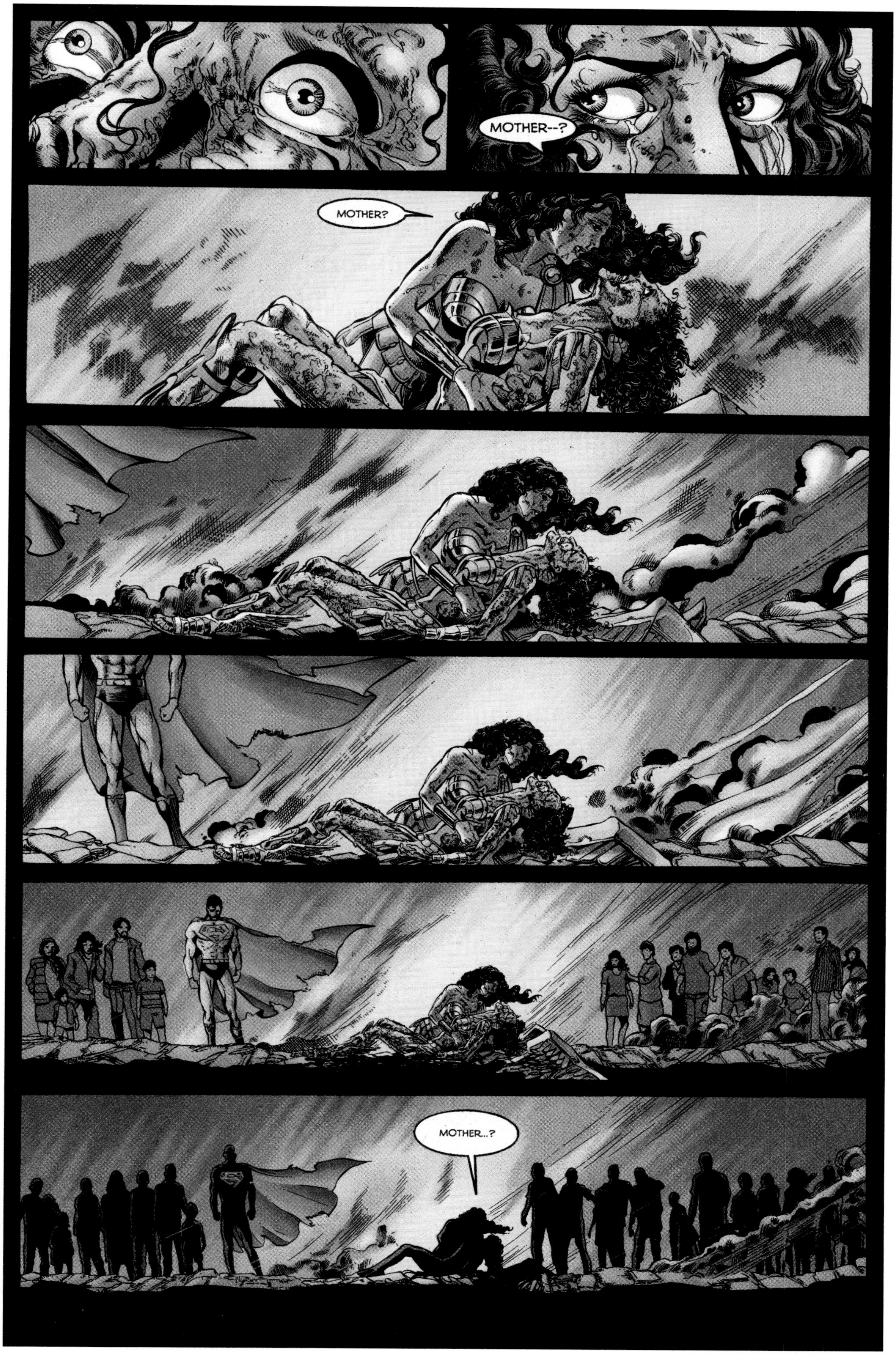
MOTHER--?
MOTHER?
MOTHER...?

Pages 50–51: A sequence from *Wonder Woman #6*, wherein Etta Candy is given a taste of life on Paradise Island, and it overwhelms the college student.

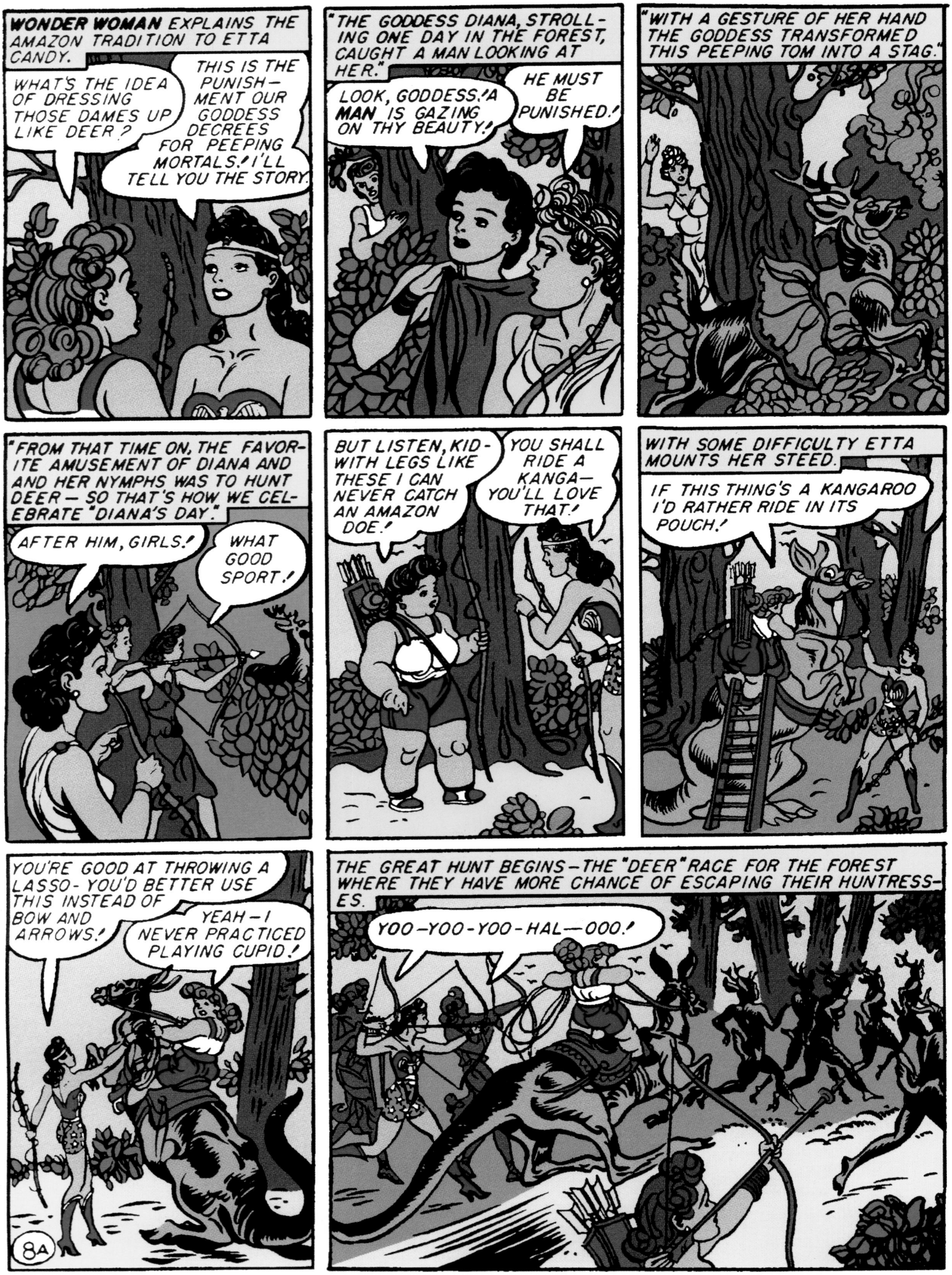

WONDER WOMAN EXPLAINS THE AMAZON TRADITION TO ETTA CANDY.
WHAT'S THE IDEA OF DRESSING THOSE DAMES UP LIKE DEER?
THIS IS THE PUNISHMENT OUR GODDESS DECREES FOR PEEPING MORTALS! I'LL TELL YOU THE STORY.
"THE GODDESS DIANA, STROLLING ONE DAY IN THE FOREST, CAUGHT A MAN LOOKING AT HER."
LOOK, GODDESS! A MAN IS GAZING ON THY BEAUTY!
HE MUST BE PUNISHED!
"WITH A GESTURE OF HER HAND THE GODDESS TRANSFORMED THIS PEEPING TOM INTO A STAG."
"FROM THAT TIME ON, THE FAVORITE AMUSEMENT OF DIANA AND AND HER NYMPHS WAS TO HUNT DEER — SO THAT'S HOW WE CELEBRATE "DIANA'S DAY."
AFTER HIM, GIRLS!
WHAT GOOD SPORT!
BUT LISTEN, KID — WITH LEGS LIKE THESE I CAN NEVER CATCH AN AMAZON DOE!
YOU SHALL RIDE A KANGA — YOU'LL LOVE THAT!
WITH SOME DIFFICULTY ETTA MOUNTS HER STEED.
IF THIS THING'S A KANGAROO I'D RATHER RIDE IN ITS POUCH!
YOU'RE GOOD AT THROWING A LASSO — YOU'D BETTER USE THIS INSTEAD OF BOW AND ARROWS!
YEAH — I NEVER PRACTICED PLAYING CUPID!
THE GREAT HUNT BEGINS — THE "DEER" RACE FOR THE FOREST WHERE THEY HAVE MORE CHANCE OF ESCAPING THEIR HUNTRESSES.
YOO-YOO-YOO-HAL—OOO!
8A

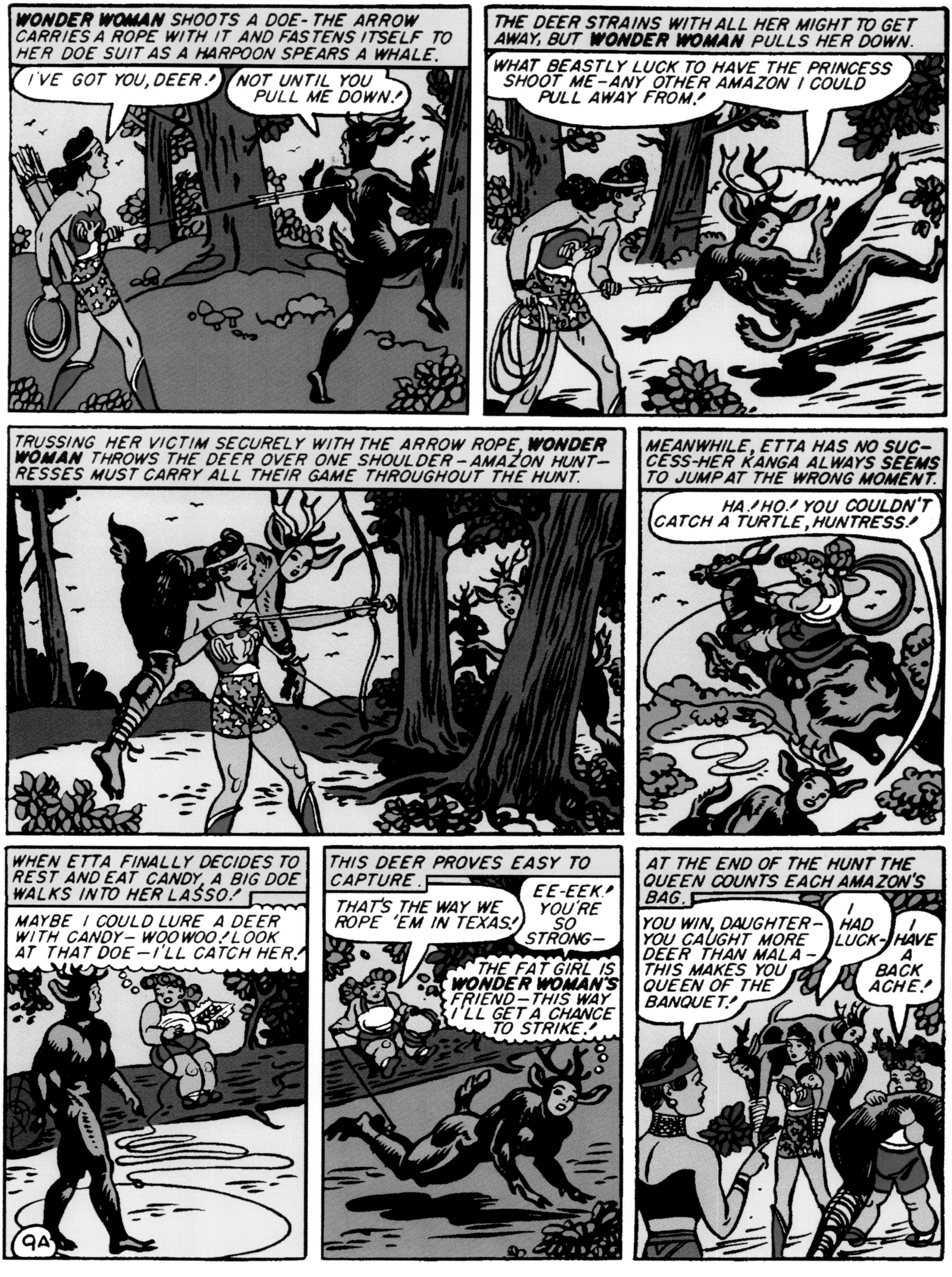

WONDER WOMAN SHOOTS A DOE-THE ARROW CARRIES A ROPE WITH IT AND FASTENS ITSELF TO HER DOE SUIT AS A HARPOON SPEARS A WHALE.
I'VE GOT YOU, DEER!
NOT UNTIL YOU PULL ME DOWN!
THE DEER STRAINS WITH ALL HER MIGHT TO GET AWAY, BUT WONDER WOMAN PULLS HER DOWN.
WHAT BEASTLY LUCK TO HAVE THE PRINCESS SHOOT ME—ANY OTHER AMAZON I COULD PULL AWAY FROM!
TRUSSING HER VICTIM SECURELY WITH THE ARROW ROPE, WONDER WOMAN THROWS THE DEER OVER ONE SHOULDER—AMAZON HUNTRESSES MUST CARRY ALL THEIR GAME THROUGHOUT THE HUNT.
MEANWHILE, ETTA HAS NO SUCCESS-HER KANGA ALWAYS SEEMS TO JUMP AT THE WRONG MOMENT.
HA! HO! YOU COULDN'T CATCH A TURTLE, HUNTRESS!
WHEN ETTA FINALLY DECIDES TO REST AND EAT CANDY, A BIG DOE WALKS INTO HER LASSO!
MAYBE I COULD LURE A DEER WITH CANDY— WOOWOO! LOOK AT THAT DOE—I'LL CATCH HER!
THIS DEER PROVES EASY TO CAPTURE.
THAT'S THE WAY WE ROPE 'EM IN TEXAS!
EE-EEK! YOU'RE SO STRONG—
THE FAT GIRL IS WONDER WOMAN'S FRIEND—THIS WAY I'LL GET A CHANCE TO STRIKE!
AT THE END OF THE HUNT THE QUEEN COUNTS EACH AMAZON'S BAG.
YOU WIN, DAUGHTER— YOU CAUGHT MORE DEER THAN MALA— THIS MAKES YOU QUEEN OF THE BANQUET!
I HAD LUCK—
I HAVE A BACK ACHE!
9A

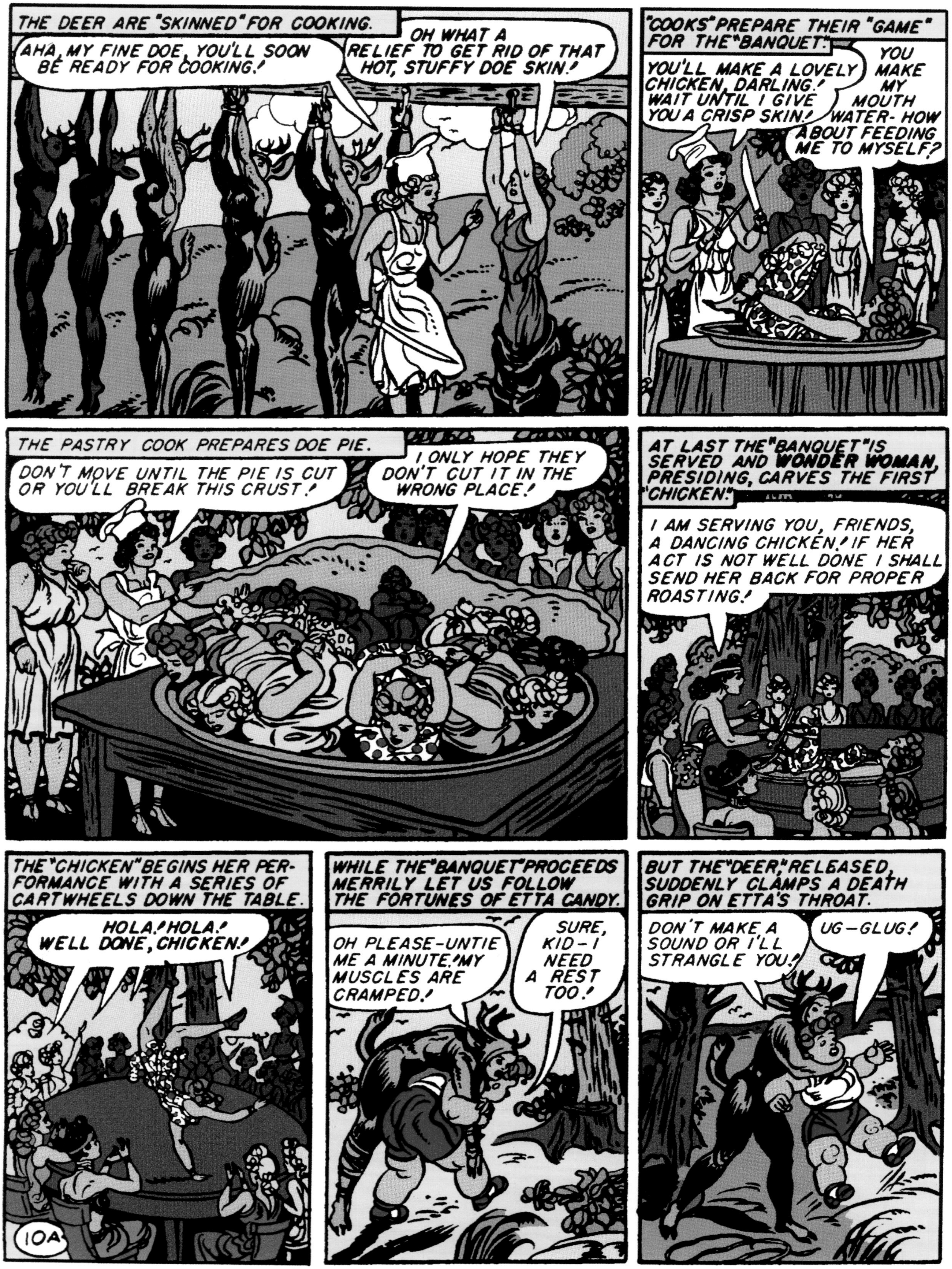

THE DEER ARE "SKINNED" FOR COOKING.
AHA, MY FINE DOE, YOU'LL SOON BE READY FOR COOKING!
OH WHAT A RELIEF TO GET RID OF THAT HOT, STUFFY DOE SKIN!
"COOKS" PREPARE THEIR "GAME" FOR THE "BANQUET."
YOU'LL MAKE A LOVELY CHICKEN, DARLING! WAIT UNTIL I GIVE YOU A CRISP SKIN!
YOU MAKE MY MOUTH WATER- HOW ABOUT FEEDING ME TO MYSELF?
THE PASTRY COOK PREPARES DOE PIE.
DON'T MOVE UNTIL THE PIE IS CUT OR YOU'LL BREAK THIS CRUST!
I ONLY HOPE THEY DON'T CUT IT IN THE WRONG PLACE!
AT LAST THE "BANQUET" IS SERVED AND WONDER WOMAN, PRESIDING, CARVES THE FIRST "CHICKEN."
I AM SERVING YOU, FRIENDS, A DANCING CHICKEN! IF HER ACT IS NOT WELL DONE I SHALL SEND HER BACK FOR PROPER ROASTING!
THE "CHICKEN" BEGINS HER PERFORMANCE WITH A SERIES OF CARTWHEELS DOWN THE TABLE.
HOLA! HOLA! WELL DONE, CHICKEN!
10A
WHILE THE "BANQUET" PROCEEDS MERRILY LET US FOLLOW THE FORTUNES OF ETTA CANDY.
OH PLEASE-UNTIE ME A MINUTE! MY MUSCLES ARE CRAMPED!
SURE, KID-I NEED A REST TOO!
BUT THE "DEER," RELEASED, SUDDENLY CLAMPS A DEATH GRIP ON ETTA'S THROAT.
DON'T MAKE A SOUND OR I'LL STRANGLE YOU!
UG-GLUG!

Left: Note the willingness of the women to be bound and somewhat humiliated in the name of celebrating womanhood, by Marston and Peter.

Below: Cover pencils for the 2008 *Who Is Wonder Woman?* collection by artist Terry Dodson.

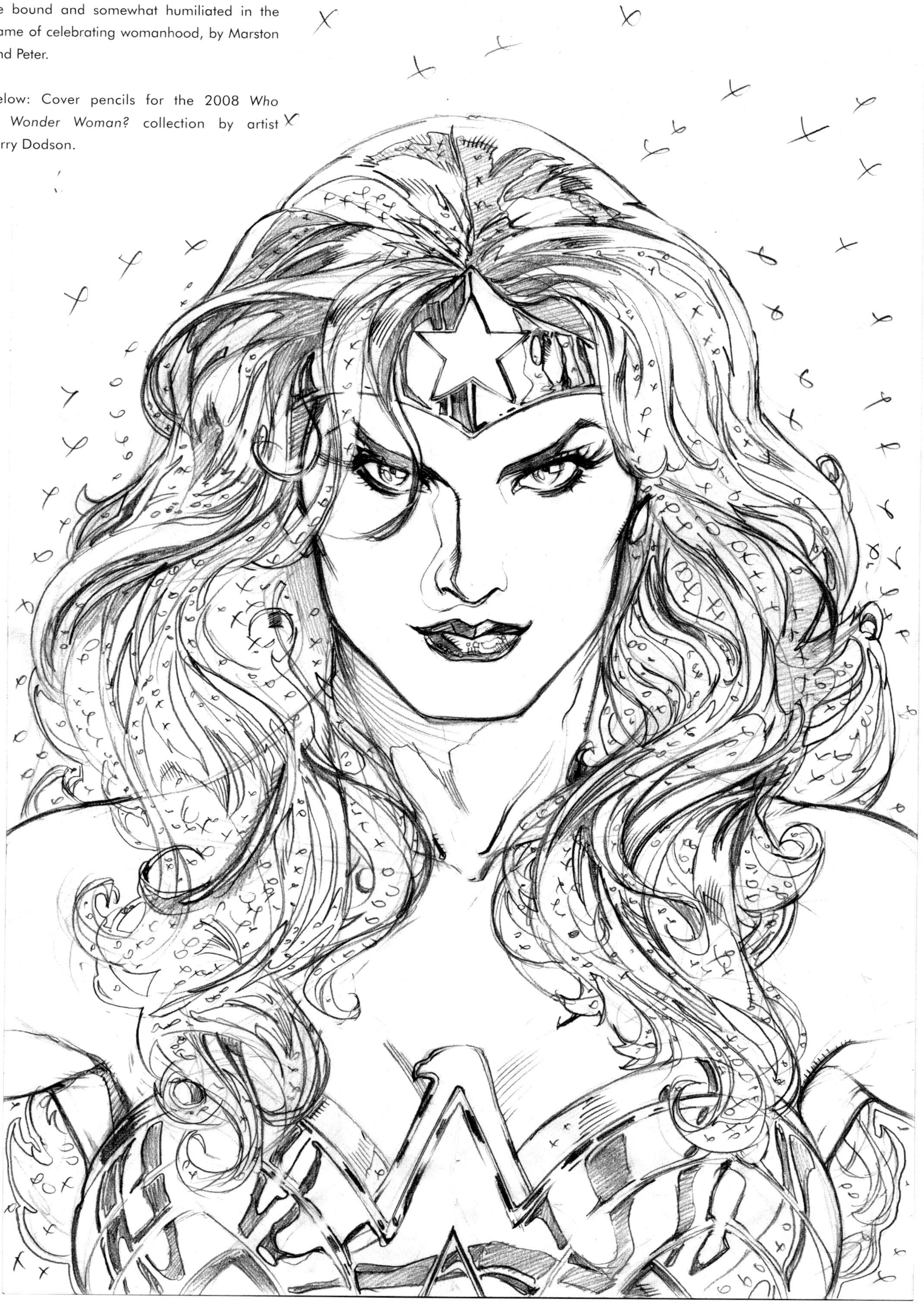

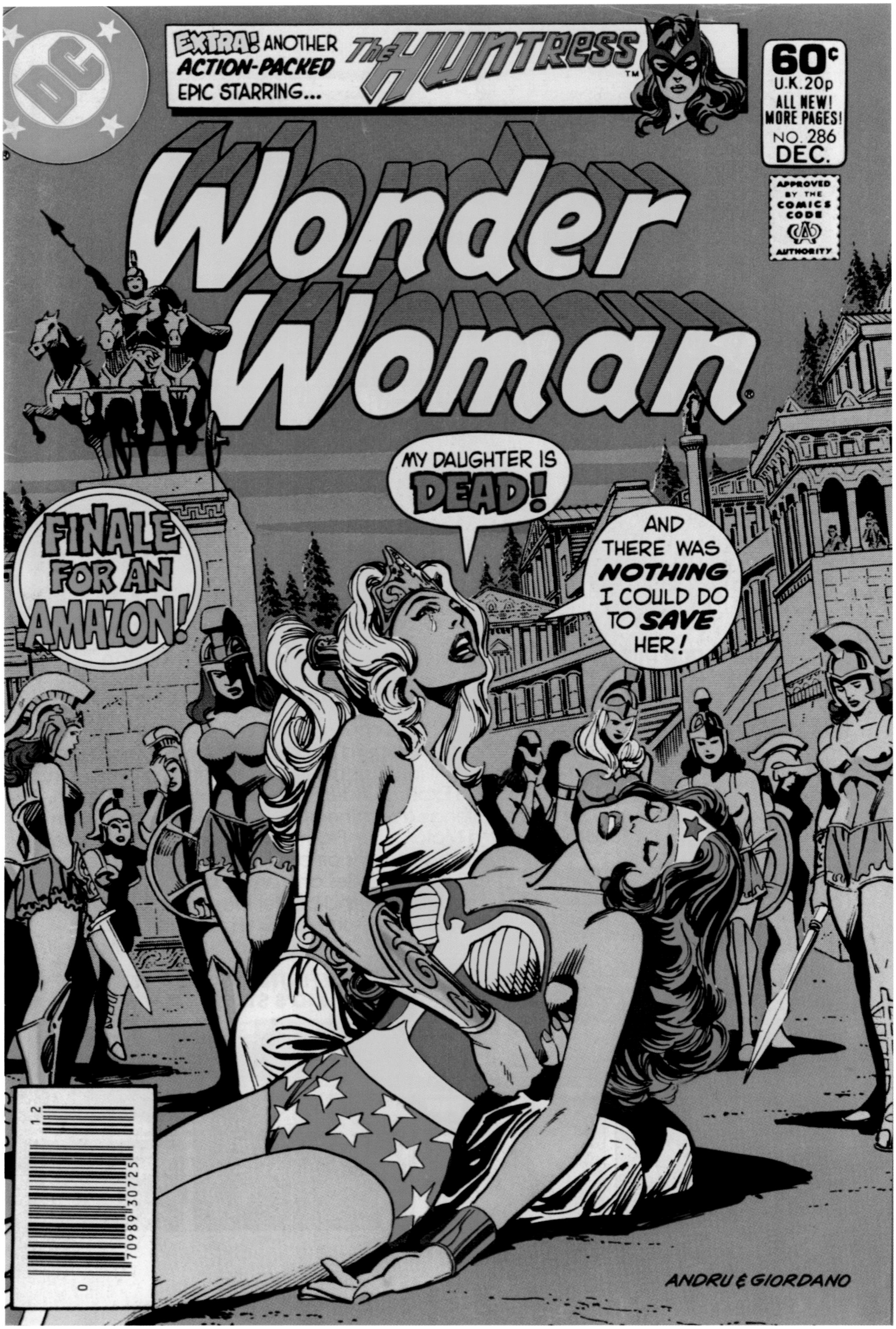
EXTRA! ANOTHER ACTION-PACKED EPIC STARRING...
The HUNTRESS
60¢
U.K.20p
ALL NEW! MORE PAGES!
NO. 286
DEC.
APPROVED BY THE COMICS CODE AUTHORITY
Wonder Woman
MY DAUGHTER IS DEAD!
AND THERE WAS NOTHING I COULD DO TO SAVE HER!
FINALE FOR AN AMAZON!
ANDRU & GIORDANO

Above: The Amazons have been depicted in a variety of ways but their warrior culture remains consistent. Cover art by Ross Andru and Dick Giordano.

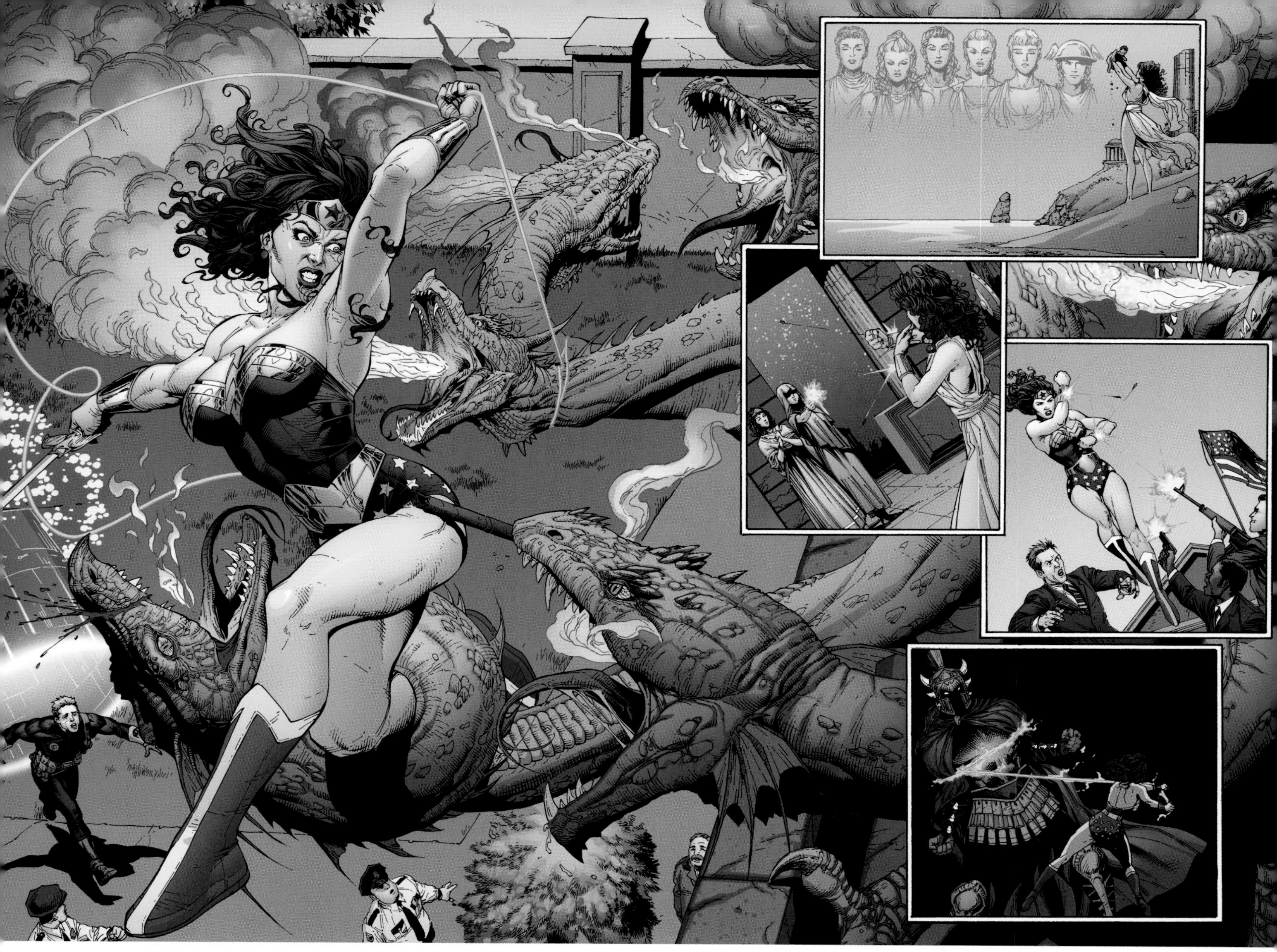

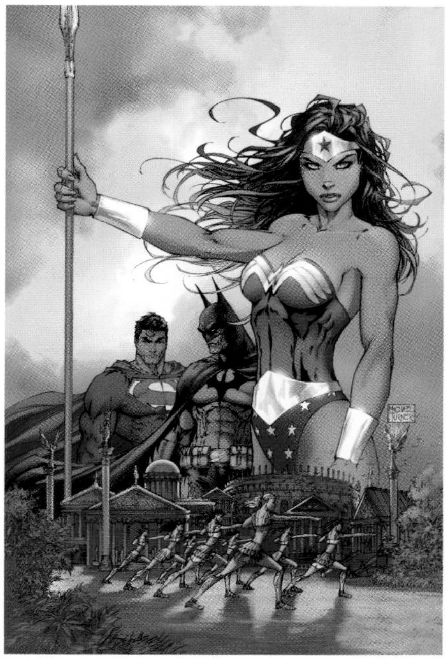

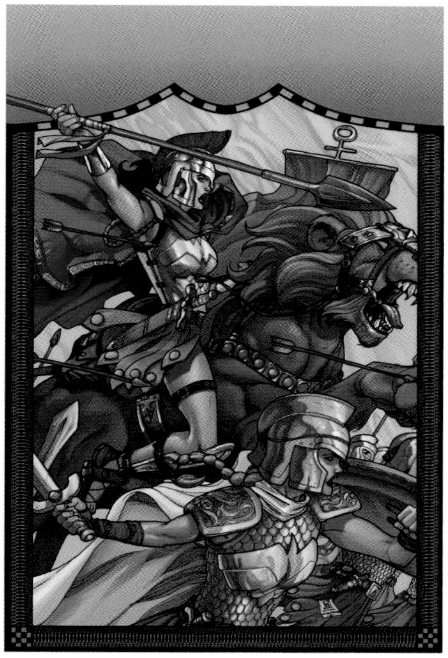

Above: A two-page sequence including origin recap panels from 2007's *Wonder Woman Annual* #1 by artists Gary Frank and Jon Sibal.

Far left: A 2004 *Superman/Batman* cover by Michael Turner showing the newly arrived Supergirl training on Themyscira.

Left: Pete Woods' cover art for *Amazons Attack!* #1 (June 2007).

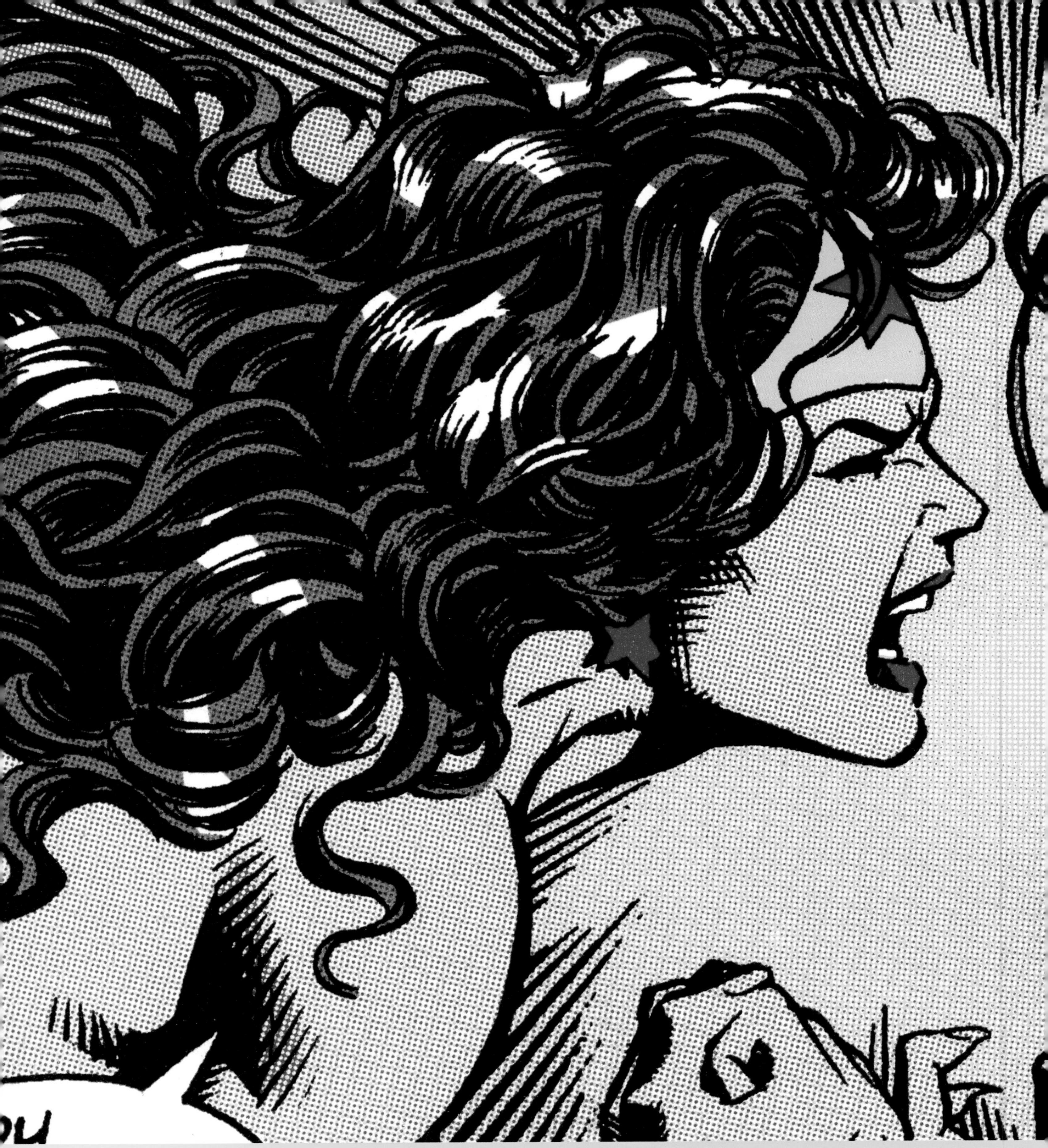

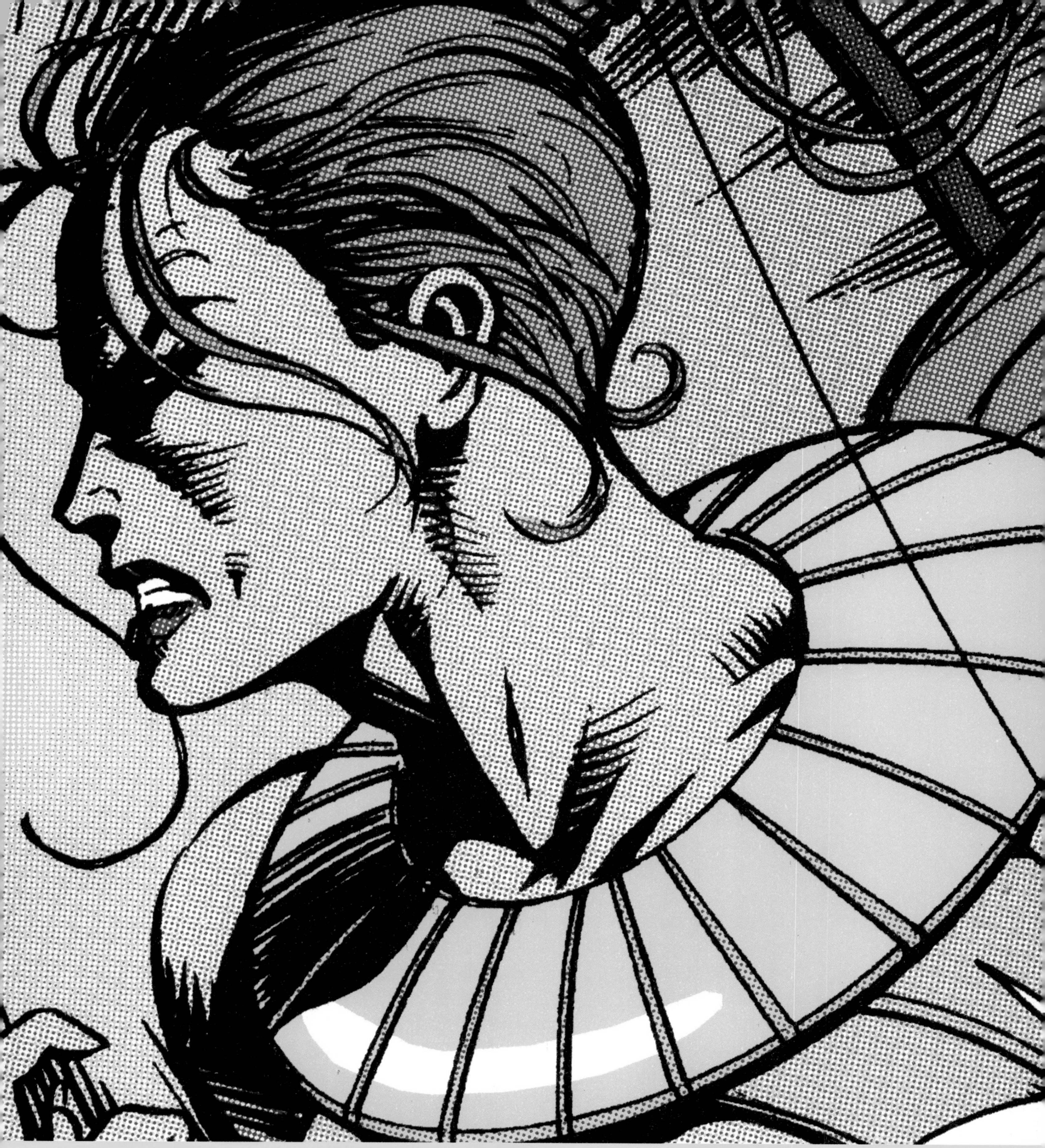

★ The Contest

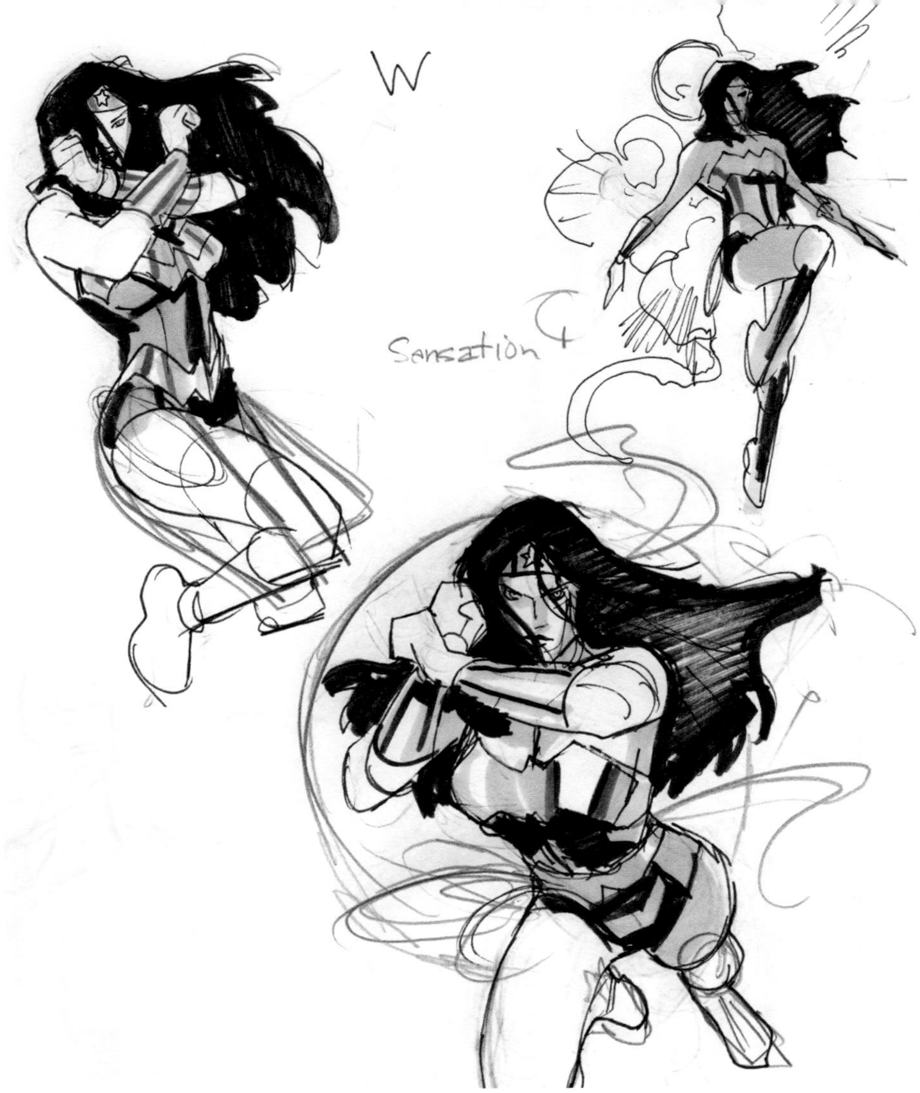
W
Sensation

Left: Character studies by Terry Dodson.

Below: An image of the Amazon Princess from a DC Comics style guide.

Right: The first time the Contest is depicted, in *All Star Comics* #8. Art by Harry G. Peter. Note that only Diana wore a mask.

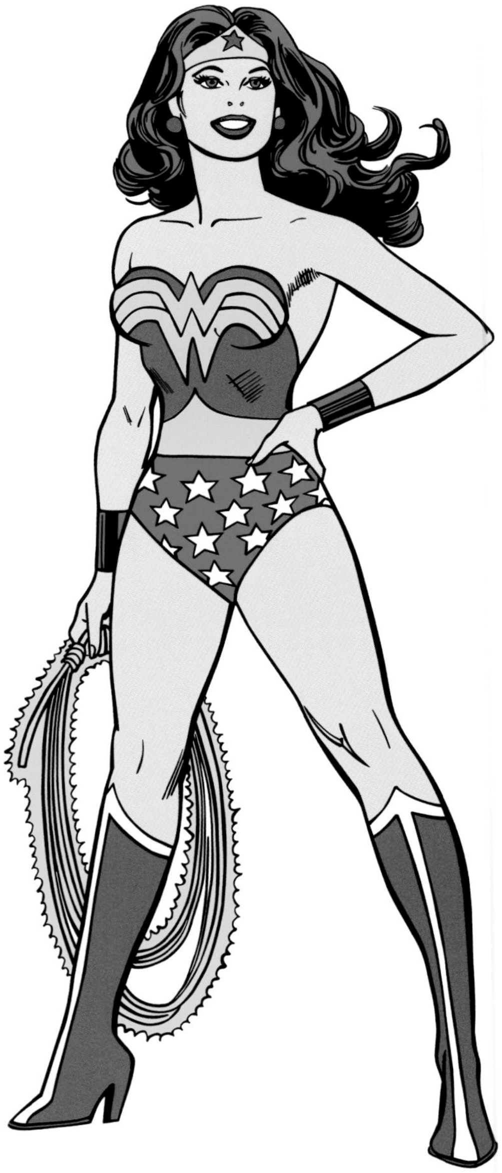

Only the threat of World War II seemed to prompt the Amazons to rejoin the world, but there was indecision over how they should best re-engage with humanity. Marston crafted an elegant solution he called the contest, a key element to Wonder Woman's origins. Whereas Superman became a hero by happenstance and Batman trained his mind and body to perfection to fight crime, Diana became a heroine out of necessity.

After Army Air Force pilot Steve Trevor crashed on Paradise Island in *All Star Comics* #8 (December 1941/January 1942), it was decided someone needed to act as the Amazons' emissary and bring him home after he healed. Queen Hippolyta decided only the very best of her subjects be given the critical assignment, so she contrived a series of challenges to select the Amazonian ambassador.

Diana was the youngest of the Amazons and at the peak of physical and mental health. She desperately wanted to participate—partly out of pride and partly because she had feelings for the handsome blond-haired man. Hippolyta, fearful of losing her daughter to the outside world, refused to allow Diana to participate.

A large stadium filled with cheering Amazons watched the volunteers take part in numerous physical tasks. Contestant number seven wore a black mask and won each event. The competition came down to only two women. To settle the matter, the mystery competitor and an Amazon named Mala played the deadly game of "bullets and bracelets," which later became a standard part of the contest storyline. When the masked Amazon won, she removed her disguise and shocked one and all when she was revealed to be Princess Diana.

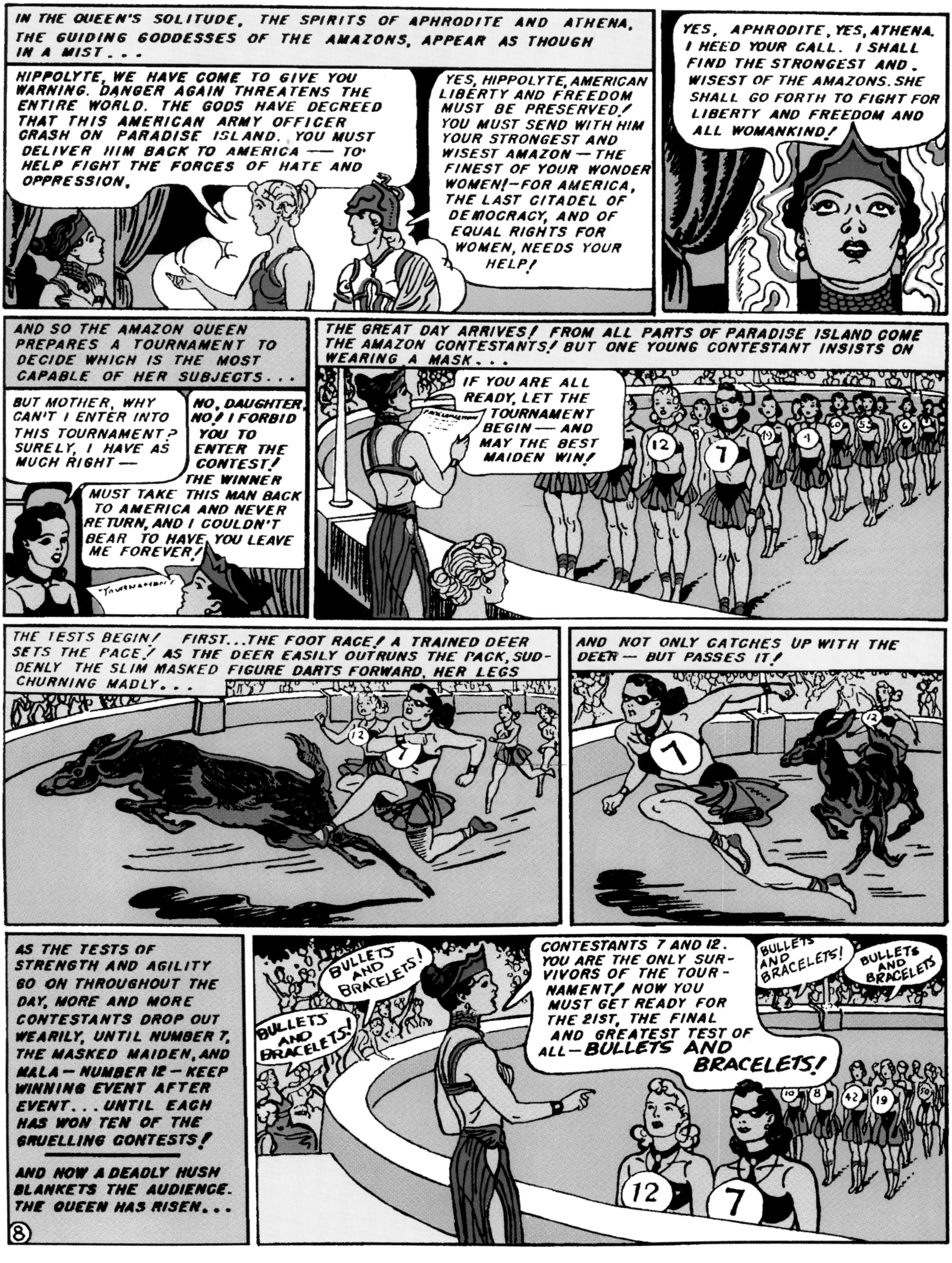
IN THE QUEEN'S SOLITUDE, THE SPIRITS OF APHRODITE AND ATHENA, THE GUIDING GODDESSES OF THE AMAZONS, APPEAR AS THOUGH IN A MIST...
HIPPOLYTE, WE HAVE COME TO GIVE YOU WARNING. DANGER AGAIN THREATENS THE ENTIRE WORLD. THE GODS HAVE DECREED THAT THIS AMERICAN ARMY OFFICER CRASH ON PARADISE ISLAND. YOU MUST DELIVER HIM BACK TO AMERICA — TO HELP FIGHT THE FORCES OF HATE AND OPPRESSION.
YES, HIPPOLYTE, AMERICAN LIBERTY AND FREEDOM MUST BE PRESERVED! YOU MUST SEND WITH HIM YOUR STRONGEST AND WISEST AMAZON — THE FINEST OF YOUR WONDER WOMEN! — FOR AMERICA, THE LAST CITADEL OF DEMOCRACY, AND OF EQUAL RIGHTS FOR WOMEN, NEEDS YOUR HELP!
YES, APHRODITE, YES, ATHENA. I HEED YOUR CALL. I SHALL FIND THE STRONGEST AND WISEST OF THE AMAZONS. SHE SHALL GO FORTH TO FIGHT FOR LIBERTY AND FREEDOM AND ALL WOMANKIND!
AND SO THE AMAZON QUEEN PREPARES A TOURNAMENT TO DECIDE WHICH IS THE MOST CAPABLE OF HER SUBJECTS...
BUT MOTHER, WHY CAN'T I ENTER INTO THIS TOURNAMENT? SURELY, I HAVE AS MUCH RIGHT —
NO, DAUGHTER, NO! I FORBID YOU TO ENTER THE CONTEST! THE WINNER MUST TAKE THIS MAN BACK TO AMERICA AND NEVER RETURN, AND I COULDN'T BEAR TO HAVE YOU LEAVE ME FOREVER!
"TOURNAMENT"
THE GREAT DAY ARRIVES! FROM ALL PARTS OF PARADISE ISLAND COME THE AMAZON CONTESTANTS! BUT ONE YOUNG CONTESTANT INSISTS ON WEARING A MASK...
IF YOU ARE ALL READY, LET THE TOURNAMENT BEGIN — AND MAY THE BEST MAIDEN WIN!
THE TESTS BEGIN! FIRST...THE FOOT RACE! A TRAINED DEER SETS THE PACE! AS THE DEER EASILY OUTRUNS THE PACK, SUDDENLY THE SLIM MASKED FIGURE DARTS FORWARD, HER LEGS CHURNING MADLY...
AND NOT ONLY CATCHES UP WITH THE DEER — BUT PASSES IT!
AS THE TESTS OF STRENGTH AND AGILITY GO ON THROUGHOUT THE DAY, MORE AND MORE CONTESTANTS DROP OUT WEARILY, UNTIL NUMBER 7, THE MASKED MAIDEN, AND MALA — NUMBER 12 — KEEP WINNING EVENT AFTER EVENT... UNTIL EACH HAS WON TEN OF THE GRUELLING CONTESTS!
AND NOW A DEADLY HUSH BLANKETS THE AUDIENCE. THE QUEEN HAS RISEN...
BULLETS AND BRACELETS!
BULLETS AND BRACELETS!
CONTESTANTS 7 AND 12. YOU ARE THE ONLY SURVIVORS OF THE TOURNAMENT! NOW YOU MUST GET READY FOR THE 21ST, THE FINAL AND GREATEST TEST OF ALL — BULLETS AND BRACELETS!
BULLETS AND BRACELETS!
BULLETS AND BRACELETS
8

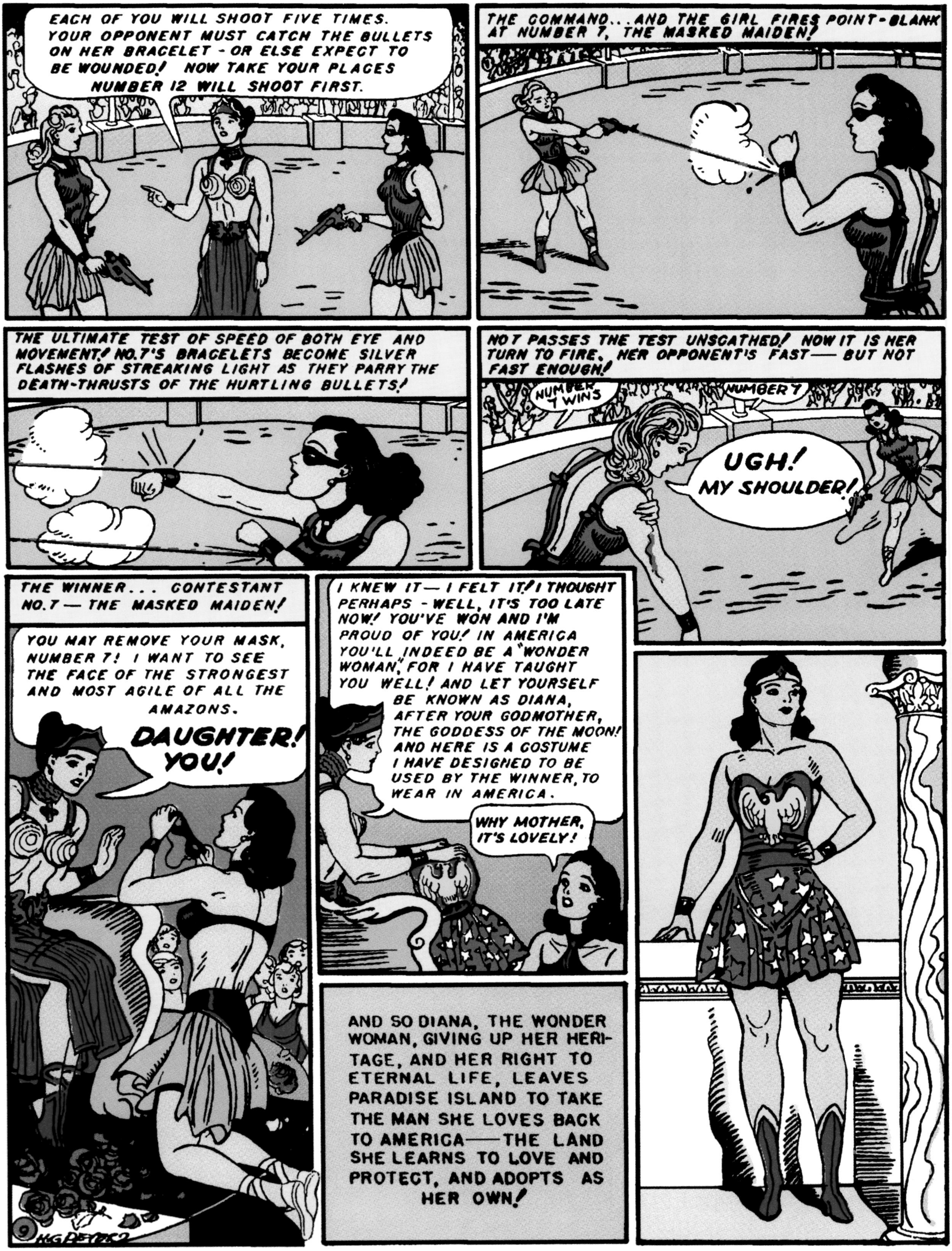
EACH OF YOU WILL SHOOT FIVE TIMES. YOUR OPPONENT MUST CATCH THE BULLETS ON HER BRACELET - OR ELSE EXPECT TO BE WOUNDED! NOW TAKE YOUR PLACES NUMBER 12 WILL SHOOT FIRST.
THE COMMAND... AND THE GIRL FIRES POINT-BLANK AT NUMBER 7, THE MASKED MAIDEN!
THE ULTIMATE TEST OF SPEED OF BOTH EYE AND MOVEMENT! NO.7'S BRACELETS BECOME SILVER FLASHES OF STREAKING LIGHT AS THEY PARRY THE DEATH-THRUSTS OF THE HURTLING BULLETS!
NO7 PASSES THE TEST UNSCATHED! NOW IT IS HER TURN TO FIRE. HER OPPONENT'S FAST— BUT NOT FAST ENOUGH!
NUMBER 7 WINS
NUMBER 7
UGH! MY SHOULDER!
THE WINNER... CONTESTANT NO.7 — THE MASKED MAIDEN!
YOU MAY REMOVE YOUR MASK, NUMBER 7! I WANT TO SEE THE FACE OF THE STRONGEST AND MOST AGILE OF ALL THE AMAZONS.
DAUGHTER! YOU!
I KNEW IT— I FELT IT! I THOUGHT PERHAPS - WELL, IT'S TOO LATE NOW! YOU'VE WON AND I'M PROUD OF YOU! IN AMERICA YOU'LL INDEED BE A "WONDER WOMAN," FOR I HAVE TAUGHT YOU WELL! AND LET YOURSELF BE KNOWN AS DIANA, AFTER YOUR GODMOTHER, THE GODDESS OF THE MOON! AND HERE IS A COSTUME I HAVE DESIGNED TO BE USED BY THE WINNER, TO WEAR IN AMERICA.
WHY MOTHER, IT'S LOVELY!
AND SO DIANA, THE WONDER WOMAN, GIVING UP HER HERITAGE, AND HER RIGHT TO ETERNAL LIFE, LEAVES PARADISE ISLAND TO TAKE THE MAN SHE LOVES BACK TO AMERICA—THE LAND SHE LEARNS TO LOVE AND PROTECT, AND ADOPTS AS HER OWN!
9
H.G.PETER

Above: Character studies by artist Terry Dodson who illustrated, with his wife Rachel Dodson, a celebrated run of covers during the 2000s. Note that in the Golden Age, the Amazons were not particularly well-toned or -muscled, whereas the modern day Wonder Woman is depicted to be a healthy, well-conditioned warrior.

Left: The Contest ends as Diana bests Mala at bullets and bracelets and wins the right to become Wonder Woman.

By then, the queen had little choice but to allow her daughter to take Trevor to Man's World, and thus began a new career as a costumed super heroine.

The thinking behind story elements such as the contest was Marston's way of exploring the superiority of women. In a 1943 issue of *The American Scholar*, he wrote, "Not even girls want to be girls so long as our feminine archetype lacks force, strength, and power. Not wanting to be girls, they don't want to be tender, submissive, and peace loving as good women are. Women's strong qualities have become despised because of their weakness. The obvious remedy is to create a feminine character with all the strength of Superman, plus all the allure of a good and beautiful woman."

The contest has been played out in every version of Wonder Woman's origin story, utilized as the challenge for the right to wear her iconic red, white, and blue outfit and tiara; or to wield her magic lasso.

Under writer Kanigher, Wonder Woman revisited the contest motif repeatedly. She was challenged by doubles of herself and fellow Amazons, and even settled problems by challenging alien invaders or common thieves to various contests, emerging victorious time and again.

When George Pérez and Greg Potter retold the story of the contest in their 1987 revamp, it was the gods who decided that an Amazon should be an emissary to Man's World. Again Diana defied her mother and easily won the contest, thereby fulfilling her destiny. This time, her wardrobe as Wonder Woman was purported to be inspired by patches and accessories worn by Steve Trevor's mother, the heroic Diana Trevor.

After the Amazons and the Bana-Mighdall were reunited, Artemis, the fiery leader of the splinter group, challenged Diana for the right to be Wonder Woman, and a new contest was held. Wearing a Proteus mask that altered her appearance, Diana faced Artemis without her gods-given powers. Diana, who was unintentionally distracted by her mother, faltered and Artemis won the final challenge to become Wonder Woman. During Artemis's brief stint as Wonder Woman, Diana remained in Man's World, adventuring in a star-spangled costume, complete with leather jacket and biker shorts, and was seen as Artemis's rival.

Without benefit of the contest, both Hippolyta and Donna Troy also briefly donned the colorful costume to serve as Wonder Woman during other periods of crises.

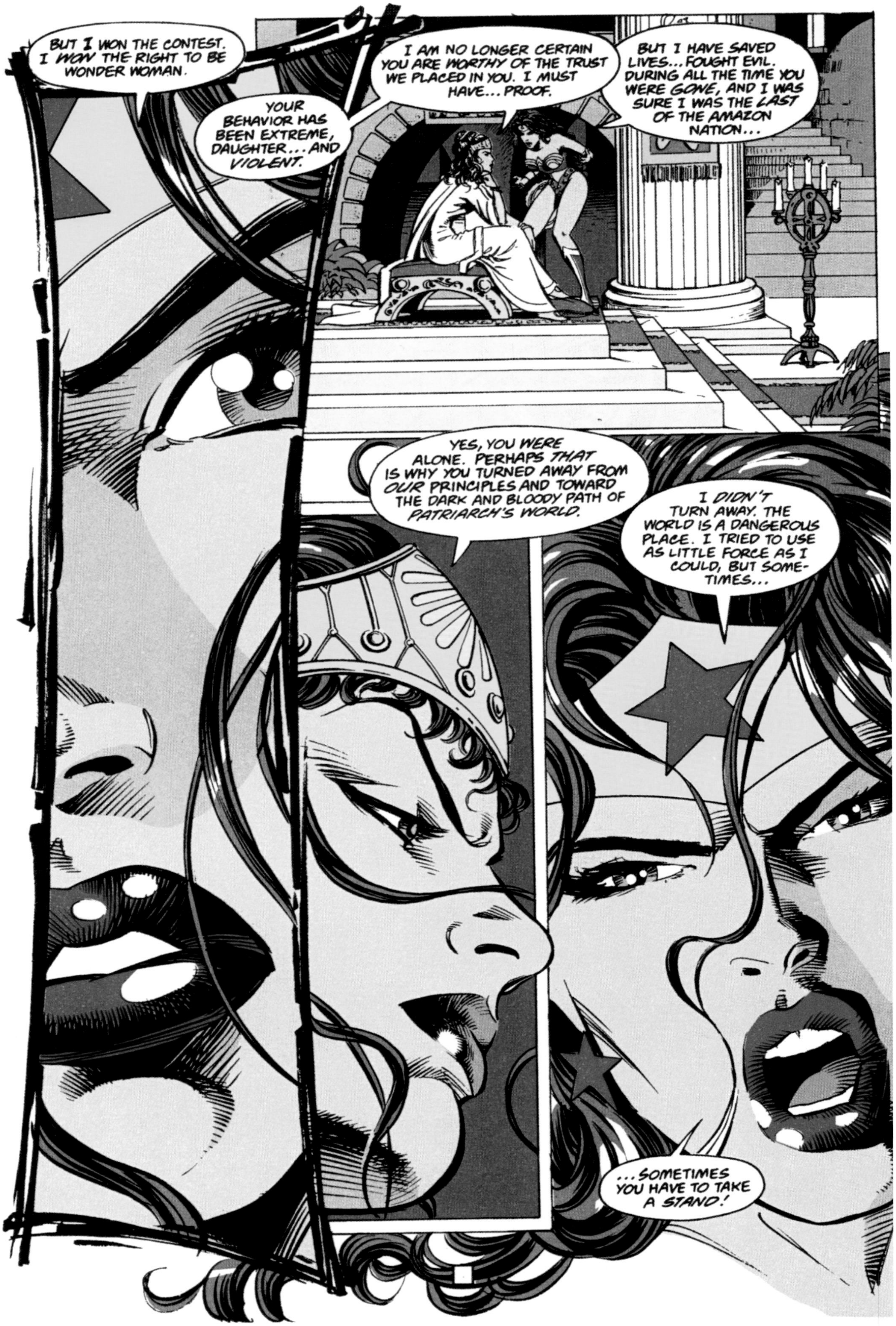
BUT I WON THE CONTEST. I WON THE RIGHT TO BE WONDER WOMAN.
YOUR BEHAVIOR HAS BEEN EXTREME, DAUGHTER... AND VIOLENT.
I AM NO LONGER CERTAIN YOU ARE WORTHY OF THE TRUST WE PLACED IN YOU. I MUST HAVE... PROOF.
BUT I HAVE SAVED LIVES... FOUGHT EVIL. DURING ALL THE TIME YOU WERE GONE, AND I WAS SURE I WAS THE LAST OF THE AMAZON NATION...
YES, YOU WERE ALONE. PERHAPS THAT IS WHY YOU TURNED AWAY FROM OUR PRINCIPLES AND TOWARD THE DARK AND BLOODY PATH OF PATRIARCH'S WORLD.
I DIDN'T TURN AWAY. THE WORLD IS A DANGEROUS PLACE. I TRIED TO USE AS LITTLE FORCE AS I COULD, BUT SOME-TIMES...
...SOMETIMES YOU HAVE TO TAKE A STAND!

Above and right: A heated exchange between mother and daughter, with Hippolyta hiding that she had a vision that showed Wonder Woman's death. Story and art by William Messner-Loebs and Mike Deodato, Jr.

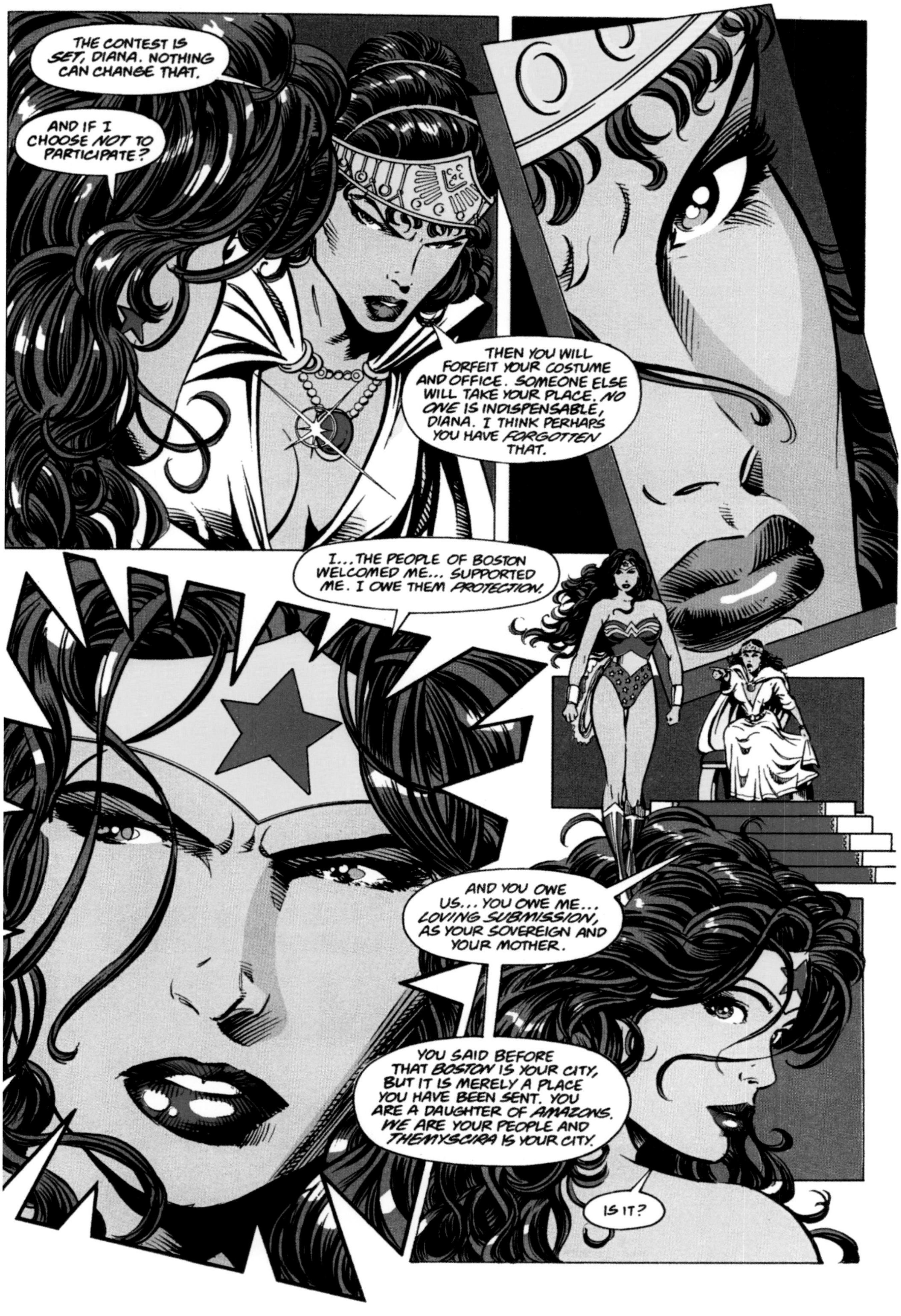
THE CONTEST IS SET, DIANA. NOTHING CAN CHANGE THAT.
AND IF I CHOOSE NOT TO PARTICIPATE?
THEN YOU WILL FORFEIT YOUR COSTUME AND OFFICE. SOMEONE ELSE WILL TAKE YOUR PLACE. NO ONE IS INDISPENSABLE, DIANA. I THINK PERHAPS YOU HAVE FORGOTTEN THAT.
I... THE PEOPLE OF BOSTON WELCOMED ME... SUPPORTED ME. I OWE THEM PROTECTION.
AND YOU OWE US... YOU OWE ME... LOVING SUBMISSION, AS YOUR SOVEREIGN AND YOUR MOTHER.
YOU SAID BEFORE THAT BOSTON IS YOUR CITY, BUT IT IS MERELY A PLACE YOU HAVE BEEN SENT. YOU ARE A DAUGHTER OF AMAZONS. WE ARE YOUR PEOPLE AND THEMYSCIRA IS YOUR CITY.
IS IT?

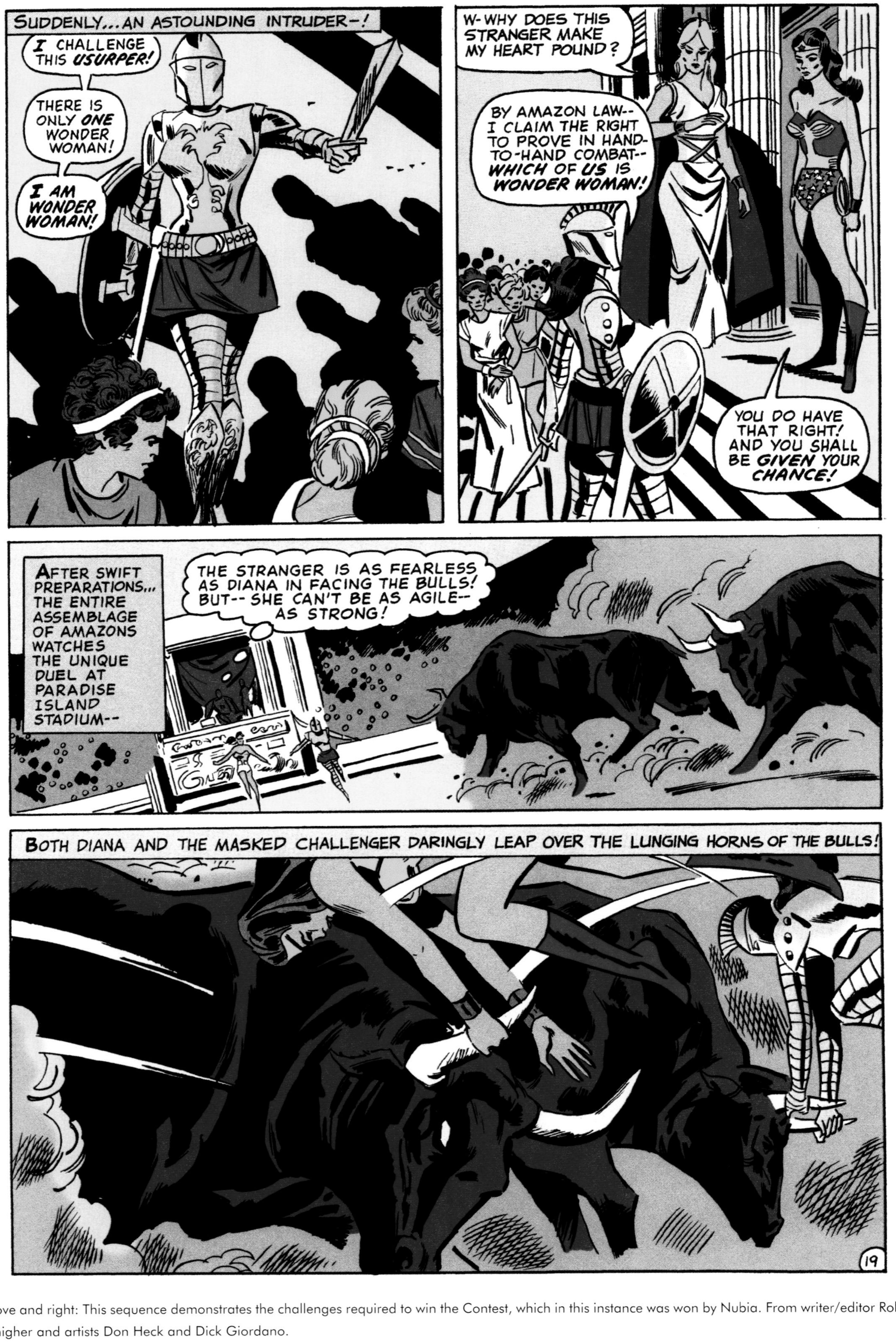
SUDDENLY...AN ASTOUNDING INTRUDER-!
I CHALLENGE THIS USURPER!
THERE IS ONLY ONE WONDER WOMAN!
I AM WONDER WOMAN!
W-WHY DOES THIS STRANGER MAKE MY HEART POUND?
BY AMAZON LAW-- I CLAIM THE RIGHT TO PROVE IN HAND-TO-HAND COMBAT-- WHICH OF US IS WONDER WOMAN!
YOU DO HAVE THAT RIGHT! AND YOU SHALL BE GIVEN YOUR CHANCE!
AFTER SWIFT PREPARATIONS... THE ENTIRE ASSEMBLAGE OF AMAZONS WATCHES THE UNIQUE DUEL AT PARADISE ISLAND STADIUM--
THE STRANGER IS AS FEARLESS AS DIANA IN FACING THE BULLS! BUT-- SHE CAN'T BE AS AGILE-- AS STRONG!
BOTH DIANA AND THE MASKED CHALLENGER DARINGLY LEAP OVER THE LUNGING HORNS OF THE BULLS!
19

Above and right: This sequence demonstrates the challenges required to win the Contest, which in this instance was won by Nubia. From writer/editor Robert Kanigher and artists Don Heck and Dick Giordano.

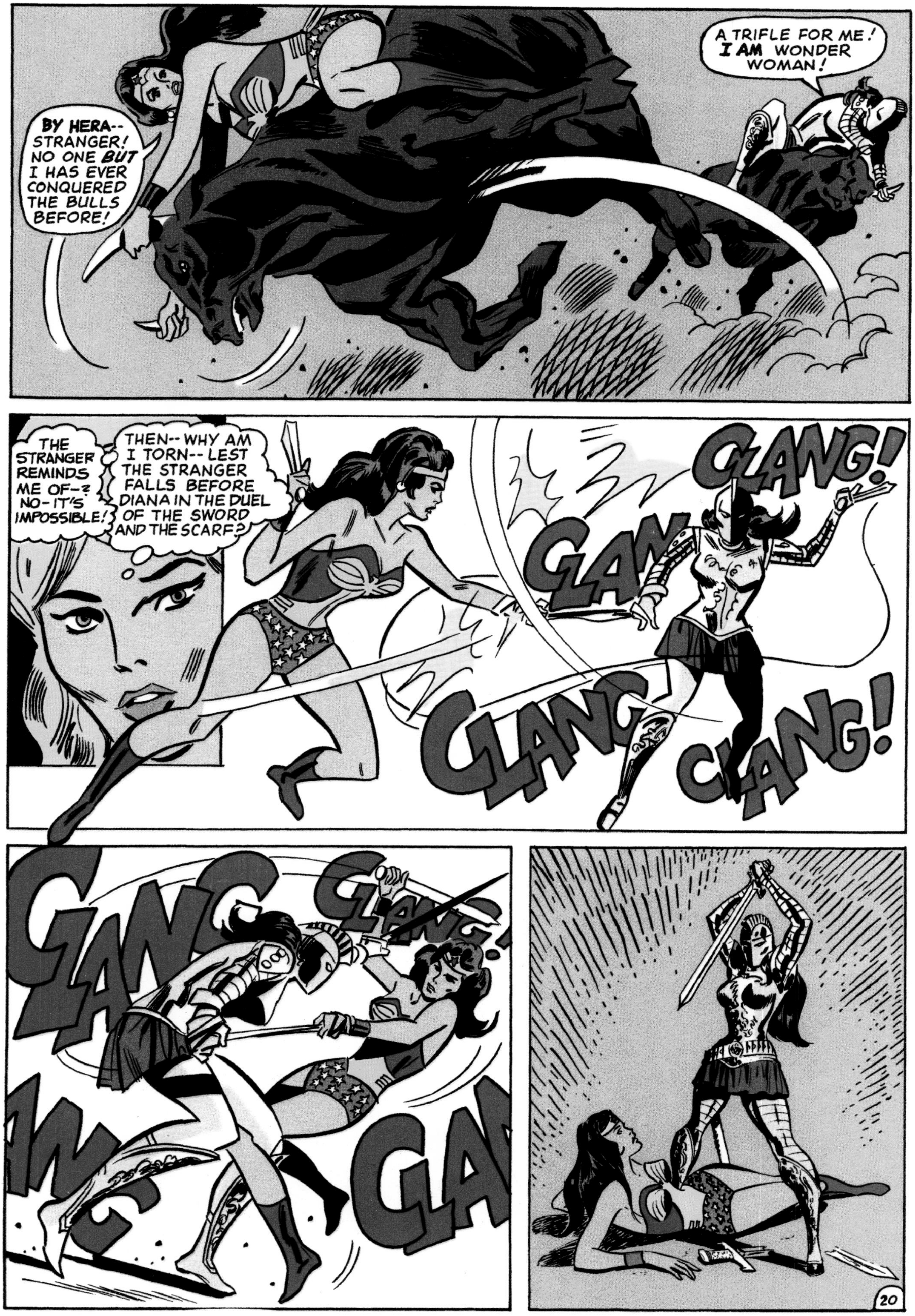
BY HERA-- STRANGER! NO ONE BUT I HAS EVER CONQUERED THE BULLS BEFORE!
A TRIFLE FOR ME! I AM WONDER WOMAN!
THE STRANGER REMINDS ME OF--? NO-IT'S IMPOSSIBLE!
THEN--WHY AM I TORN--LEST THE STRANGER FALLS BEFORE DIANA IN THE DUEL OF THE SWORD AND THE SCARF?
CLANG!
CLANG!
CLANG!
20

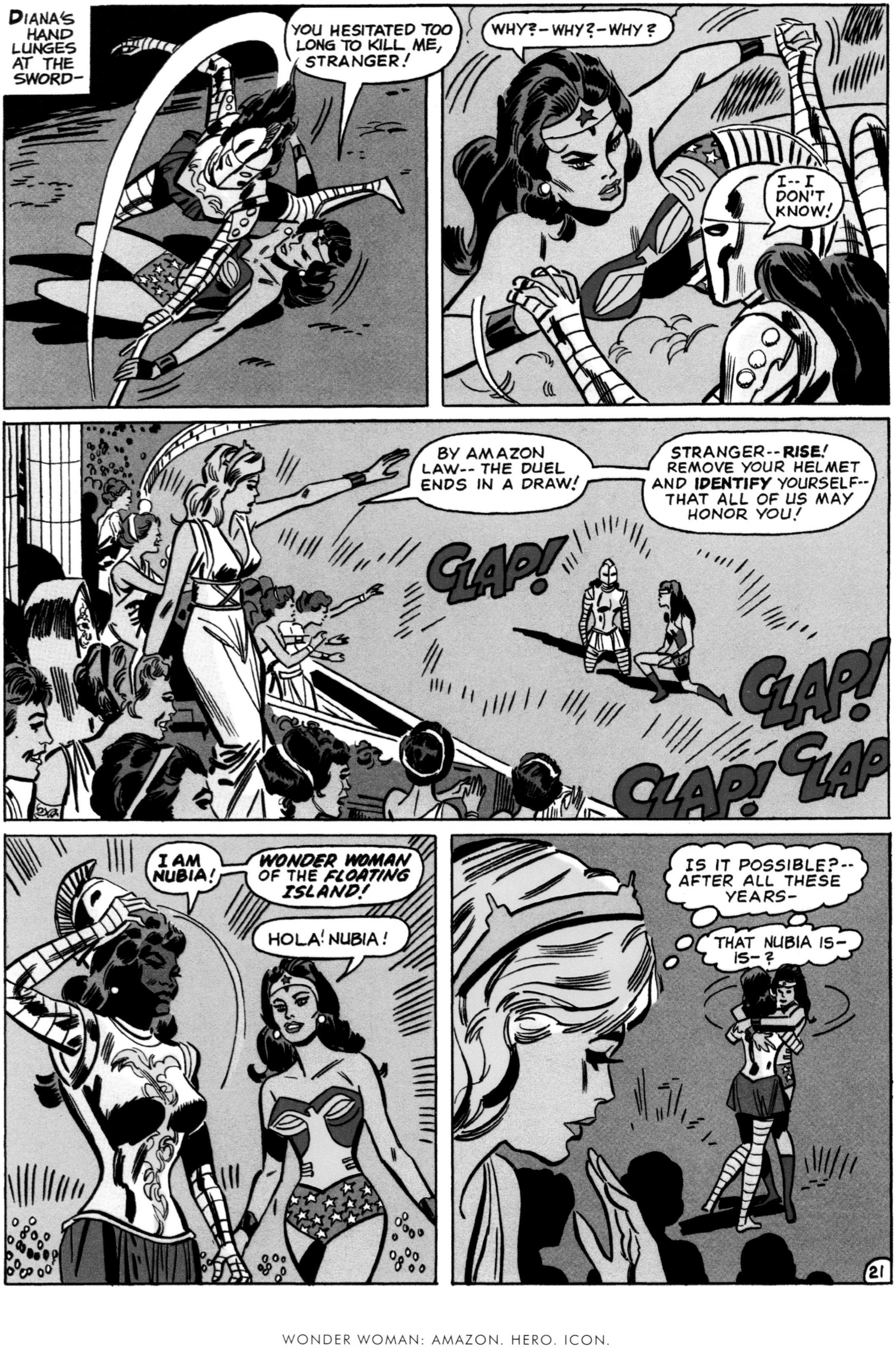
DIANA'S HAND LUNGES AT THE SWORD-
YOU HESITATED TOO LONG TO KILL ME, STRANGER!
WHY?-WHY?-WHY?
I--I DON'T KNOW!
BY AMAZON LAW-- THE DUEL ENDS IN A DRAW!
STRANGER--RISE! REMOVE YOUR HELMET AND IDENTIFY YOURSELF-- THAT ALL OF US MAY HONOR YOU!
CLAP!
CLAP!
CLAP!
CLAP
I AM NUBIA!
WONDER WOMAN OF THE FLOATING ISLAND!
HOLA! NUBIA!
IS IT POSSIBLE?-- AFTER ALL THESE YEARS-
THAT NUBIA IS- IS-?
21

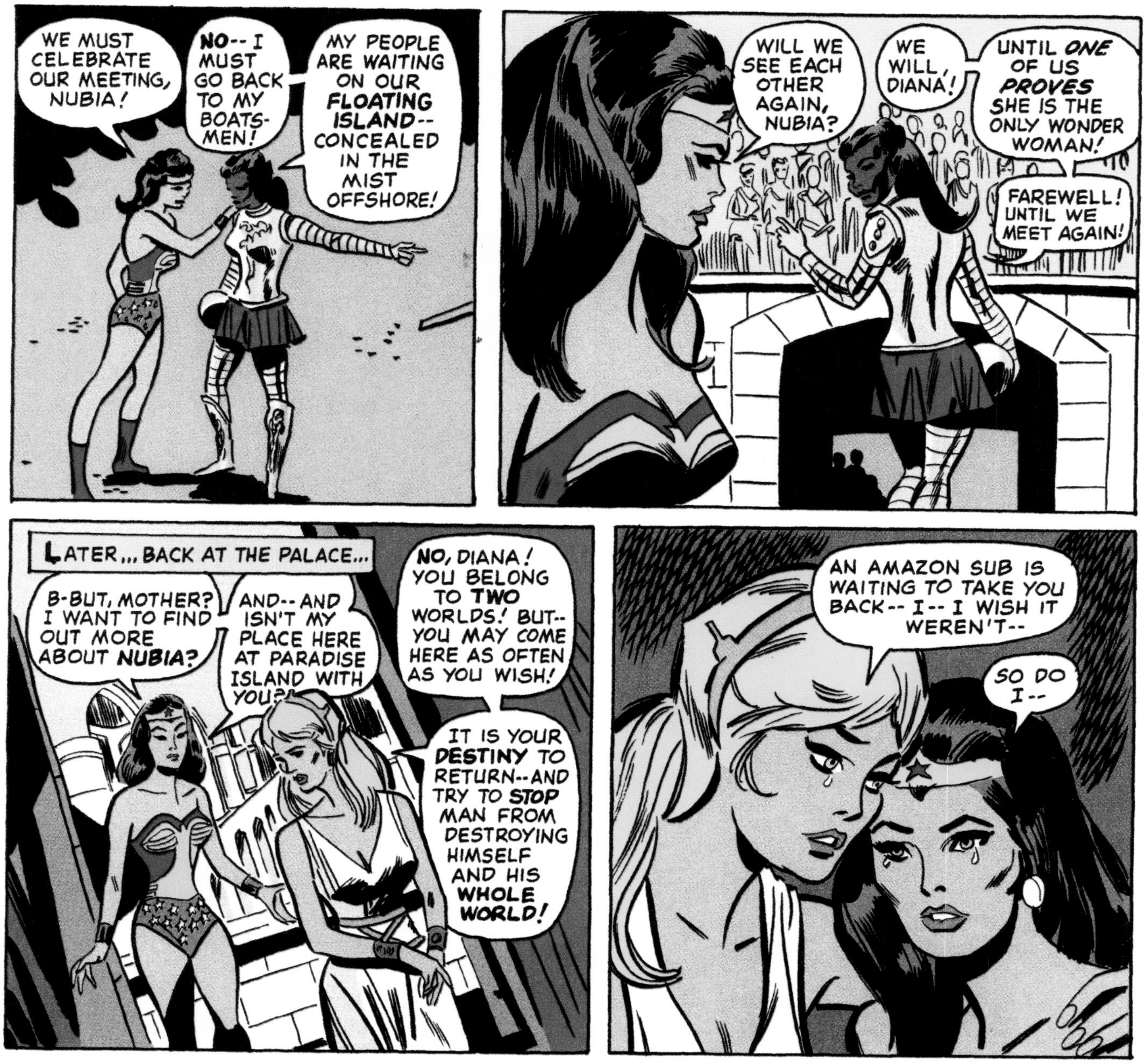
WE MUST CELEBRATE OUR MEETING, NUBIA!
NO-- I MUST GO BACK TO MY BOATS-MEN!
MY PEOPLE ARE WAITING ON OUR FLOATING ISLAND-- CONCEALED IN THE MIST OFFSHORE!
WILL WE SEE EACH OTHER AGAIN, NUBIA?
WE WILL, DIANA!
UNTIL ONE OF US PROVES SHE IS THE ONLY WONDER WOMAN!
FAREWELL! UNTIL WE MEET AGAIN!
LATER... BACK AT THE PALACE...
B-BUT, MOTHER? I WANT TO FIND OUT MORE ABOUT NUBIA?
AND-- AND ISN'T MY PLACE HERE AT PARADISE ISLAND WITH YOU?!
NO, DIANA! YOU BELONG TO TWO WORLDS! BUT-- YOU MAY COME HERE AS OFTEN AS YOU WISH!
IT IS YOUR DESTINY TO RETURN--AND TRY TO STOP MAN FROM DESTROYING HIMSELF AND HIS WHOLE WORLD!
AN AMAZON SUB IS WAITING TO TAKE YOU BACK-- I-- I WISH IT WEREN'T--
SO DO I--

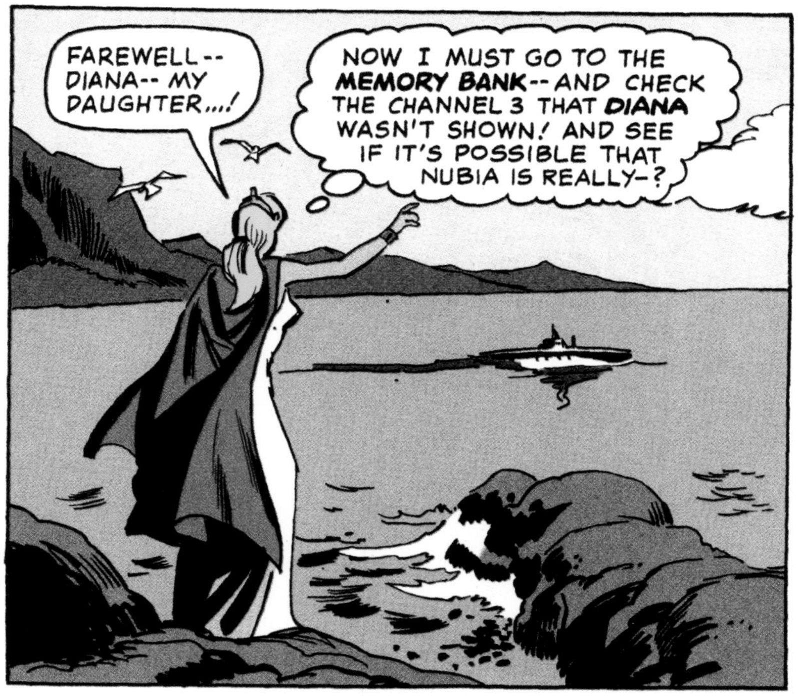
FAREWELL-- DIANA-- MY DAUGHTER...!
NOW I MUST GO TO THE MEMORY BANK-- AND CHECK THE CHANNEL 3 THAT DIANA WASN'T SHOWN! AND SEE IF IT'S POSSIBLE THAT NUBIA IS REALLY-?

Nubia has darker skin than any previous Amazon. It started a subplot that eventually revealed she was a second child fashioned from clay and gifted with life by the gods.

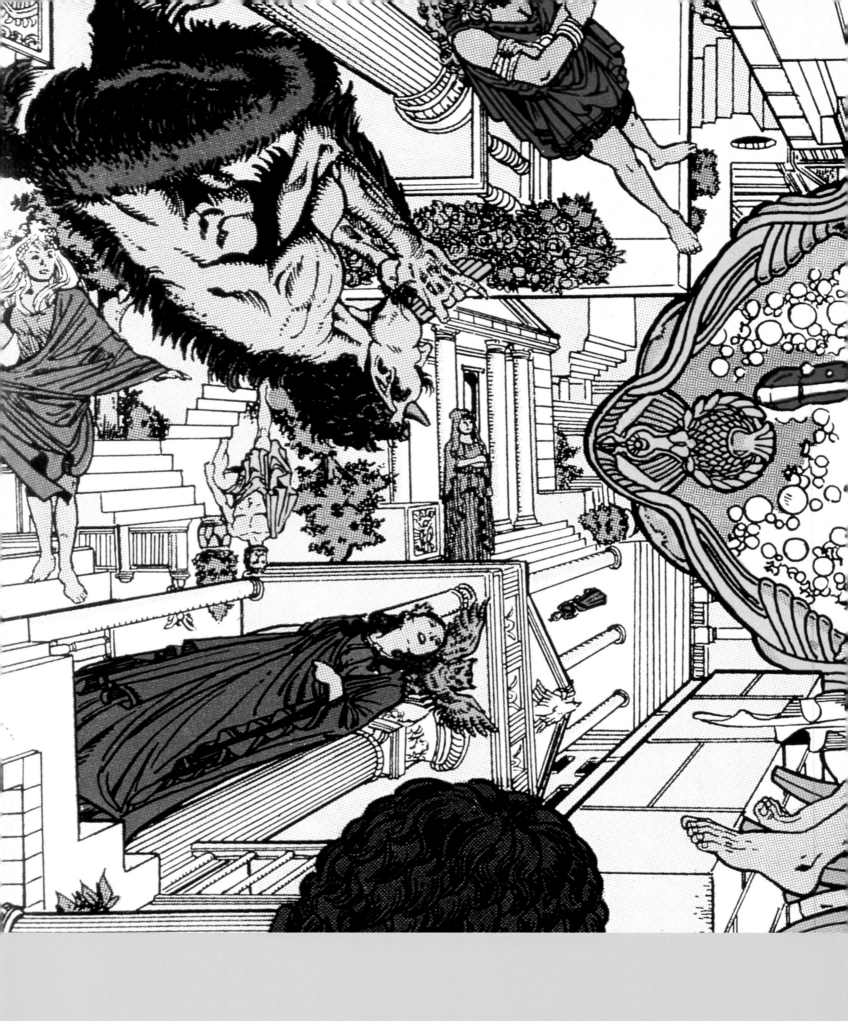

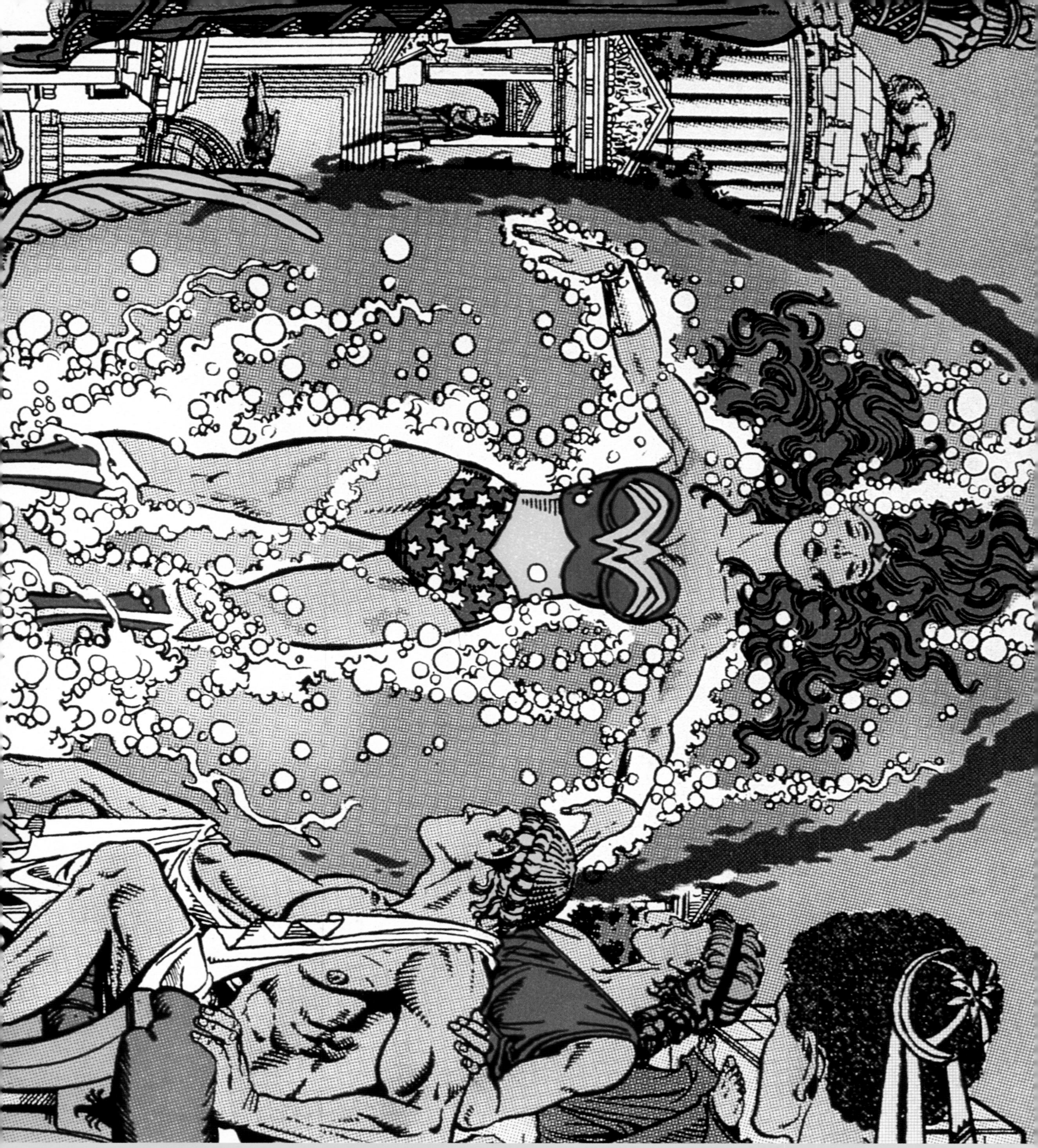

★ The Olympians

"THAT ENERGY CREATED, IN TIME, A RACE OF BEINGS WHO CAME TO THINK OF THEMSELVES AS GODS, LIKE US...
"AND WHOSE POWERS AND INFLUENCE GENERATED ON EARTH A GOLDEN AGE...

While Marston used much Greek mythology to craft Diana and the Amazons, he rarely used the gods themselves, with the notable exception of Ares/Mars, the god of war. Sure, Aphrodite was a patron to the Amazons and other gods periodically turned up, but rarely did they interfere in the doings of Wonder Woman while she supported the United States during the Second World War.

Wonder Woman's exploits were not limited to encounters with the Greek pantheon. In the years after World War II, until Marston's death in 1947, she also encountered Norse gods and Irish leprechauns.

When Robert Kanigher took over as writer/editor, he too eschewed the gods and goddesses. When they did turn up during Wonder Woman's first three decades under his direction, it was an odd mix of their Greek and Roman incarnations.

The gods didn't play a really significant role in the *Wonder Woman* comic books until the mid-1970s, when Martin Pasko wrote the series and Aphrodite appeared to help resurrect a dead Steve Trevor. Subsequent writers, including Jack C. Harris and Gerry Conway, also used the gods in the classic Marston mold.

In the wake of a cosmic house cleaning, the top three super heroes—Superman, Batman, and Wonder Woman—were updated in conjunction with DC Comics' fiftieth anniversary. Building on Greg Potter's ideas, plotter/penciler George Pérez pushed the notions and insisted the new series stick to Greek mythology. Les Daniels noted in *Wonder Woman: The Complete History*, "Pérez rejected the thought that the love goddess

Above and right: It wasn't until the 1987 revamp of Wonder Woman before the Greek gods and goddesses of myth truly appeared as otherworldly entities. In these images from George Pérez and Bruce Patterson it is clear that Mount Olympus and its inhabitants do things just a bit differently than mere mortals.

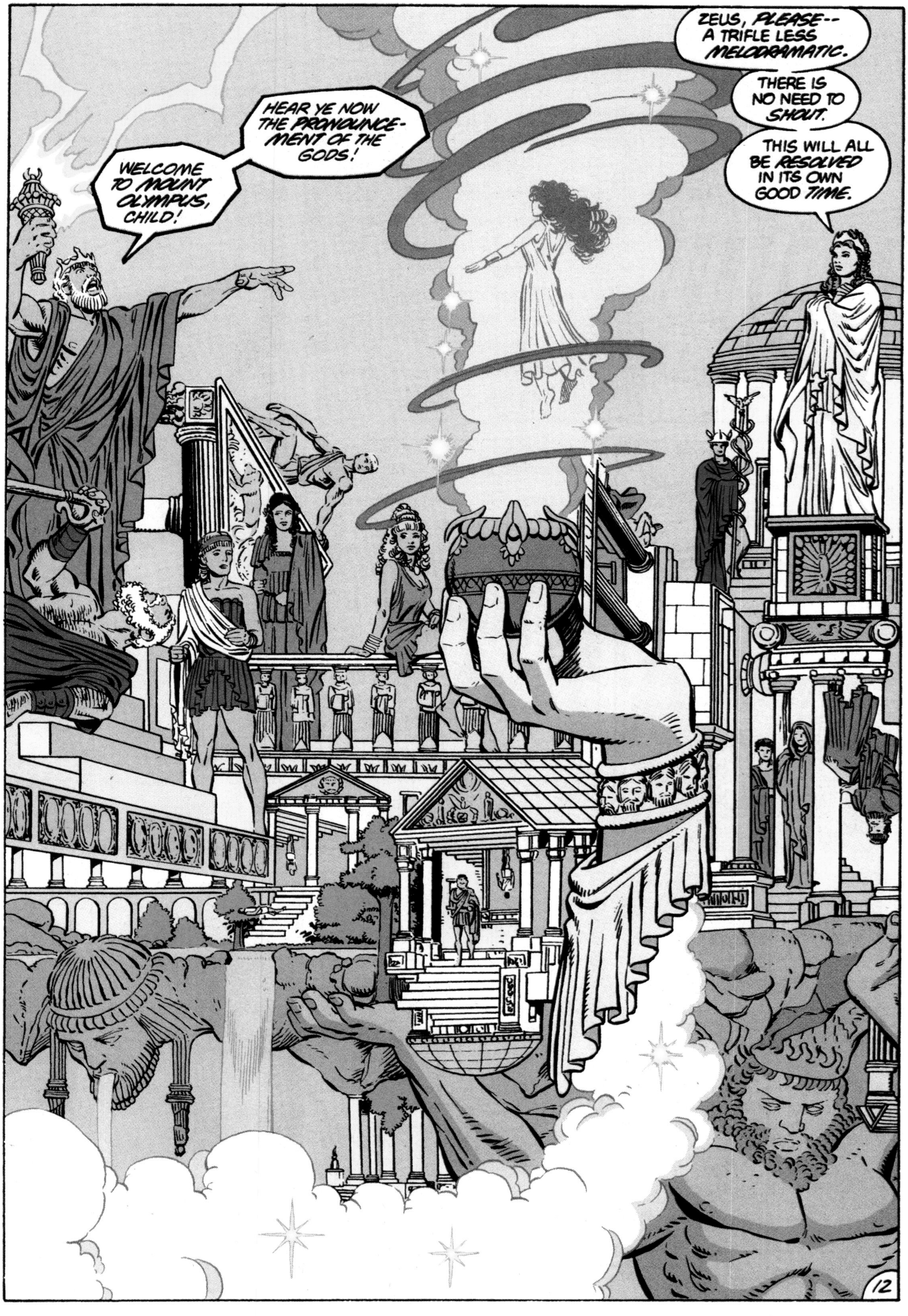
WELCOME TO MOUNT OLYMPUS, CHILD!
HEAR YE NOW THE PRONOUNCEMENT OF THE GODS!
ZEUS, PLEASE-- A TRIFLE LESS MELODRAMATIC.
THERE IS NO NEED TO SHOUT.
THIS WILL ALL BE RESOLVED IN ITS OWN GOOD TIME.
12

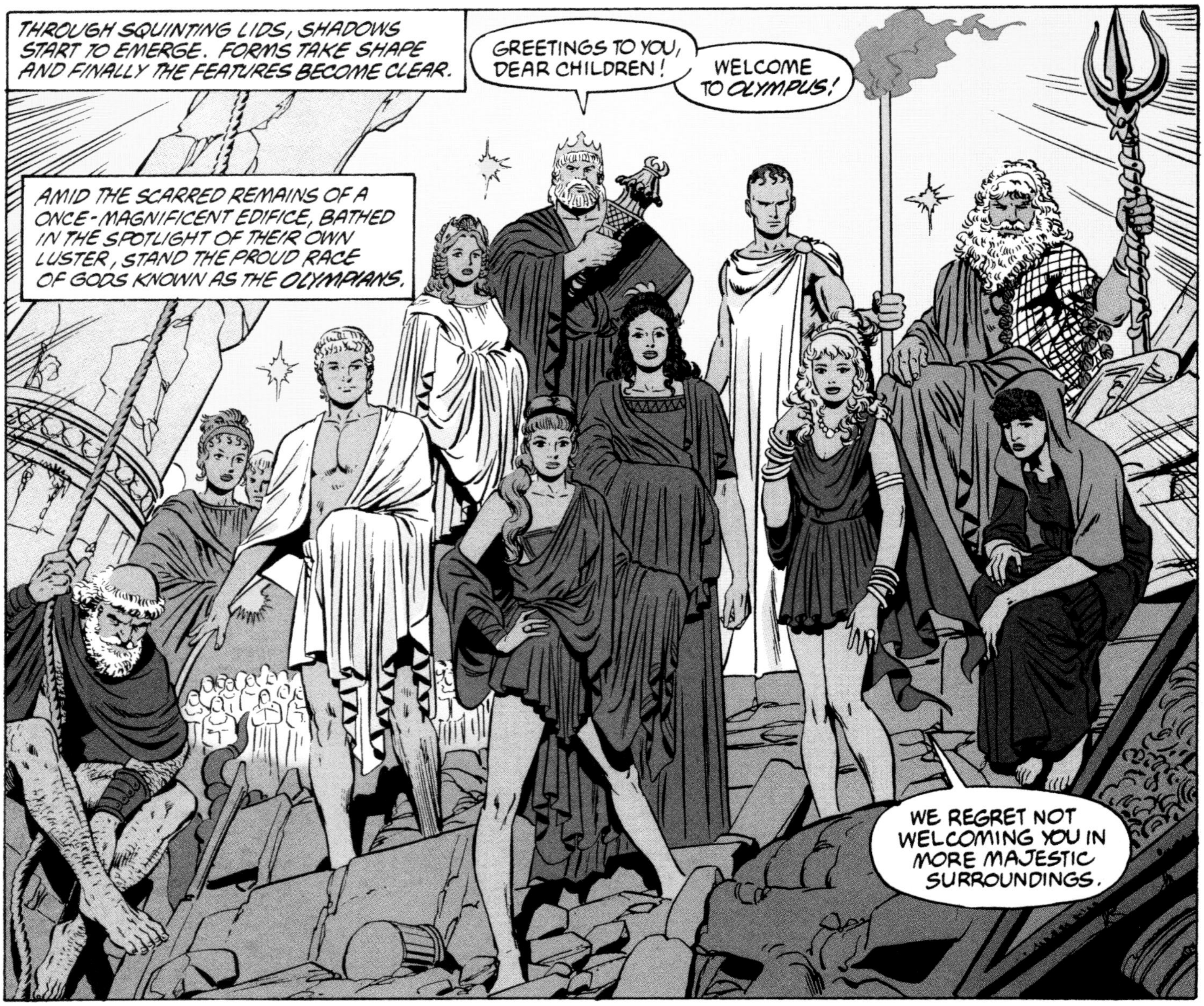
THROUGH SQUINTING LIDS, SHADOWS START TO EMERGE. FORMS TAKE SHAPE AND FINALLY THE FEATURES BECOME CLEAR.
GREETINGS TO YOU, DEAR CHILDREN!
WELCOME TO OLYMPUS!
AMID THE SCARRED REMAINS OF A ONCE-MAGNIFICENT EDIFICE, BATHED IN THE SPOTLIGHT OF THEIR OWN LUSTER, STAND THE PROUD RACE OF GODS KNOWN AS THE OLYMPIANS.
WE REGRET NOT WELCOMING YOU IN MORE MAJESTIC SURROUNDINGS.

Aphrodite could have been the leading patron of the Amazons, and doubtless would have rejected Marston's notion that women would tame men through erotic enslavement, if it had been more explicit."

Since the 1986 relaunch, the gods and goddesses of Mount Olympus have been regular players in Diana's life, for good or ill. DC's internal mythology acknowledged the various pantheons of gods from multiple cultures, sometimes working in concert and other times working against one another. The company's unique pantheon, dubbed the New Gods, played a major role in Pérez's early stories. Darkseid, the malevolent god of Apokolips, actually took his quest for universal dominance to Olympus and leveled the realm, despite the involvement of both Wonder Woman and Superman.

Of all the gods, Ares interfered with Diana most often. Ares sought to plunge Man's World into eternal warfare. On Themyscira, Doom's Doorway was opened more than once, threatening to set free all manner of mythological terrors from Hades's realm were it not for the vigilant Amazons.

The Amazons' lord, Zeus, was pivotal to an early multiparter in the reboot, wherein Diana rebuffed his amorous advances and was forced to face a "challenge of the gods" to prove her continued worth as Wonder Woman. As a result, Zeus also removed the portal to Hades. Pérez's final story arc brought the various pantheons into conflict, courtesy of the evil sorceress Circe. Diana reduced to her clay form but, thanks in large part to a pyrrhic flame maintained by the god Hephaestus and his Roman counterpart Vulcan, she was recreated by her mother and eventually defeated Circe.

Above: Another look at the Olympic pantheon as illustrated by George Pérez and Bruce Patterson.

Right: When John Byrne became writer/artist he continued to depict an Escher-like Mount Olympus, adding his own touches with ornamental heads of the gods sprinkled throughout the structure.

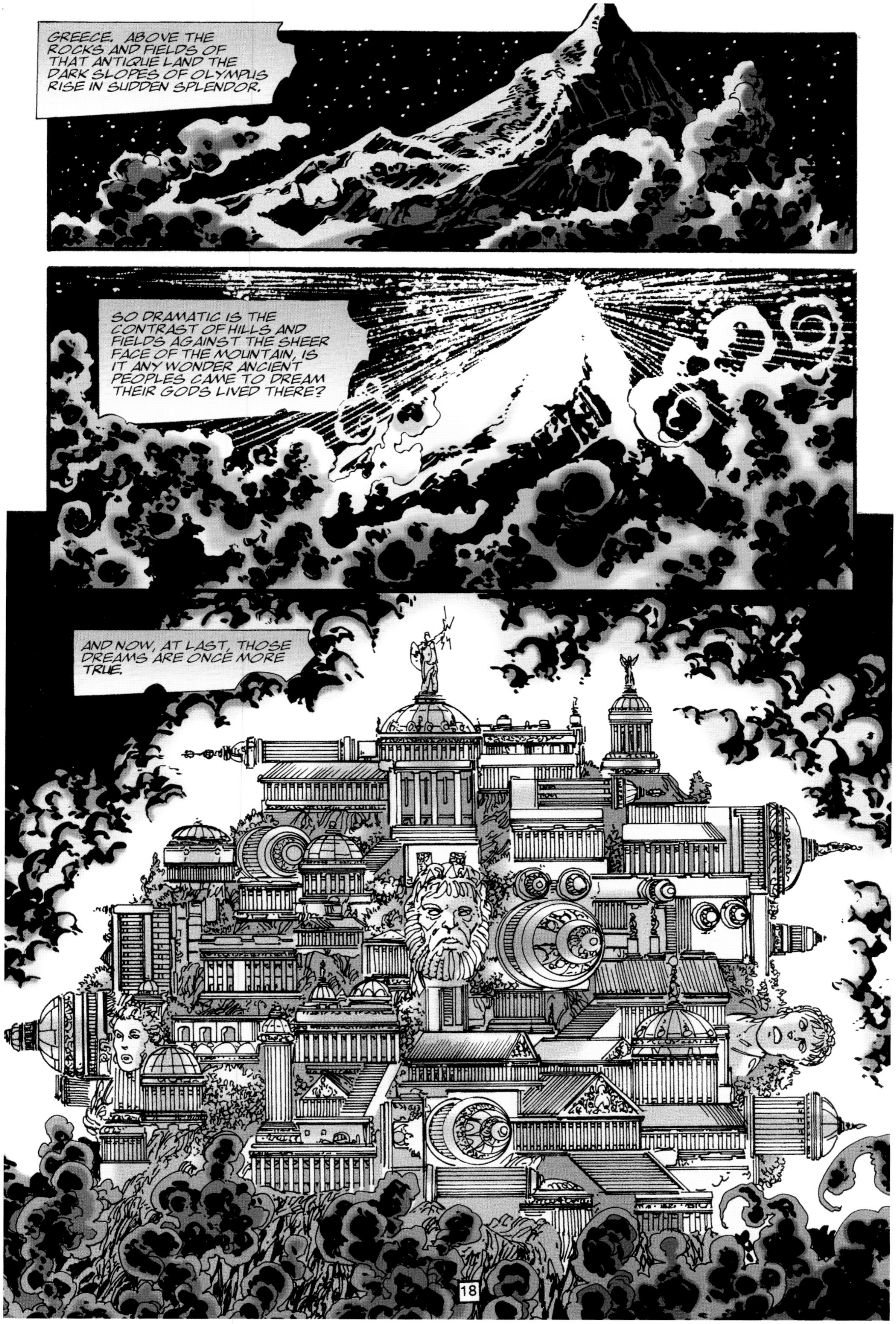
GREECE. ABOVE THE ROCKS AND FIELDS OF THAT ANTIQUE LAND THE DARK SLOPES OF OLYMPUS RISE IN SUDDEN SPLENDOR.
SO DRAMATIC IS THE CONTRAST OF HILLS AND FIELDS AGAINST THE SHEER FACE OF THE MOUNTAIN, IS IT ANY WONDER ANCIENT PEOPLES CAME TO DREAM THEIR GODS LIVED THERE?
AND NOW, AT LAST, THOSE DREAMS ARE ONCE MORE TRUE.
18

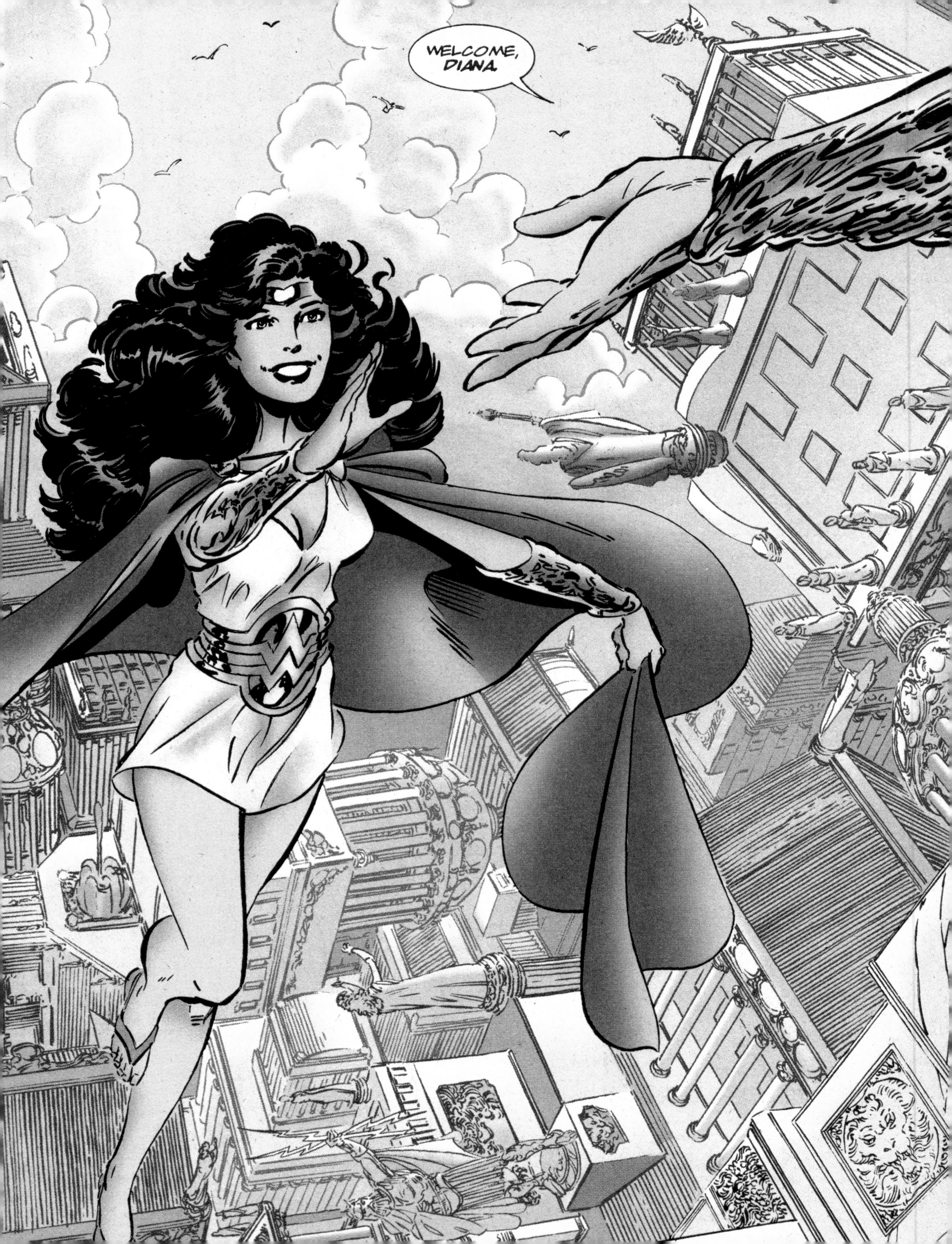
WELCOME, DIANA.

WE HAVE BEEN GONE FROM HER LIFE LONG ENOUGH.

IT'S TIME WE FINALLY REVEAL OURSELVES TO *OLYMPUS'* GREATEST CHAMPION... ...AND *WELCOME* HER HOME.

Left: Diana is welcomed to Mount Olympus, about to be named goddess of truth during story arc from writer/artist John Byrne.

Above: Writer/penciller Phil Jimenez restored the Olympic Pantheon to Diana's life.

Page 76: the god Pan attempts to seduce the Amazon Princess in this sequence from Mike Deodato, Jr.

Page 77: Cronus and his cult of worshippers threaten Wonder Woman. Art by Yanick Paquette and Bob McLeod.

When John Byrne became the series' writer/artist in 1995, he took the arc one step farther by killing Diana but rewarding her career by having her spirit arrive on Olympus, where she was greeted as Diana, goddess of truth. After acclimating to her new-found role, Diana decided she wasn't ready to stop being a super heroine. "Now that I am a goddess," she proclaimed in *Wonder Woman #136* (August 1998), "with power and immortality beyond the measure of humanity, there has never been a better time for Diana of Themyscira to once more claim the name of Wonder Woman!"

Byrne crafted a story to explain why *Wonder Woman* had featured both Greek and Roman versions of the same gods and goddess. He used the cosmic New God named Darkseid as the catalyst, explaining that Darkseid traveled to Earth centuries ago and manipulated Europeans into worshipping the gods by using two different sets of names. Since the various deities derived their power based on the number of worshippers, this resulted in a weakening of the Greek gods' powers. Darkseid no longer considered the Greek pantheon a threat to his plans for conquest.

In time, Diana's refusal to abstain from helping her mortal friends led Zeus to renounce her godhood and return her to Earth. Rather than play a passive observer, the Amazon princess gratefully accepted this "punishment."

The gods have been an essential part of Wonder Woman's story. Beginning in 2003 with writer Greg Rucka, they adapted to modern dress and technology, even using laptops in lieu of scrolls. However, their political shenanigans never let up. For example, a vengeful Athena, who promised Ares control of the Underworld, maneuvered Zeus out of power for a time. Ares used Wonder Woman's struggles against Hades as she was attempting to rescue the spirit of Hermes to sneak up and stab the ruler of the dead in the back, killing the god.

The gods proved fickle throughout the years, which was in keeping with the real world Greek mythology. It was ultimately revealed that Zeus was Cassie Sandsmark's father and that her destiny was to become the second Wonder Girl. Zeus had previously granted and withdrew boons to his worshippers seemingly at whim until his comeuppance at Athena's hand.

Athena's good name was tarnished when the evil New God Granny Goodness masqueraded as Athena and convinced Hippolyta to wage an unwarranted war on America, which damaged the Amazons' reputation. Wonder Woman and Wonder Girl were instrumental in ending the Amazons' misguided attack.

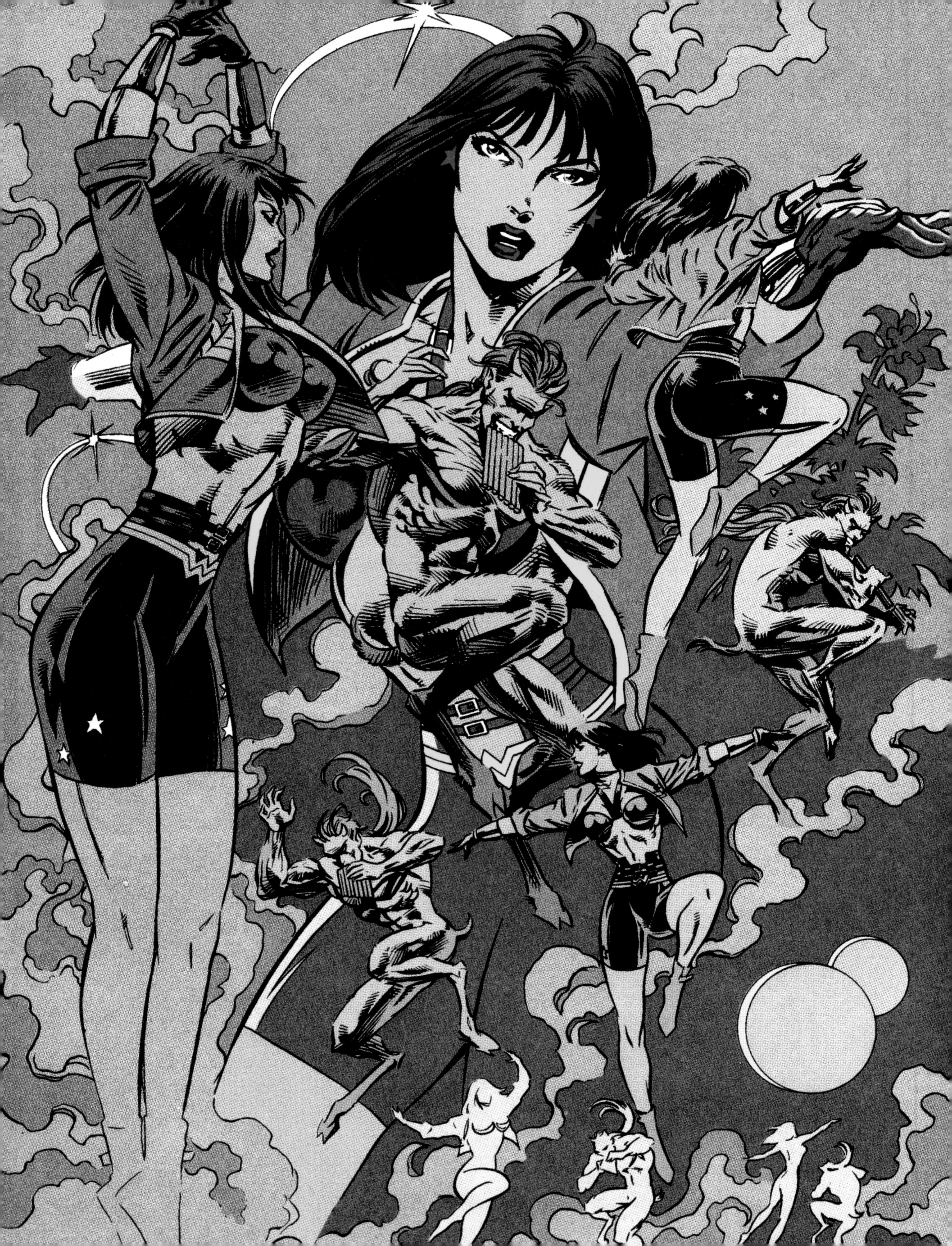

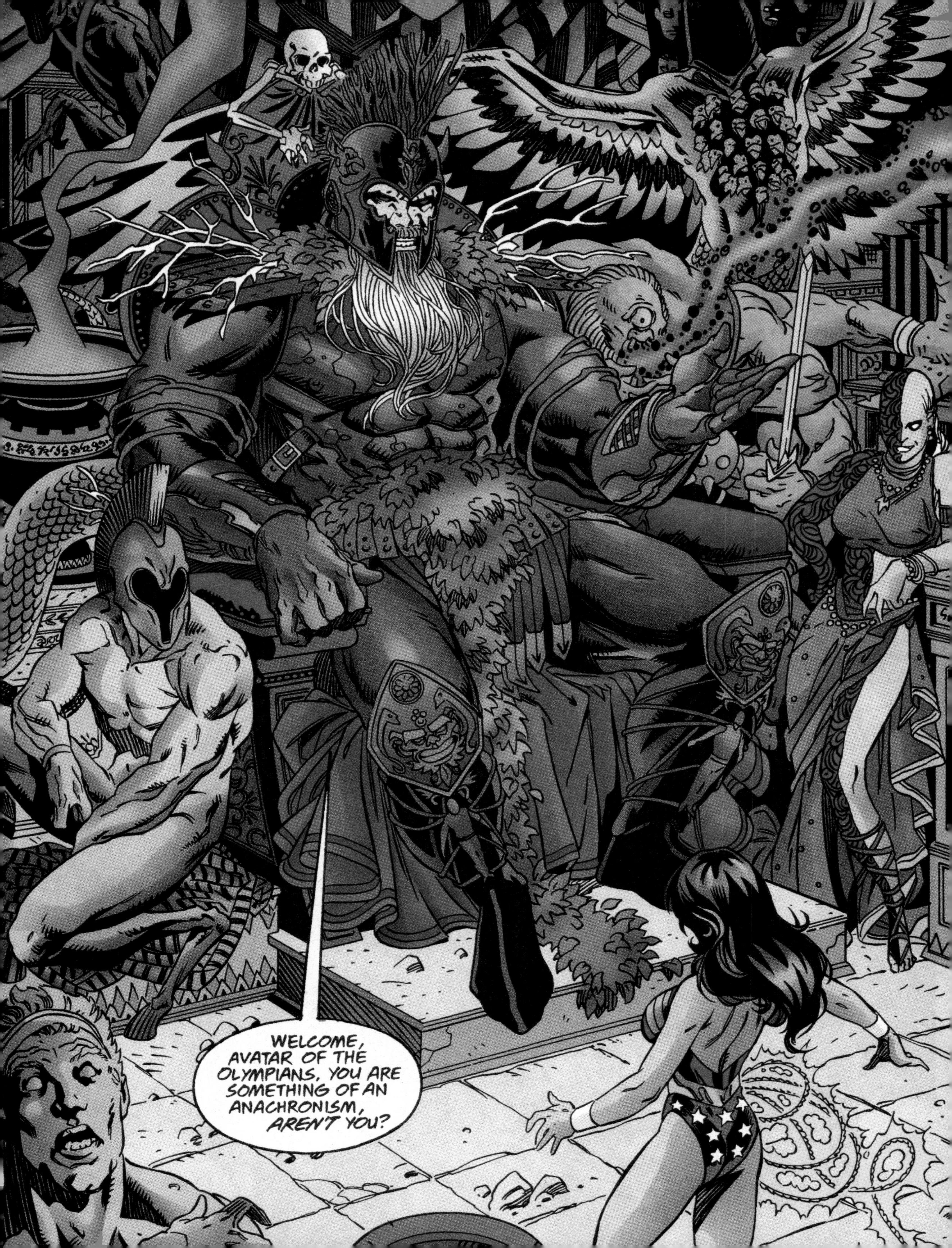
WELCOME, AVATAR OF THE OLYMPIANS. YOU ARE SOMETHING OF AN ANACHRONISM, AREN'T YOU?

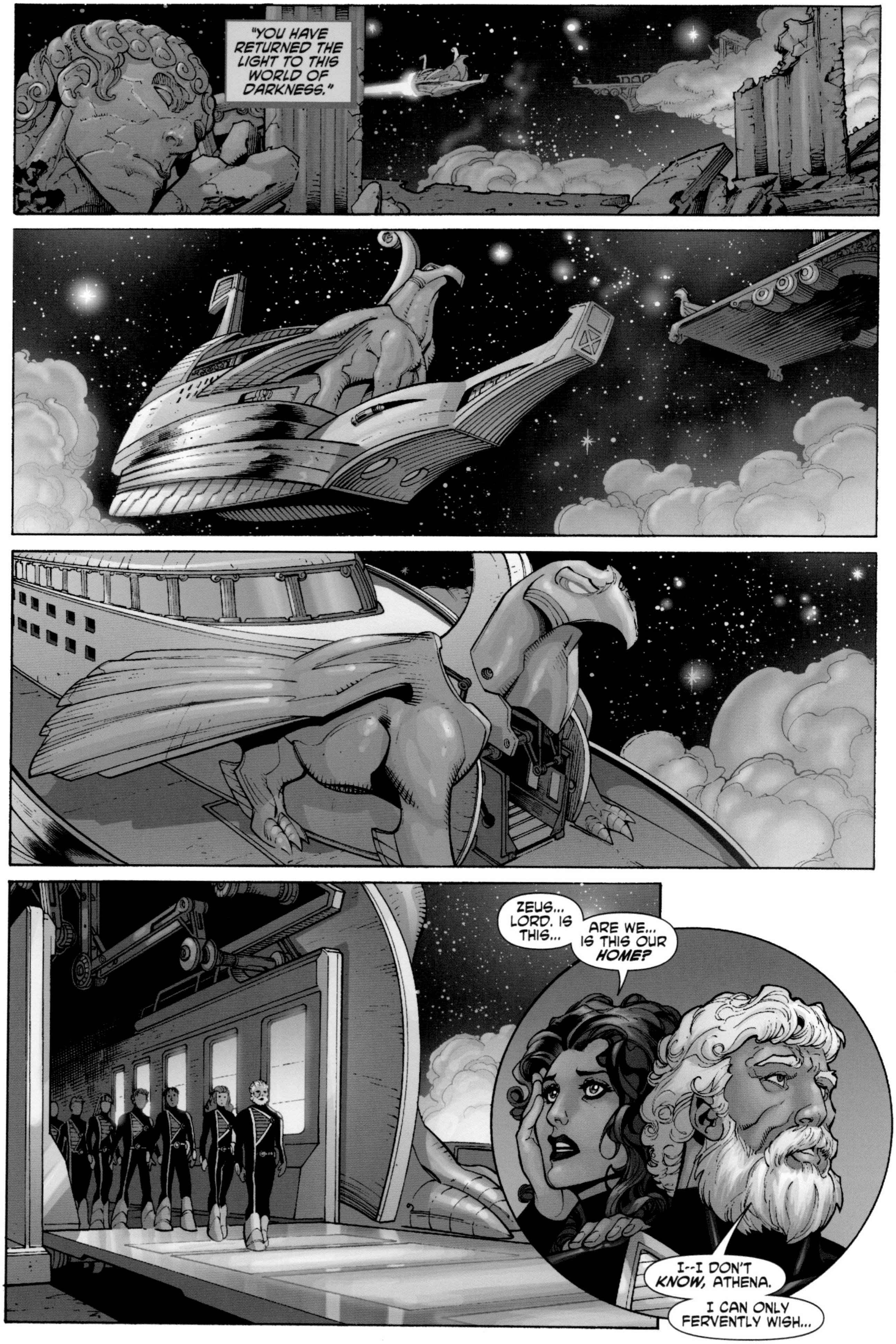
"YOU HAVE RETURNED THE LIGHT TO THIS WORLD OF DARKNESS."
ZEUS... LORD. IS THIS...
ARE WE... IS THIS OUR HOME?
I--I DON'T KNOW, ATHENA.
I CAN ONLY FERVENTLY WISH...

Above and right: When the gods fall from favor, even Mount Olympus is no longer sacrosanct, as seen in these pages from *Wonder Woman* [third series] #26. Art by Aaron Lopresti and Matt Ryan.

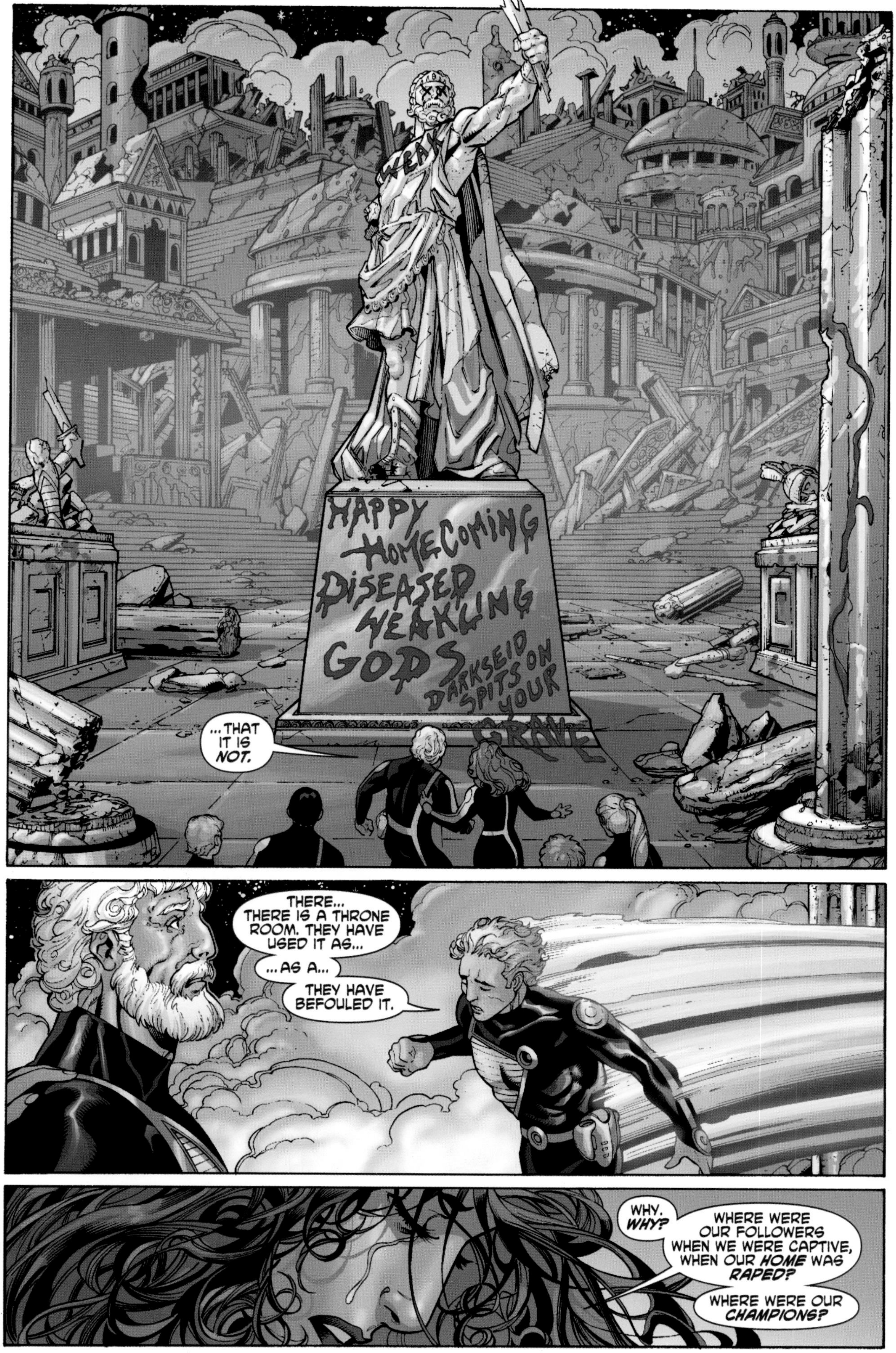
HAPPY HOMECOMING
DISEASED WEAKLING GODS
DARKSEID SPITS ON YOUR GRAVE
...THAT IT IS NOT.
THERE... THERE IS A THRONE ROOM. THEY HAVE USED IT AS...
...AS A...
THEY HAVE BEFOULED IT.
WHY. WHY?
WHERE WERE OUR FOLLOWERS WHEN WE WERE CAPTIVE, WHEN OUR HOME WAS RAPED?
WHERE WERE OUR CHAMPIONS?

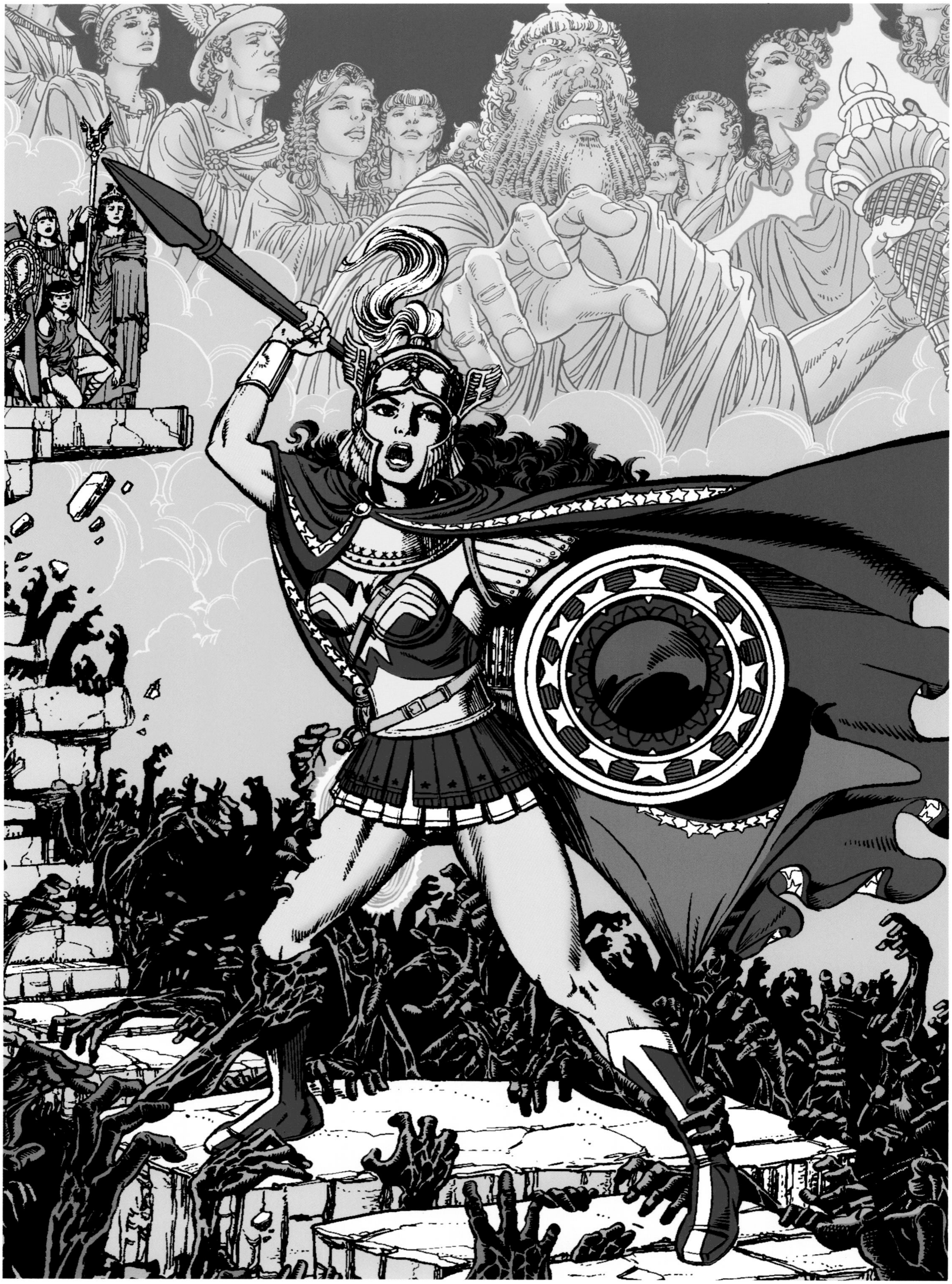

A cover detail from 1987's *Wonder Woman* #10, which contained the "Challenge of the Gods" storyline. In 1987, her entire life was started afresh courtesy of writer Greg Potter and artist George Pérez.

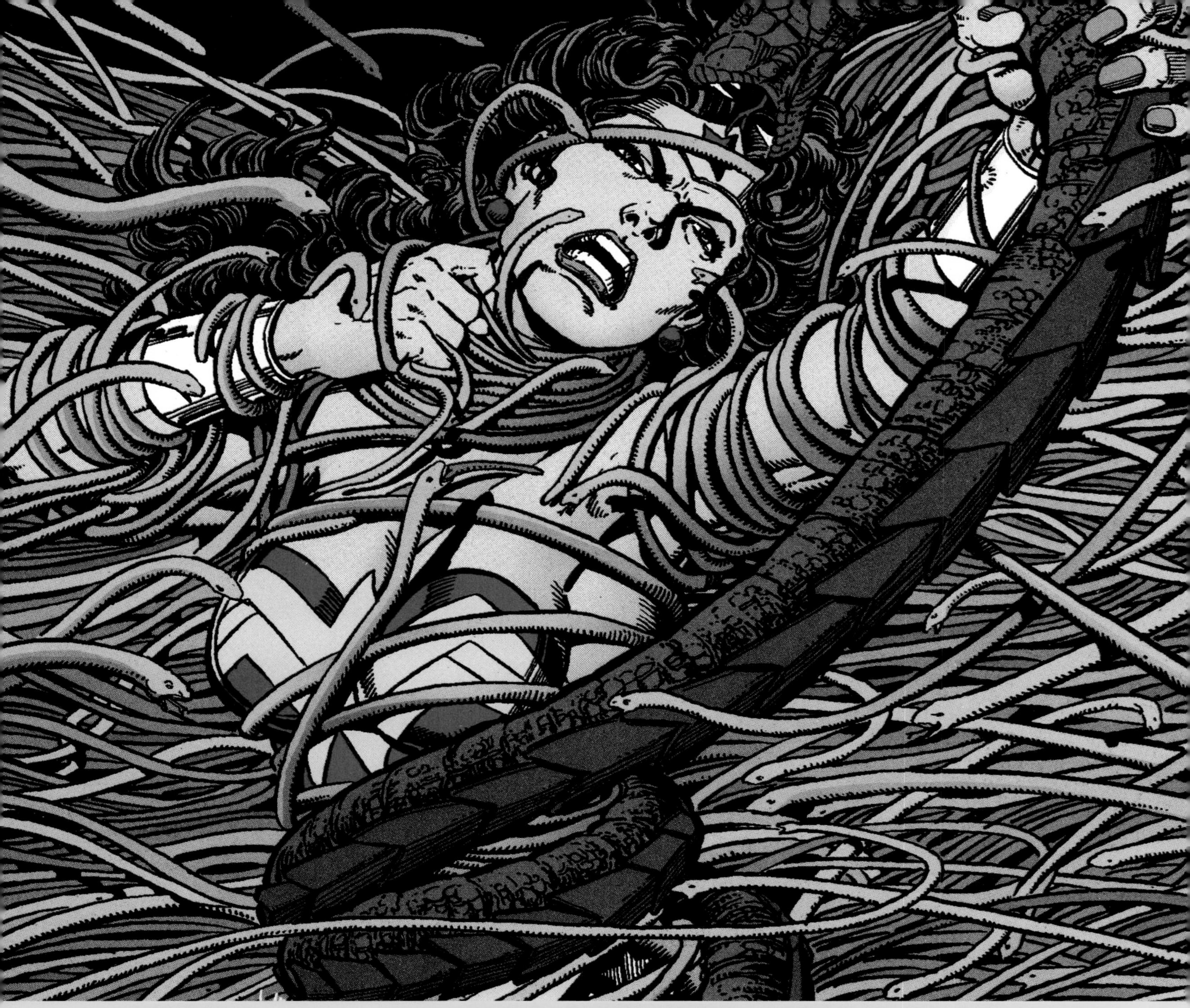

George Pérez

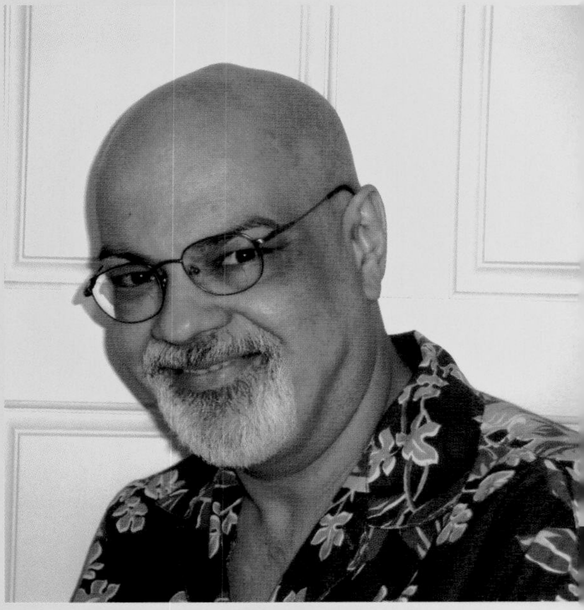

George Pérez, born in 1953, was a comic-fan-turned-artist, breaking into the field at age twenty. He went on to become one of the most popular comics illustrators of the modern age. His storytelling and design skills are never better than when he is illustrating scenes involving armies of heroes and villains. As a result, he is well known for his work on *Justice League of America*, *The New Teen Titans*, *Fantastic Four*, and *The Avengers*. He illustrated DC's fiftieth anniversary maxiseries *Crisis on Infinite Earths*, which led to a multiple-year stint as writer/artist on *Wonder Woman*. More recently he has drawn such major event titles as *JLA/Avengers* and *Final Crisis: Legion of Three Worlds*.

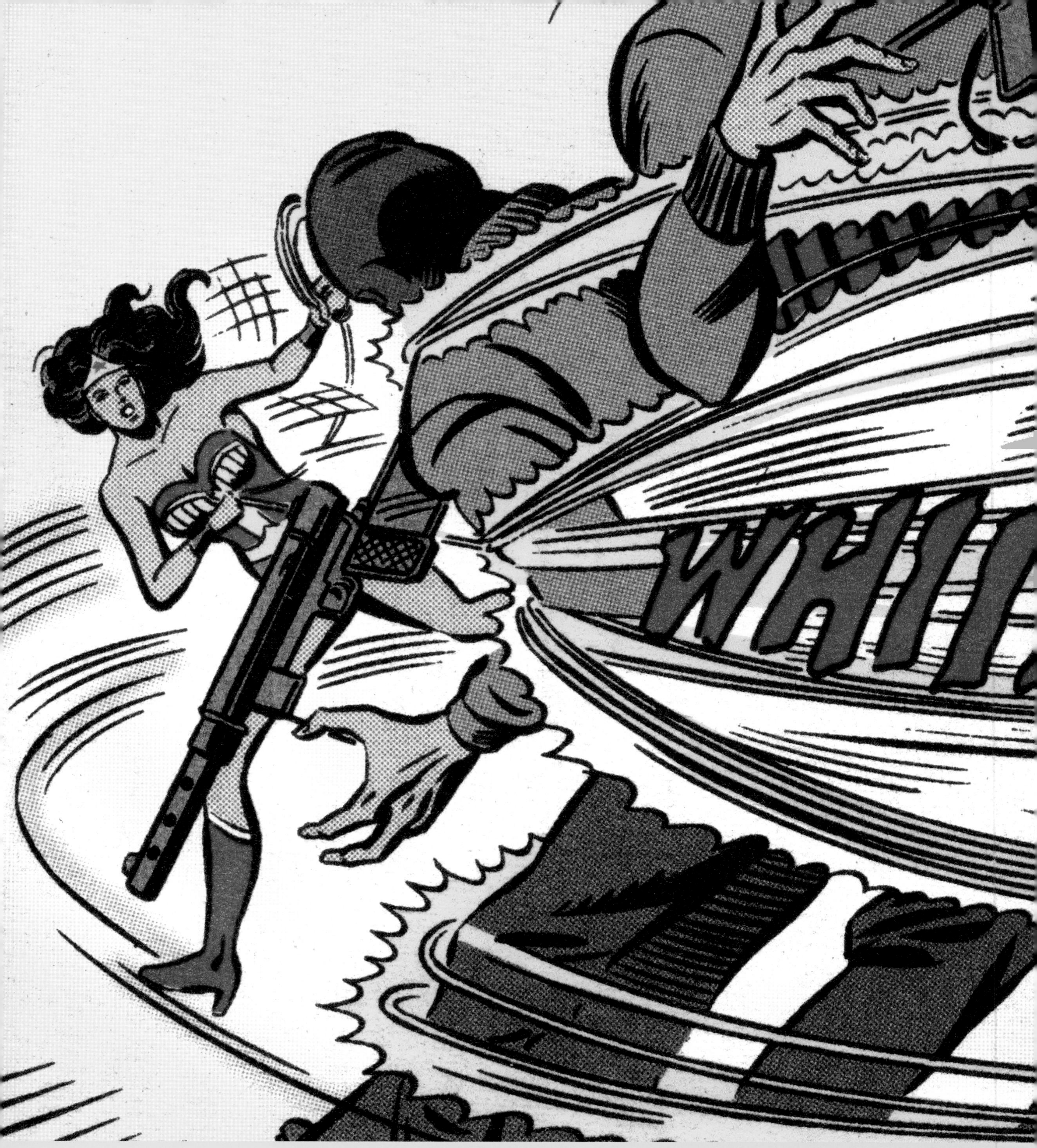
WHII

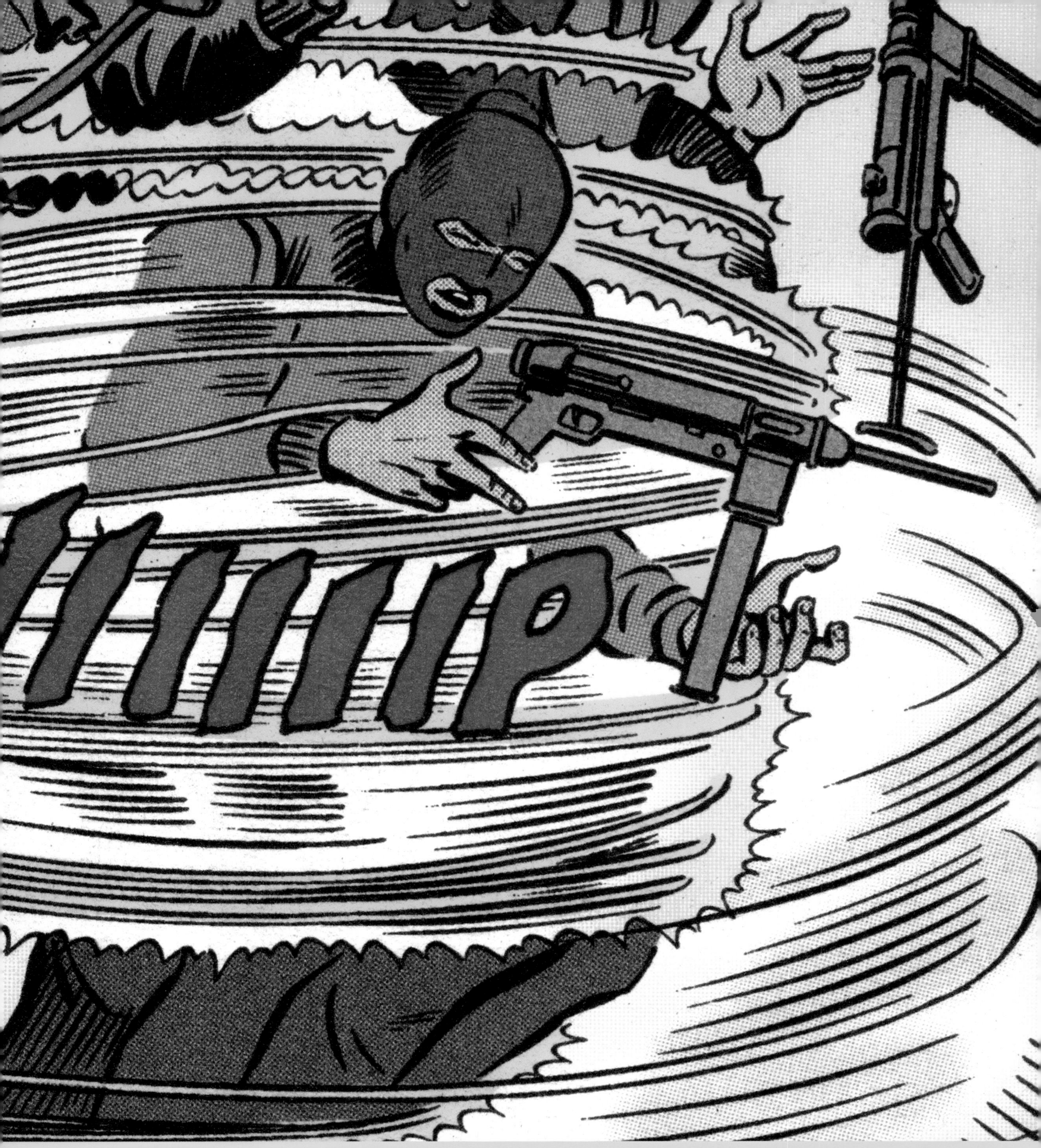

★ Tools of the Trade

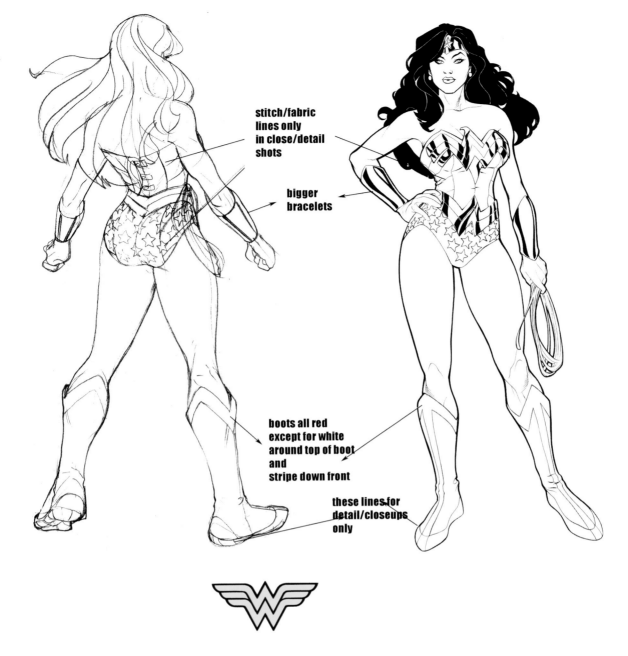

stitch/fabric
lines only
in close/detail
shots

bigger
bracelets

boots all red
except for white
around top of boot
and
stripe down front

these lines for
detail/closeups
only

Wonder Woman is the product of a warrior culture, and thus wouldn't journey to Man's World unarmed. Marston wisely developed a number of tools for her to use.

It all begins with the bracelets, said to be forged from the dense metal amazonium, and strong enough to repel bullets. During the Pérez retelling, Hippolyta insisted all Amazons wear them as a reminder of their time as slaves to Hercules. As seen in her origin, winning the "bullets and bracelets" challenge allowed Diana to be the Amazons' champion, and the game has since become part of Wonder Woman's legend.

Queen Hippolyta warned her daughter that should her bracelets be bound together, Diana would lose her gods-given powers. Time and again, Marston saw to it that Wonder Woman was bound and enslaved, a recurring theme that actually caused some concern for All American's editorial offices. During the 1940s, letters would arrive calling attention to the frequency with which Wonder Woman and her fellow female compatriots found themselves bound and confined. Marston worried editor Mayer and others with the dubious contention that "confinement to [Wonder Woman] and the Amazons is just a sporting game, an actual enjoyment of being subdued. This, my dear friend, is the one truly great contribution of my Wonder Woman strip to moral education of the young. The only hope for peace is to watch people who are full of pep and unbound force to *enjoy* being bound, Women are exciting for this one reason—it is the secret of women's allure—women *enjoy* submission, being bound. This I bring out in the Paradise Island sequences where the girls beg for chains and enjoy wearing them."

Imagine Marston espousing those thoughts today!

Above: Character designs for the Amazon Princess by artist Terry Dodson.

Right: Stuart Immonen drew this pin-up image, which was included in the *Wonder Woman: Down to Earth* graphic novel, collecting the start of writer Greg Rucka's run on the title.

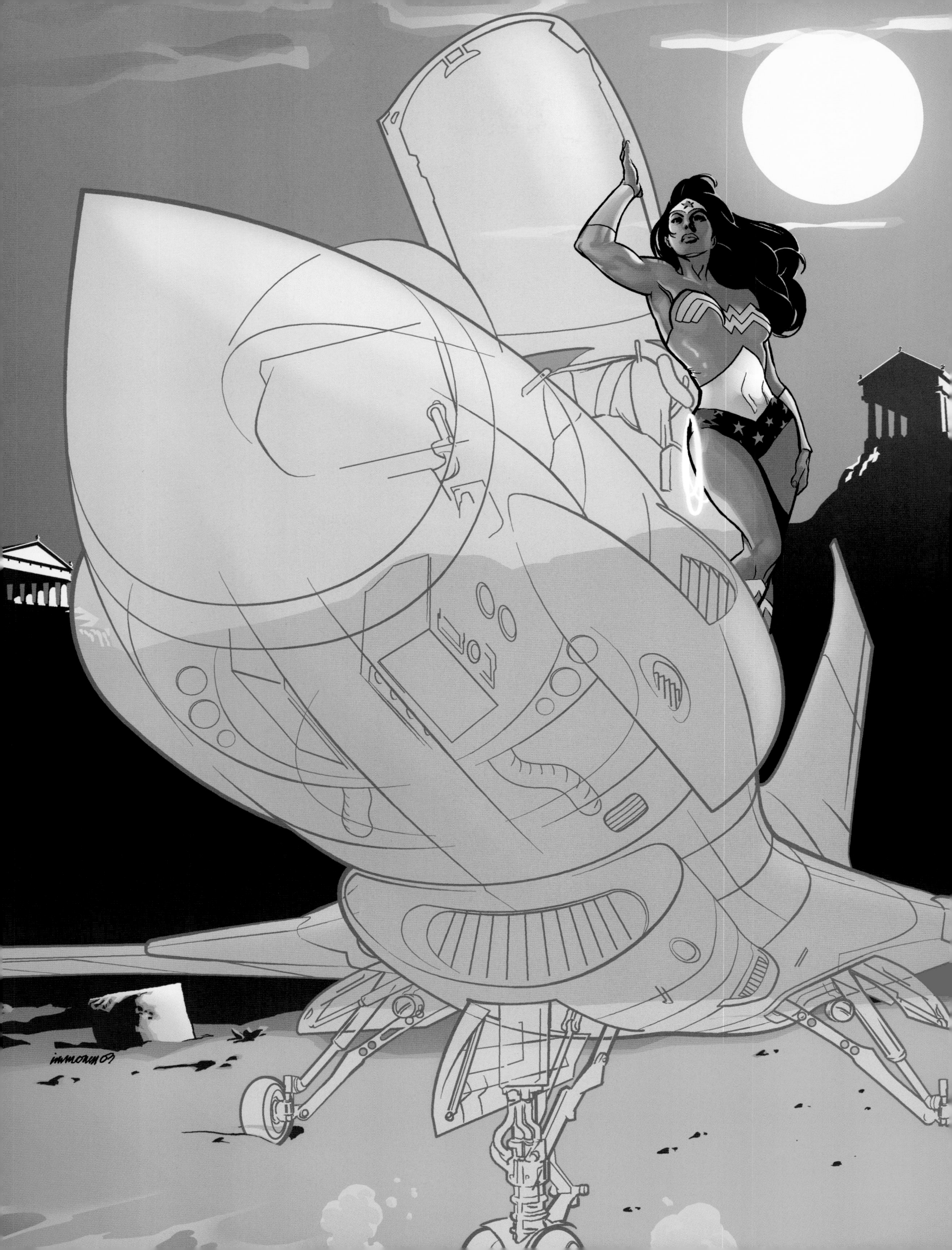

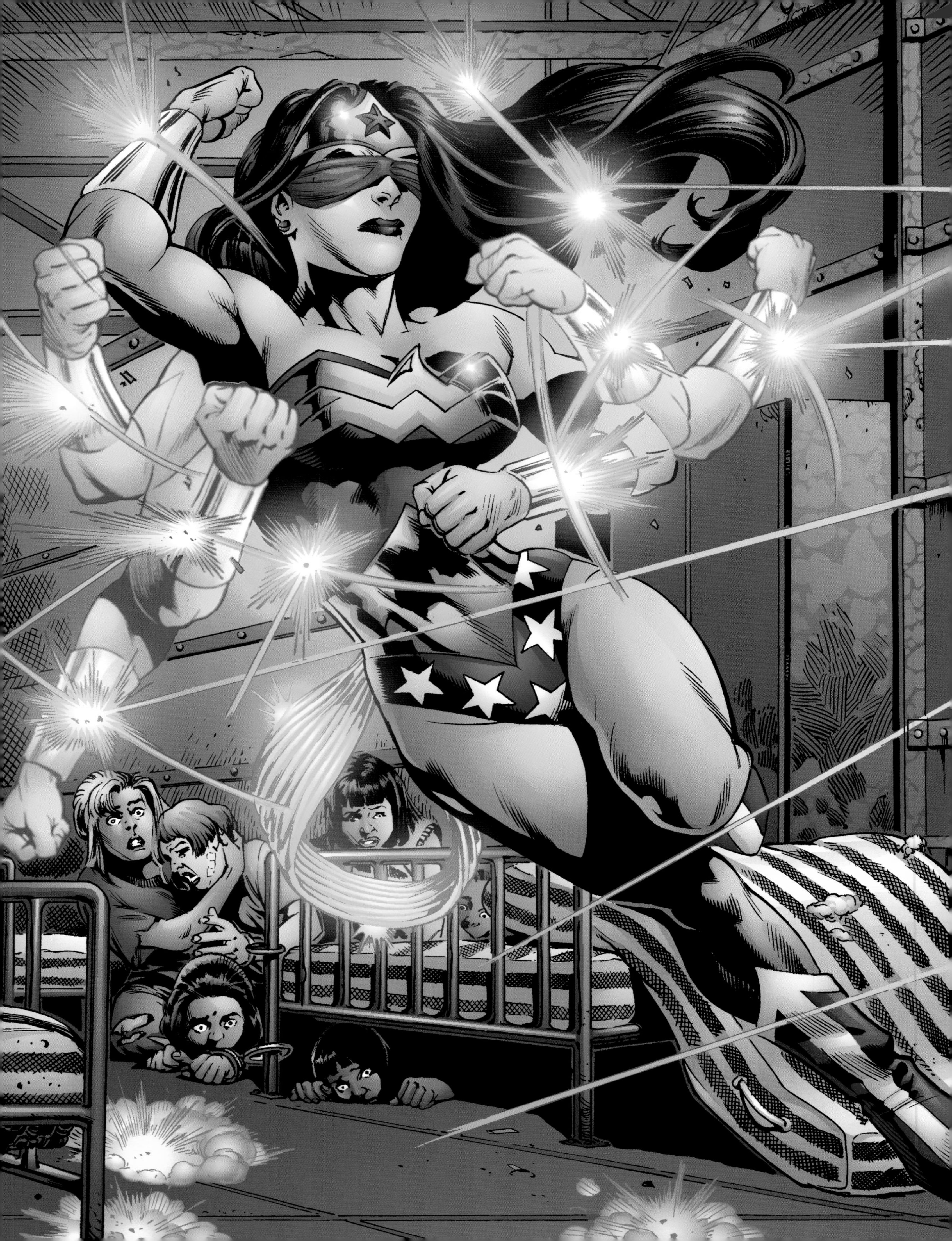

Left: Even blind, Wonder Woman is so well trained that she can effortlessly play bullets and bracelets while protecting the innocent. Art by Rags Morales and Michael Bair.

Right: cover art to *Wonder Woman* [third series] #19, art by Bernard Chang, showing that her modern day vambraces are strong enough to withstand energy blasts.

Below: Style guide art.

Under Kanigher and others, the bondage elements vanished entirely, and Marston's penchant for themes of submission and domination is viewed with an odd fondness, given what Marston and Peter got away with for years.

Today, Wonder Woman's silver bracelets—now called vambraces and resembling gauntlets—are said to be forged by Hephaestus from pieces of Zeus's shield. As a result, they can absorb tremendous impact or, when struck together, can cause a concussive force, able to make even Superman's ears bleed.

Atop Wonder Woman's head rests the golden tiara with its red star, denoting her rank as princess of Paradise Island. Through the years it has been used as a boomerang and a cutting instrument. The star has also acted as a port, allowing the Amazon princess to tether with various devices, and was apparently where her JLA communicator was stored.

Her best-known accoutrement is her golden lasso, also known as the Lasso of Truth, or the magic lasso. The lasso was introduced in her seventh appearance, *Sensation Comics* #6 (June 1942) and was part of the Amazonian game of "girl-roping," performed while riding fantastical giant animals called kangas.

Given Marston's work with lie detectors and human psychology, it makes perfect sense that he would invent a tool like the lasso, even though no such item existed in either Greek or Roman myth. In the Pérez reboot, the lasso was forged by Hephaestus from the golden girdle of Gaea and was a gift from Hestia. The lasso can expand its length with near-infinite elasticity, and anyone it touches is compelled to tell the truth. The golden glow is referred to as the Fires of Hestia and indicates its incredible power at work.

WONDER WOMAN HAULS HER AMAZON PLANE TO THE ROOF OF THE OLD BARN WHERE SHE KEEPS IT HIDDEN.

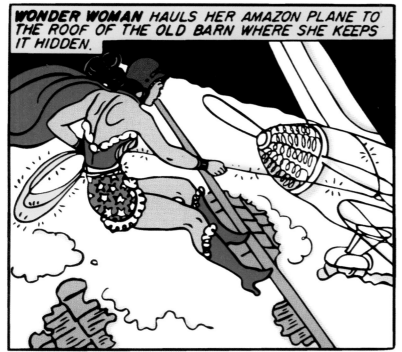

LIFTING THE HEAVILY LOADED PLANE OVER HER HEAD, THE MIGHTY AMAZON PREPARES TO LAUNCH IT LIKE A HUMAN CATAPULT.

HURLING HER PLANE HIGH INTO THE AIR, **WONDER WOMAN** DIRECTS IT BY MENTAL RADIO.

RISE TO 1000 FEET - COURSE NORTH-NORTH EAST!

CLIMBING INTO HER PLANE, **WONDER WOMAN** FLIES TO THE TENEMENT DISTRICT WHERE PETE ALLEN LIVES.

AS THE FLYING AMAZON REACHES PETE'S TENEMENT HOME, SHE LETS DOWN HER AERIAL LADDER.

I'LL KEEP MY PLANE CIRCLING OVERHEAD WHILE I FILL STOCKINGS FOR PETE AND GERTIE AND OTHER CHILDREN IN THIS HOUSE.

③

LUCKY THESE TENEMENT ROOFS ARE FLAT— IT'S CHILD'S PLAY TO LAND ON THEM!

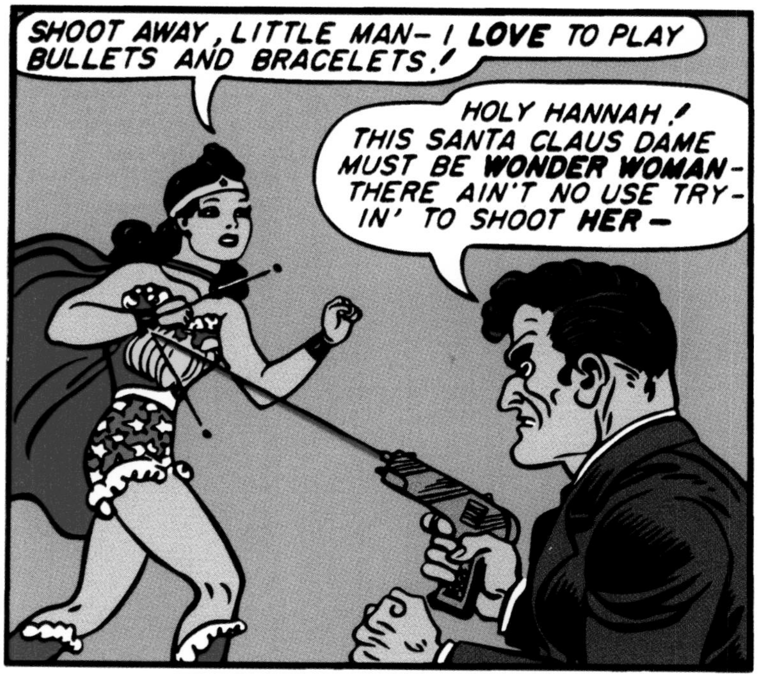
SHOOT AWAY, LITTLE MAN– I LOVE TO PLAY BULLETS AND BRACELETS!
HOLY HANNAH! THIS SANTA CLAUS DAME MUST BE WONDER WOMAN– THERE AIN'T NO USE TRY-IN' TO SHOOT HER–

Left and right: In this holiday tale from Marston and Peter, Wonder Woman substitutes for Santa Claus, complete with fur-trimmed costume. Note that the robot plane is a propeller model that needs a push from Wonder Woman in order to take flight.

Supposedly unbreakable, the lasso has actually been severed on more than one occasion, a symbol of the threat posed by Wonder Woman's respective foes. The lasso was vulnerable to breaking during times when the nature of the truth was challenged. For example, during a JLA mission, Wonder Woman believed Rama Khan falsely confessed. The Bizarro creature couldn't understand the nature of truth, and this complete lack of understanding caused the lasso to snap in two.

In other instances, the lasso was strong enough to hold Superman, Captain Marvel, Hercules, and even the god Ares. Its nigh-invulnerable properties has also made it a conductor of magical energies. During her days as a goddess, Wonder Woman even used the lasso to heal Donna Troy's fractured mind.

Gail Simone, who took over *Wonder Woman* in 2007, said the lasso is "a deadly weapon that not only binds you and follows its mistress's commands, [but] the damned thing can see into your soul."

In recent years, Wonder Woman has occasionally been called to war and has donned impenetrable golden armor, inspired in design by an eagle and crafted by fellow Amazon Pallas. A sword was another creation by Hephaestus, and the wings on the armor could be retracted when not in use or spread out to provide additional protection.

To travel freely, Wonder Woman first left Paradise Island via an invisible plane that responded to her mental commands. Differing accounts said the plane was a creation of the Amazons or was the legendary Pegasus magically transformed for Diana's use. Through the years the plane was modified in design to more closely resemble American air technology, so the propeller version that was first employed gave way to a sleek jet plane. Under writer Kanigher, Wonder Woman began to soar on air currents and had less use for the plane. Still, hangar space within the JLA's mountain headquarters was reserved for the invisible jet.

Diana was gifted with a sentient life form from the Lansinar, a race that once lived on Earth's surface eons ago and was rescued from certain death by the Amazon princess. Responding to her thoughts, the lightweight disc-shaped entity, which first appeared in *Wonder Woman* #115 (November 1996), could alter its size, shape, and density. This provided her with not only a new invisible jet, but it could become a high-powered motorcycle, a chariot and two horses, or even a headquarters (dubbed the Wonder Dome). Years later, the life form sacrificed its existence to protect Themyscira from a mammoth tidal wave. It lost its sentience but remained in the shape of the invisible plane as of *Wonder Woman* #201 (April 2004). Wonder Woman's fellow Amazons were inspired to build her a real invisible jet. The Lansinarians were asked to contribute some of its technology to help build the jet, and it has remained in her arsenal of incredible accessories.

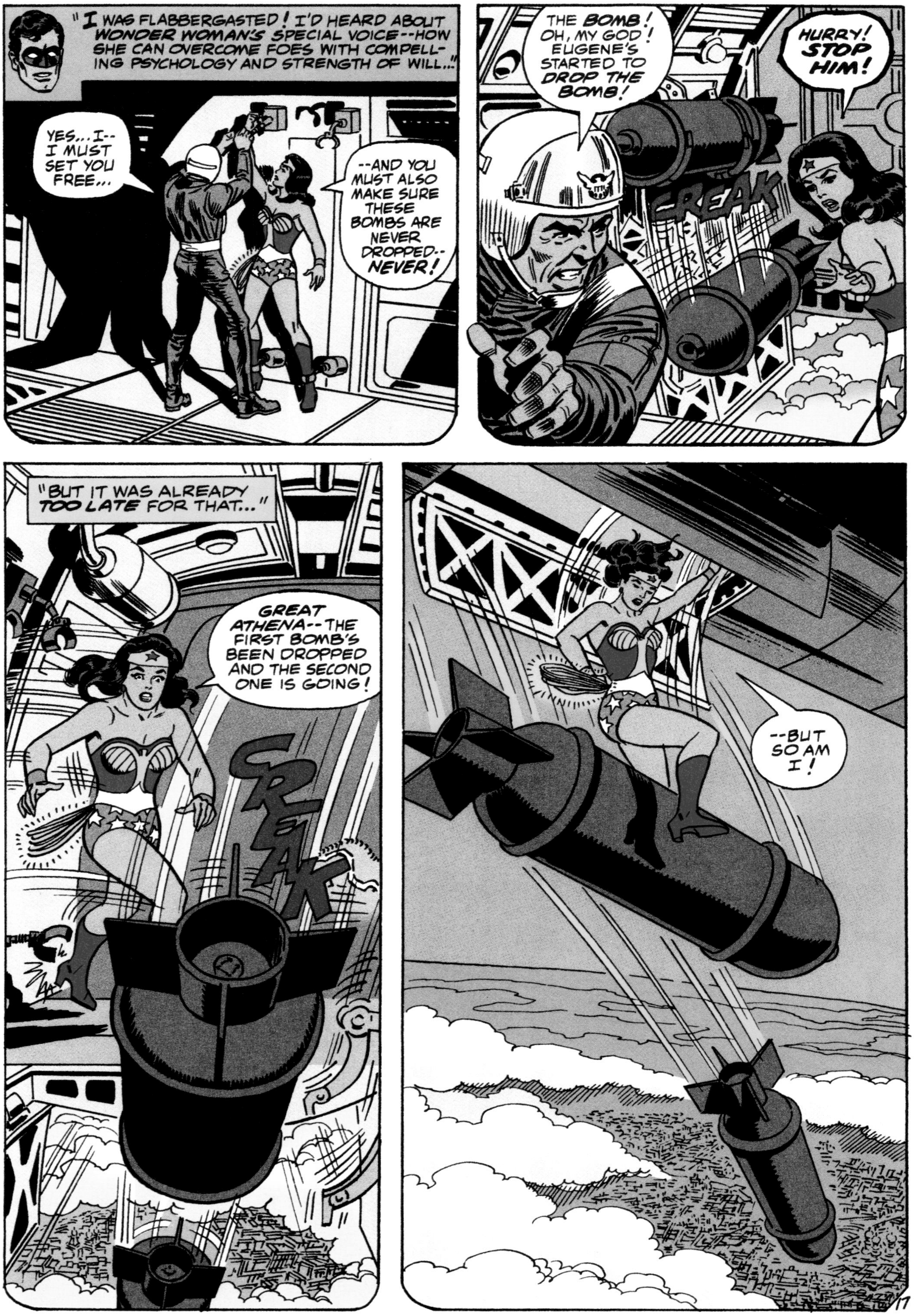
"I WAS FLABBERGASTED! I'D HEARD ABOUT WONDER WOMAN'S SPECIAL VOICE--HOW SHE CAN OVERCOME FOES WITH COMPELLING PSYCHOLOGY AND STRENGTH OF WILL..."
YES... I-- I MUST SET YOU FREE...
--AND YOU MUST ALSO MAKE SURE THESE BOMBS ARE NEVER DROPPED-- NEVER!
THE BOMB! OH, MY GOD! EUGENE'S STARTED TO DROP THE BOMB!
HURRY! STOP HIM!
CREAK
"BUT IT WAS ALREADY TOO LATE FOR THAT..."
GREAT ATHENA--THE FIRST BOMB'S BEEN DROPPED AND THE SECOND ONE IS GOING!
CREAK
--BUT SO AM I!
17

Above and right: When Wonder Woman reapplied for admission to the Justice League, a different member monitored her exploits. Here, Green Lantern narrates his teammate's quick thinking in using her magic lasso in an unconventional manner. Art by Curt Swan and Frank Giacoia (signed as Phil Zupa).

"SHE STOOD UP ON THE BACK OF THAT 20-MEGATON MONSTER, SPINNING HER LASSO LIKE A RODEO CHAMPION..."
ARTEMIS GUIDE MY AIM!
"...AND SHE LATCHED ONTO THE TAIL OF THAT OTHER WARHEAD AS IF IT WERE A WILD-EYED STEER!"
"NEXT MOMENT, THE ROBOT PLANE ZOOMED IN FROM OVER THE HORIZON AND..."
THERE! GOT BOTH OF THEM!
I PRAY THE GOLDEN LASSO IS STRETCHABLE AND INDESTRUCTIBLE ENOUGH TO PERFORM A MIRACLE!
NOW TO SPIN A PAIR OF GOLDEN COCOONS AROUND THE TWO WARHEADS...
...AND PULL ON BOTH ENDS TO PUT THE BOMBS UNDER PRESSURE!
18

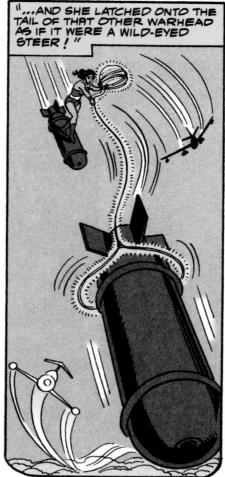

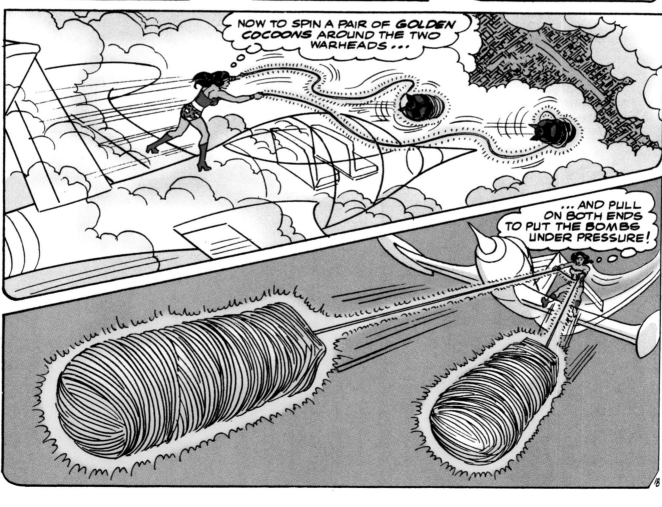

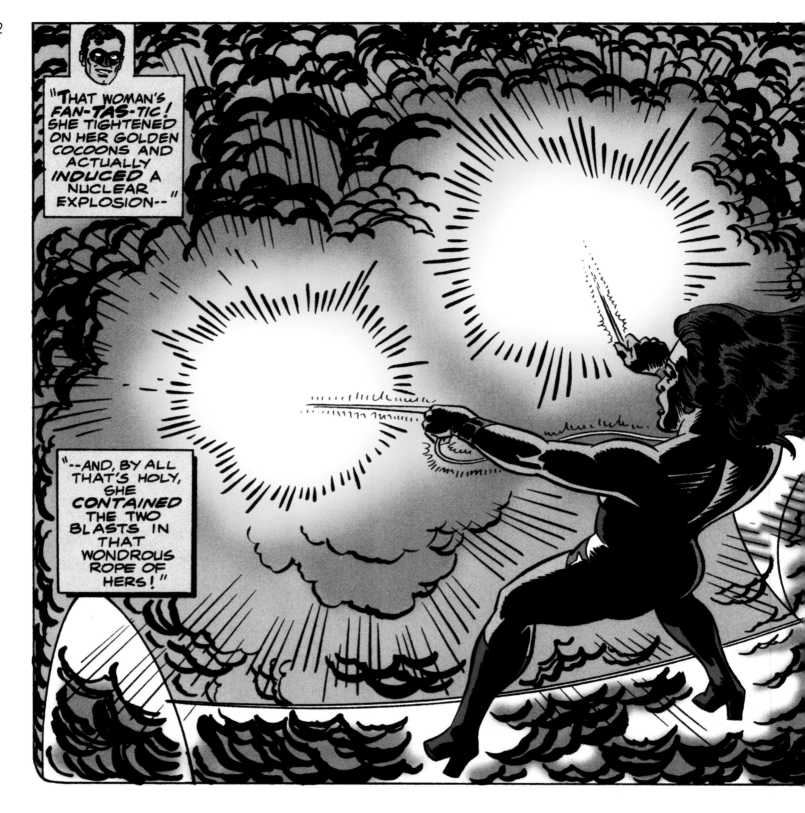

"THAT WOMAN'S *FAN-TAS-TIC!* SHE TIGHTENED ON HER GOLDEN COCOONS AND ACTUALLY *INDUCED* A NUCLEAR EXPLOSION--"

"--AND, BY ALL THAT'S HOLY, SHE *CONTAINED* THE TWO BLASTS IN THAT WONDROUS ROPE OF HERS!"

Above: As the story reached its climax, readers could see that Wonder Woman's lasso could not be snapped by anything—even a nuclear explosion.

Right: John Byrne wanted to write Wonder Woman's invisible plane back into her arc. He crafted a story, in which she was given a piece of alien technology that would transform into any shape she desired. The bottom panel depicts a man she knew as Champion but who turned out to be Hercules, back and looking for revenge again the Amazons.

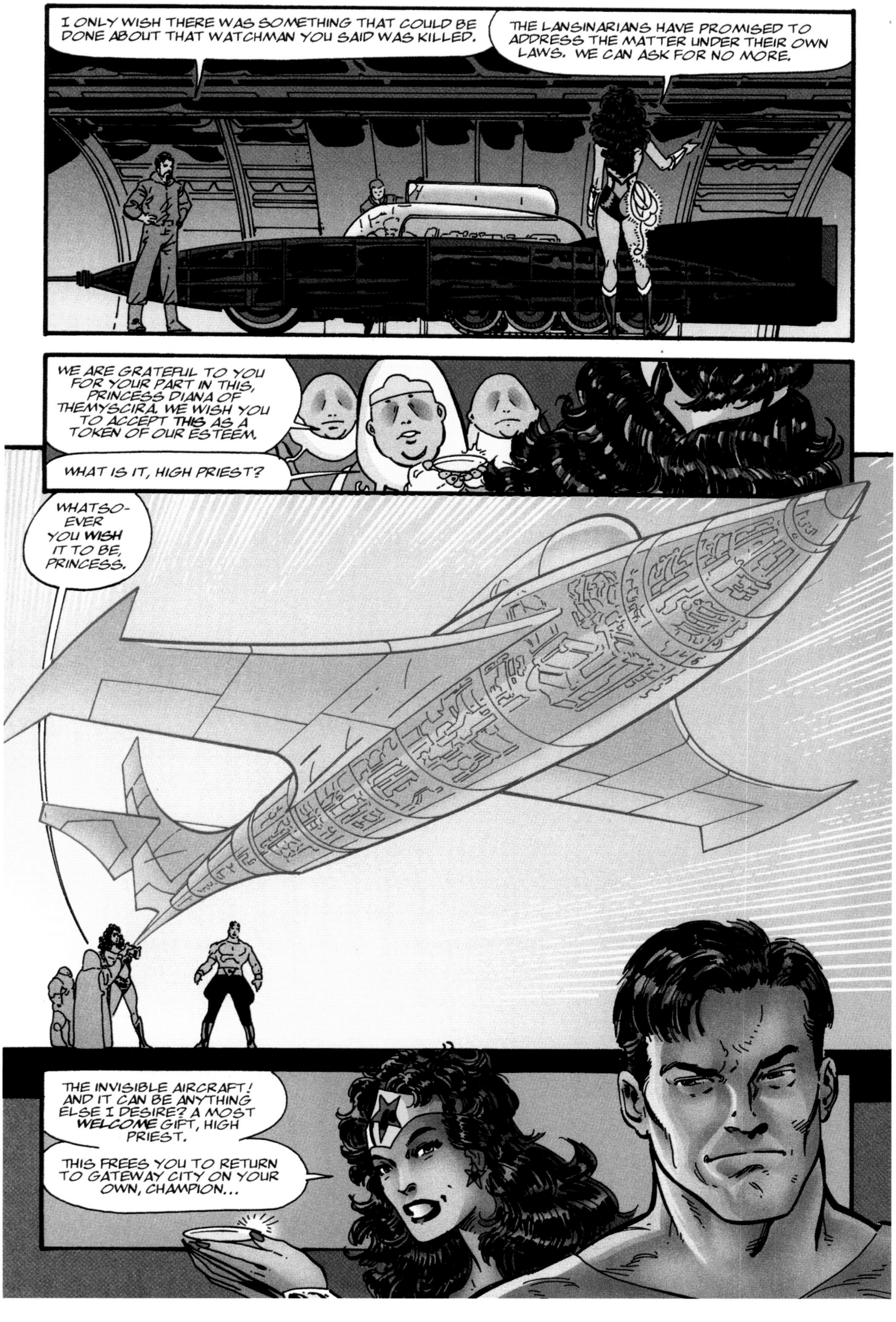
I ONLY WISH THERE WAS SOMETHING THAT COULD BE DONE ABOUT THAT WATCHMAN YOU SAID WAS KILLED.
THE LANSINARIANS HAVE PROMISED TO ADDRESS THE MATTER UNDER THEIR OWN LAWS. WE CAN ASK FOR NO MORE.
WE ARE GRATEFUL TO YOU FOR YOUR PART IN THIS, PRINCESS DIANA OF THEMYSCIRA. WE WISH YOU TO ACCEPT THIS AS A TOKEN OF OUR ESTEEM.
WHAT IS IT, HIGH PRIEST?
WHATSO-EVER YOU WISH IT TO BE, PRINCESS.
THE INVISIBLE AIRCRAFT! AND IT CAN BE ANYTHING ELSE I DESIRE? A MOST WELCOME GIFT, HIGH PRIEST.
THIS FREES YOU TO RETURN TO GATEWAY CITY ON YOUR OWN, CHAMPION...

EN ROUTE, **WONDER WOMAN'S** MENTAL RADIO SPEAKS.

CALLING **WONDER WOMAN** — INVADING SPACE SHIP BELONGS TO MARS! HAVE NO FURTHER INFORMATION — PRISONERS KEPT CLOSELY CONFINED AND BLINDFOLDED ——

ON PARADISE ISLAND, QUEEN HIPPOLYTE HELPS HER DAUGHTER OPERATE THE MAGIC SPHERE.

YOU'VE GOT IT — THERE'S MARS' SPACE SHIP ON THE VIEW PLATE!

THANK APHRODITE! NOW WE CAN TRACE THE SHIP TO ITS BASE!

MARS IS HEADING FOR THE MOON — HE MUST HAVE CAPTURED IT AND MADE IT DARK!

BUT **WHAT'S** HAPPENED TO DIANA, GODDESS OF THE MOON, AND HER MAIDENS? DAUGHTER, YOU MUST GO THERE IMMEDIATELY!

MOTHER, I WANT TO TAKE PAULA WITH ME — I MAY NEED HER SCIENTIFIC GENIUS.

VERY WELL, DARLING — PAULA IS NOW FREE TO LEAVE PARADISE ISLAND AND GO ANYWHERE YOU COMMAND!

THE GIRLS MOUNT A **SKY KANGA**, AN ANIMAL BRED BY THE AMAZONS FOR SHORT SPACE TRIPS.

HOW DO KANGAS BREATHE IN SPACE?

THEY HAVE RESERVE-AIR LUNGS — BUT **WE** NEED THESE OXYGEN MASKS!

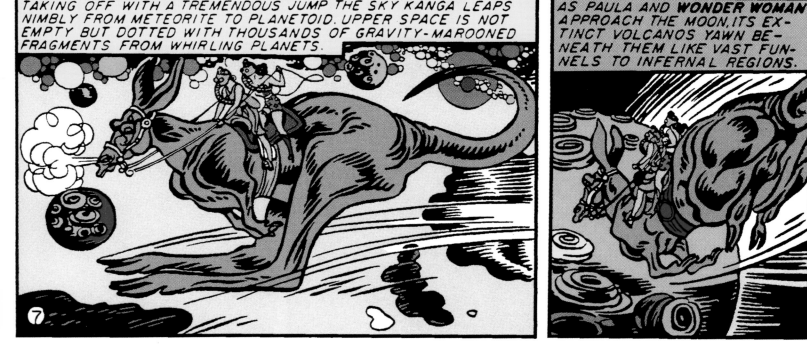

TAKING OFF WITH A TREMENDOUS JUMP THE SKY KANGA LEAPS NIMBLY FROM METEORITE TO PLANETOID. UPPER SPACE IS NOT EMPTY BUT DOTTED WITH THOUSANDS OF GRAVITY-MAROONED FRAGMENTS FROM WHIRLING PLANETS.

7

AS PAULA AND **WONDER WOMAN** APPROACH THE MOON, ITS EXTINCT VOLCANOS YAWN BENEATH THEM LIKE VAST FUNNELS TO INFERNAL REGIONS.

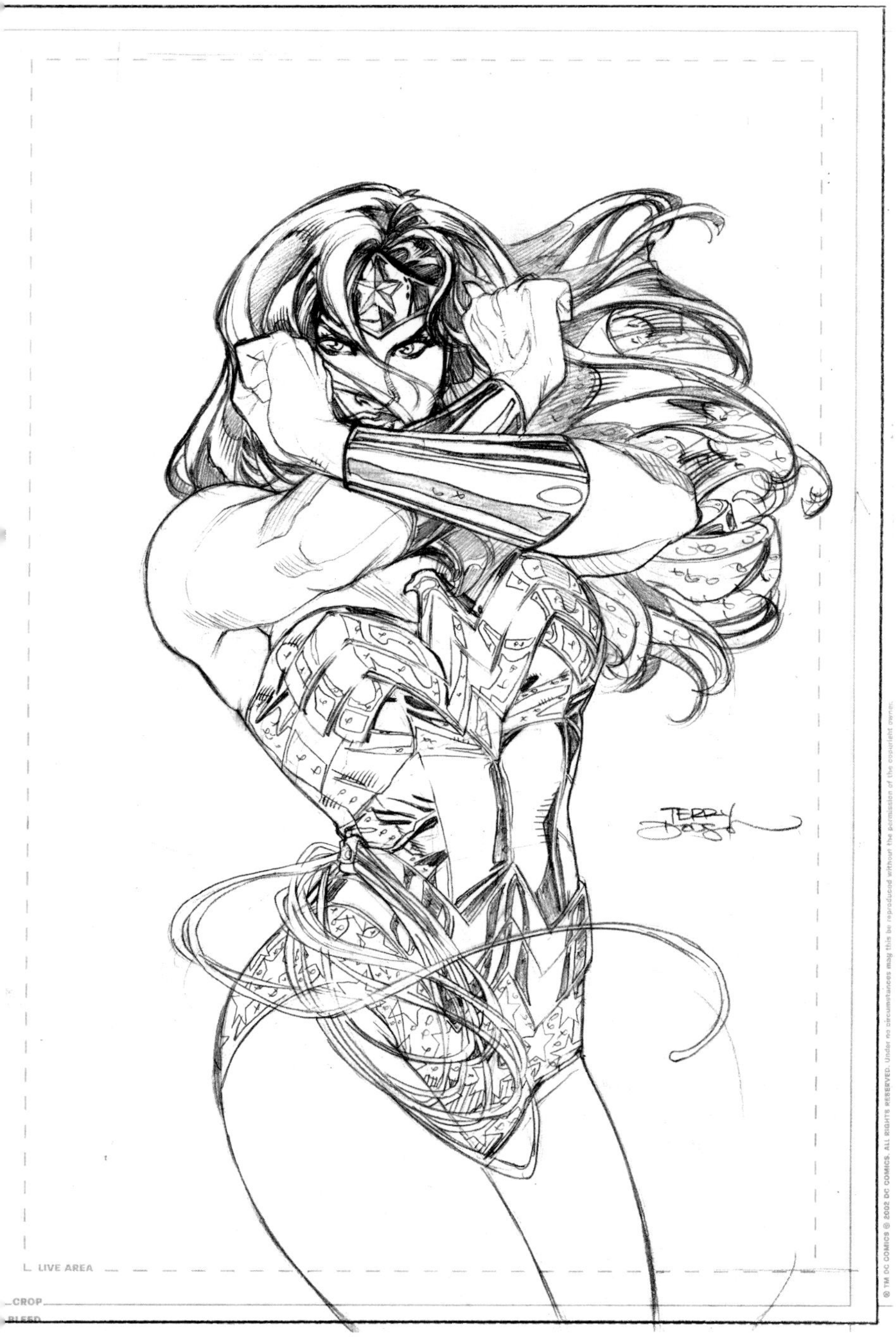
LIVE AREA
CROP

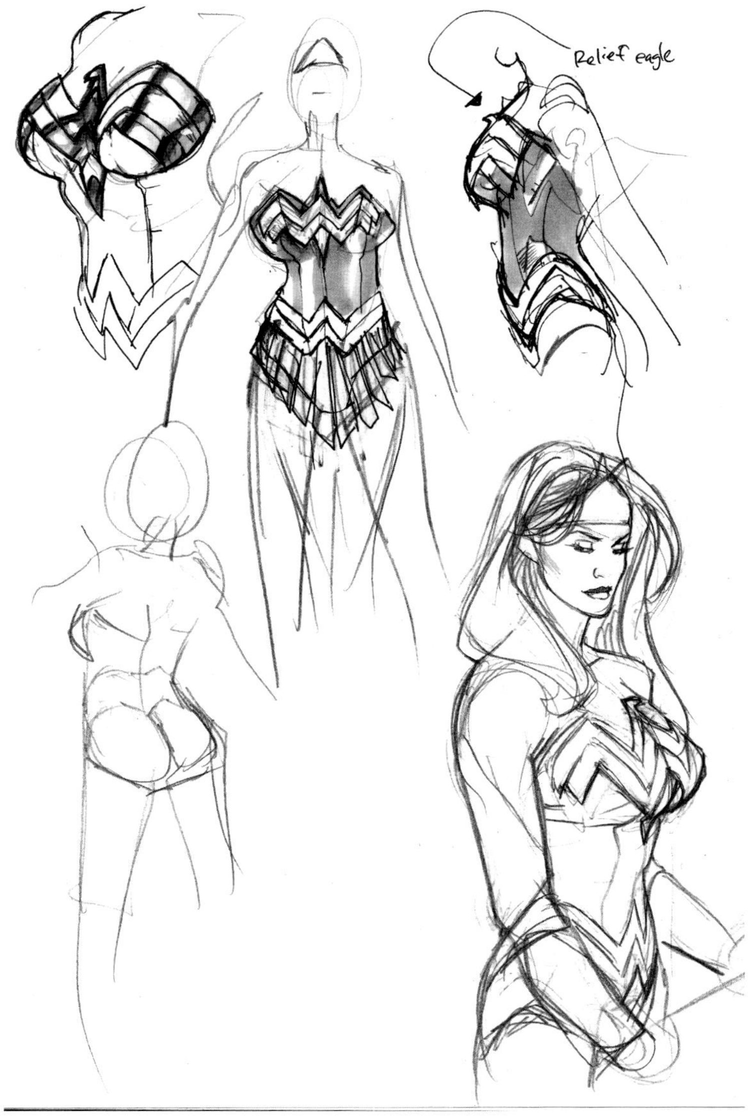
Relief eagle

Above: Pencil art for a cover by Terry Dodson, who also drew the character studies.

Left: Marston played fast and loose with science, as seen in this sequence. Wonder Woman and Paula von Gunther survive the vacuum of space with mere oxygen masks, while the kanga had lungs powerful enough to propel them across the solar system.

Right: Another piece of seldom-seen style guide artwork.

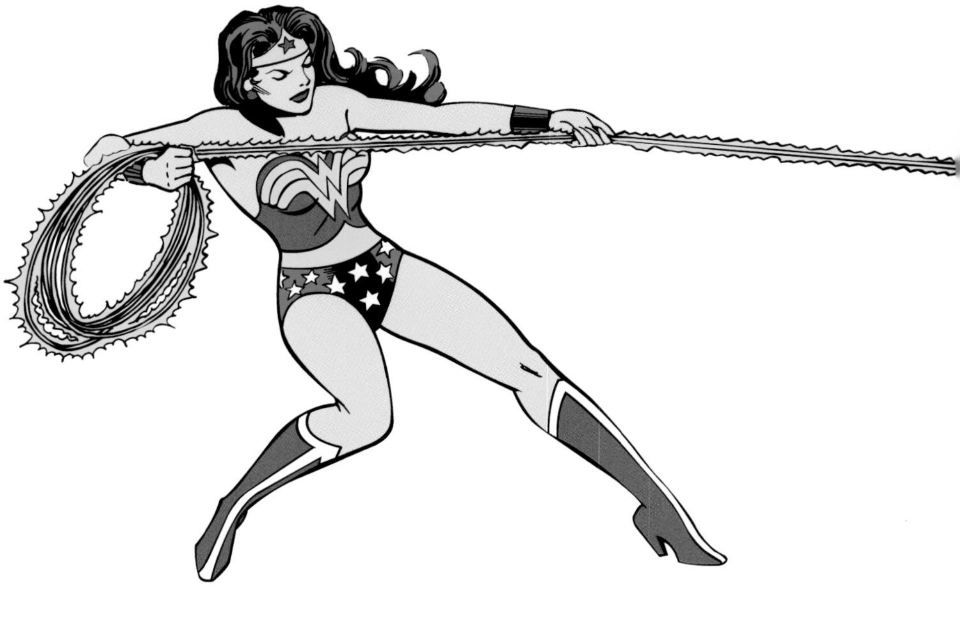

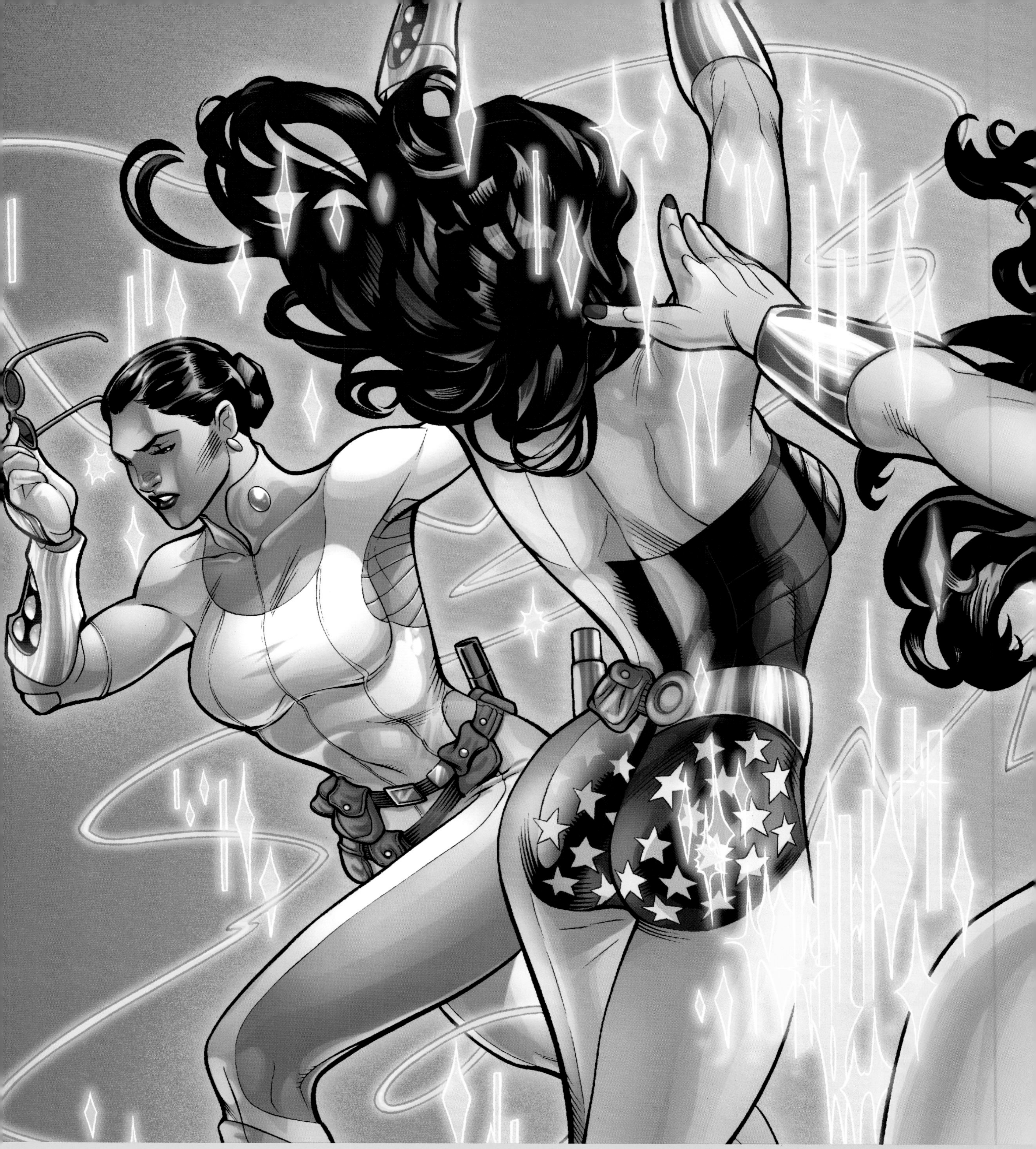

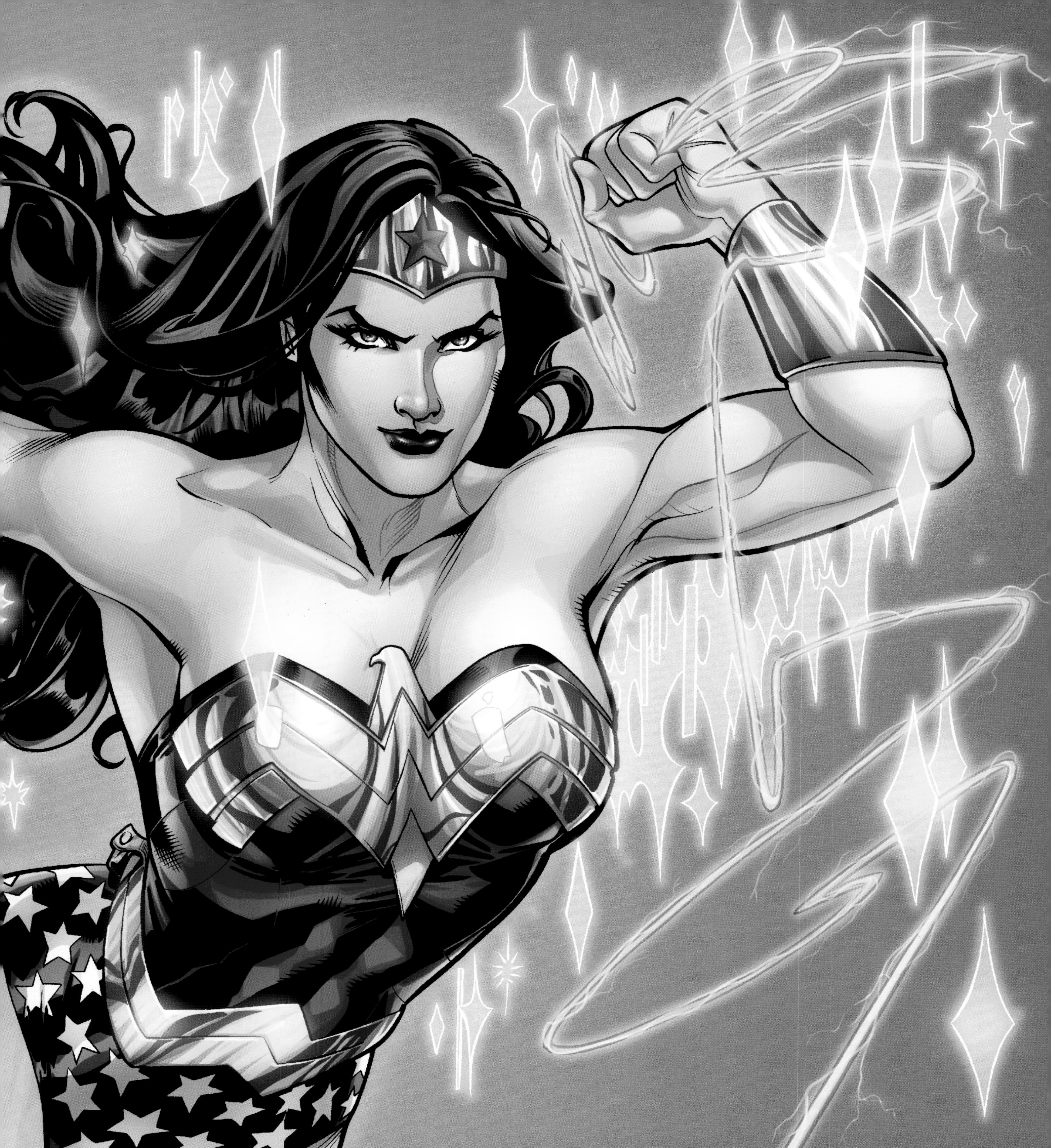

★ Coming To Man's World

One would think that after being raised on an island filled with fabulous-looking, powerful women, Diana's arrival in Man's World would be a culture shock. After all, she was coming to America during the waning days of the Great Depression, and had never experienced the sights, sounds, and smells of a big city.

Instead of being shocked, she never looked back and took to her new life with enthusiasm and energy. First, she performed a "bullets and bracelets" promotion and earned a substantial sum of money, something Diana quickly learned was necessary in "Man's World." Soon after, Diana decided on the need for a civilian identity, which was essential in comic book stories at the time. She met army nurse Diana Prince, who was pining for her fiancé in South America. Flush with cash, Diana bought Prince's identity and entered the United States Army as Colonel Philip Darnell's secretary, which allowed her to be close to Steve Trevor.

In time, Diana Prince rose through the ranks to become a major, despite her frequent absences to defend justice as Wonder Woman. Diana was largely a colorless personality, with no distinct character from her costumed alter ego, and everyone accepted her benign guise with little or no question.

When writer Martin Pasko set the 1976 comic-book adventures back to World War II, which reflected the television series, they depicted the parallel world known as Earth-2. In this version, Diana Prince was a WAVES yeoman, working under Major Steve Trevor.

Above: The traditional whirling magical transformation from one guise into another, from a classic DC Comics style guide.

Right: When Wonder Woman was reintroduced in 1987, she was placed in Boston. Once she went public, the media couldn't get enough of her. The woman featured in the bottom three panels was promoter Mindy Mayer, who tried to help the Amazon acclimate to Patriarch's World. Art by George Pérez.

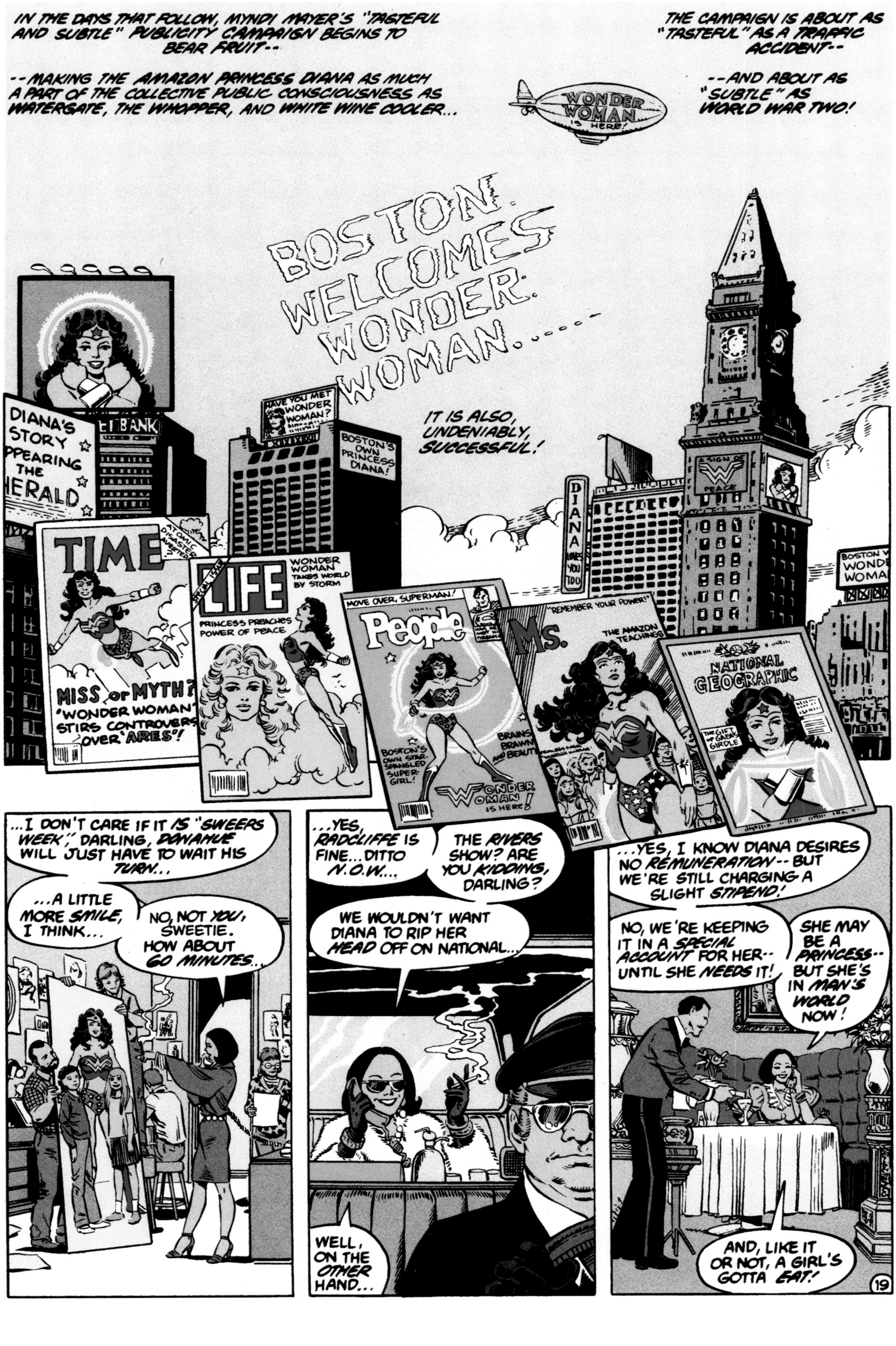

IN THE DAYS THAT FOLLOW, MYNDI MAYER'S "TASTEFUL AND SUBTLE" PUBLICITY CAMPAIGN BEGINS TO BEAR FRUIT--
--MAKING THE AMAZON PRINCESS DIANA AS MUCH A PART OF THE COLLECTIVE PUBLIC CONSCIOUSNESS AS WATERGATE, THE WHOPPER, AND WHITE WINE COOLER...
THE CAMPAIGN IS ABOUT AS "TASTEFUL" AS A TRAFFIC ACCIDENT--
--AND ABOUT AS "SUBTLE" AS WORLD WAR TWO!
WONDER WOMAN IS HERE!
BOSTON WELCOMES WONDER WOMAN......
IT IS ALSO, UNDENIABLY, SUCCESSFUL!
DIANA'S STORY PPEARING THE HERALD
HAVE YOU MET WONDER WOMAN?
BOSTON'S OWN PRINCESS DIANA!
A SIGN OF PEACE
DIANA LOVES YOU TOO
BOSTON WONDE WOMA
TIME
ATOMIC DISASTER AVERTED?
MISS OR MYTH? 'WONDER WOMAN' STIRS CONTROVERS OVER 'ARES'!
LIFE
SPECIAL ISSUE
WONDER WOMAN TAKES WORLD BY STORM
PRINCESS PREACHES POWER OF PEACE
MOVE OVER, SUPERMAN!
People
BOSTON'S OWN STAR-SPANGLED SUPER-GIRL!
BRAINS BRAWN AND BEAUTY
WONDER WOMAN IS HERE!
Ms.
"REMEMBER YOUR POWER!"
THE AMAZON TEACHINGS
NATIONAL GEOGRAPHIC
THE GIFT OF GAEA'S GIRDLE
...I DON'T CARE IF IT IS "SWEEPS WEEK," DARLING, DONAHUE WILL JUST HAVE TO WAIT HIS TURN...
...A LITTLE MORE SMILE, I THINK...
NO, NOT YOU, SWEETIE. HOW ABOUT 60 MINUTES...
...YES, RADCLIFFE IS FINE...DITTO N.O.W....
THE RIVERS SHOW? ARE YOU KIDDING, DARLING?
WE WOULDN'T WANT DIANA TO RIP HER HEAD OFF ON NATIONAL...
WELL, ON THE OTHER HAND...
...YES, I KNOW DIANA DESIRES NO REMUNERATION--BUT WE'RE STILL CHARGING A SLIGHT STIPEND!
NO, WE'RE KEEPING IT IN A SPECIAL ACCOUNT FOR HER--UNTIL SHE NEEDS IT!
SHE MAY BE A PRINCESS--BUT SHE'S IN MAN'S WORLD NOW!
AND, LIKE IT OR NOT, A GIRL'S GOTTA EAT!
19

TOO BAD I HAD TO WASTE TIME DESTROYING THAT MONSTER **FEAR**! THE ASTRAL KIDNAPERS HAVE DISAPPEARED - I'LL NEED HELP! I'LL GO TO HOLLIDAY COLLEGE - IF ETTA AND THE GIRLS ARE ASLEEP, I CAN USE THEM—

AT HOLLIDAY COLLEGE, SURE ENOUGH, THE AMAZON PRINCESS MEETS THE ASTRAL FORMS OF ETTA AND HER GIRLS.

APHRODITE WITH YOU, GIRLS! I NEED YOUR HELP!

HOORAY, IT'S **WONDER WOMAN**! HEY, WHATCHA DOIN' HERE IN DREAMLAND, KID?

SHUT UP, GIRLS - I BETCHA **WONDER WOMAN'S** GOT AN ASSIGNMENT FOR US!

YOU'RE RIGHT! WE MUST FIND PRISON CASTLE WHERE MARIE IS HELD CAPTIVE. I WILL PROCEED WITHOUT DISGUISE, HOPING THAT SPIRIT KIDNAPERS WILL TRY TO CAPTURE ME. YOU GIRLS WILL FOLLOW DISGUISED AS BIRDS!

WOO WOO! I'LL MAKE A SWELL SWAN!

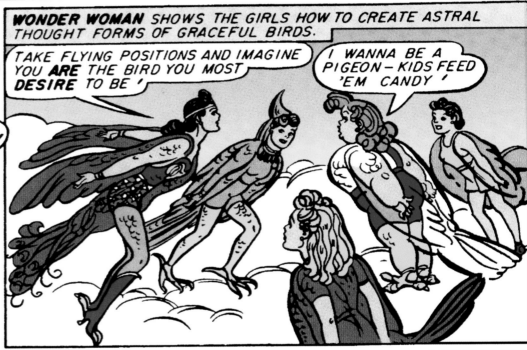

WONDER WOMAN SHOWS THE GIRLS HOW TO CREATE ASTRAL THOUGHT FORMS OF GRACEFUL BIRDS.

TAKE FLYING POSITIONS AND IMAGINE YOU **ARE** THE BIRD YOU MOST **DESIRE** TO BE!

I WANNA BE A PIGEON - KIDS FEED 'EM CANDY!

WONDER WOMAN LEADS HER FLIGHT OF RARE BIRDS OVER THE ASTRAL PLANE.

⑩

SUDDENLY, AHEAD, APPEARS A LOVELY OASIS, INVITING THE TIRED ASTRAL TRAVELER TO REST.

AHA - SO **THIS** IS THEIR TRAP! I'LL PRETEND TO FALL FOR IT.

JAP BOMBING PLANES RUN INTO AN AMBUSH OF AMERICAN FIGHTERS AND ARE SHOT DOWN BY THE DOZEN IN FLAMES.

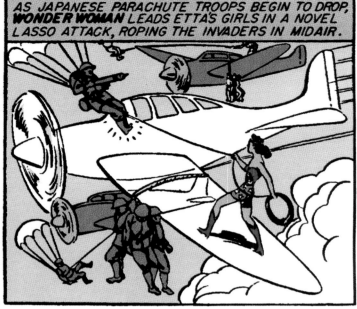

AS JAPANESE PARACHUTE TROOPS BEGIN TO DROP, **WONDER WOMAN** LEADS ETTA'S GIRLS IN A NOVEL LASSO ATTACK, ROPING THE INVADERS IN MIDAIR.

Left: Etta Candy and her sorority sisters were recurring players throughout the 1940s, ready to forego their studies in order to help Wonder Woman. In this sequence, they mastered a heretofore unknown ability to transform. Art by Harry G. Peter.

Above: Wonder Woman rarely got herself involved in World War II despite her work for the armed forces, but she would rescue those in need. Art by Harry G. Peter.

While enjoying globetrotting and intergalactic derring-do during comics' Golden Age, Wonder Woman seemed at home in every culture. Any thought of using her "fish out of water" perspective was ignored by Marston and Kanigher. Instead, Diana Prince and Wonder Woman enjoyed escapes and adventures fighting evil in all its forms.

Diana had a nice support system in the form of the highly excitable Etta Candy. Etta, overweight and often seen clutching a box of chocolates, befriended the Amazon Princess in *Sensation Comics* #2 (February 1942). She eventually earned Diana's trust and was brought along on cases. At one point Diana asked Etta for an army to help her struggle against Dr. Poison, so Etta found one hundred college-aged women and formed the Holliday Girls of the Holliday College for Women.

Marston seemed to delight in the sorority antics of his day, including "baby parties," where coeds dressed as infants, and he played out the scene in the comics. The brash Etta led the Holliday Girls through sheer force of personality, but never lorded her relationship with Wonder Woman over her fellow members of Beta Lambda. She was always ready for a fight, and Etta's trademark "woo, woo" let readers know there was action to come.

By 1950, Kanigher had enough of Candy and her confection-named family, as well as the Holliday girls, so they were both abandoned. Etta and the Holliday Girls finally resurfaced in the 1960s. In a 1980 makeover, Etta was briefly Diana's roommate, and Etta's final appearance was during Wonder Woman's modern-day reincarnation as a career military officer who eventually married Steve Trevor. Etta confronted body type issues when she encountered Wonder Woman, which sent a vital message to the female readership.

Diana Prince remained largely an unformed character through the years, until she renounced her powers in 1968. Hippolyta told her that the magic that had sustained the Amazons had been exhausted, and they had to move to another dimension. Diana, though, chose to remain on Earth. By then, Diana Prince *was* Wonder Woman and was an adventurous female, out to make it on her own without benefit of godly interference. Guided by the wise I-Ching, she adventured around the world, aiding the troubled and confounding the schemes of Dr. Cyber.

After she regained her powers with the return of Paradise Island and the Amazons in 1972, Diana went through numerous professions as writers tried to find a definitive career and personality to differentiate her from other better-known heroes. As a result, she was a United Nations translator before becoming a field agent for the UN's Crisis Bureau. She later trained to become an astronaut based in Houston, but never really did much with the restrictions placed on her time. Instead, she returned to the United Nations before giving her identity a makeover and finding her way back to the military. This time Diana was a captain in the air force, working at the Pentagon's Special Assignments Bureau.

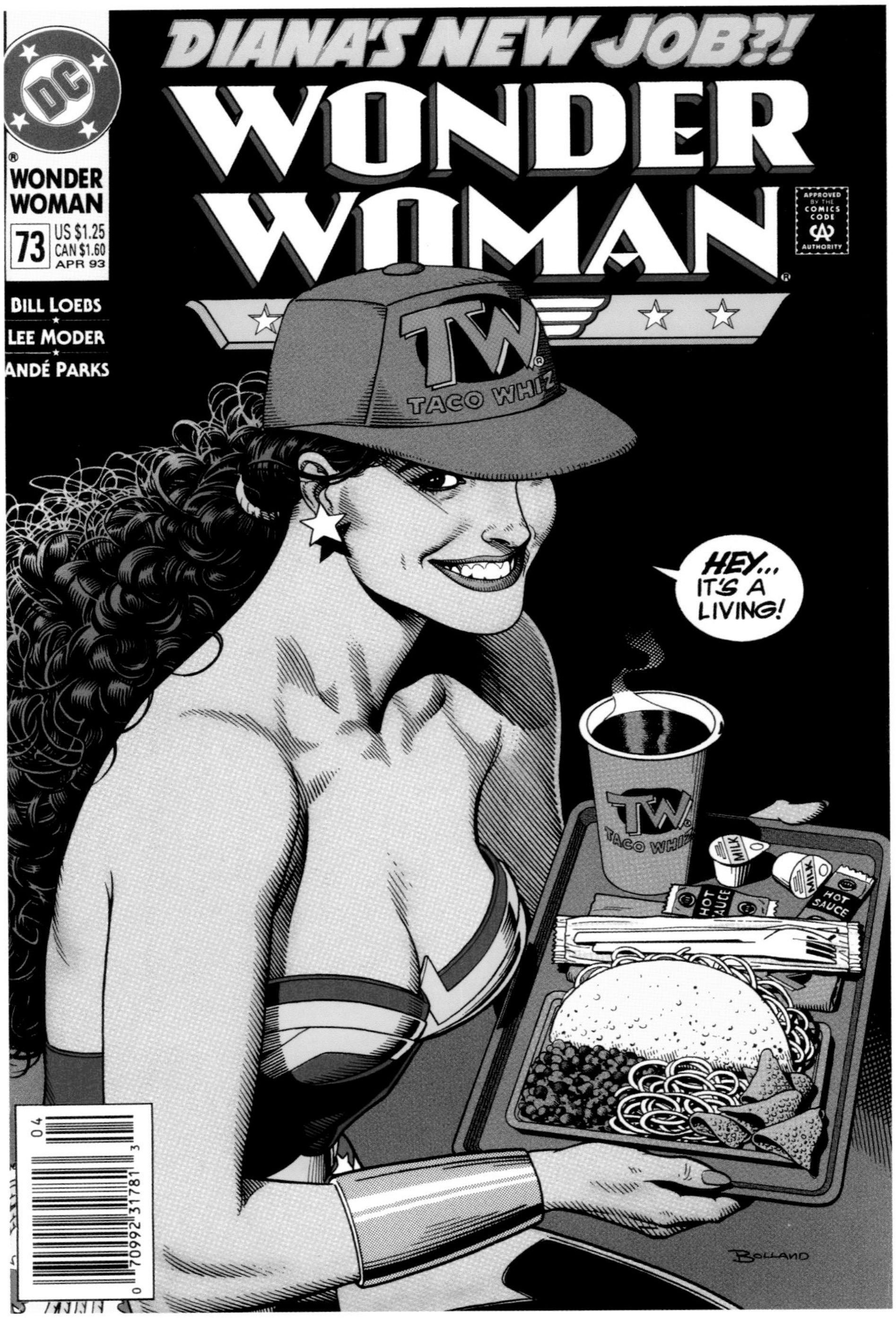

DIANA'S NEW JOB?!
WONDER WOMAN
WONDER WOMAN
73 US $1.25 CAN $1.60 APR 93
BILL LOEBS
LEE MODER
ANDÉ PARKS
TW TACO WHIZ
HEY... IT'S A LIVING!
HOT SAUCE
MILK
BOLLAND

Left: When Diana needed an income, she worked for a time as a minimum-wage employee for the Taco Whiz chain, as seen in this classic cover by Brian Bolland.

Below: Character studies in marker by Terry Dodson.

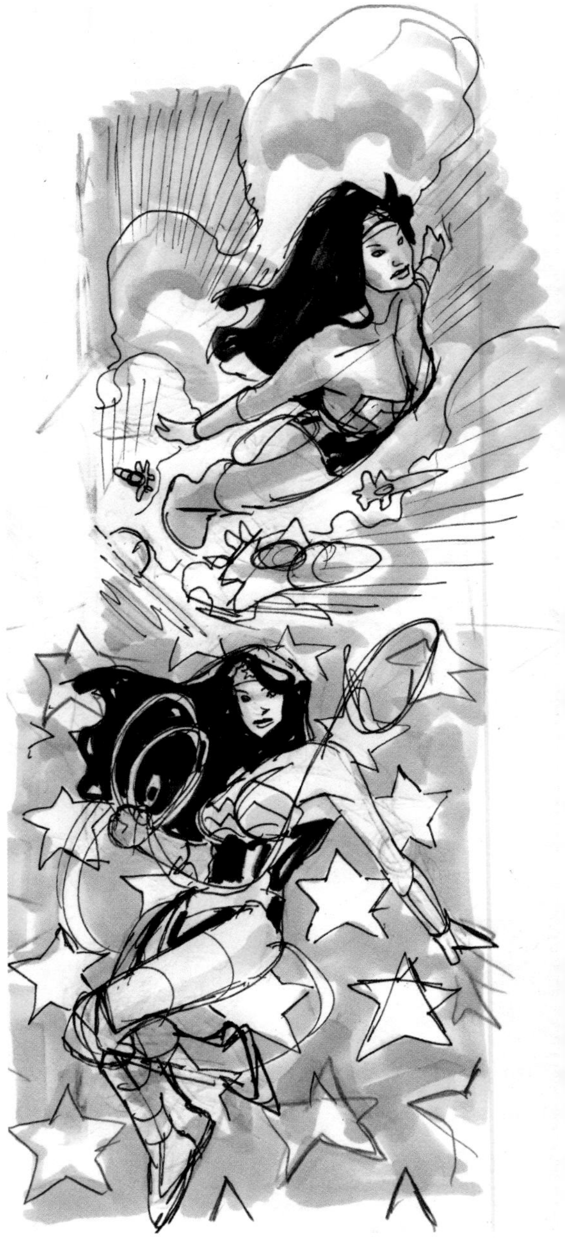

Right: Yanick Paquette and Bob McLeod illustrate Diana's ire at the 1940s portrayal of Wonder Woman. Hippolyta had actually journeyed back in time to adventure as Wonder Woman during this storyline—a nod to her Golden Age adventures.

Her reintroduction in 1986 finally allowed writers to explore what it must have been like to enter a new world with little time to prepare. Diana was an ambassador and was therefore simply known as Diana of Themyscira. From time to time, though, she used "Diana Prince" when an alias was required.

Still, she didn't immediately appear in her iconic outfit in public. Instead, she had numerous adventures before a well-choreographed series of events allowed her to show up as a one-man cavalry at the climax of a DC Universe–wide crossover known as *Legends*.

Diana remained a representative from Themyscira and a heroine for many years, until storylines demanded she resume her alter ego. Once more she assumed the identity of Diana Prince, this time working for the Department of Meta-human Affairs. She was partnered with Tom Tresser, who briefly became a romantic interest. In *Wonder Woman Annual* #1 (2007), writer Gail Simone had the villain Circe enchant Diana, which allowed Circe to steal Diana's power and let her be either the mortal Diana Prince or the immortal heroine Wonder Woman. The scheme was contrived as a way to avenge the women Wonder Woman had failed to aid throughout the years. With or without powers, Diana continued to fight for truth and justice, and managed to regain her abilities. She proved once and for all the woman herself was a wonder.

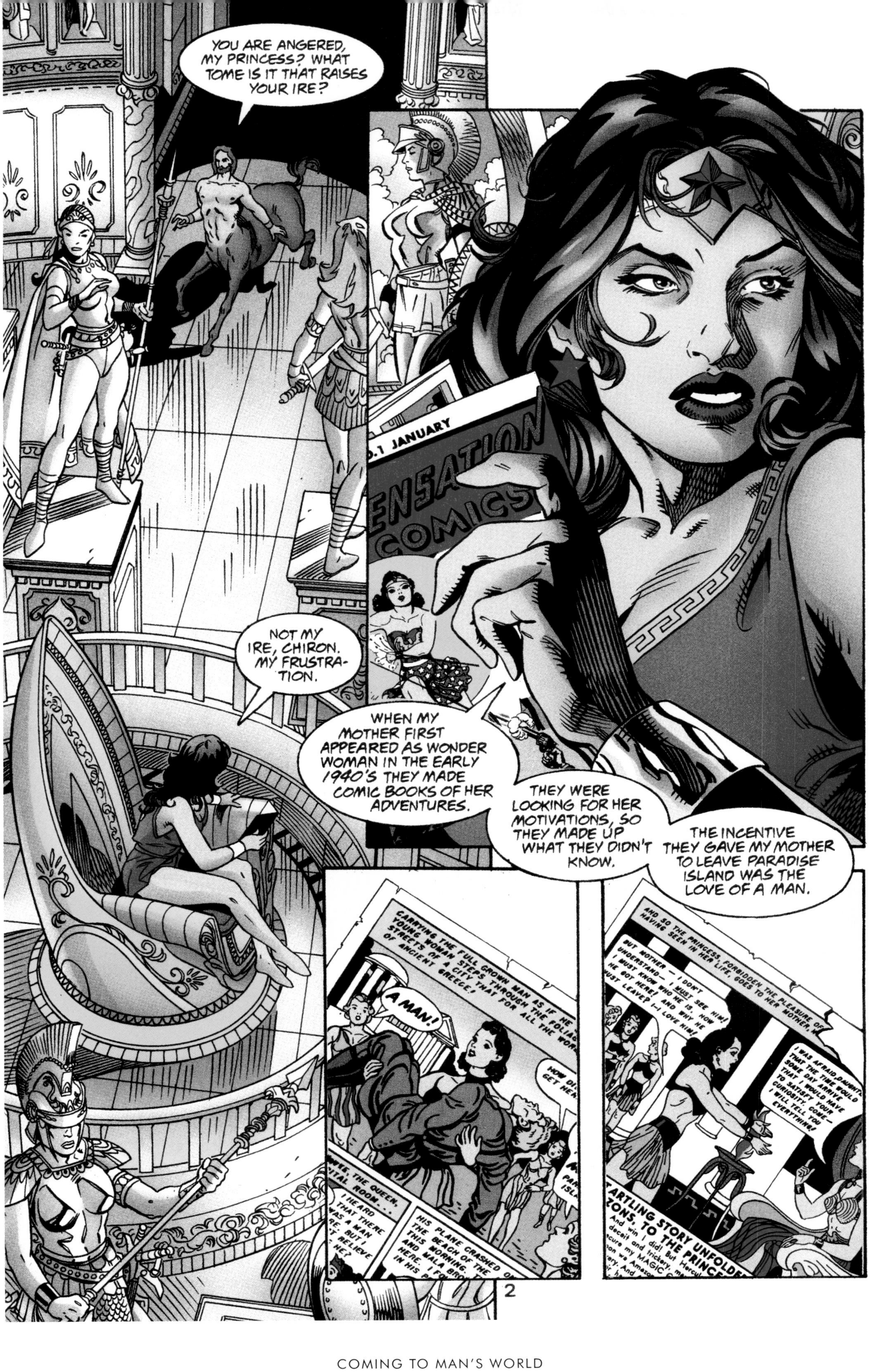
YOU ARE ANGERED, MY PRINCESS? WHAT TOME IS IT THAT RAISES YOUR IRE?
NOT MY IRE, CHIRON. MY FRUSTRATION.
WHEN MY MOTHER FIRST APPEARED AS WONDER WOMAN IN THE EARLY 1940'S THEY MADE COMIC BOOKS OF HER ADVENTURES.
THEY WERE LOOKING FOR HER MOTIVATIONS, SO THEY MADE UP WHAT THEY DIDN'T KNOW.
THE INCENTIVE THEY GAVE MY MOTHER TO LEAVE PARADISE ISLAND WAS THE LOVE OF A MAN.
A MAN!
2

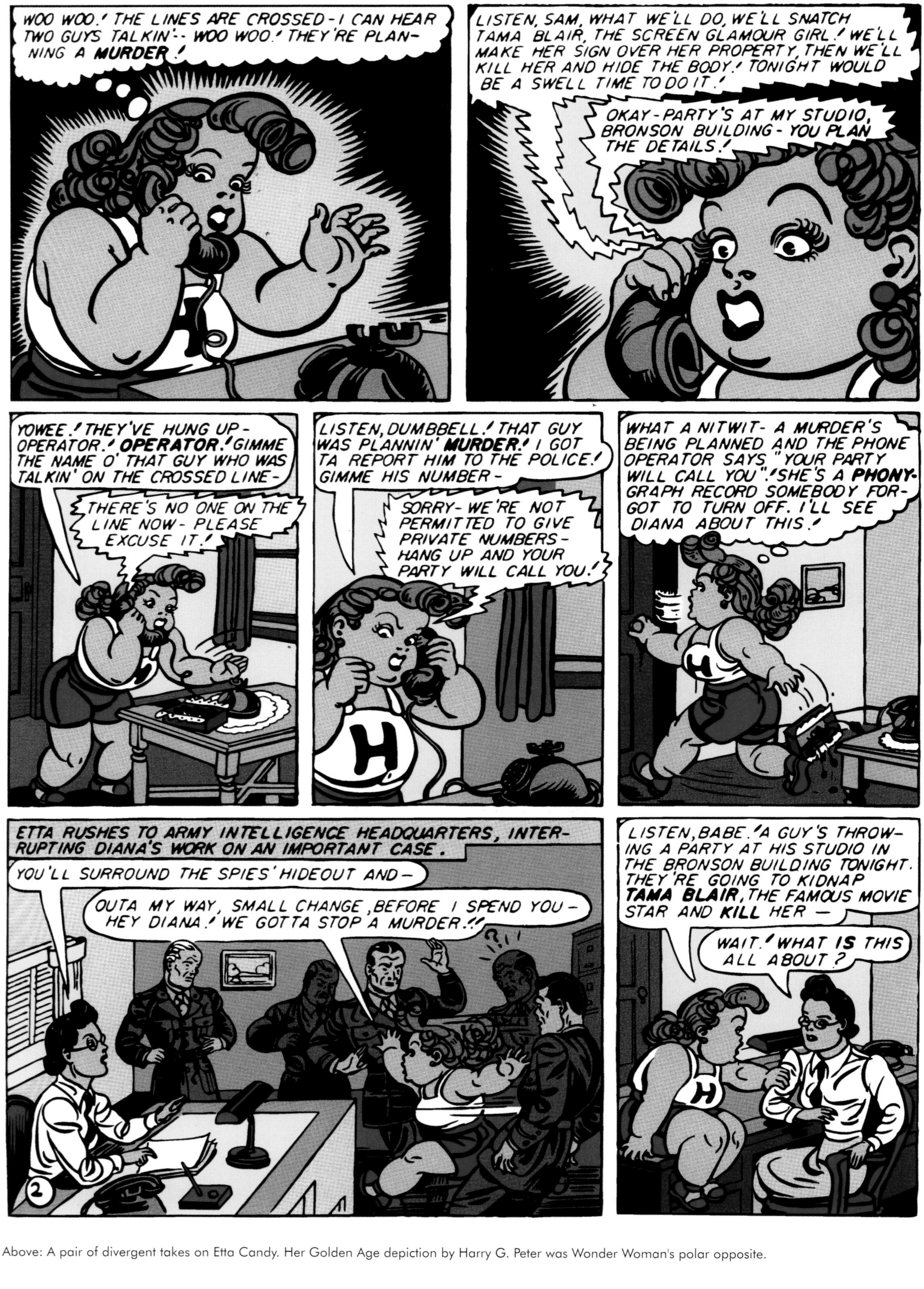
WOO WOO! THE LINES ARE CROSSED - I CAN HEAR TWO GUYS TALKIN' -- WOO WOO! THEY'RE PLANNING A MURDER!
LISTEN, SAM, WHAT WE'LL DO, WE'LL SNATCH TAMA BLAIR, THE SCREEN GLAMOUR GIRL! WE'LL MAKE HER SIGN OVER HER PROPERTY, THEN WE'LL KILL HER AND HIDE THE BODY! TONIGHT WOULD BE A SWELL TIME TO DO IT!
OKAY - PARTY'S AT MY STUDIO, BRONSON BUILDING - YOU PLAN THE DETAILS!
YOWEE! THEY'VE HUNG UP - OPERATOR! OPERATOR! GIMME THE NAME O' THAT GUY WHO WAS TALKIN' ON THE CROSSED LINE -
THERE'S NO ONE ON THE LINE NOW - PLEASE EXCUSE IT!
LISTEN, DUMBBELL! THAT GUY WAS PLANNIN' MURDER! I GOT TA REPORT HIM TO THE POLICE! GIMME HIS NUMBER -
SORRY - WE'RE NOT PERMITTED TO GIVE PRIVATE NUMBERS - HANG UP AND YOUR PARTY WILL CALL YOU!
WHAT A NITWIT - A MURDER'S BEING PLANNED AND THE PHONE OPERATOR SAYS "YOUR PARTY WILL CALL YOU"! SHE'S A PHONYGRAPH RECORD SOMEBODY FORGOT TO TURN OFF. I'LL SEE DIANA ABOUT THIS!
ETTA RUSHES TO ARMY INTELLIGENCE HEADQUARTERS, INTERRUPTING DIANA'S WORK ON AN IMPORTANT CASE.
YOU'LL SURROUND THE SPIES' HIDEOUT AND -
OUTA MY WAY, SMALL CHANGE, BEFORE I SPEND YOU - HEY DIANA! WE GOTTA STOP A MURDER!!
2
LISTEN, BABE! A GUY'S THROWING A PARTY AT HIS STUDIO IN THE BRONSON BUILDING TONIGHT. THEY'RE GOING TO KIDNAP TAMA BLAIR, THE FAMOUS MOVIE STAR AND KILL HER -
WAIT! WHAT IS THIS ALL ABOUT?

Above: A pair of divergent takes on Etta Candy. Her Golden Age depiction by Harry G. Peter was Wonder Woman's polar opposite.

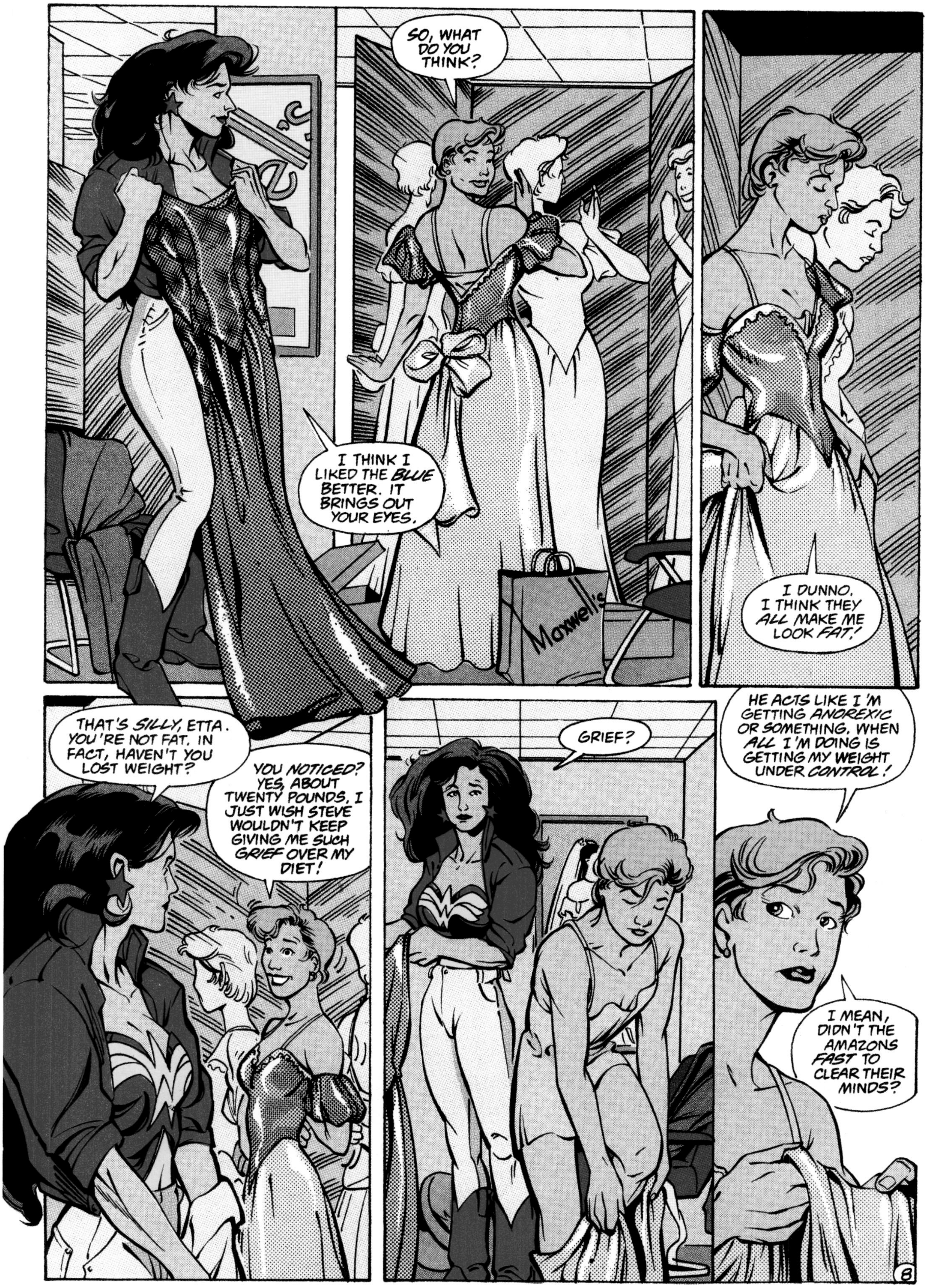
SO, WHAT DO YOU THINK?
I THINK I LIKED THE BLUE BETTER. IT BRINGS OUT YOUR EYES.
I DUNNO. I THINK THEY ALL MAKE ME LOOK FAT!
THAT'S SILLY, ETTA. YOU'RE NOT FAT. IN FACT, HAVEN'T YOU LOST WEIGHT?
YOU NOTICED? YES, ABOUT TWENTY POUNDS. I JUST WISH STEVE WOULDN'T KEEP GIVING ME SUCH GRIEF OVER MY DIET!
GRIEF?
HE ACTS LIKE I'M GETTING ANOREXIC OR SOMETHING, WHEN ALL I'M DOING IS GETTING MY WEIGHT UNDER CONTROL!
I MEAN, DIDN'T THE AMAZONS FAST TO CLEAR THEIR MINDS?
8

Above: In modern times, Etta felt she couldn't compare to the Amazon Princess and developed an eating disorder. Art by Lee Moder, Ande Parks, and Aaron McClellan.

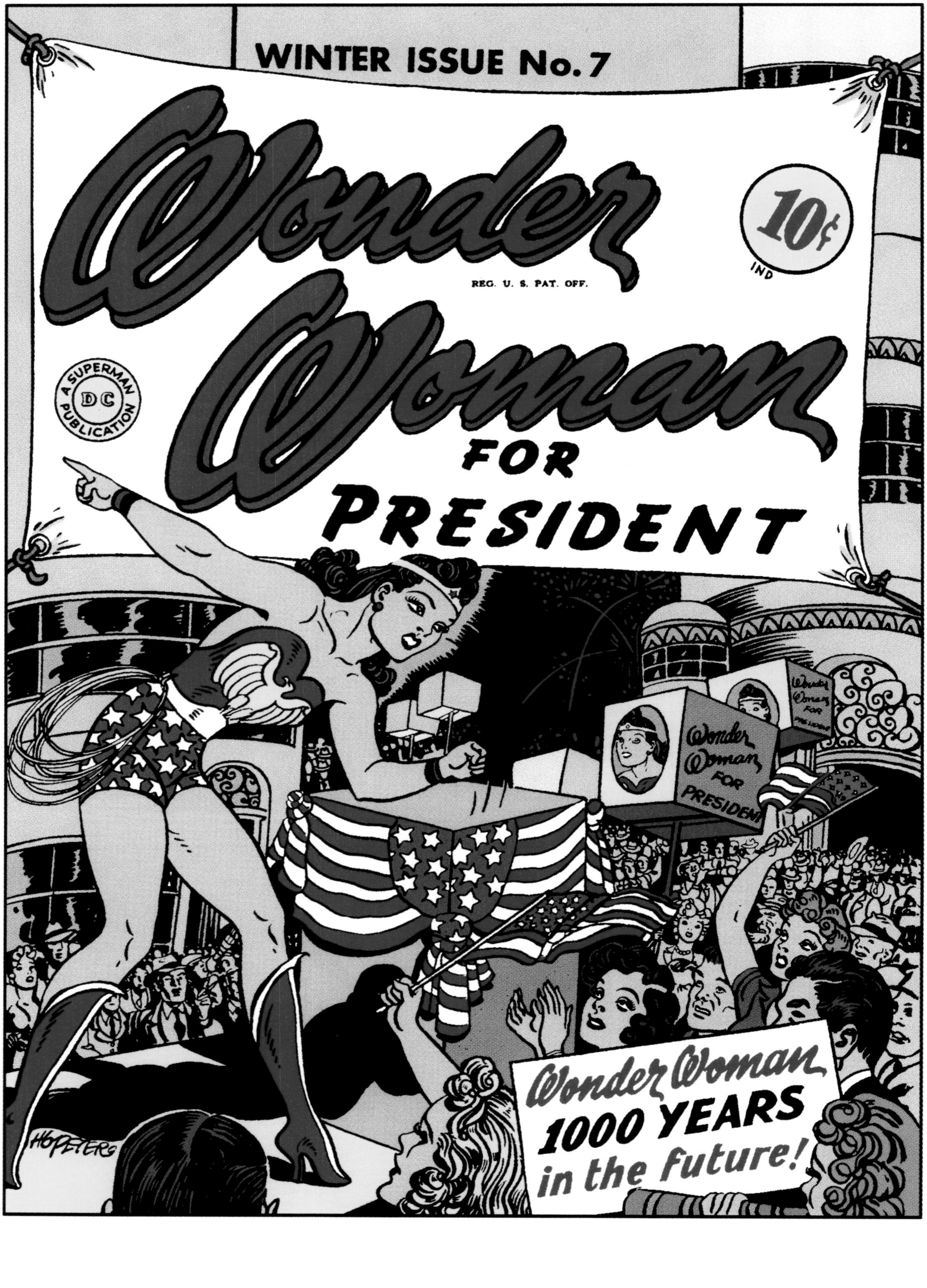
WINTER ISSUE No.7
Wonder Woman
REG. U. S. PAT. OFF.
10¢
IND
A SUPERMAN DC PUBLICATION
FOR
PRESIDENT
Wonder Woman
FOR
PRESIDENT
Wonder Woman 1000 YEARS in the future!
HG PETERS

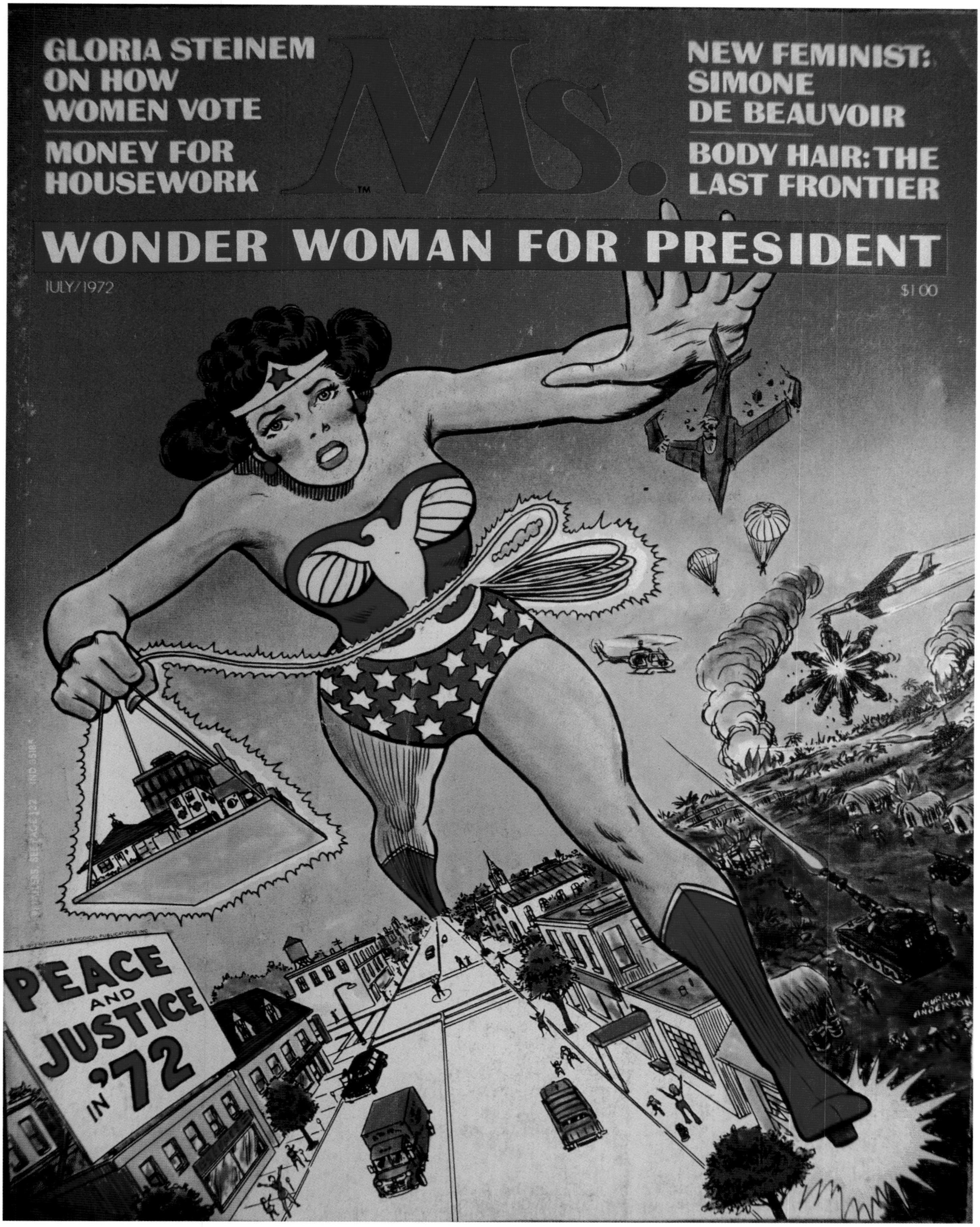
GLORIA STEINEM
ON HOW
WOMEN VOTE
MONEY FOR
HOUSEWORK
Ms.
NEW FEMINIST:
SIMONE
DE BEAUVOIR
BODY HAIR: THE
LAST FRONTIER
WONDER WOMAN FOR PRESIDENT
JULY/1972
$1.00
PEACE
AND
JUSTICE
IN '72

Left: In a fanciful story from 1943, Marston and Peter predict that Wonder Woman would become President one thousand years in the future.

Above: It made perfect sense for *Ms. Magazine* to nominate the Amazon Princess for the Oval Office in their inaugural issue. Cover art by Murphy Anderson.

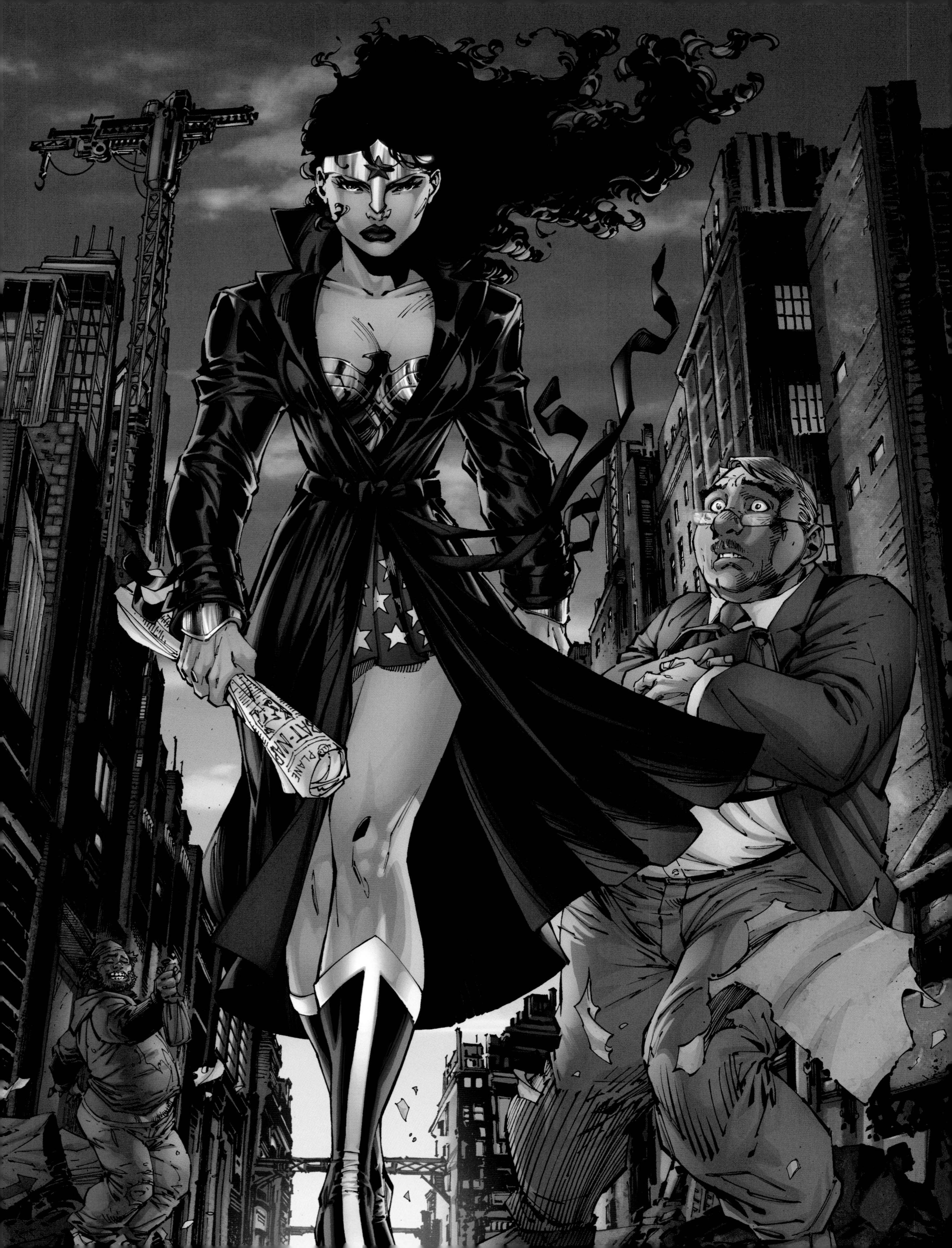
PLANE

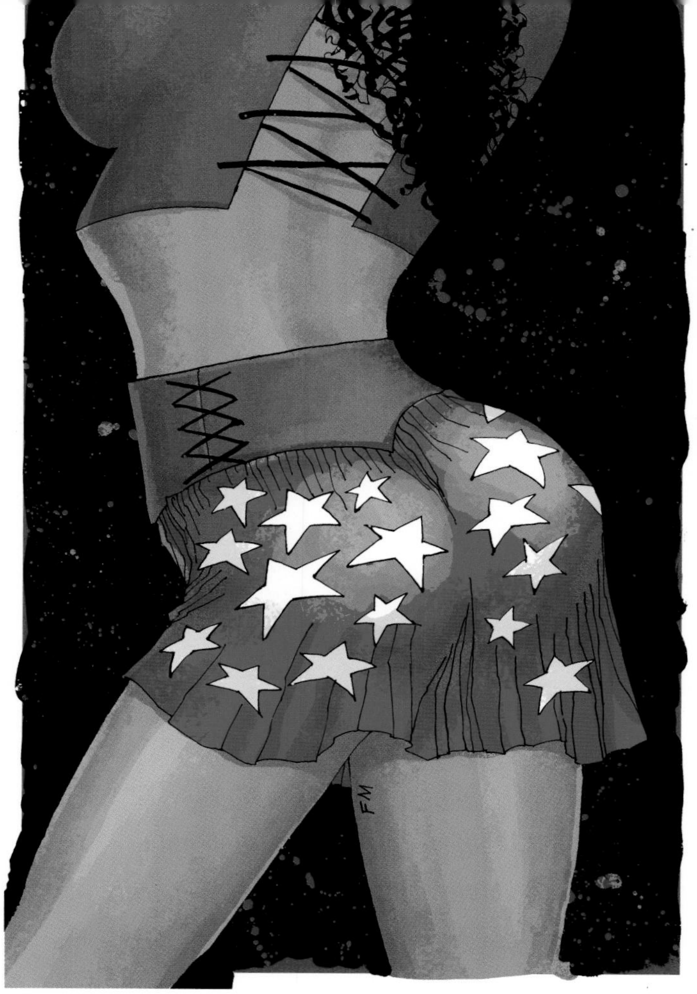

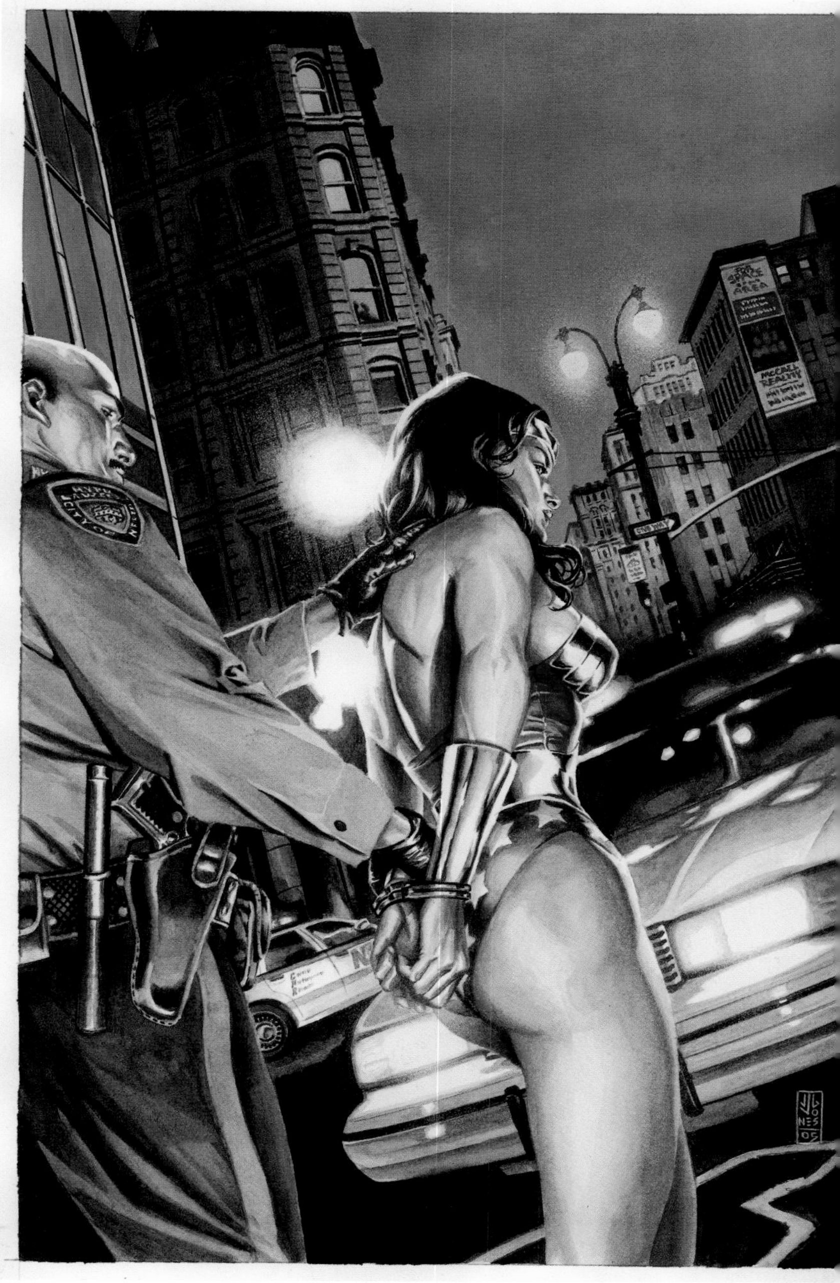

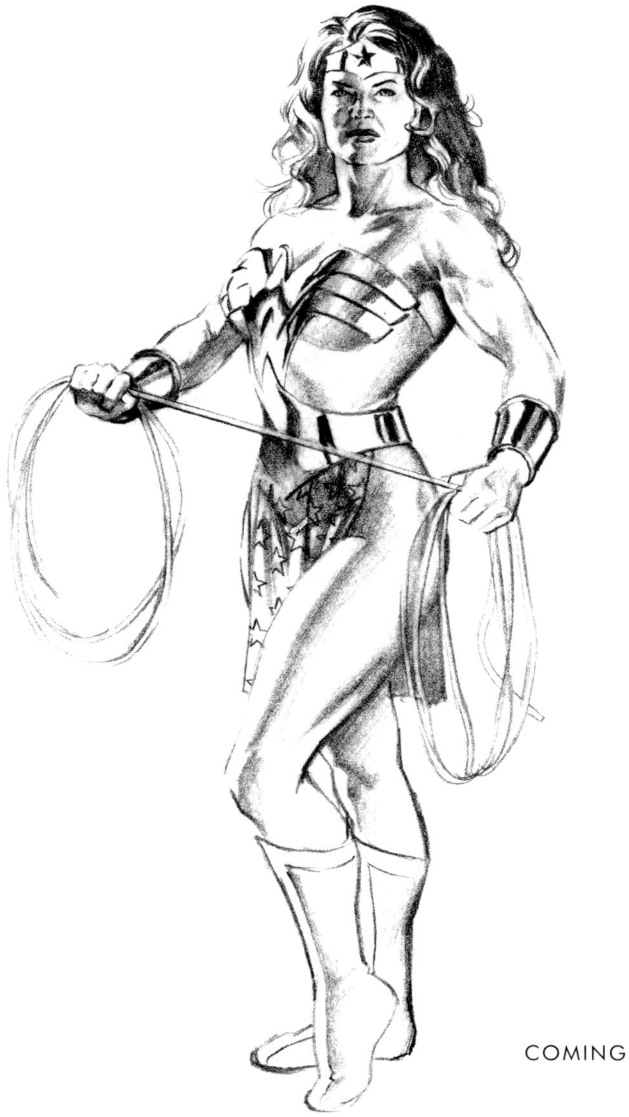

Far left: Don't mess with this Amazon. Wonder Woman stalks the city streets in this image from artists Jim Lee and Scott Williams.

Above left: A saucy look at Wonder Woman, courtesy of Frank Miller.

Above right: J. G. Jones's cover painting shows Wonder Woman being taken into police custody after snapping the neck of the madman Maxwell Lord.

Left: A pencil study of the super heroine by Alex Ross as part of his preparation to paint the *Kingdom Come* miniseries.

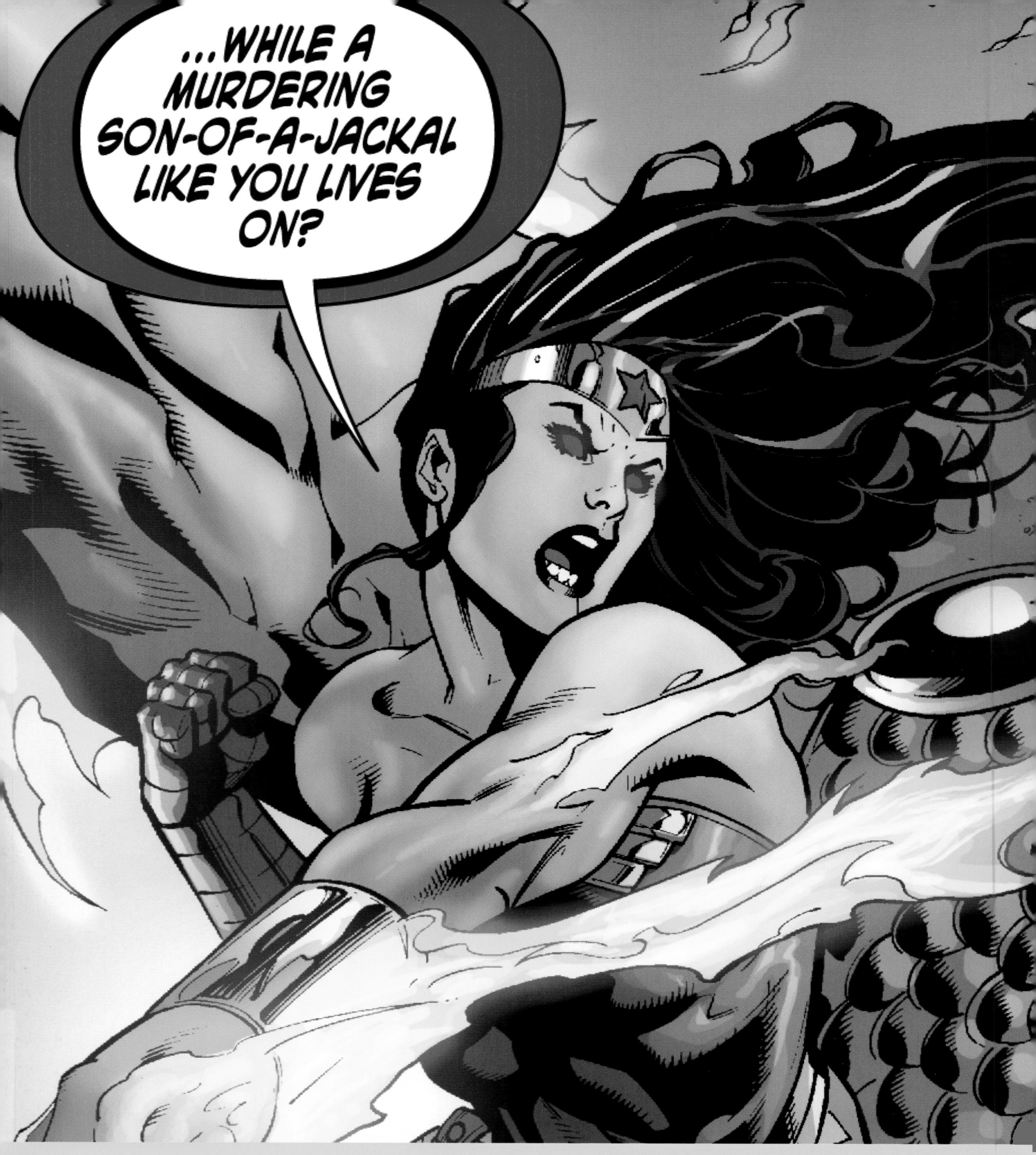
...WHILE A MURDERING SON-OF-A-JACKAL LIKE YOU LIVES ON?

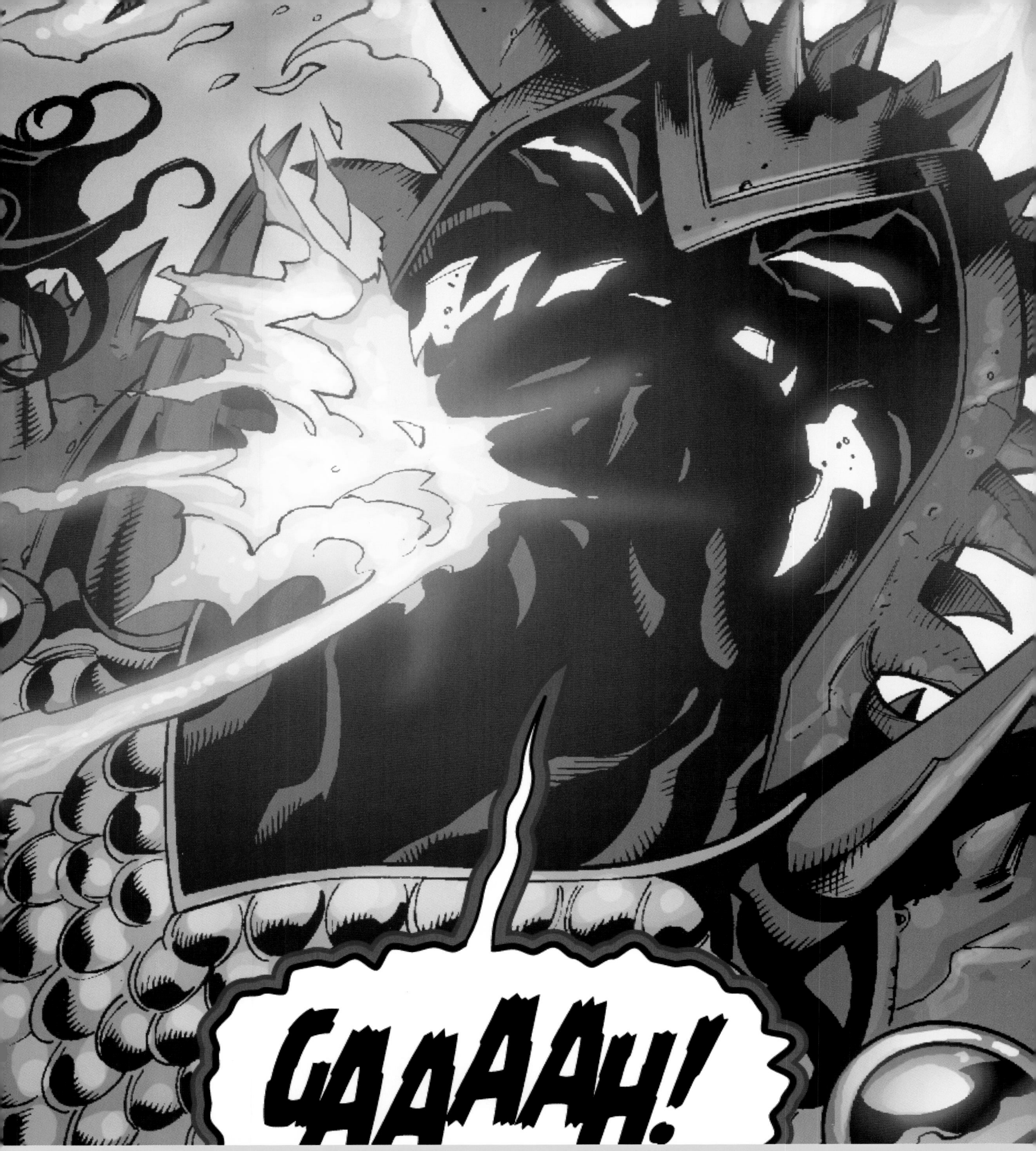
GAAAAH!

★ The Opponents

AS THE AMAZON SLIPS TO THE FLOOR UNCONSCIOUS, PAULA BINDS HER SECURELY WITH THE MAGIC LASSO.
I LEARNED IN AMAZON PRISON HOW A GIRL SHOULD BE TIED—NOT EVEN **WONDER WOMAN** CAN ESCAPE **THESE** BONDS!

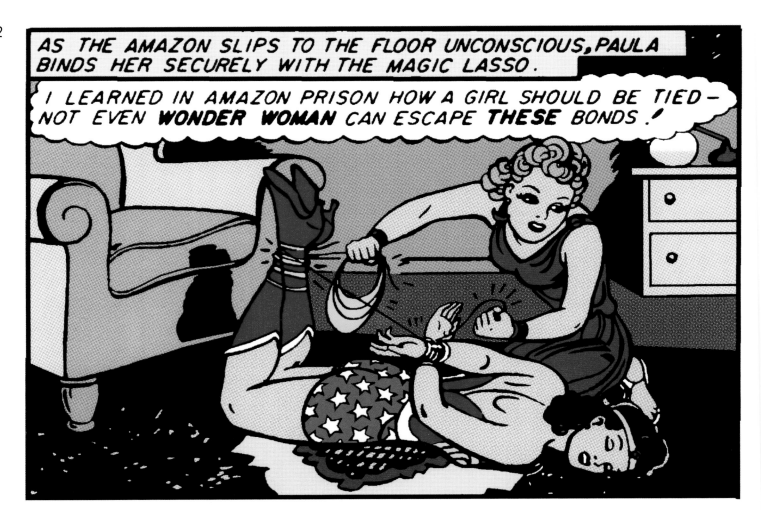

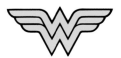

While Superman has Lex Luthor and Batman the Joker, Wonder Woman has had less memorable rogues, not for lack of trying. Fans of the *Super Friends* cartoons will probably remember Giganta and the Cheetah, but Wonder Woman's live-action series ignored her comic-book foes altogether.

Her first costumed opponent, Dr. Poison, arrived in *Sensation Comics* #2 (February 1942), the first in a line of doctors to plague the Amazon. Dr. Poison was an enemy saboteur and quickly forgotten, to be replaced by others such as Dr. Cyber, Dr. Moon, and most importantly, Dr. Psycho. Marston wrote what he knew, using Psycho to pit numerous psychological ploys against the heroine. Psycho, who first arrived in *Wonder Woman* #5 (June/July 1943), was a misogynistic dwarf who used his talents to commit murder and assorted mayhem. Throughout the years, writers after Marston used Dr. Psycho to engage Wonder Woman in twisted psychological duels.

In almost every early encounter, Wonder Woman, Etta Candy, and others found themselves captive, bound, and confined. The theme, Marston argued, was dramatic for readers while appearing less violent, which he saw as a good thing for his young readers. He was ignoring the effects the recurring bondage imagery might have on these developing minds. Even editor Sheldon Mayer tried to have Marston tone down the bondage imagery, especially after complaints began to arrive. The good doctor held his ground and was ready—nay eager—to engage his critics. In the end, the frequent images of the Amazon princess bound and prostrated recurred until Marston's death. Additionally, Marston instructed artist Harry G. Peter to add attractive slave women to do the villains' bidding.

Above: Paula von Gunther was a Nazi agent and recurring nemesis before she was rehabilitated by the Amazons. Golden Age Wonder Woman managed to find herself bound up and at another's mercy with frightening regularity.

Right: A good look at the many foes the Golden Age Wonder Woman battled. From left: King Blackfu, the Cheetah, Giganta, Dr. Psycho, the Duke of Deception, and actor Bedwin Footh.

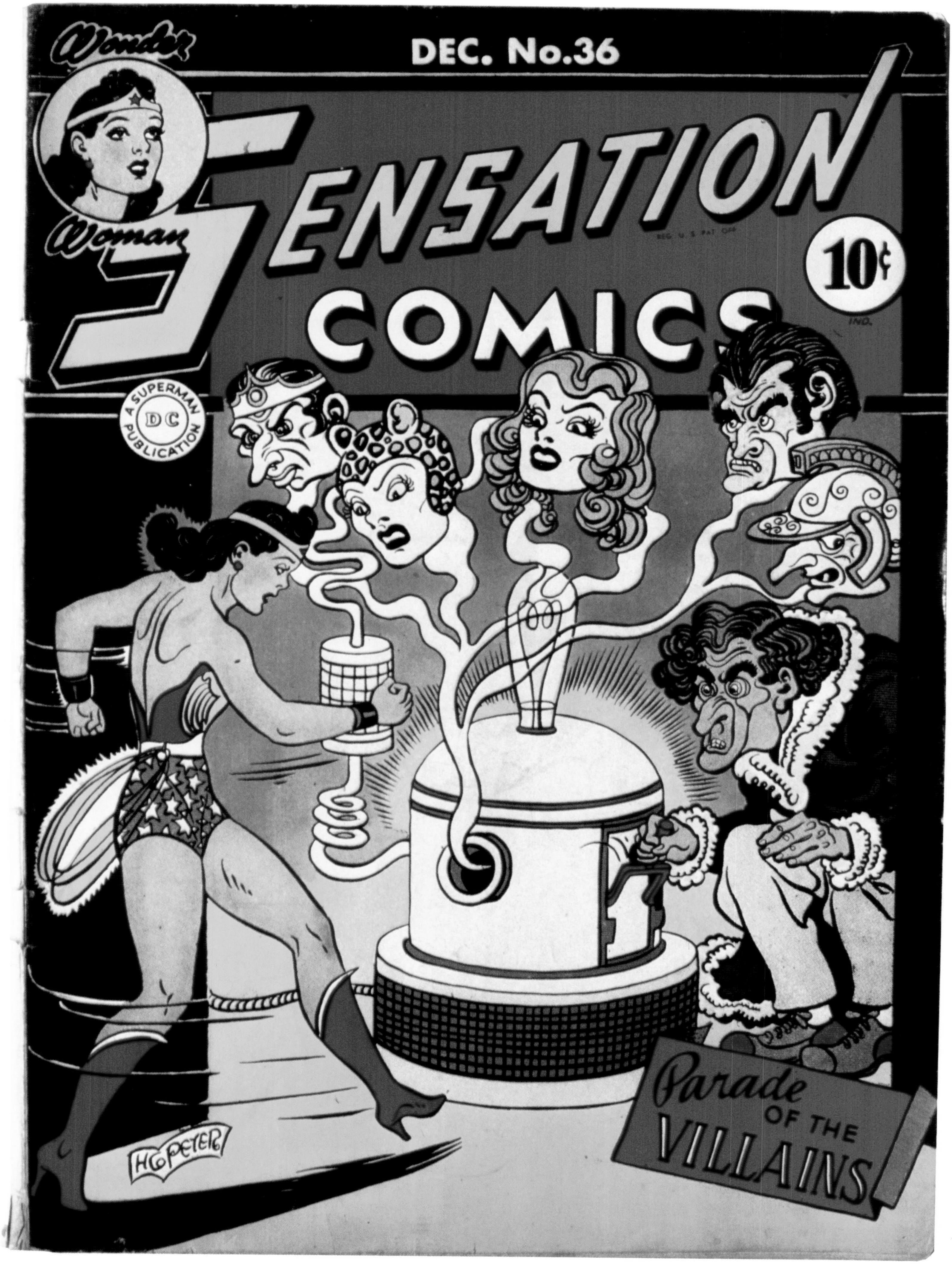

Wonder Woman
DEC. No.36
SENSATION COMICS
10¢
A SUPERMAN DC PUBLICATION
Parade OF THE VILLAINS
HG PETER

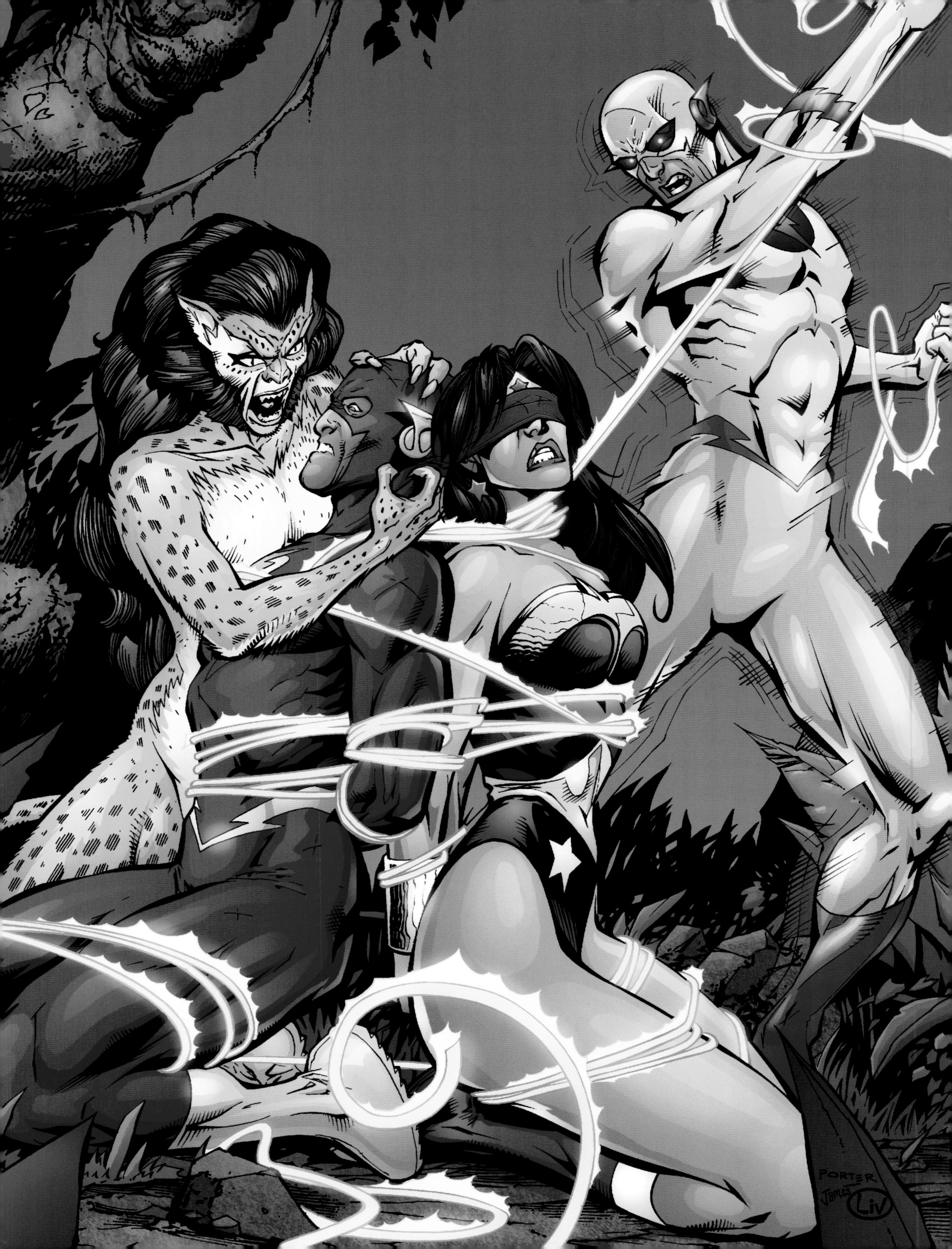
PORTER
James
Liv

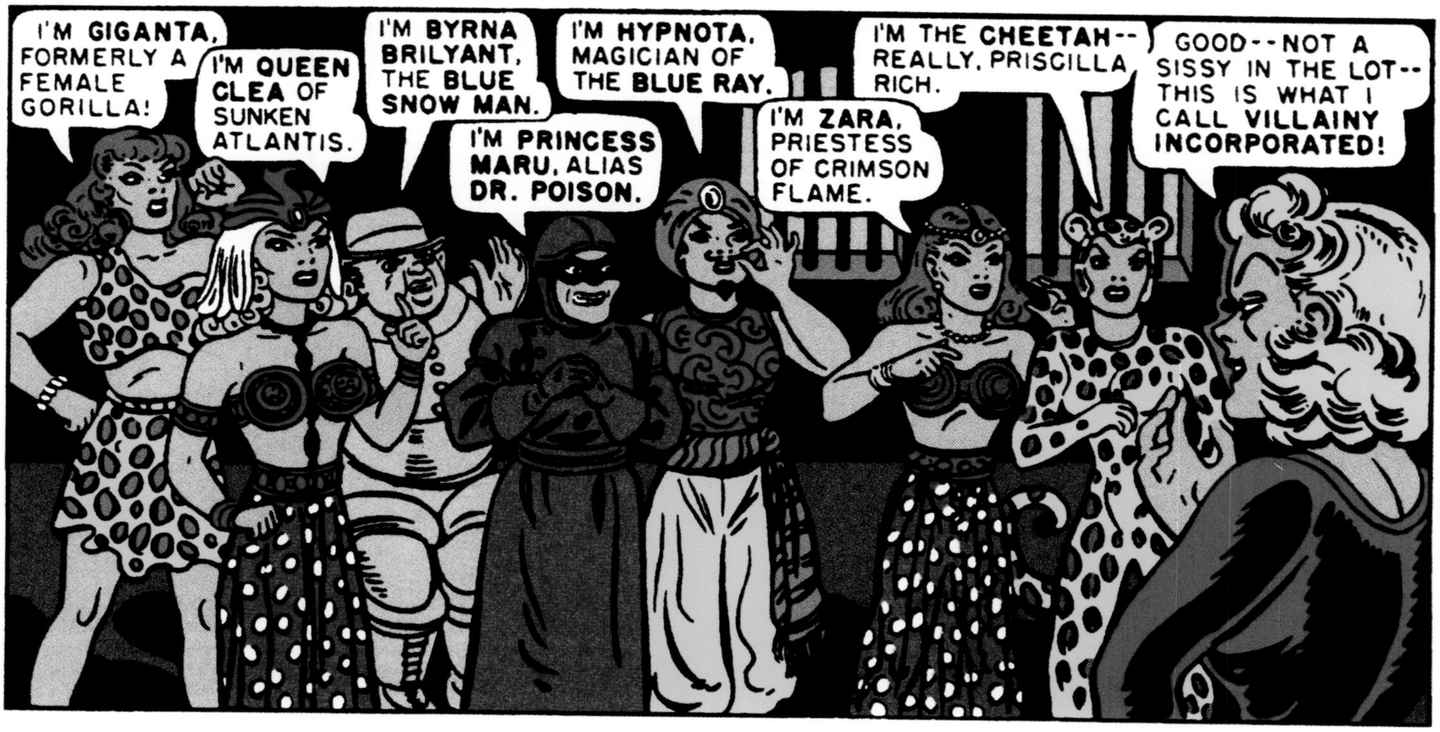
I'M GIGANTA, FORMERLY A FEMALE GORILLA!
I'M QUEEN CLEA OF SUNKEN ATLANTIS.
I'M BYRNA BRILYANT, THE BLUE SNOW MAN.
I'M PRINCESS MARU, ALIAS DR. POISON.
I'M HYPNOTA, MAGICIAN OF THE BLUE RAY.
I'M ZARA, PRIESTESS OF CRIMSON FLAME.
I'M THE CHEETAH-- REALLY, PRISCILLA RICH.
GOOD--NOT A SISSY IN THE LOT-- THIS IS WHAT I CALL VILLAINY INCORPORATED!

Left: The Flash and Wonder Woman found themselves trapped by their deadliest foes, the Cheetah and Zoom, in this cover from Howard Porter and Livesay.

Above: Wonder Woman's Golden Age Rogues Gallery may not be as colorful as Batman's, but they frequently posed trouble for the Amazon Princess under Marston and Peter.

Interestingly, when feminist Gloria Steinem wrote an introduction to the 1972 *Wonder Woman*, a collection of Golden Age stories, she ignored the entire bondage theme.

Baroness Paula von Gunther was Princess Diana's first significant recurring foe, but after being sentenced to an extended stay on Paradise Island, she was transformed from Axis agent to benevolent friend. Paula constructed numerous devices to help others from her secret laboratory under the Holliday College for Girls. Her most amazing device may have been the matter transporter, which allowed Wonder Woman to complete a mission on Venus.

Her most memorable female foe, though, was Pricilla Rich, the Cheetah, who was introduced in an issue after Dr. Psycho's introduction. She suffered from both an inferiority complex and a split personality. After perceiving that the Amazon snubbed her at an affair, Rich donned the spotted catsuit to commit robberies and to destroy Wonder Woman. In modern times, there have been mystical elements added to the villain, along with others who would use the Cheetah name and outfit, but Priscilla Rich has become one of the deadliest villains the Amazon princess has had to contend with.

The sorceress Circe was one of the most dangerous and persistent opponents used by contemporary Wonder Woman comic book writers. Her spells caused death and destruction, and Circe continually sought to make Wonder Woman suffer greatly before Diana could be killed. In one instance, depicted in *Wonder Woman* #175 (December 2001), Circe goaded Wonder Woman to kill her while the world watched. Tempted as she was, Diana instead offered her an open hand of peace. Although the Amazon emerged triumphant time and again, there was usually a price to be paid each time.

However, former JLA benefactor Maxwell Lord was less fortunate. The insane Lord, despite possessing telepathic powers, was hell-bent on eradicating meta-humans from the Earth. He launched a scheme to use cybernetic humans, dubbed OMACs, to kill them. When confronted by Wonder Woman, Superman, and Batman, Lord took control of the Man of Steel's mind and had him beat the Dark Knight to near-death. Unable to free Superman from Lord's mental control, the Amazon warrior instinctively employed her training and killed Lord, snapping his neck. The act, caught on camera, was broadcast worldwide and later had Wonder Woman defending her actions before the World Court.

Marston worked hard to introduce numerous foes for his heroine, building a Rogues Gallery that was colorful, if not memorable. When Robert Kanigher took over after Marston's death, he largely ignored the villains (save for the Duke of Deception and a character called the Angle Man) Marston had created in favor of one-time invading aliens, scheming criminals and other uninvolving foes. Wonder Woman spent countless pages

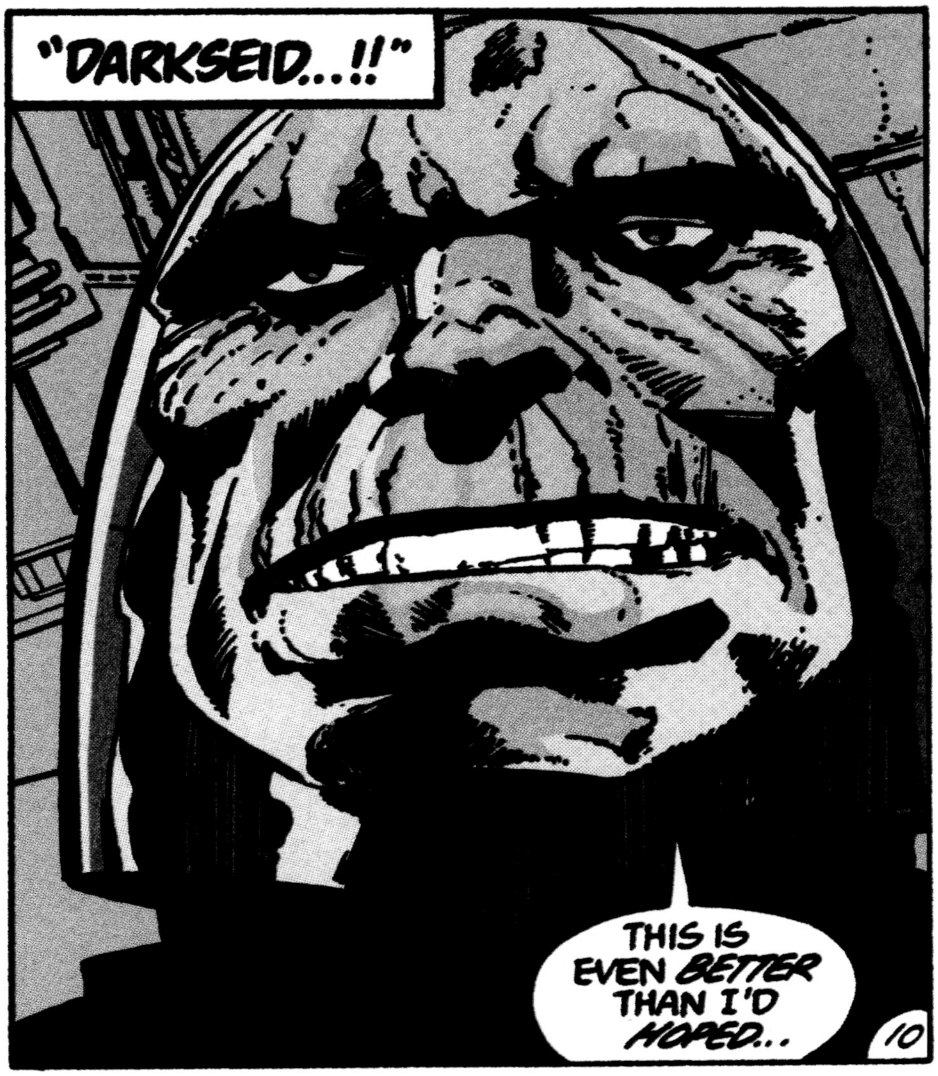
"DARKSEID...!!"
THIS IS EVEN BETTER THAN I'D HOPED...
10

Left: Darkseid, lord of Apokolips, sought to ensure the denizens of Mount Olympus would not interfere in his scheme to obtain the Anti-Life Equation and conquer mankind. As told in stories from George Pérez and John Byrne, Wonder Woman and Superman saw to it he failed.

Right: The 100-armed creature from the underworld, Cottus, proved to be a challenge for the Amazon Princess. Story by Greg Rucka and art by Drew Johnson, James Raiz, Sean Phillips, and Ray Snyder.

protecting her double identity or battling various duplicates who were magical, mechanical, or extraordinary. One particular example involved Tracy's Day Parade balloons in the shapes of prehistoric creatures and the Amazon princess. Both were flying into the atmostphere, and the balloons were found by would-be alien conquerors and animated in order to attack the Earth. Wonder Woman defeated each animated balloon, including her helium-filled doppelgänger, as depicted in *Wonder Woman* #114 (May 1960).

In his waning months on the title, Kanigher unsuccessfully brought back the rogues from Marston's days in an attempt to raise the sales. After Kanigher left the staff, writers Denny O'Neil and Mike Sekowsky also ignored the familiar foes, instead opting to introduce the recurring threat of Dr. Cyber. As the 1970s dawned and Wonder Woman's adventures reverted to the days of World War II, new Nazi threats arrived, such as Baron Blitzkrieg.

More powerful and magical enemies were on hand during Wonder Woman's revival in 1987. Ares stood center stage for many of these storylines, but Wonder Woman's cavalcade of enemies was supplemented by the White Magician and new versions of the Silver Swan and Dr. Poison, and monsters plucked from Greek mythology, including the Cyclops, Minotaur and Echinda. Wonder Woman's encounters involved the major creatures, including the spirit of Ixion, who was reportedly Earth's first mass murderer; and the minor creatures, such as Rockface and Plassma.

These days Wonder Woman's opponents are a mix drawn from Greek myth, her own nearly seventy-year history, and the rest of the DC Universe, and who are constantly testing her mettle and her ideals.

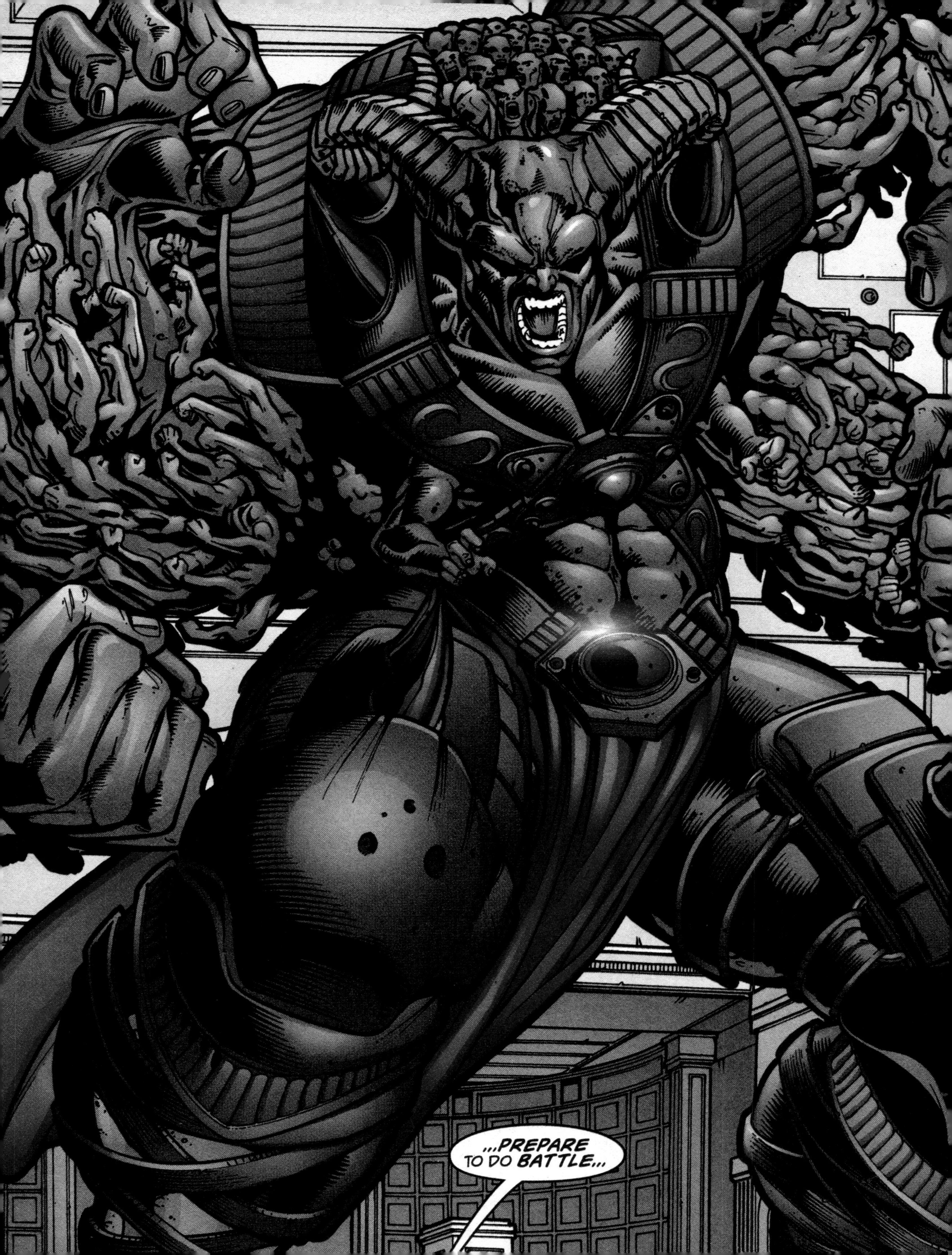
...PREPARE TO DO BATTLE...

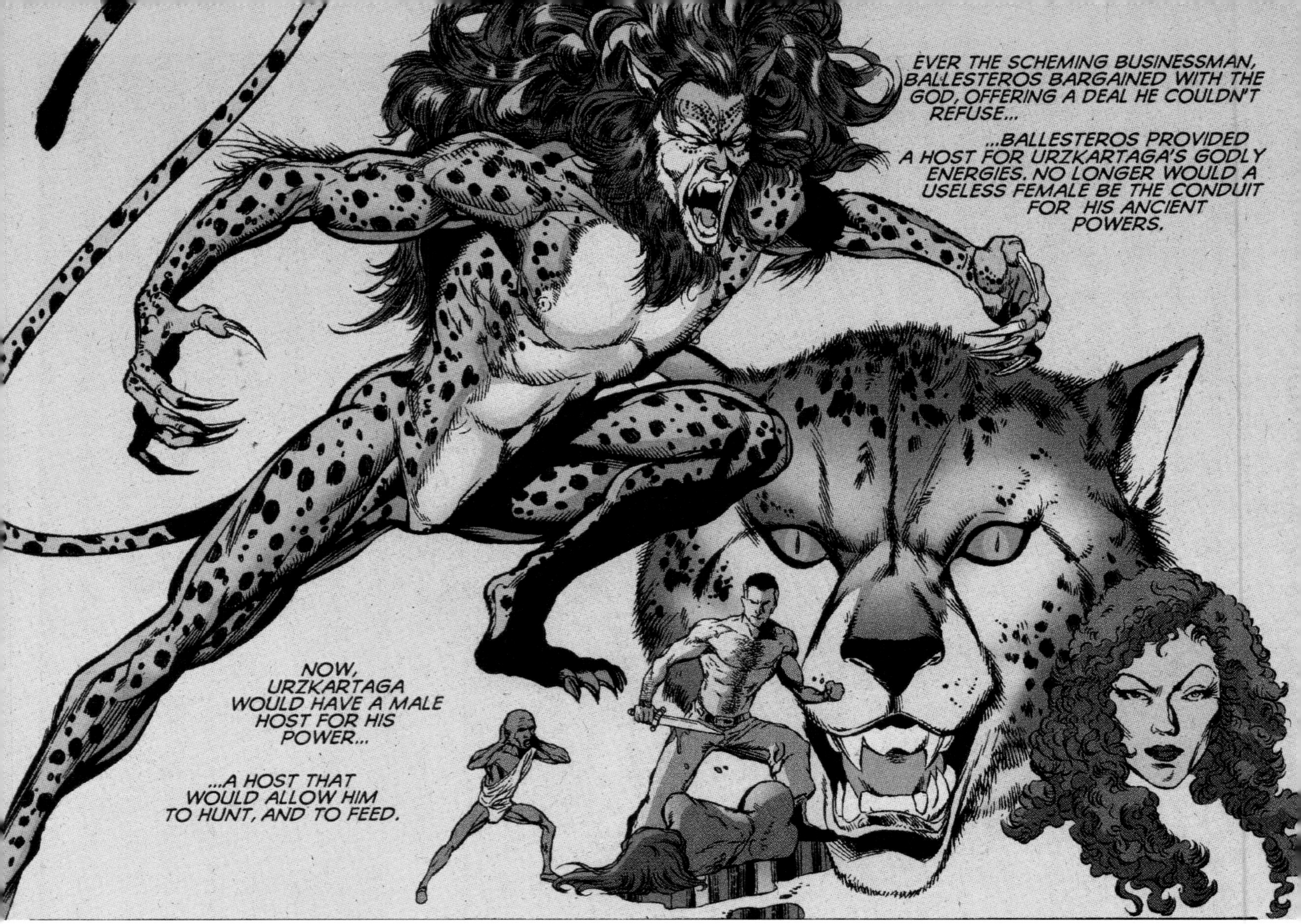
EVER THE SCHEMING BUSINESSMAN, BALLESTEROS BARGAINED WITH THE GOD, OFFERING A DEAL HE COULDN'T REFUSE...
...BALLESTEROS PROVIDED A HOST FOR URZKARTAGA'S GODLY ENERGIES. NO LONGER WOULD A USELESS FEMALE BE THE CONDUIT FOR HIS ANCIENT POWERS.
NOW, URZKARTAGA WOULD HAVE A MALE HOST FOR HIS POWER...
...A HOST THAT WOULD ALLOW HIM TO HUNT, AND TO FEED.

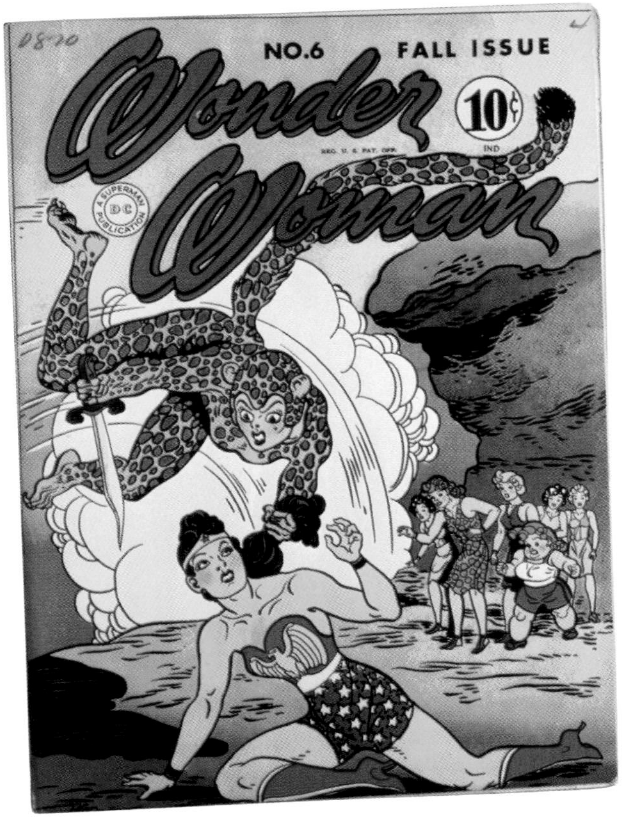
NO.6
FALL ISSUE
Wonder Woman
10¢
A SUPERMAN DC PUBLICATION

Above: Originally, the Cheetah was merely Priscilla Rich in a catsuit. After a 1980s revamp, the Cheetah had mystically-derived strength and ferocity. In time, two women and a man managed to obtain the power and became deadly opponents to Wonder Woman. Art here by Phil Jimenez and Andy Lanning.

Left: A look at the acrobatic Rich as the Cheetah. Cover by Harry G. Peter.

Right: Ares, god of war, became a primary threat to Wonder Woman and Earth's inhabitants after the 1987 revamp. Art by Shawn Atkinson and Ande Parks.

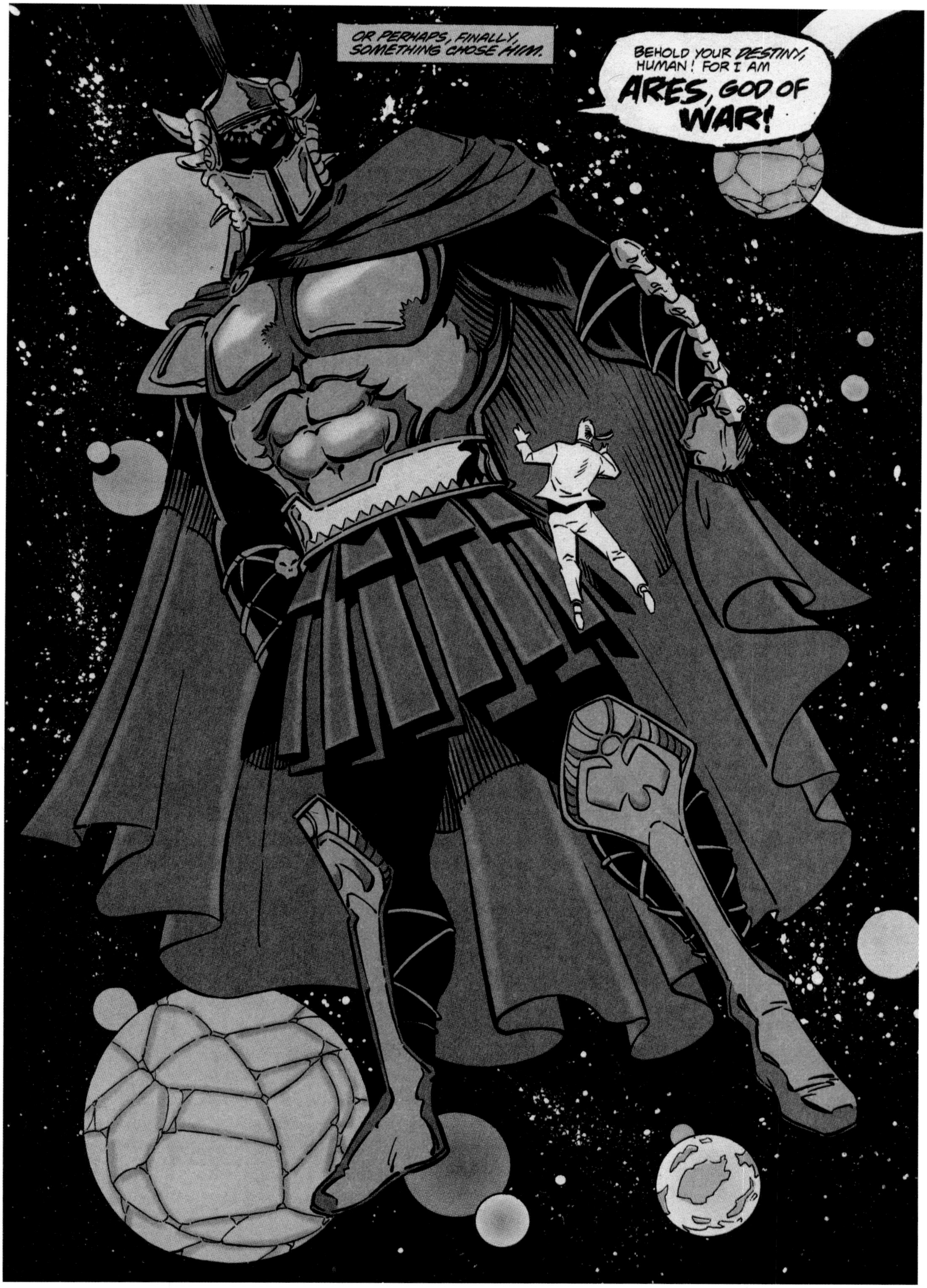
OR PERHAPS, FINALLY, SOMETHING CHOSE HIM.
BEHOLD YOUR DESTINY, HUMAN! FOR I AM ARES, GOD OF WAR!

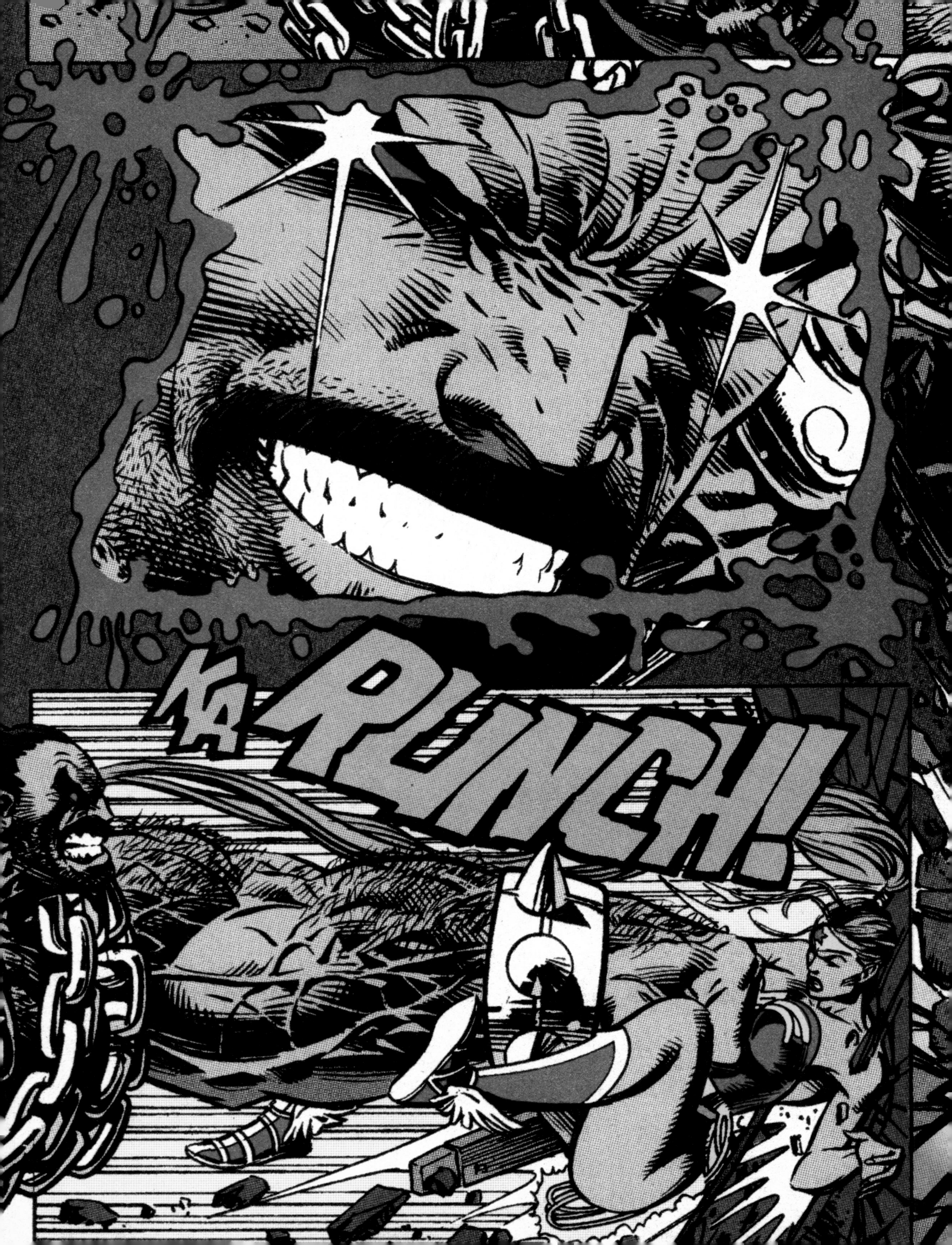
KA PUNCH!

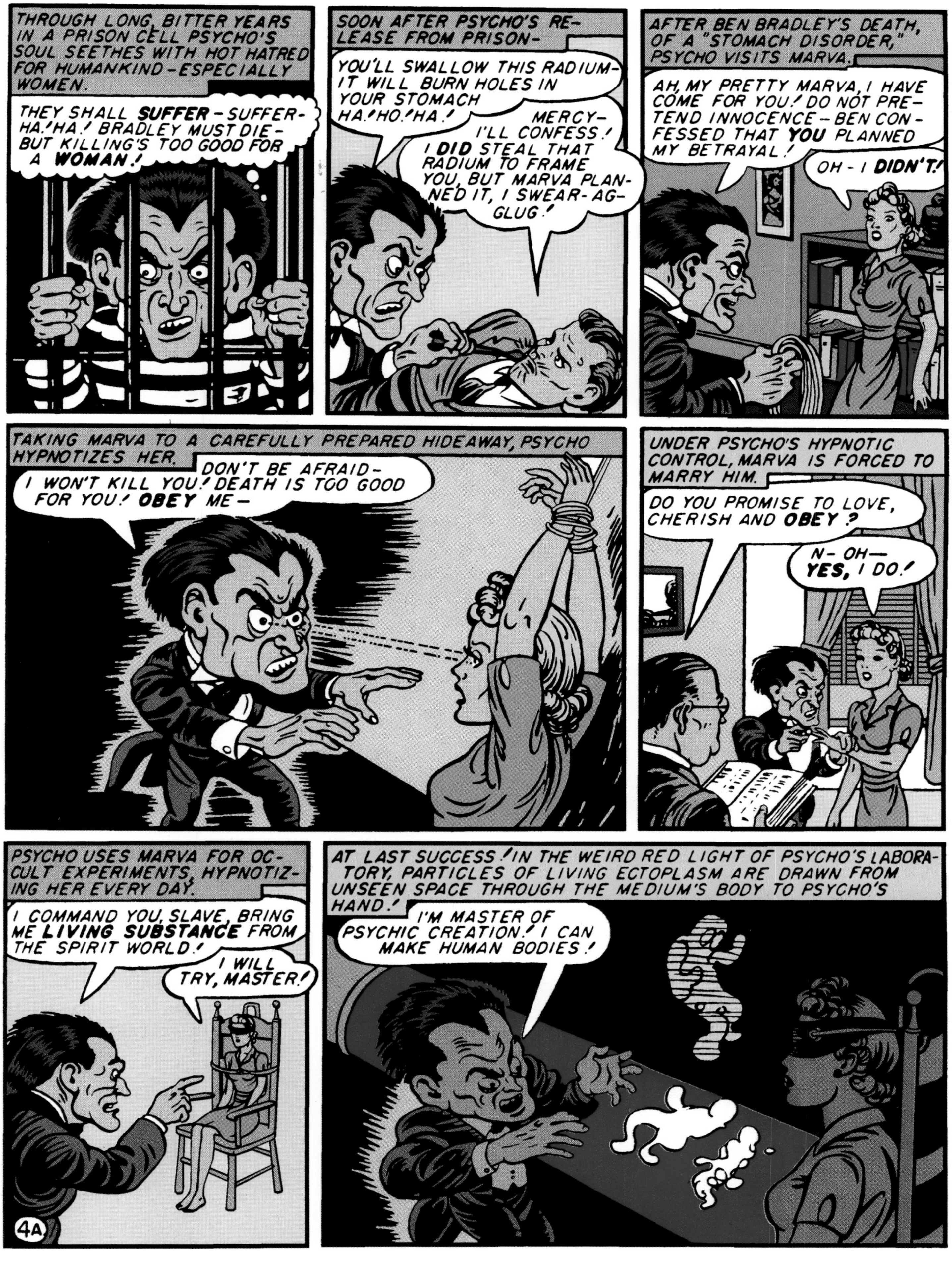
THROUGH LONG, BITTER YEARS IN A PRISON CELL PSYCHO'S SOUL SEETHES WITH HOT HATRED FOR HUMANKIND - ESPECIALLY WOMEN.
THEY SHALL SUFFER - SUFFER - HA! HA! BRADLEY MUST DIE - BUT KILLING'S TOO GOOD FOR A WOMAN!
SOON AFTER PSYCHO'S RELEASE FROM PRISON-
YOU'LL SWALLOW THIS RADIUM - IT WILL BURN HOLES IN YOUR STOMACH HA! HO! HA!
MERCY - I'LL CONFESS! I DID STEAL THAT RADIUM TO FRAME YOU, BUT MARVA PLANNED IT, I SWEAR - AG- GLUG!
AFTER BEN BRADLEY'S DEATH, OF A "STOMACH DISORDER," PSYCHO VISITS MARVA.
AH, MY PRETTY MARVA, I HAVE COME FOR YOU! DO NOT PRETEND INNOCENCE - BEN CONFESSED THAT YOU PLANNED MY BETRAYAL!
OH - I DIDN'T!
TAKING MARVA TO A CAREFULLY PREPARED HIDEAWAY, PSYCHO HYPNOTIZES HER.
DON'T BE AFRAID - I WON'T KILL YOU! DEATH IS TOO GOOD FOR YOU! OBEY ME -
UNDER PSYCHO'S HYPNOTIC CONTROL, MARVA IS FORCED TO MARRY HIM.
DO YOU PROMISE TO LOVE, CHERISH AND OBEY?
N- OH - YES, I DO!
PSYCHO USES MARVA FOR OCCULT EXPERIMENTS, HYPNOTIZING HER EVERY DAY.
I COMMAND YOU, SLAVE, BRING ME LIVING SUBSTANCE FROM THE SPIRIT WORLD!
I WILL TRY, MASTER!
4A
AT LAST SUCCESS! IN THE WEIRD RED LIGHT OF PSYCHO'S LABORATORY, PARTICLES OF LIVING ECTOPLASM ARE DRAWN FROM UNSEEN SPACE THROUGH THE MEDIUM'S BODY TO PSYCHO'S HAND!
I'M MASTER OF PSYCHIC CREATION! I CAN MAKE HUMAN BODIES!

Left: A fearsome figure, the Chauvinist, was powerful foe to Wonder Woman, who was Artemis, leader of the Bana-Mighdall branch of the Amazons during this arc. Art by Mike Deodato, Jr.

Above: Dr. Psycho overcame his diminutive limitations by mastering hypnosis and psychology, toying with people, and compelling them to do his bidding. Art by Harry G. Peter.

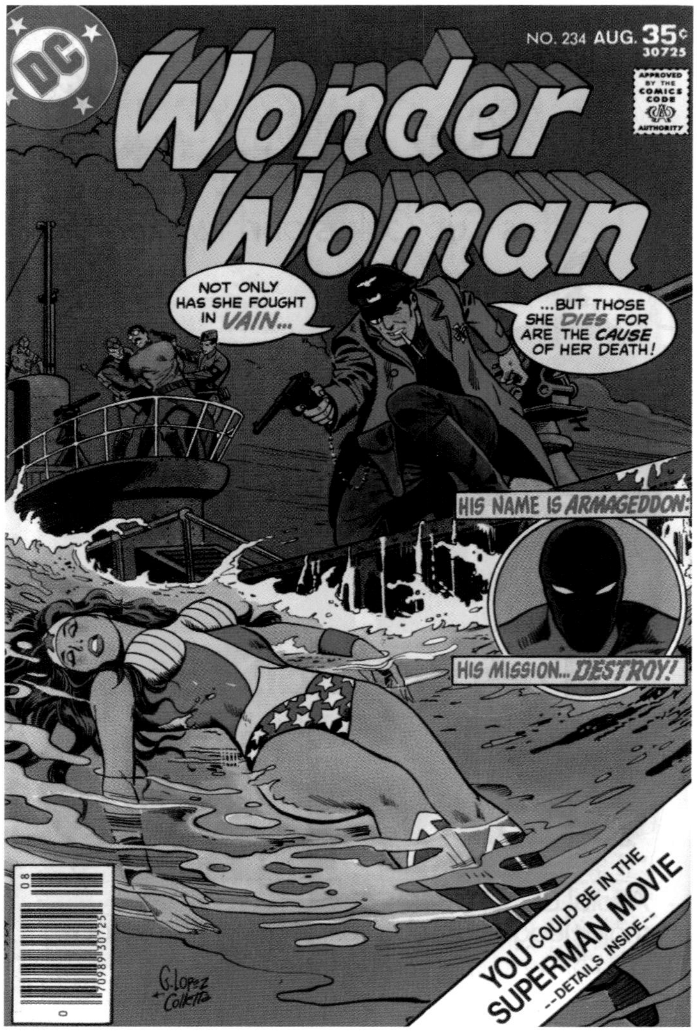
NO. 234 AUG. 35¢
30725
Wonder Woman
NOT ONLY HAS SHE FOUGHT IN VAIN...
...BUT THOSE SHE DIES FOR ARE THE CAUSE OF HER DEATH!
HIS NAME IS ARMAGEDDON:
HIS MISSION...DESTROY!
YOU COULD BE IN THE SUPERMAN MOVIE
--DETAILS INSIDE--

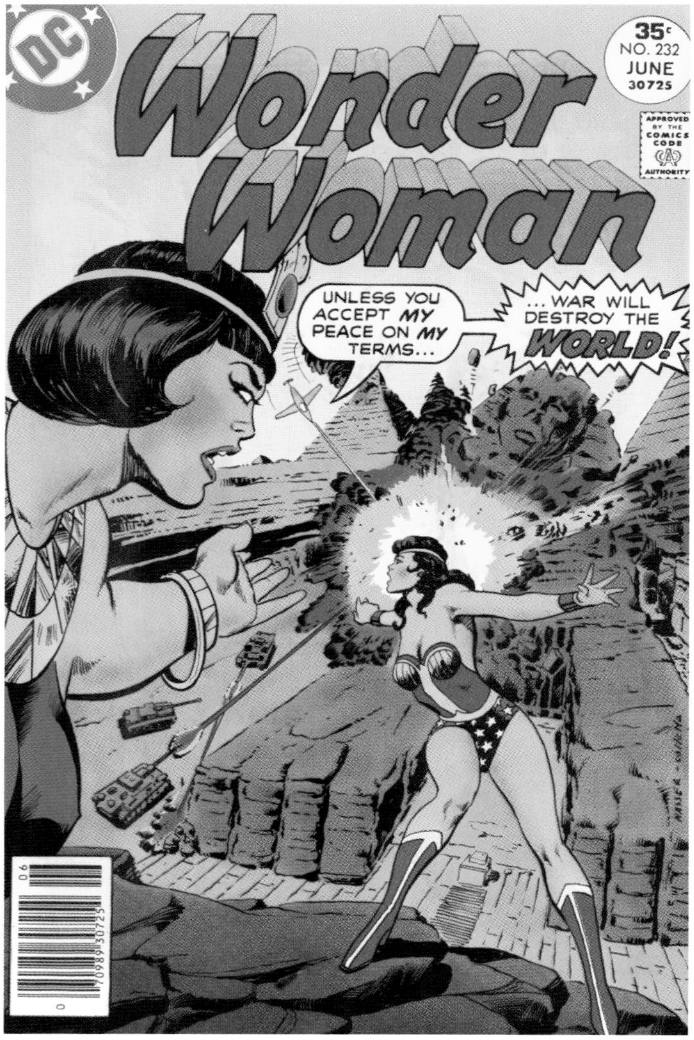
35¢
NO. 232
JUNE
30725
Wonder Woman
UNLESS YOU ACCEPT MY PEACE ON MY TERMS...
...WAR WILL DESTROY THE WORLD!

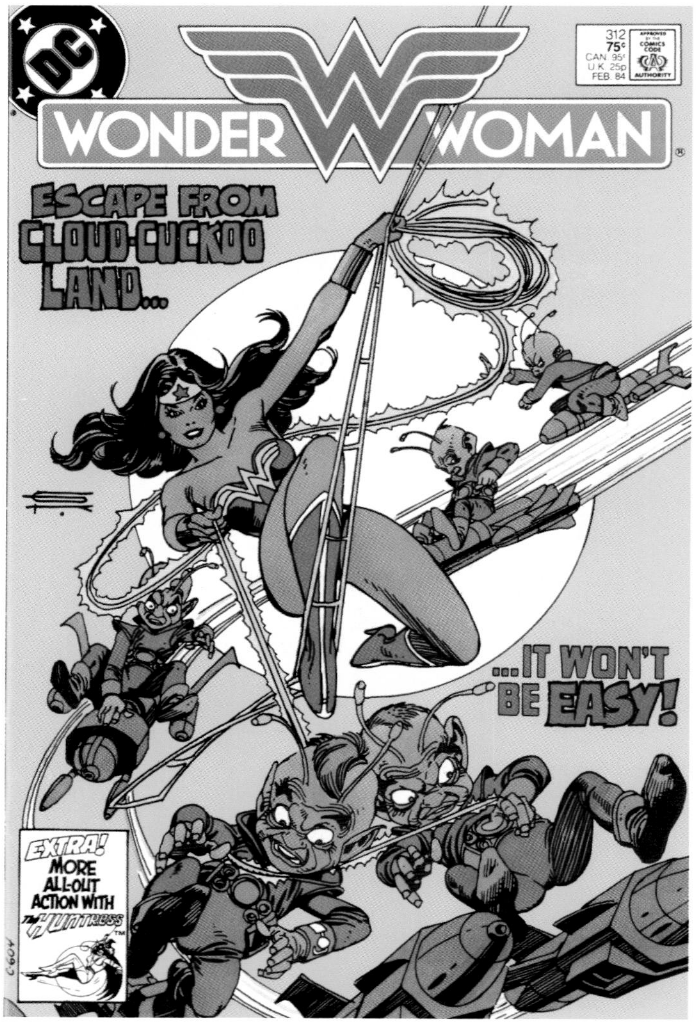
312
75¢
CAN. 95¢
U.K. 25p
FEB. 84
WONDER WOMAN
ESCAPE FROM CLOUD-CUCKOO LAND...
...IT WON'T BE EASY!
EXTRA! MORE ALL-OUT ACTION WITH THE HUNTRESS

Clockwise from left: Wonder Woman's opponents in the late 1970s and 1980s may have been challenging but were far from memorable. Covers by José Luis Garcia Lopez and Vince Colletta, Michael Nasser, and Gil Kane.

Right: A close-up of a 1960s foe from artists Mike Sekowsky and Dick Giordano.

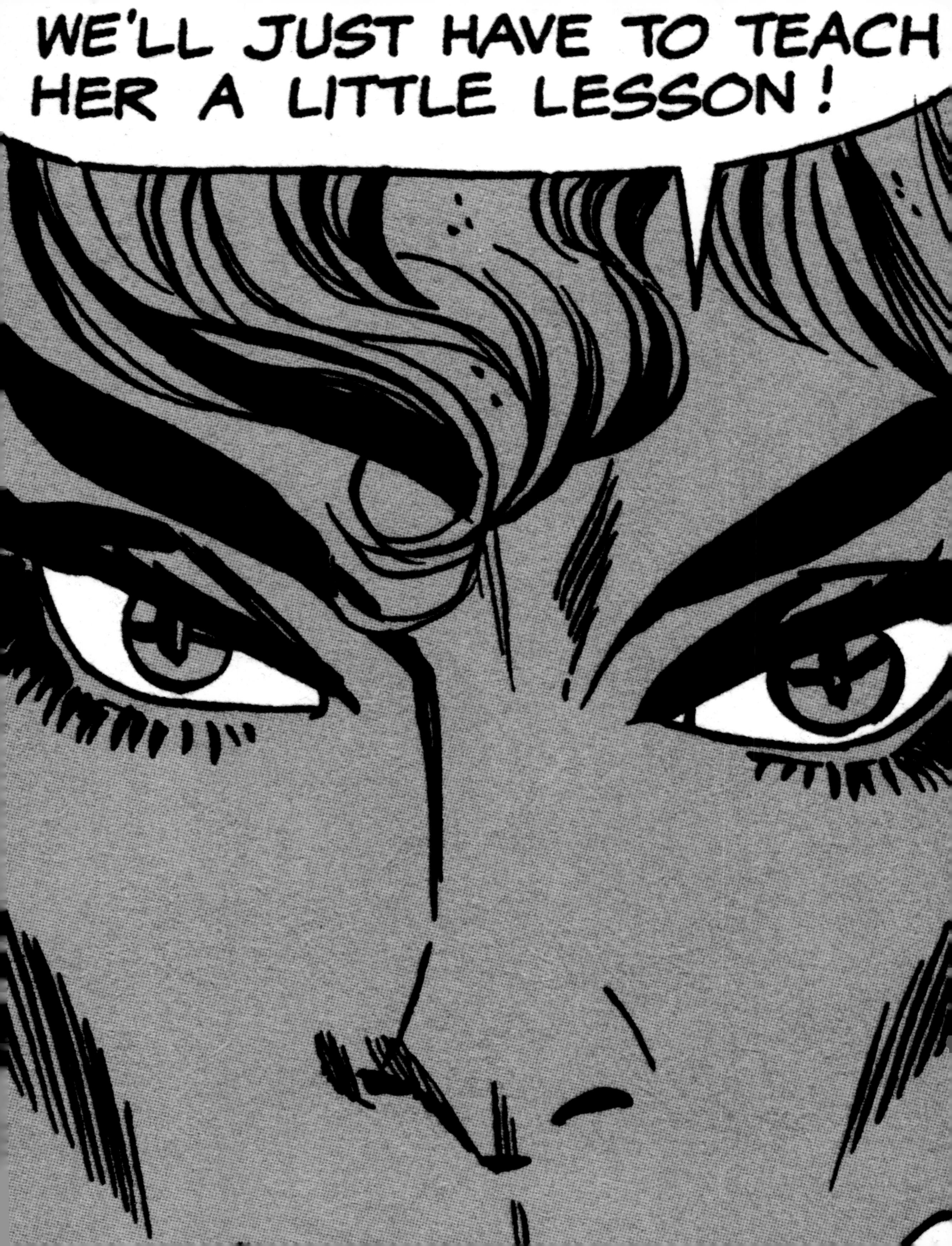
WE'LL JUST HAVE TO TEACH HER A LITTLE LESSON!

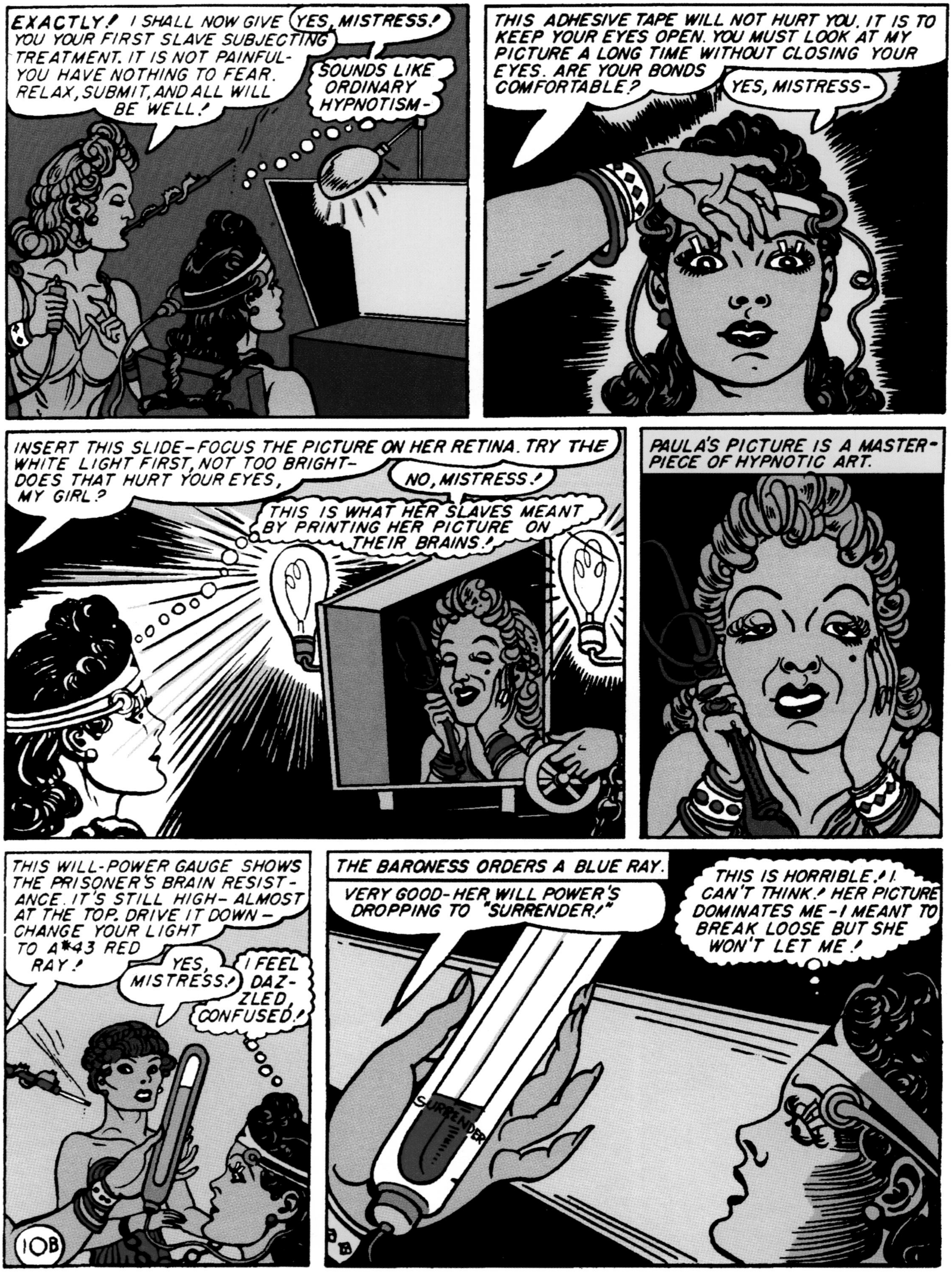
EXACTLY! I SHALL NOW GIVE YOU YOUR FIRST SLAVE SUBJECTING TREATMENT. IT IS NOT PAINFUL- YOU HAVE NOTHING TO FEAR. RELAX, SUBMIT, AND ALL WILL BE WELL!
YES, MISTRESS!
SOUNDS LIKE ORDINARY HYPNOTISM-
THIS ADHESIVE TAPE WILL NOT HURT YOU. IT IS TO KEEP YOUR EYES OPEN. YOU MUST LOOK AT MY PICTURE A LONG TIME WITHOUT CLOSING YOUR EYES. ARE YOUR BONDS COMFORTABLE?
YES, MISTRESS-
INSERT THIS SLIDE-FOCUS THE PICTURE ON HER RETINA. TRY THE WHITE LIGHT FIRST, NOT TOO BRIGHT- DOES THAT HURT YOUR EYES, MY GIRL?
NO, MISTRESS!
THIS IS WHAT HER SLAVES MEANT BY PRINTING HER PICTURE ON THEIR BRAINS!
PAULA'S PICTURE IS A MASTER-PIECE OF HYPNOTIC ART.
THIS WILL-POWER GAUGE SHOWS THE PRISONER'S BRAIN RESIST-ANCE. IT'S STILL HIGH- ALMOST AT THE TOP. DRIVE IT DOWN- CHANGE YOUR LIGHT TO A #43 RED RAY!
YES, MISTRESS!
I FEEL DAZ-ZLED, CONFUSED!
10B
THE BARONESS ORDERS A BLUE RAY.
VERY GOOD- HER WILL POWER'S DROPPING TO "SURRENDER!"
SURRENDER
THIS IS HORRIBLE! I CAN'T THINK! HER PICTURE DOMINATES ME- I MEANT TO BREAK LOOSE BUT SHE WON'T LET ME!

Above: Paula von Gunther has Wonder Woman trapped once more: this time, she attempts to enslave the super heroine.

Right: Terry and Rachel Dodson's cover to *Wonder Woman* [third series] #4 (November 2006) shows the Amazon Princess bound by the evil sorceress Circe.

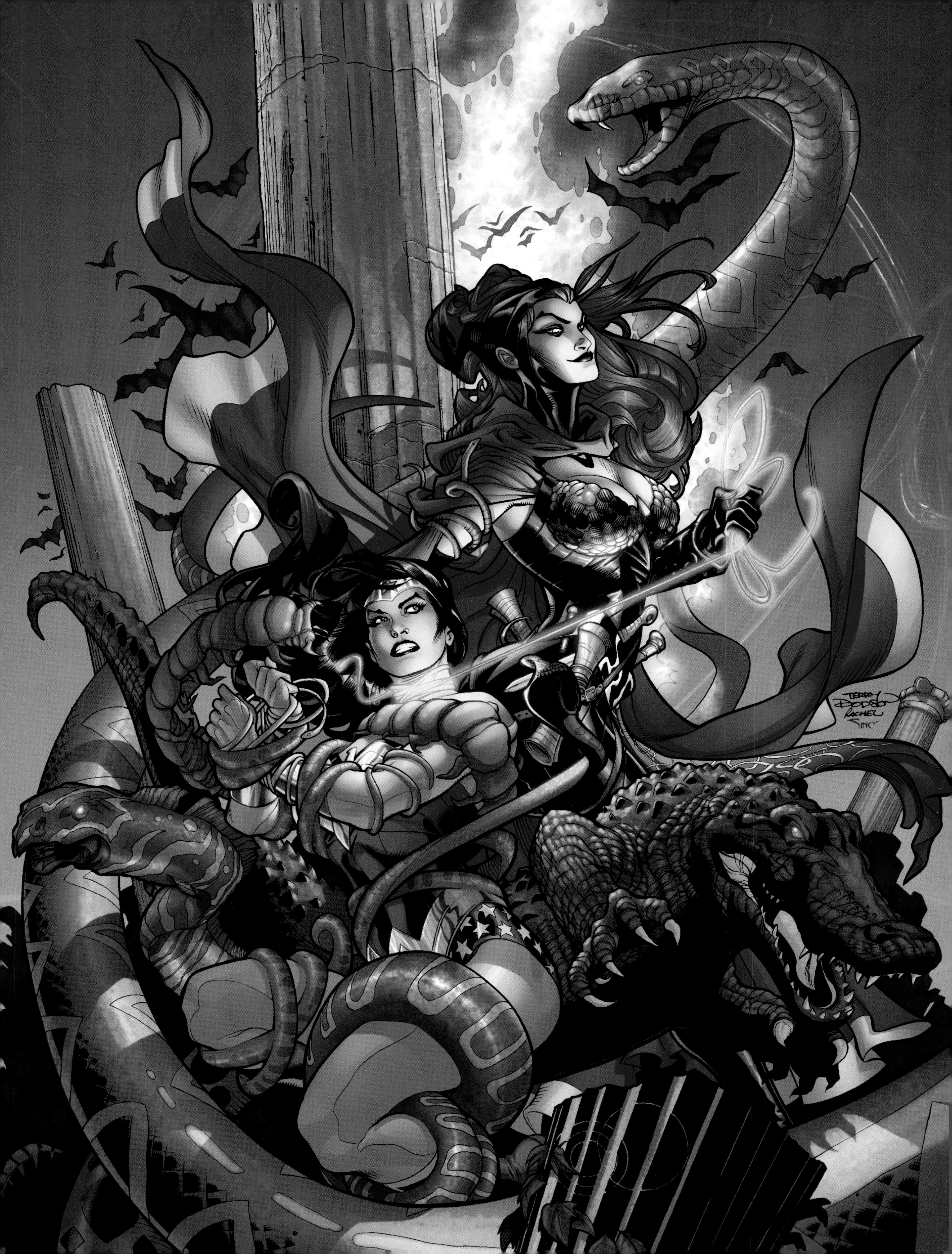
TERRY
DODSON
RACHEL

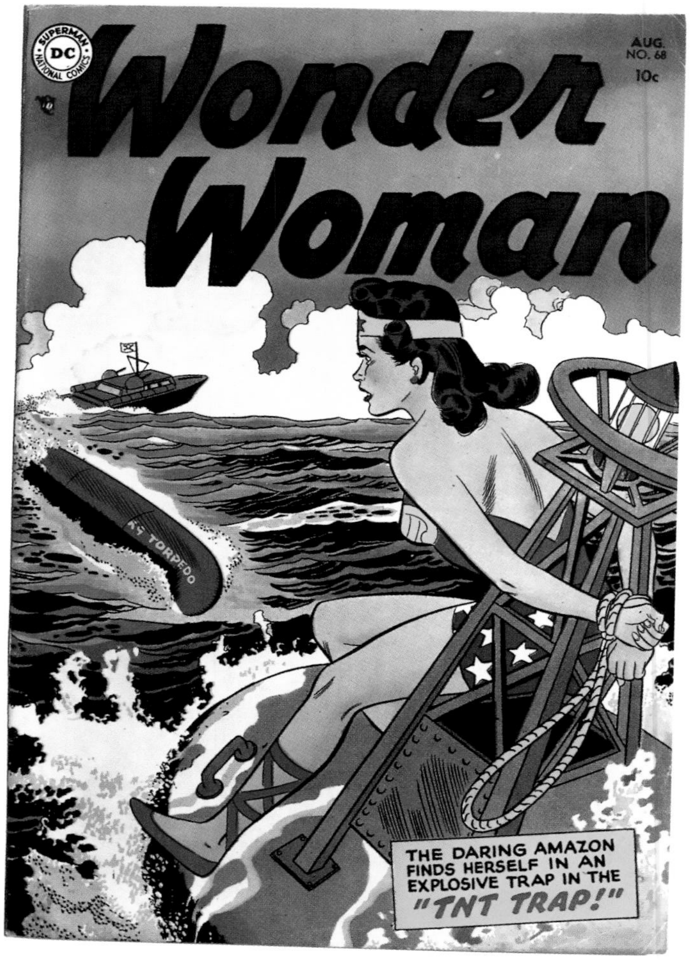
Wonder Woman
AUG. NO. 68
10c
THE DARING AMAZON FINDS HERSELF IN AN EXPLOSIVE TRAP IN THE "TNT TRAP!"

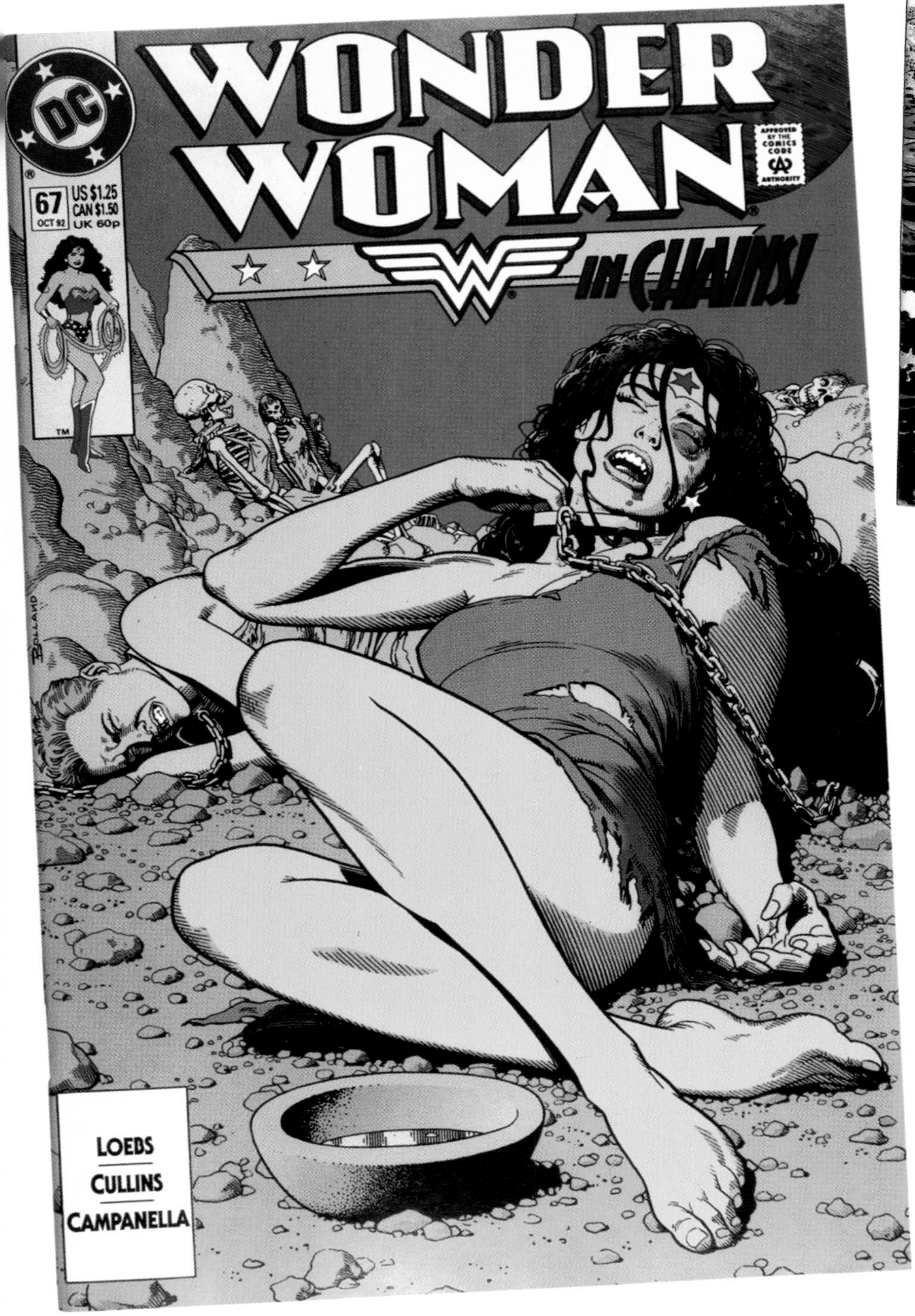
WONDER WOMAN
67
US $1.25
CAN $1.50
OCT 92
UK 60p
IN CHAINS!
LOEBS
CULLINS
CAMPANELLA

Above: The bondage theme became old hat by this point, but the danger is no less deadly in this cover from Irv Novick, one of the first artists to draw the character after Peter's tenure.

Left: For almost one year, Wonder Woman traveled in space and fought for justice on other planets. The fight for freedom was not an easy one, as seen when she found herself enslaved on a cruel alien planet. Cover by Brian Bolland.

Right: A look at the cover process of Terry and Rachel Dodson. Note the foes behind her in the image above left and above right.

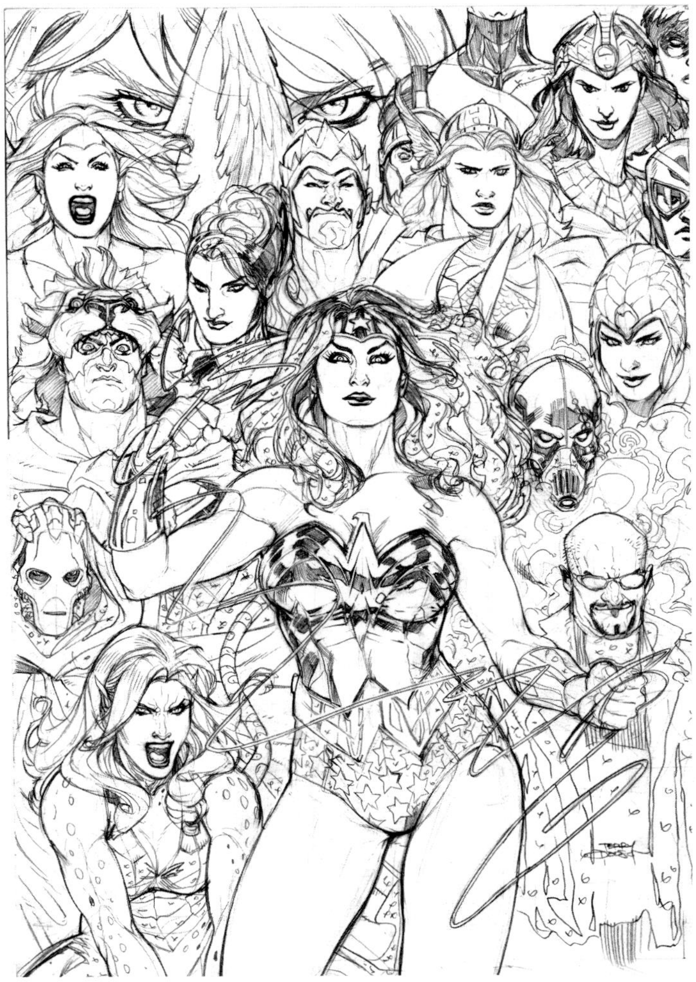

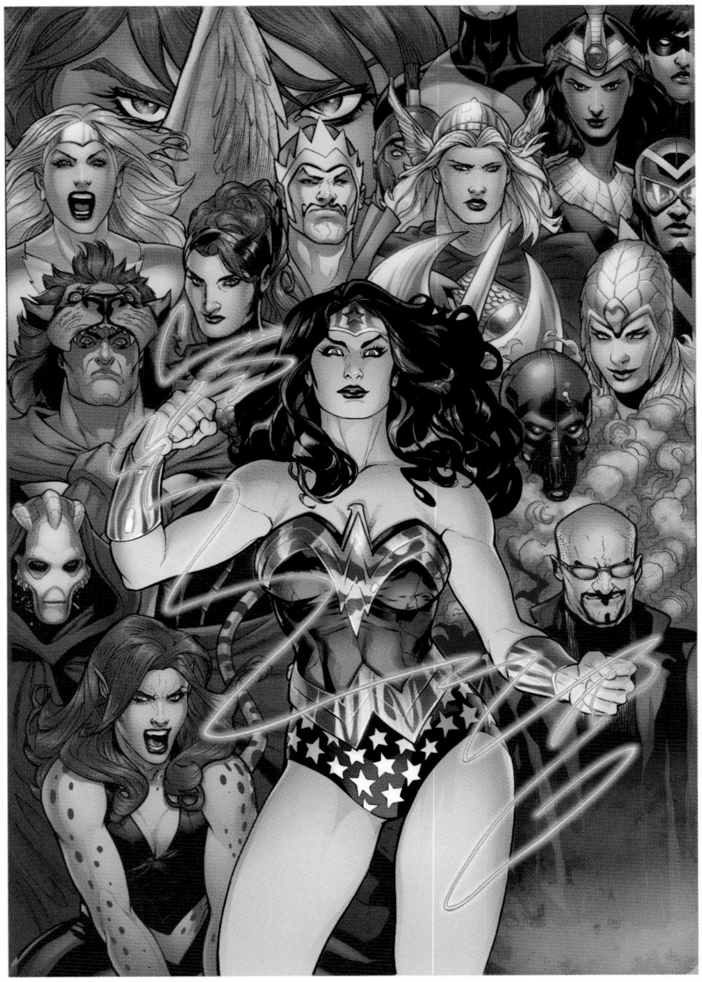

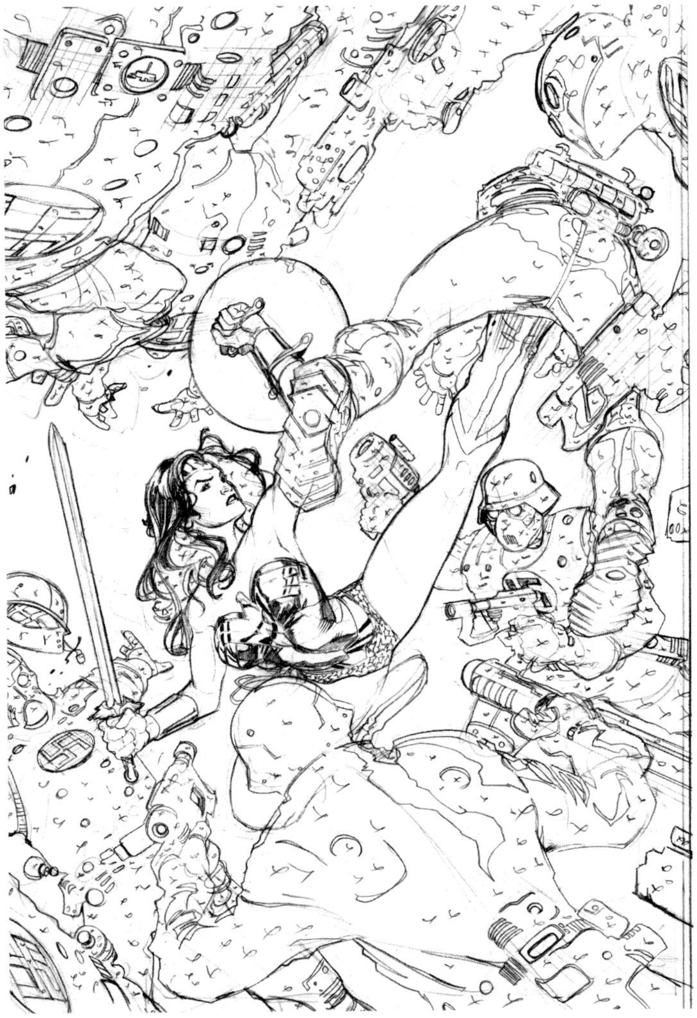

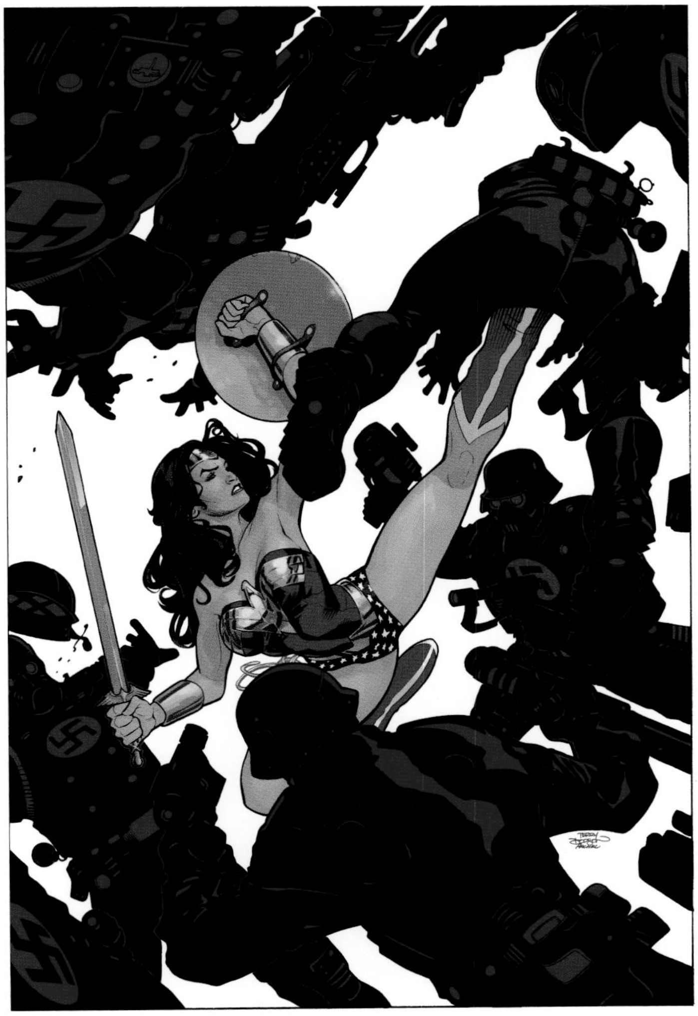

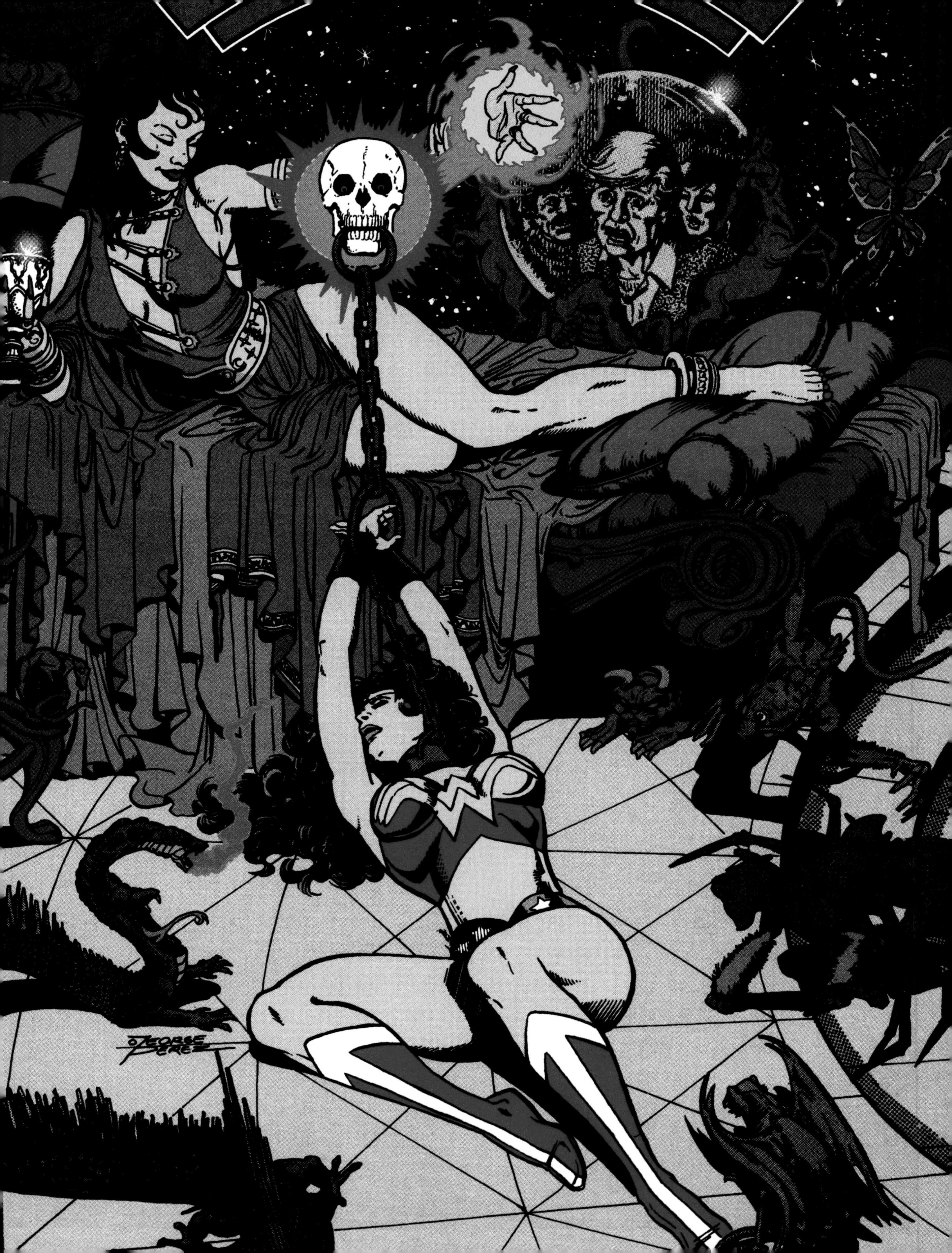
©GEORGE PEREZ

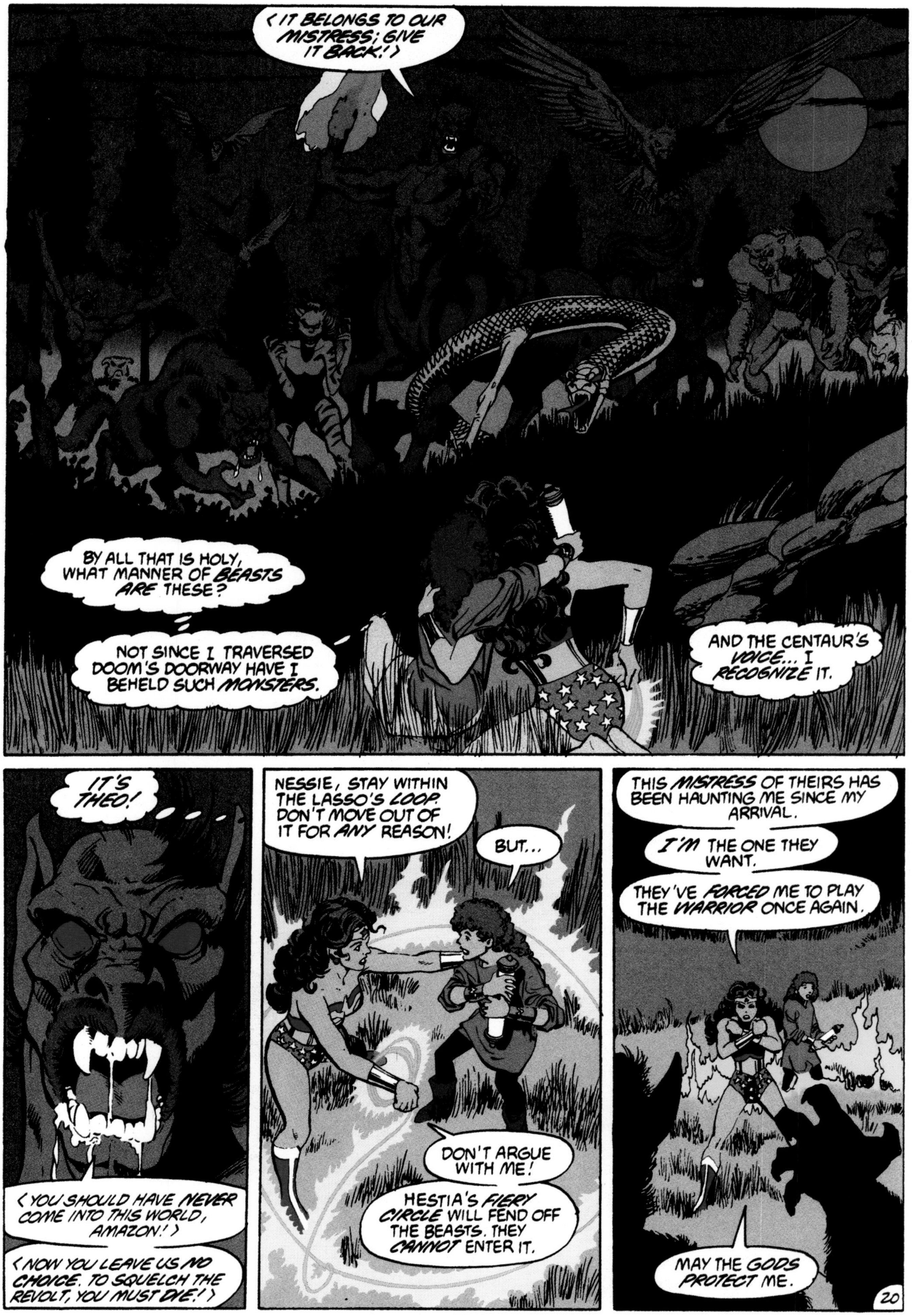

< IT BELONGS TO OUR MISTRESS; GIVE IT BACK! >
BY ALL THAT IS HOLY, WHAT MANNER OF BEASTS ARE THESE?
NOT SINCE I TRAVERSED DOOM'S DOORWAY HAVE I BEHELD SUCH MONSTERS.
AND THE CENTAUR'S VOICE... I RECOGNIZE IT.
IT'S THEO!
< YOU SHOULD HAVE NEVER COME INTO THIS WORLD, AMAZON! >
< NOW YOU LEAVE US NO CHOICE. TO SQUELCH THE REVOLT, YOU MUST DIE! >
NESSIE, STAY WITHIN THE LASSO'S LOOP. DON'T MOVE OUT OF IT FOR ANY REASON!
BUT...
DON'T ARGUE WITH ME!
HESTIA'S FIERY CIRCLE WILL FEND OFF THE BEASTS. THEY CANNOT ENTER IT.
THIS MISTRESS OF THEIRS HAS BEEN HAUNTING ME SINCE MY ARRIVAL.
I'M THE ONE THEY WANT.
THEY'VE FORCED ME TO PLAY THE WARRIOR ONCE AGAIN.
MAY THE GODS PROTECT ME.
20

Left: Circe's arrival spelled serious trouble for Wonder Woman. Cover by George Pérez.

Above: The Cheetah recruited other beastly hunters, threatening Wonder Woman and her friend, the teenager Vanessa Kapetelis.

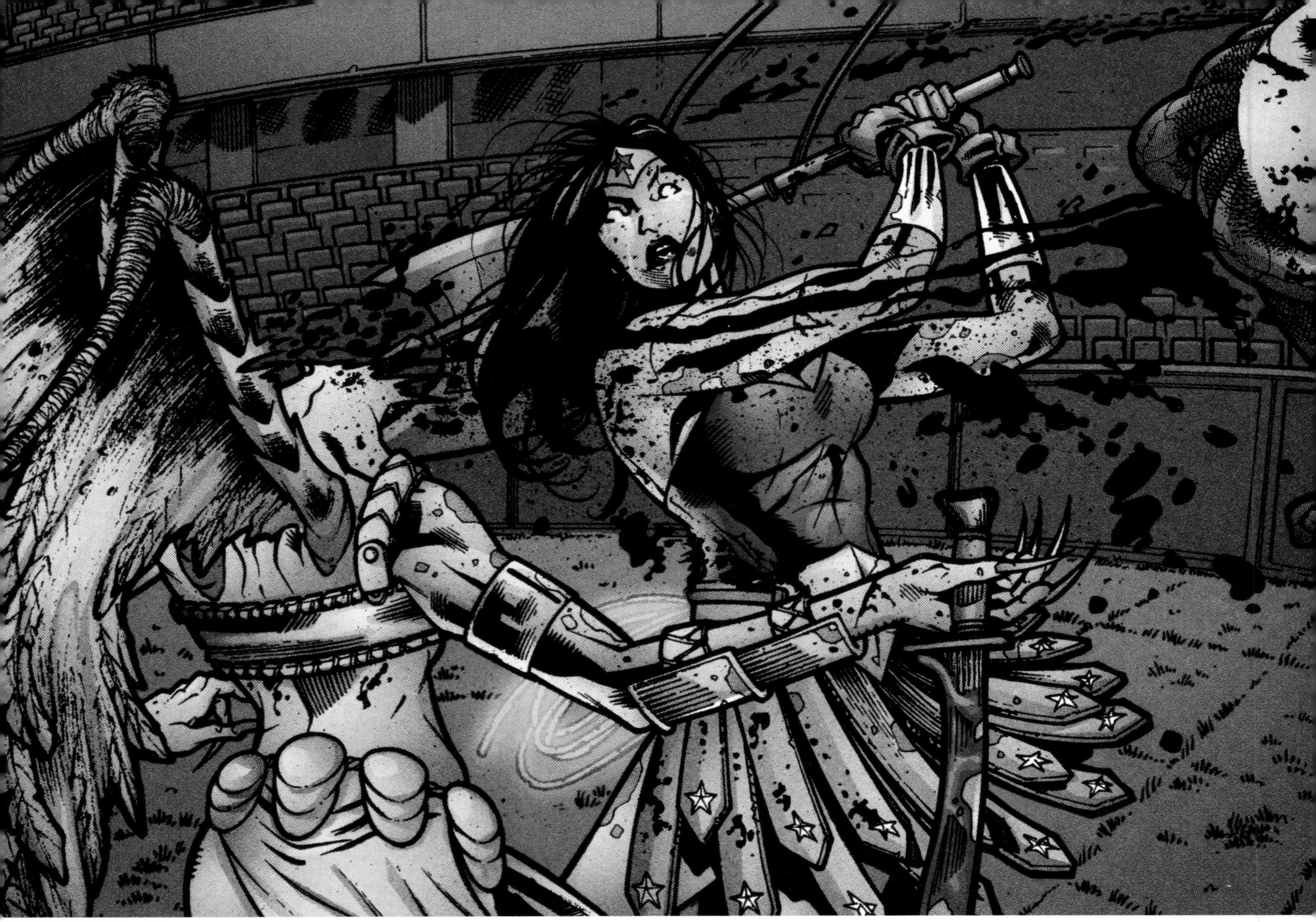

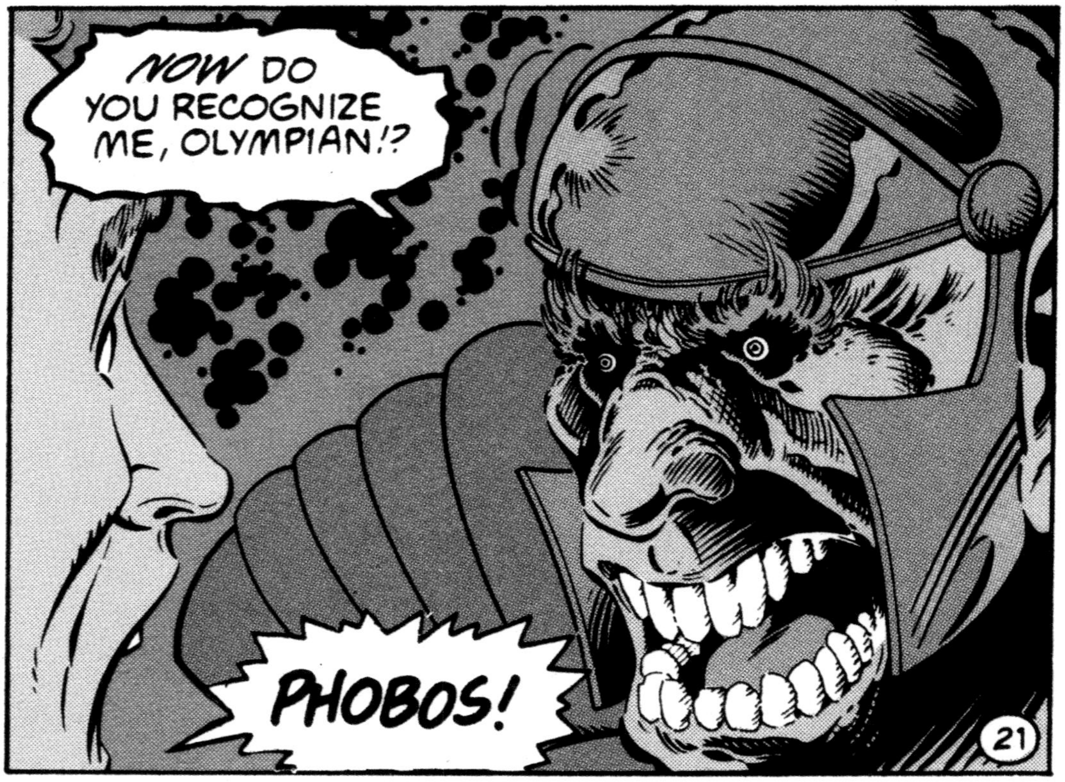
NOW DO YOU RECOGNIZE ME, OLYMPIAN!?
PHOBOS!
21

Above: With the entire world watching, a blinded Wonder Woman beheaded the deadly Medousa in this climactic moment from artists Drew Johnson and Ray Snyder.

Left: George Pérez mined the Greek myths for new challenges, such as crafting the arrival of Phobos.

Right: In this taut sequence from Pérez, Wonder Woman struggles to free her friend Julia Kapetelis from the creature Echidna.

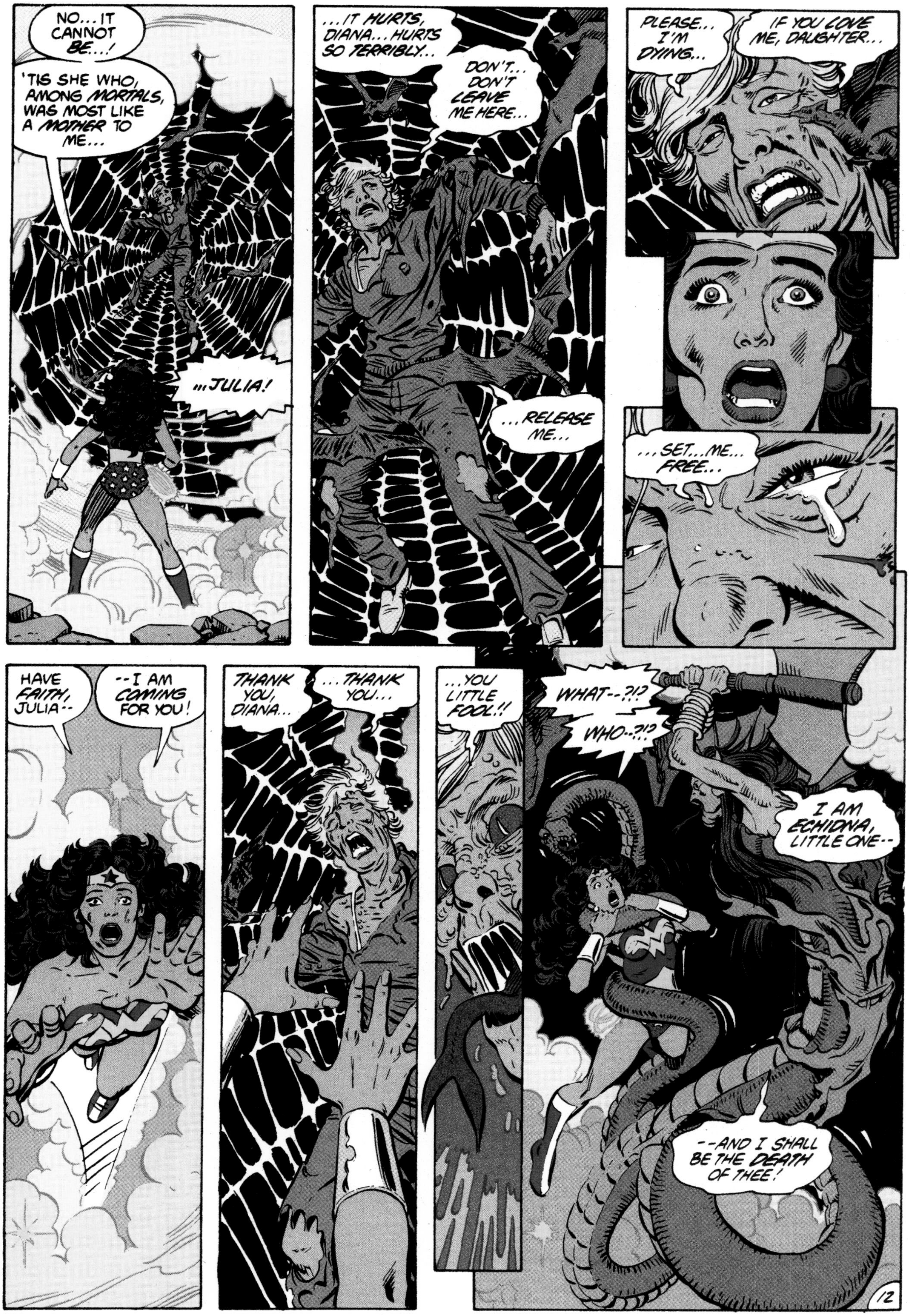
NO... IT CANNOT BE...!
'TIS SHE WHO, AMONG MORTALS, WAS MOST LIKE A MOTHER TO ME...
...JULIA!
...IT HURTS, DIANA... HURTS SO TERRIBLY...
DON'T... DON'T LEAVE ME HERE...
...RELEASE ME...
PLEASE... I'M DYING...
IF YOU LOVE ME, DAUGHTER...
...SET...ME... FREE...
HAVE FAITH, JULIA--
--I AM COMING FOR YOU!
THANK YOU, DIANA...
...THANK YOU...
...YOU LITTLE FOOL!!
WHAT--?!?
WHO--?!?
I AM ECHIDNA, LITTLE ONE--
--AND I SHALL BE THE DEATH OF THEE!
12

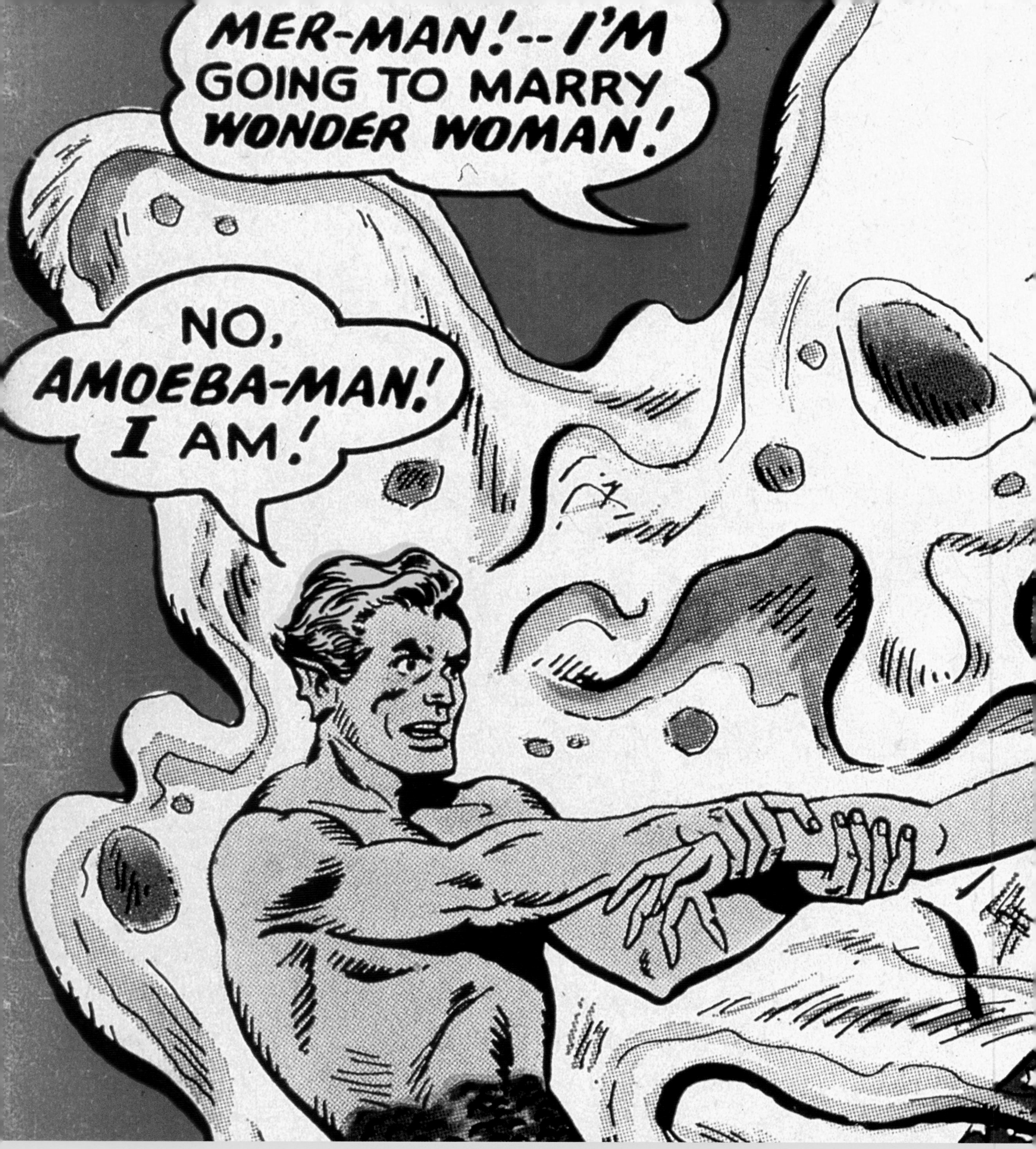
MER-MAN!--I'M GOING TO MARRY WONDER WOMAN!
NO, AMOEBA-MAN! I AM!

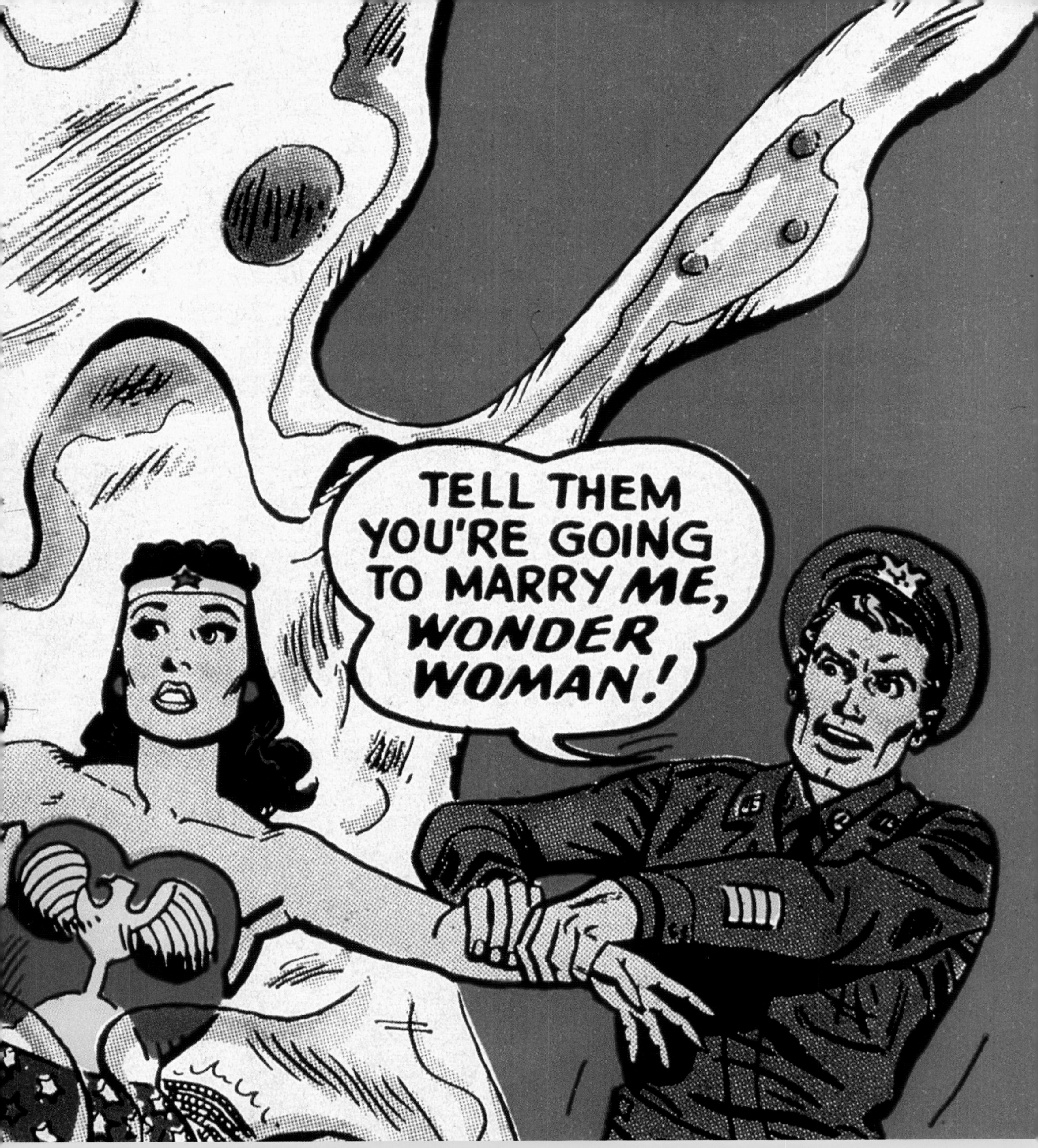
TELL THEM YOU'RE GOING TO MARRY *ME*, *WONDER WOMAN!*

★ The Lovers

I STILL DON'T UNDERSTAND HOW THAT HUMAN HARPY CONTROLLED ME-THANK HEAVEN YOU BROKE HER SPELL!
I HAD TO BECOME A HELPLESS WOMAN TO DO IT— I OWE THE BARONESS ONE FOR THAT!

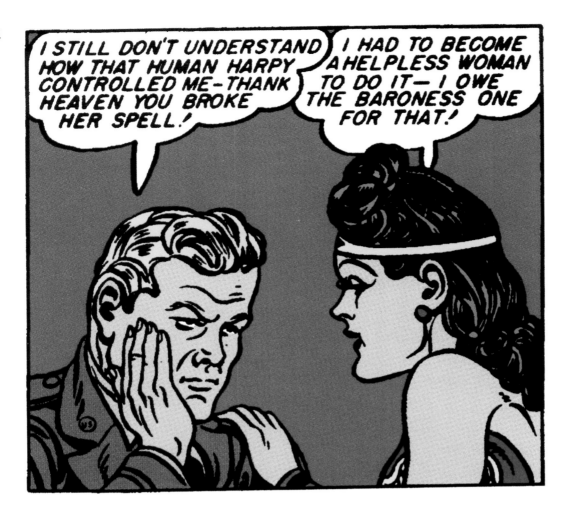

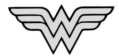

We all know about Steve Trevor, one of the few constants in Wonder Woman's life. He was the reason Diana left Paradise Island for the first time, but interestingly, most writers have admitted they had no idea what to do with him. In fact, the one thing that kept happening to the poor guy was that he was repeatedly killed for dramatic impact and to clear the stage for a hopefully more engaging romantic interest.

Steve first died when Denny O'Neil killed him in a hail of bullets during a robbery in 1968. He was resurrected by the goddess Aphrodite as a part of editor Julius Schwartz's efforts to revitalize the title in the mid-1970s. Steve was quickly killed once more by successors of Schwartz, who deemed the character a bore. His second resurrection was a mystic sleight of hand as the gods brought a Steve Trevor to earth from a parallel universe to become a part of Diana's life.

Steve pined for Wonder Woman right from his arrival on Paradise Island, and when *Sensation Comics* refocused its contents to more closely resemble the popular romance comics of the 1950s, his marriage proposals grew more frequent. In *Sensation Comics* #97 (May/June 1950), Wonder Woman, while serving as romance editor of the *Daily Globe*, was asked again by Steve for her hand in marriage. She consulted Aphrodite's Law and learned she'd be required to give up her Amazon powers and identity if she were to marry Steve. The world needed Wonder Woman more than Steve Trevor, and he was told no yet again.

By the early 1960s, DC introduced the notion of parallel worlds, which set Wonder Woman's adventures, from her 1941 debut through to the end of Harry G. Peter's

Above: From the beginning, Steve Trevor held a special place in Wonder Woman's life. He was the catalyst that propelled her from resident of Paradise Island to champion in Man's World. Art by Harry G. Peter.

Right: In the 1960s, writer/editor Robert Kanigher told tales of Diana's youth and introduced her teen romantic rivals Mer-Boy and Bird-Boy. Cover art by Ross Andru and Mike Esposito.

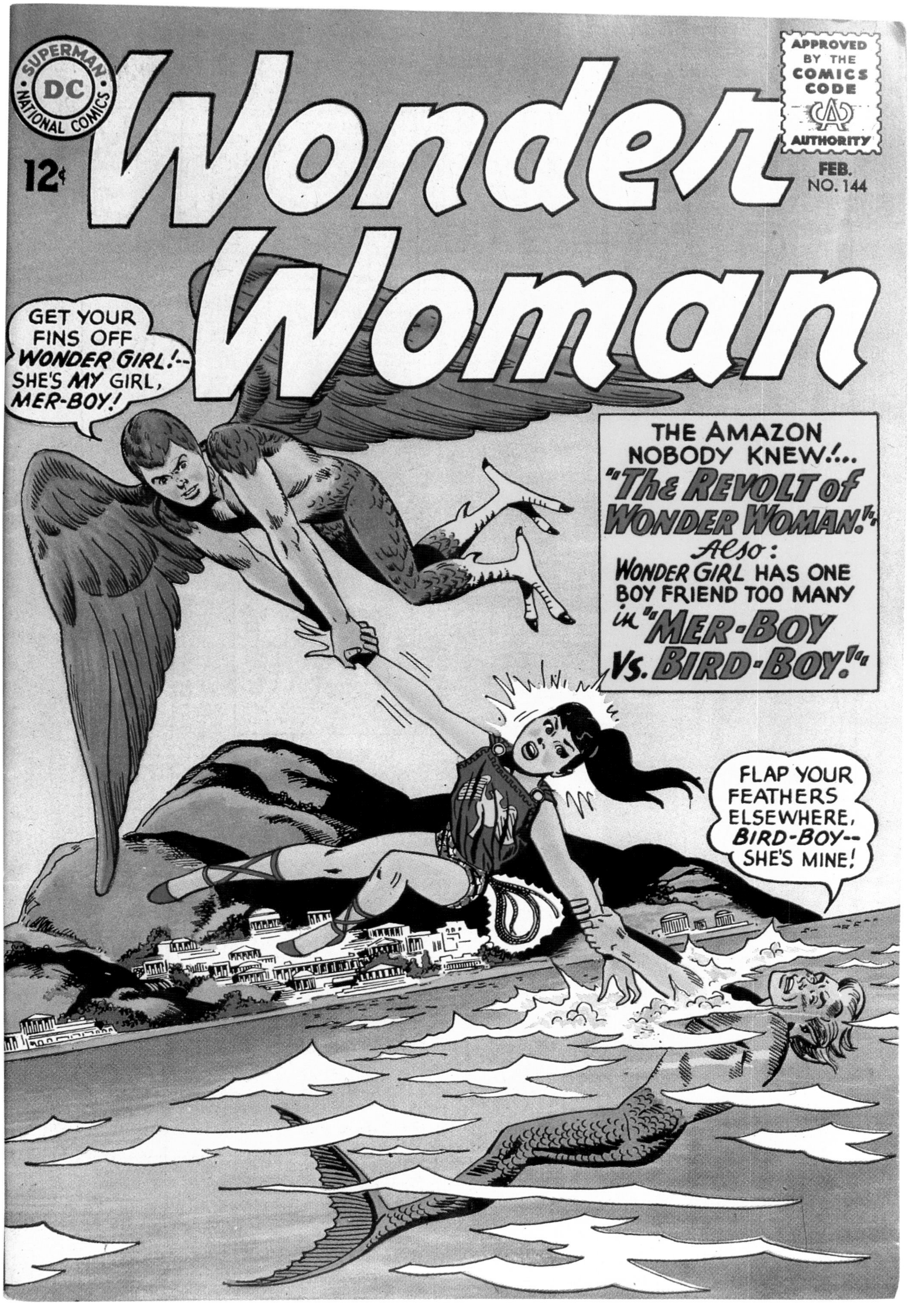
SUPERMAN DC NATIONAL COMICS
APPROVED BY THE COMICS CODE AUTHORITY
Wonder Woman
12¢
FEB. NO. 144
GET YOUR FINS OFF WONDER GIRL!-- SHE'S MY GIRL, MER-BOY!
THE AMAZON NOBODY KNEW!... "The REVOLT of WONDER WOMAN!" Also: WONDER GIRL HAS ONE BOY FRIEND TOO MANY in "MER-BOY Vs. BIRD-BOY!"
FLAP YOUR FEATHERS ELSEWHERE, BIRD-BOY-- SHE'S MINE!

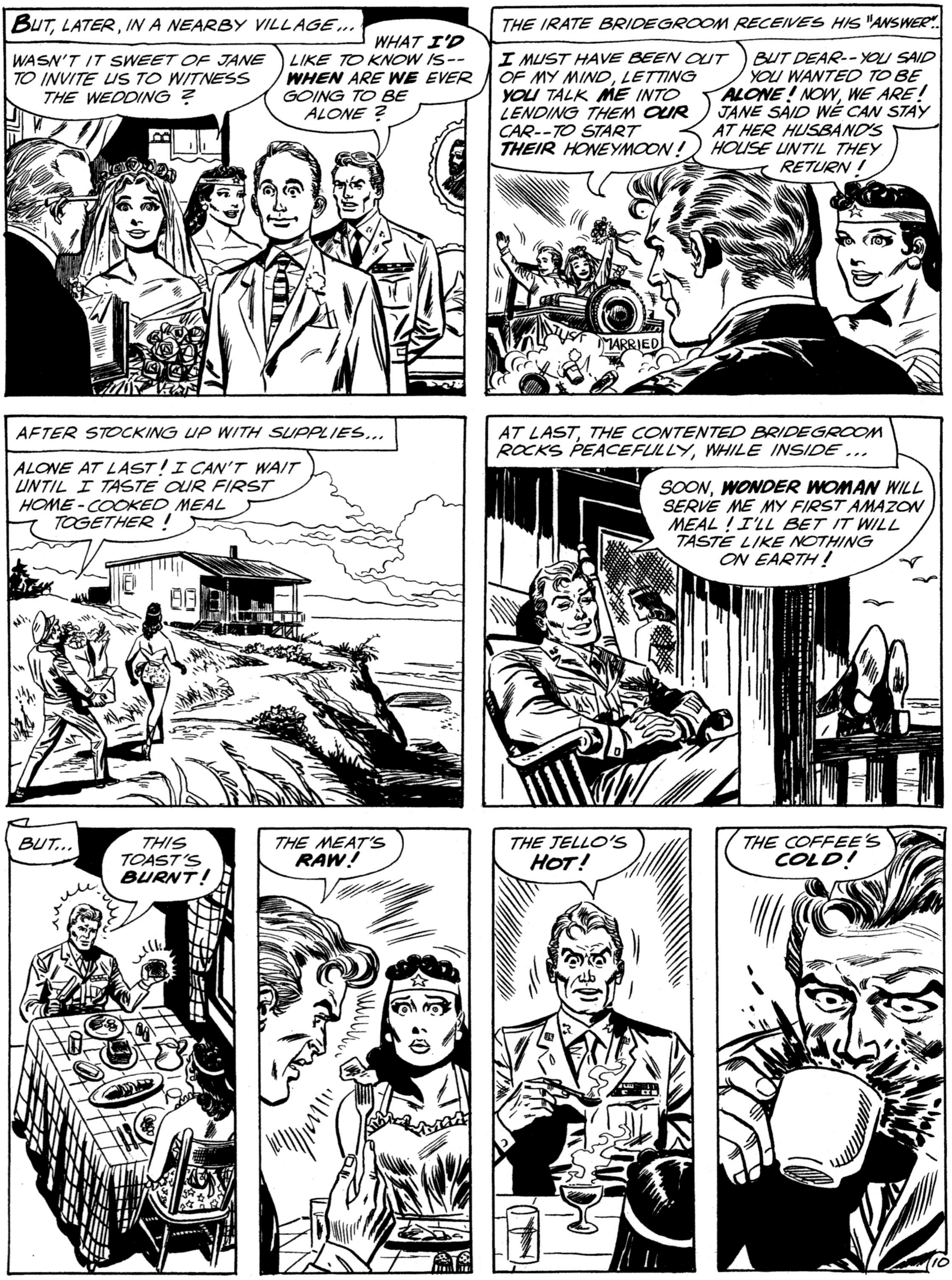
BUT, LATER, IN A NEARBY VILLAGE...
WASN'T IT SWEET OF JANE TO INVITE US TO WITNESS THE WEDDING ?
WHAT I'D LIKE TO KNOW IS-- WHEN ARE WE EVER GOING TO BE ALONE ?
THE IRATE BRIDEGROOM RECEIVES HIS "ANSWER"...
I MUST HAVE BEEN OUT OF MY MIND, LETTING YOU TALK ME INTO LENDING THEM OUR CAR--TO START THEIR HONEYMOON !
BUT DEAR--YOU SAID YOU WANTED TO BE ALONE ! NOW, WE ARE ! JANE SAID WE CAN STAY AT HER HUSBAND'S HOUSE UNTIL THEY RETURN !
JUST MARRIED
AFTER STOCKING UP WITH SUPPLIES...
ALONE AT LAST ! I CAN'T WAIT UNTIL I TASTE OUR FIRST HOME-COOKED MEAL TOGETHER !
AT LAST, THE CONTENTED BRIDEGROOM ROCKS PEACEFULLY, WHILE INSIDE...
SOON, WONDER WOMAN WILL SERVE ME MY FIRST AMAZON MEAL ! I'LL BET IT WILL TASTE LIKE NOTHING ON EARTH !
BUT...
THIS TOAST'S BURNT !
THE MEAT'S RAW !
THE JELLO'S HOT !
THE COFFEE'S COLD !
10

Above and right: Robert Kanigher, Ross Andru and Mike Esposito showed readers one possible disastrous outcome of the marriage of Wonder Woman to Steve Trevor. Thankfully, it was all a dream.

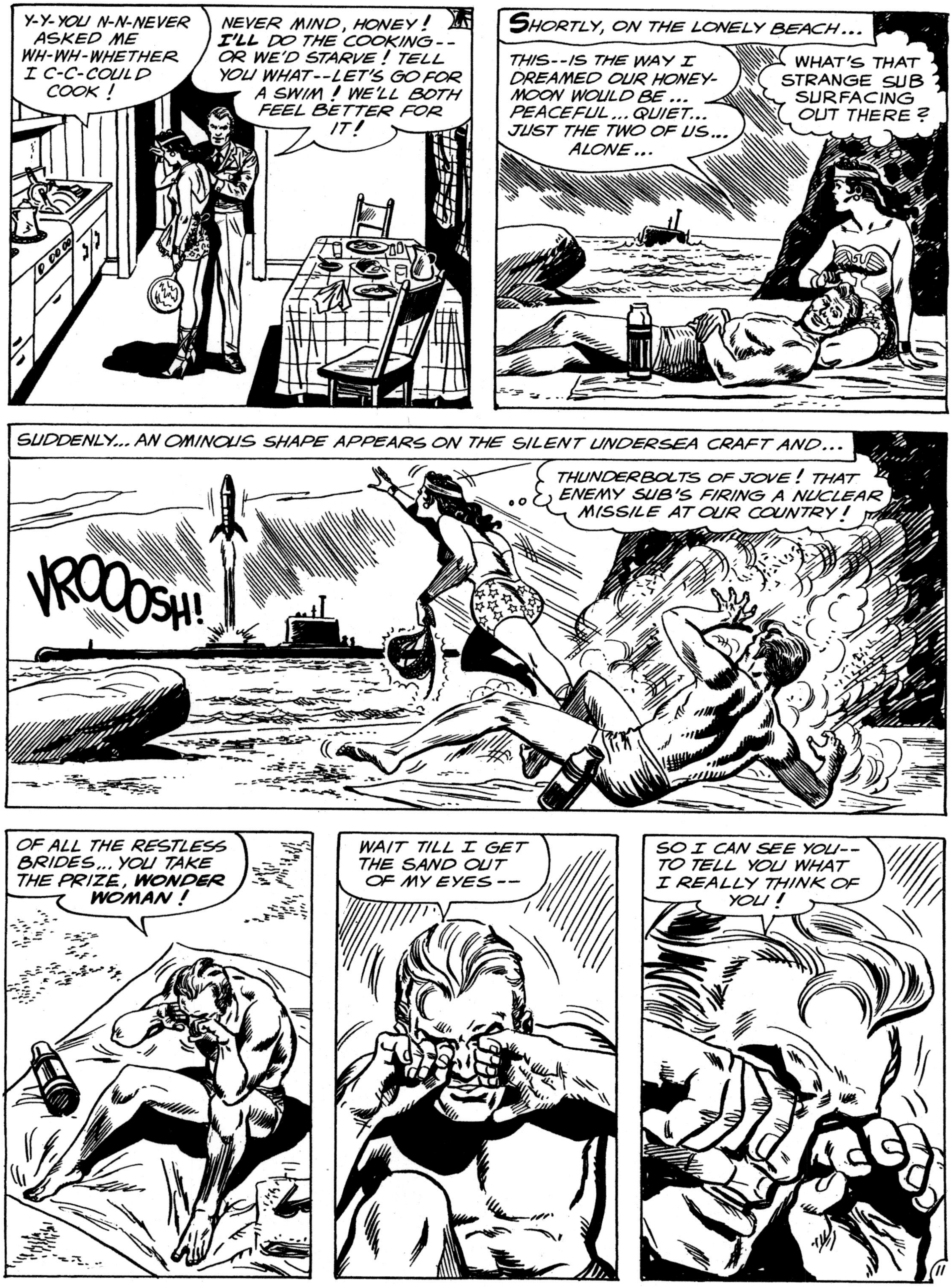
Y-Y-YOU N-N-NEVER ASKED ME WH-WH-WHETHER I C-C-COULD COOK!
NEVER MIND, HONEY! I'LL DO THE COOKING-- OR WE'D STARVE! TELL YOU WHAT--LET'S GO FOR A SWIM! WE'LL BOTH FEEL BETTER FOR IT!
SHORTLY, ON THE LONELY BEACH...
THIS--IS THE WAY I DREAMED OUR HONEY-MOON WOULD BE... PEACEFUL... QUIET... JUST THE TWO OF US... ALONE...
WHAT'S THAT STRANGE SUB SURFACING OUT THERE?
SUDDENLY... AN OMINOUS SHAPE APPEARS ON THE SILENT UNDERSEA CRAFT AND...
THUNDERBOLTS OF JOVE! THAT ENEMY SUB'S FIRING A NUCLEAR MISSILE AT OUR COUNTRY!
VROOOSH!
OF ALL THE RESTLESS BRIDES... YOU TAKE THE PRIZE, WONDER WOMAN!
WAIT TILL I GET THE SAND OUT OF MY EYES--
SO I CAN SEE YOU-- TO TELL YOU WHAT I REALLY THINK OF YOU!
11

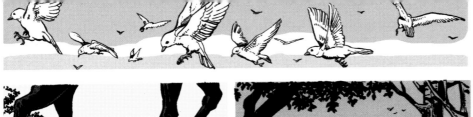

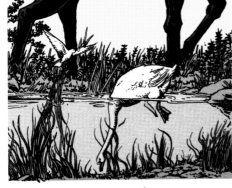

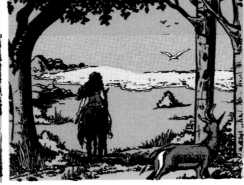

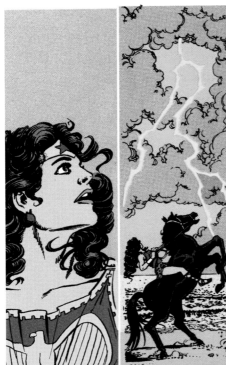

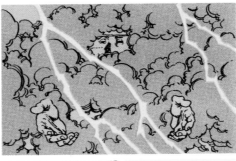

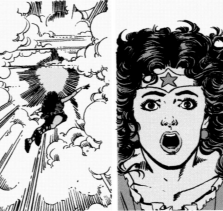

Left and right: In 1988, the potential for romance between Superman and Wonder Woman was finally explored in a subplot that ran in *Wonder Woman, Superman,* and *Action Comics*. Art by George Pérez.

Below: Adam Hughes illustrates what a super-romance might look like.

WONDER WOMAN
141
LUKE
PAQUETTE
MCLEOD
TRINITY • Part 2 of 2

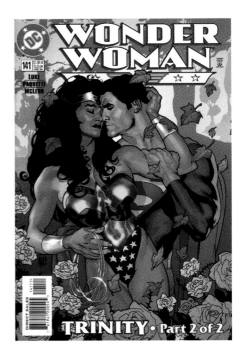

run as artist with *Wonder Woman* #97 (April 1958) on Earth-2. Her exploits from the 1960s through 1985 were said to occur on Earth-1. As a result, to celebrate the publication of *Wonder Woman* #300 (February 1983), the Wonder Woman and Steve Trevor of Earth-2 were finally wed. Later, the cosmic event called the Crisis on Infinite Earths was designed to collapse the parallel universes into one cohesive reality, and in *Wonder Woman* #329 (February 1986) Earth-1's Diana and Steve also married.

Why wouldn't Wonder Woman want to be with the powerful Superman instead of the not-so-powerful Steve Trevor? The revamp in 1987 addressed the issue that readers had been wondering about for several decades. At the time, writer/artist John Byrne was handling the Man of Steel in *Superman* and *Action Comics*. He collaborated with *Wonder Woman*'s George Pérez to explore the notion of Wonder Woman and Superman's relationship. The Last Son of Krypton was captivated by the Amazon upon meeting, dreaming about her and finally asking her for a date some time later. That first outing, in *Action Comics* #600, was spoiled when Darkseid attacked Mount Olympus, dragging the would-be lovers into the fight.

It took *Kingdom Come*, a story about a potential future for Earth's heroes by writer Mark Waid and painter Alex Ross, before the two could truly explore their feelings. The Joker had viciously killed Lois Lane, thereby clearing the way for the heroes to reconnect. By the story's end, the couple learned that they would be expecting their first

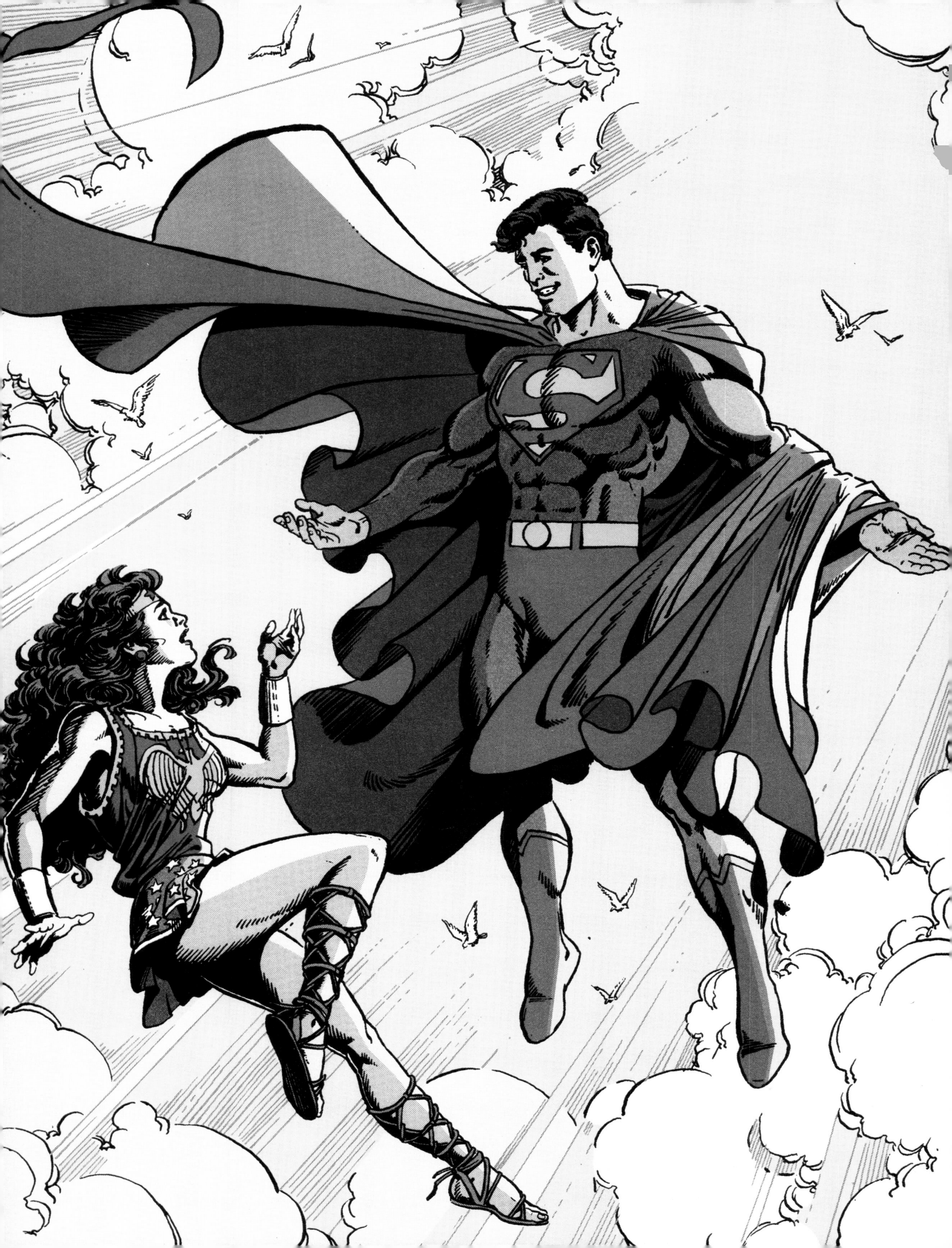

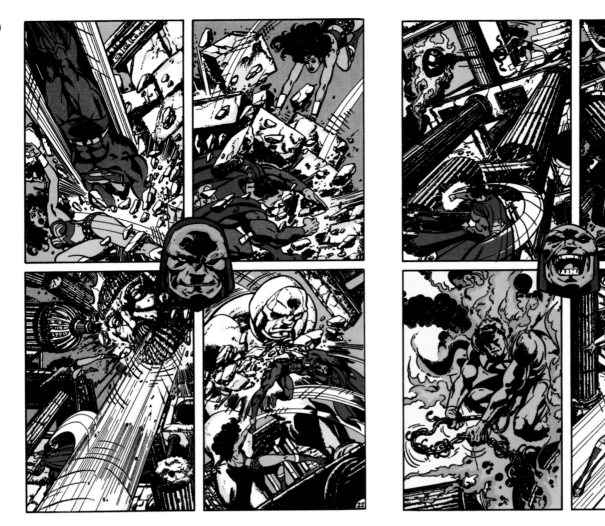

child. They decide to share the good news with Batman, but the Dark Knight cleverly deduced the fact on his own.

Kanigher spent the 1950s and 1960s increasingly adding romance into his story-lines. He even introduced rival suitors for Wonder Woman, which included Mer-Man and Bird-Man. The 1970s and 1980s saw other short-lived prospects, such as detective Jonny Double, astronaut Mike Bailey, and military officer Keith Griggs. Following the 1987 retelling, most men in the series were more interested in Wonder Woman than she in them, such as Boston police inspector Ed Indelicato and Gateway City police officer Mike Schorr.

Diana's first real romance was Trevor Barnes, an African-American who met the princess while working for the United Nations Rural Development Organization. In the hands of writer/artist Phil Jimenez, Barnes was a well-rounded figure and worthy suitor to the Amazon Princess. He remained by her side until he sacrificed himself to save humanity by containing in his body the entity known as the Shattered God, which rapidly aged him until he died of old age. Zeus rewarded Barnes by transforming him into a life-giving rainfall and returning him to the earth to replenish lands that had been scorched by the Shattered God.

Her next long-term romance was a most unlikely one with former spy-turned-operative for the Department of Meta-human Affairs, Tom Tresser. He was brash, cocky, and seemingly ill-suited for a princess, but he continually showed Wonder Woman his remarkable courage. His greatest challenge came when he arrived on Themyscira to obtain permission from Hippolyta to pursue the romance. She dubbed him Sir Thomas of Cleveland, named him an Amazon, and gave him the rank of guardsman, out of respect for her daughter. In the summer of 2009, however, Diana was pushed to her limits by the villain Genocide and finally had to admit she did not actually love Tresser. The relationship quickly and sadly fell apart.

Above: In *Action Comics* #600, Wonder Woman and Superman attempt to go on a date but their night is interrupted by Darkseid's attack on Mount Olympus. Art by John Byrne and George Pérez.

Right: After her revamp in 1987, Diana didn't have a real romance until the early 2000s. She found love with Trevor Barnes and clearly Diana makes every effort to be a good guest and warm presence in this page from writer/penciller Phil Jimenez and inker Andy Lanning.

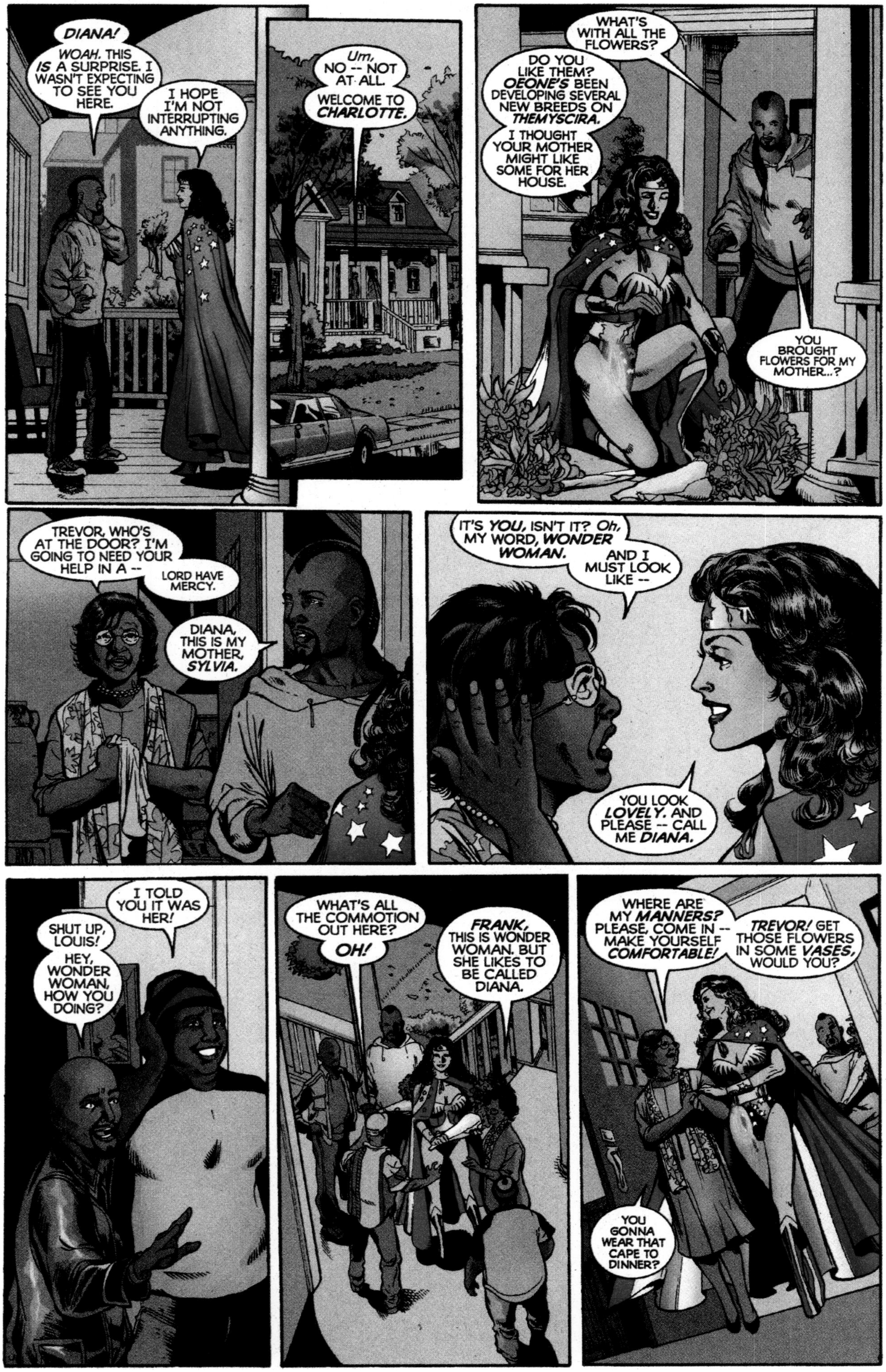
DIANA!
WOAH. THIS IS A SURPRISE. I WASN'T EXPECTING TO SEE YOU HERE.
I HOPE I'M NOT INTERRUPTING ANYTHING.
Um, NO -- NOT AT ALL.
WELCOME TO CHARLOTTE.
WHAT'S WITH ALL THE FLOWERS?
DO YOU LIKE THEM? OEONE'S BEEN DEVELOPING SEVERAL NEW BREEDS ON THEMYSCIRA.
I THOUGHT YOUR MOTHER MIGHT LIKE SOME FOR HER HOUSE.
YOU BROUGHT FLOWERS FOR MY MOTHER...?
TREVOR, WHO'S AT THE DOOR? I'M GOING TO NEED YOUR HELP IN A --
LORD HAVE MERCY.
DIANA, THIS IS MY MOTHER, SYLVIA.
IT'S YOU, ISN'T IT? Oh, MY WORD, WONDER WOMAN.
AND I MUST LOOK LIKE --
YOU LOOK LOVELY. AND PLEASE -- CALL ME DIANA.
I TOLD YOU IT WAS HER!
SHUT UP, LOUIS!
HEY, WONDER WOMAN, HOW YOU DOING?
WHAT'S ALL THE COMMOTION OUT HERE?
OH!
FRANK, THIS IS WONDER WOMAN. BUT SHE LIKES TO BE CALLED DIANA.
WHERE ARE MY MANNERS? PLEASE, COME IN -- MAKE YOURSELF COMFORTABLE!
TREVOR! GET THOSE FLOWERS IN SOME VASES, WOULD YOU?
YOU GONNA WEAR THAT CAPE TO DINNER?

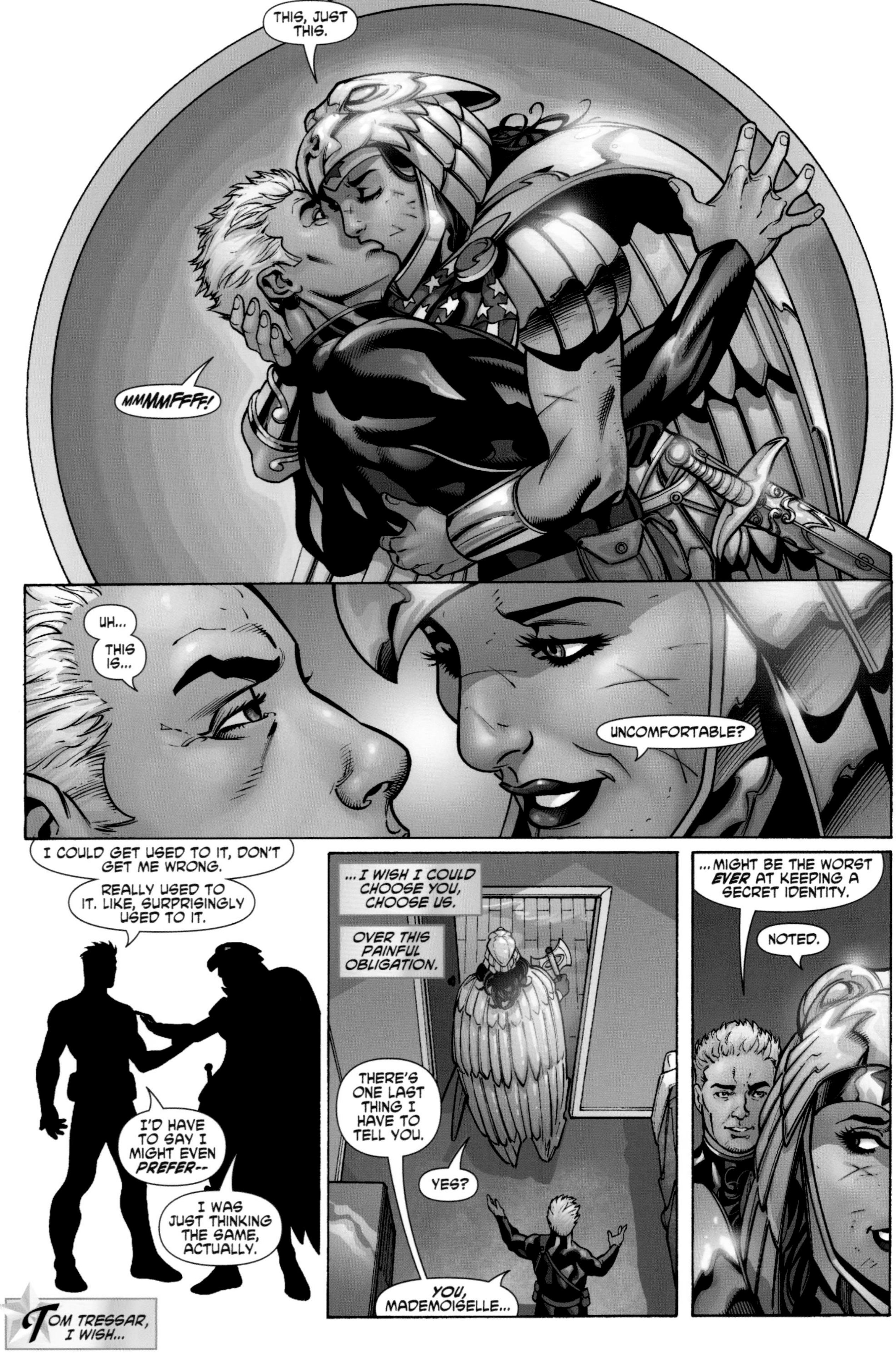
THIS, JUST THIS.
MMMMFFFF!
UH... THIS IS...
UNCOMFORTABLE?
I COULD GET USED TO IT, DON'T GET ME WRONG.
REALLY USED TO IT. LIKE, SURPRISINGLY USED TO IT.
I'D HAVE TO SAY I MIGHT EVEN PREFER--
JUST THINKING THE SAME, ACTUALLY.
TOM TRESSAR, I WISH...
...I WISH I COULD CHOOSE YOU, CHOOSE US.
OVER THIS PAINFUL OBLIGATION.
THERE'S ONE LAST THING I HAVE TO TELL YOU.
YES?
YOU, MADEMOISELLE...
...MIGHT BE THE WORST EVER AT KEEPING A SECRET IDENTITY.
NOTED.

Above: Diana, in full Amazonian battle armor, shows her affection for Tom Tresser in this sequence by Aaron Lopresti and Matt Ryan.

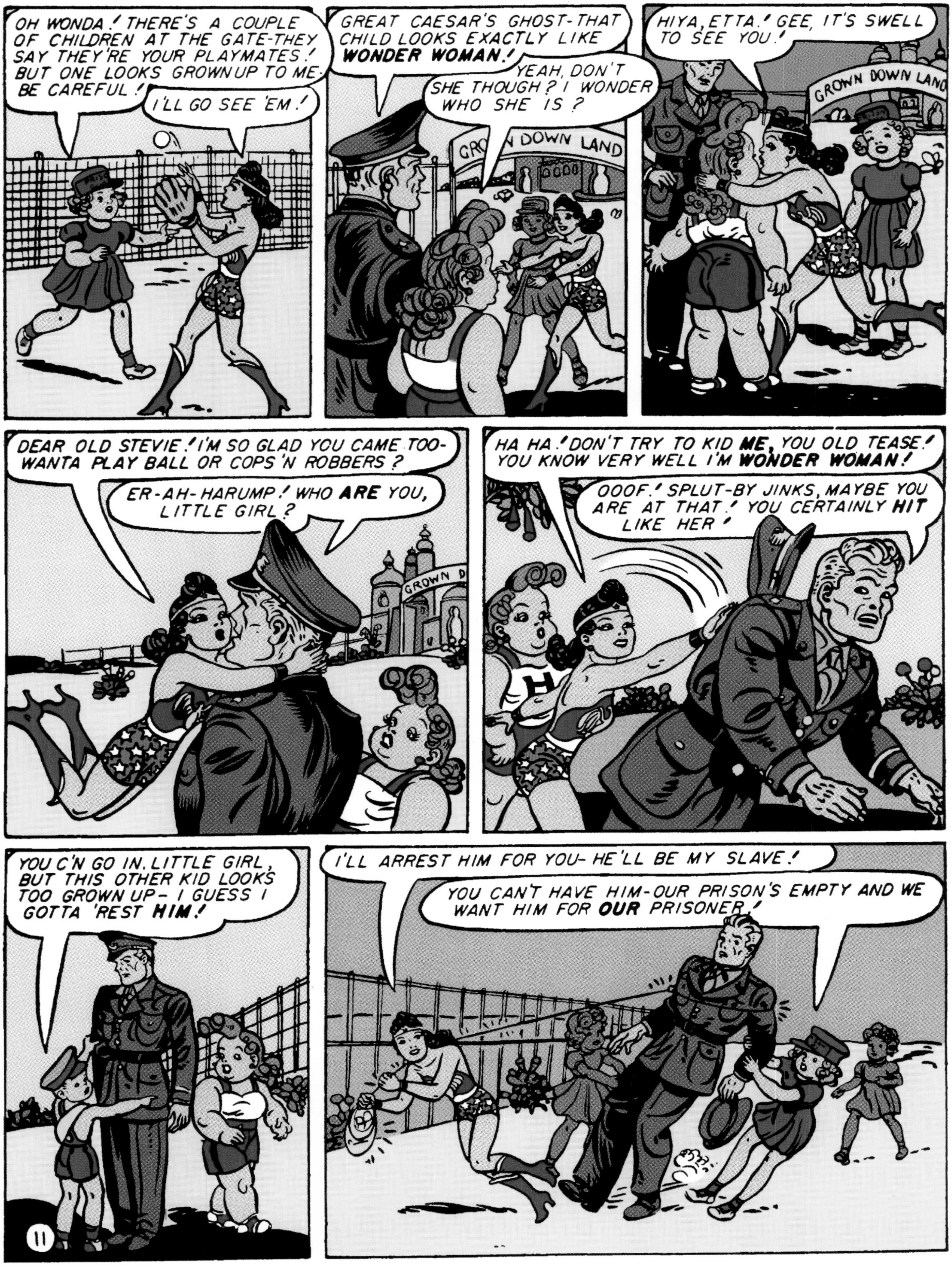

OH WONDA! THERE'S A COUPLE OF CHILDREN AT THE GATE-THEY SAY THEY'RE YOUR PLAYMATES! BUT ONE LOOKS GROWNUP TO ME-BE CAREFUL!
I'LL GO SEE 'EM!
GREAT CAESAR'S GHOST-THAT CHILD LOOKS EXACTLY LIKE WONDER WOMAN!
YEAH, DON'T SHE THOUGH? I WONDER WHO SHE IS?
GROWN DOWN LAND
HIYA, ETTA! GEE, IT'S SWELL TO SEE YOU!
GROWN DOWN LAND
DEAR OLD STEVIE! I'M SO GLAD YOU CAME TOO-WANTA PLAY BALL OR COPS 'N ROBBERS?
ER-AH-HARUMP! WHO ARE YOU, LITTLE GIRL?
HA HA! DON'T TRY TO KID ME, YOU OLD TEASE! YOU KNOW VERY WELL I'M WONDER WOMAN!
OOOF! SPLUT-BY JINKS, MAYBE YOU ARE AT THAT! YOU CERTAINLY HIT LIKE HER!
YOU C'N GO IN. LITTLE GIRL, BUT THIS OTHER KID LOOKS TOO GROWN UP- I GUESS I GOTTA 'REST HIM!
11
I'LL ARREST HIM FOR YOU- HE'LL BE MY SLAVE!
YOU CAN'T HAVE HIM-OUR PRISON'S EMPTY AND WE WANT HIM FOR OUR PRISONER!

Above: In a bizarre twist, Wonder Woman is reduced to the size of a young teen but doesn't realize it when she encounters Steve Trevor and Etta Candy in this sequence by Harry G. Peter.

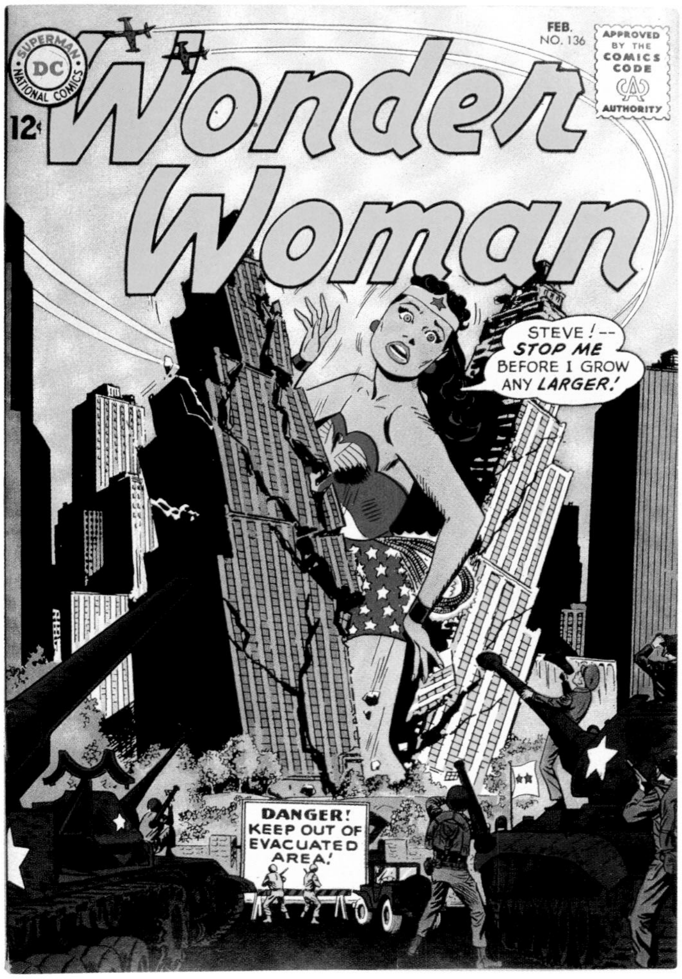
SUPERMAN DC NATIONAL COMICS
FEB. NO. 136
APPROVED BY THE COMICS CODE AUTHORITY
12¢
Wonder Woman
STEVE!-- STOP ME BEFORE I GROW ANY LARGER!
DANGER! KEEP OUT OF EVACUATED AREA!

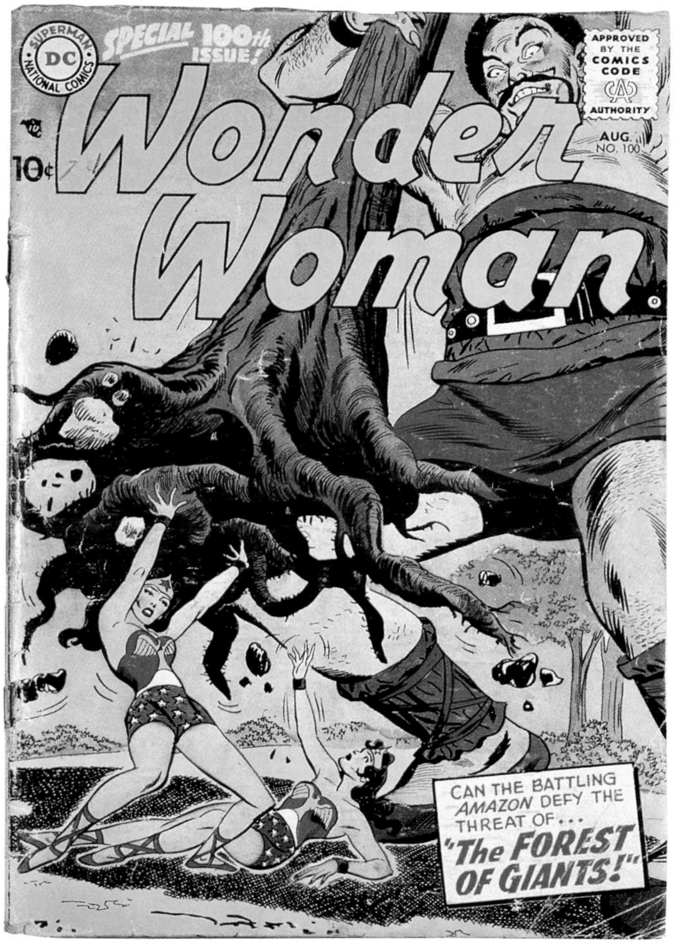
SUPERMAN DC NATIONAL COMICS
SPECIAL 100th ISSUE!
APPROVED BY THE COMICS CODE AUTHORITY
10¢
AUG. NO. 100
Wonder Woman
CAN THE BATTLING AMAZON DEFY THE THREAT OF...
"The FOREST OF GIANTS!"

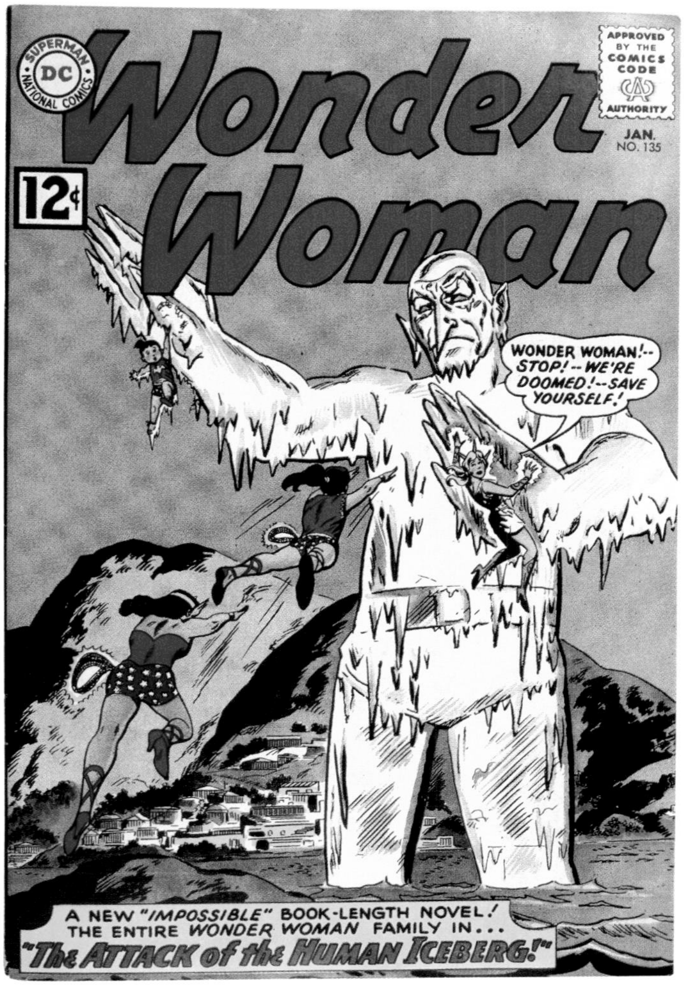
SUPERMAN DC NATIONAL COMICS
APPROVED BY THE COMICS CODE AUTHORITY
JAN. NO. 135
12¢
Wonder Woman
WONDER WOMAN!-- STOP!--WE'RE DOOMED!--SAVE YOURSELF!
A NEW "IMPOSSIBLE" BOOK-LENGTH NOVEL! THE ENTIRE WONDER WOMAN FAMILY IN...
"The ATTACK of the HUMAN ICEBERG!"

This page: Covers from the classic art team of Ross Andru and Mike Esposito, demonstrating their dynamic layout and design sense in addition to drawing in the style of Harry G. Peter. These covers also demonstrate writer/editor Robert Kanigher's predilection for pitting Wonder Woman against doppelgängers and bizarre threats as opposed to the more conventional Rogues Gallery.

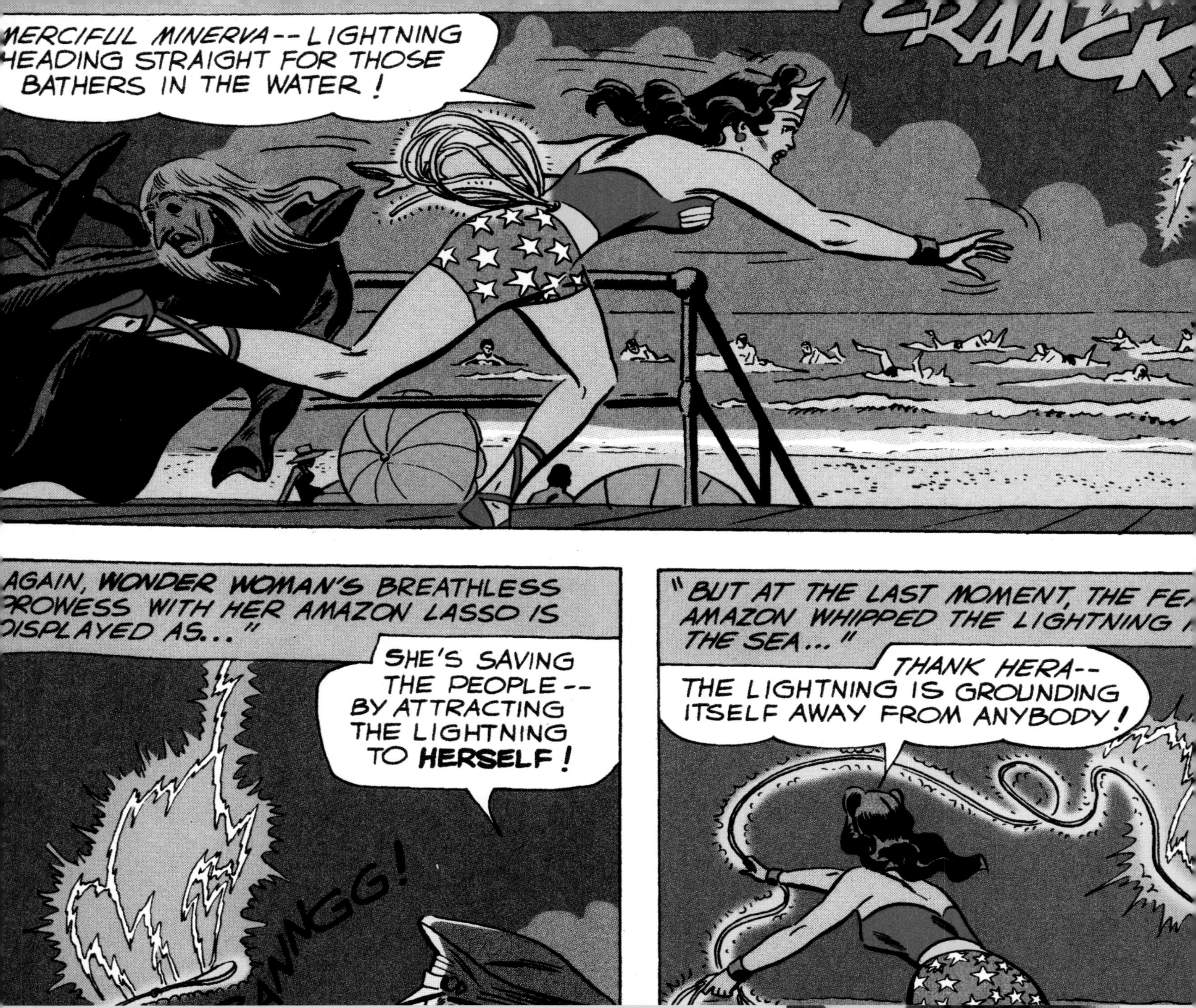
MERCIFUL MINERVA--LIGHTNING HEADING STRAIGHT FOR THOSE BATHERS IN THE WATER!
CRAAACK
AGAIN, WONDER WOMAN'S BREATHLESS PROWESS WITH HER AMAZON LASSO IS DISPLAYED AS..."
SHE'S SAVING THE PEOPLE-- BY ATTRACTING THE LIGHTNING TO HERSELF!
"BUT AT THE LAST MOMENT, THE FE AMAZON WHIPPED THE LIGHTNING THE SEA..."
THANK HERA-- THE LIGHTNING IS GROUNDING ITSELF AWAY FROM ANYBODY!

Ross Andru & Mike Esposito

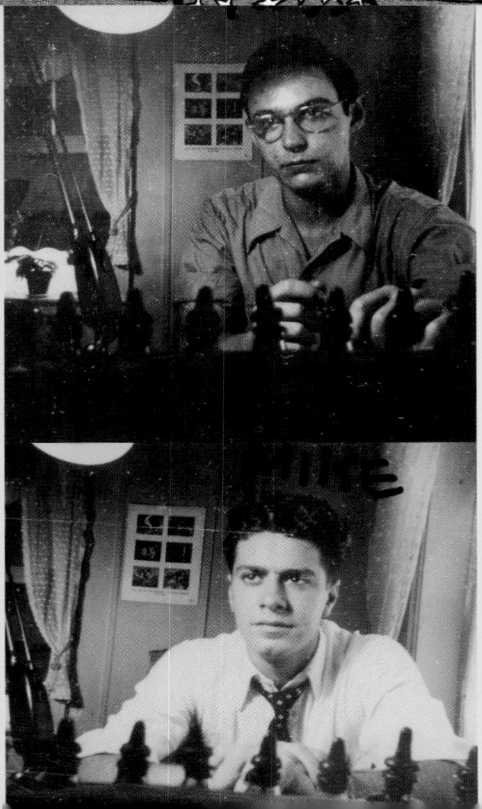

One of the most famous and prolific artistic teams in comic book history, Ross Andru and Mike Esposito's pairing was one that quickly developed into an easy working relationship. This allowed them to produce countless comic books, comic strips, and humor magazines. Andru (1927–1993) studied animation but began drawing strips. He started with "Tarzan," and went on to handle every major hero at both DC Comics and Marvel Comics. Esposito (1927–) also wanted to be an animator, but fell into comic book illustration instead, beginning his work in 1951 with Andru. In addition to their lengthy run on *Wonder Woman*, Andru and Esposito helped Kanigher develop "The War That Time Forgot," the Metal Men, and the 1970s incarnation of Rose and Thorn.

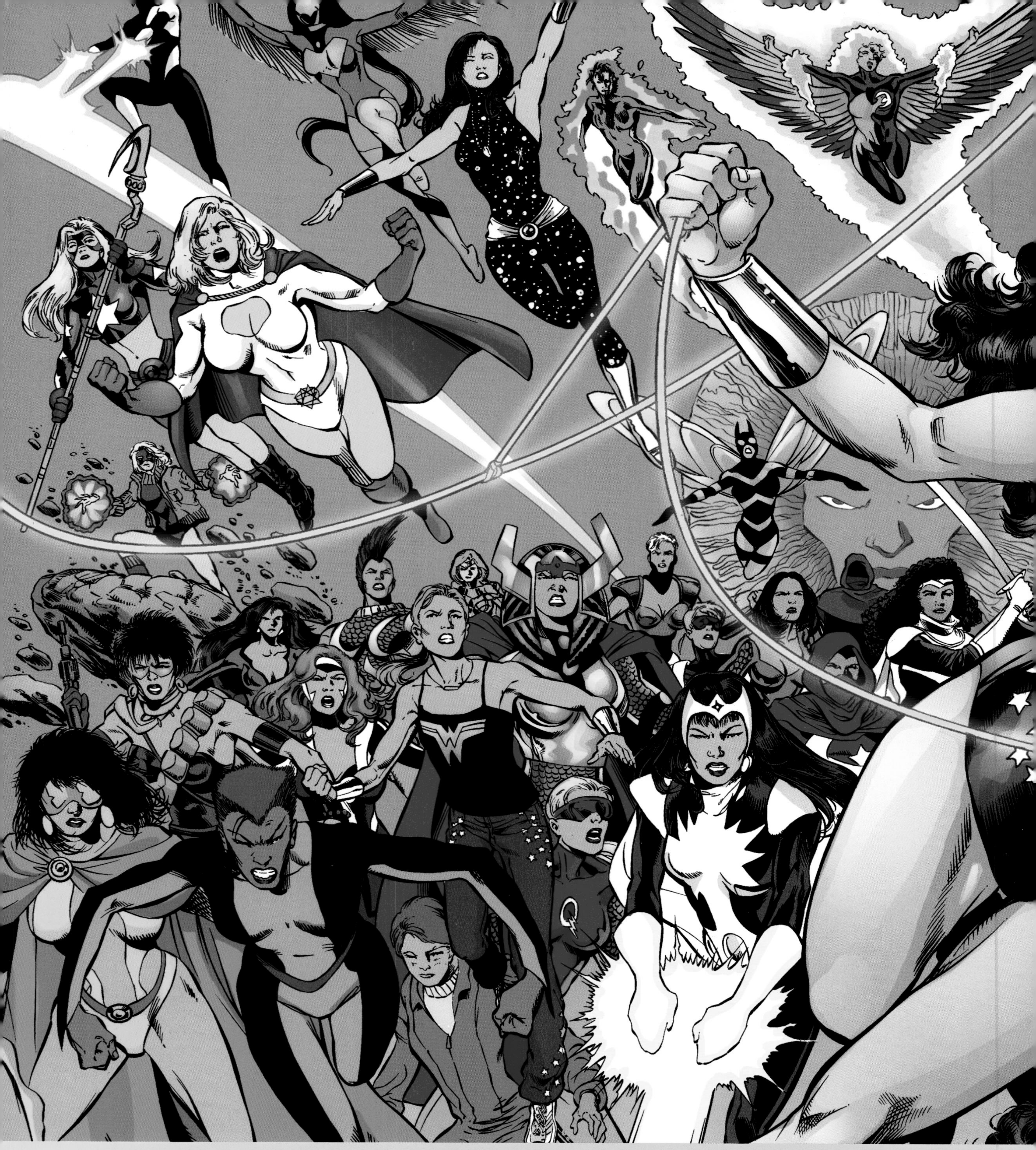

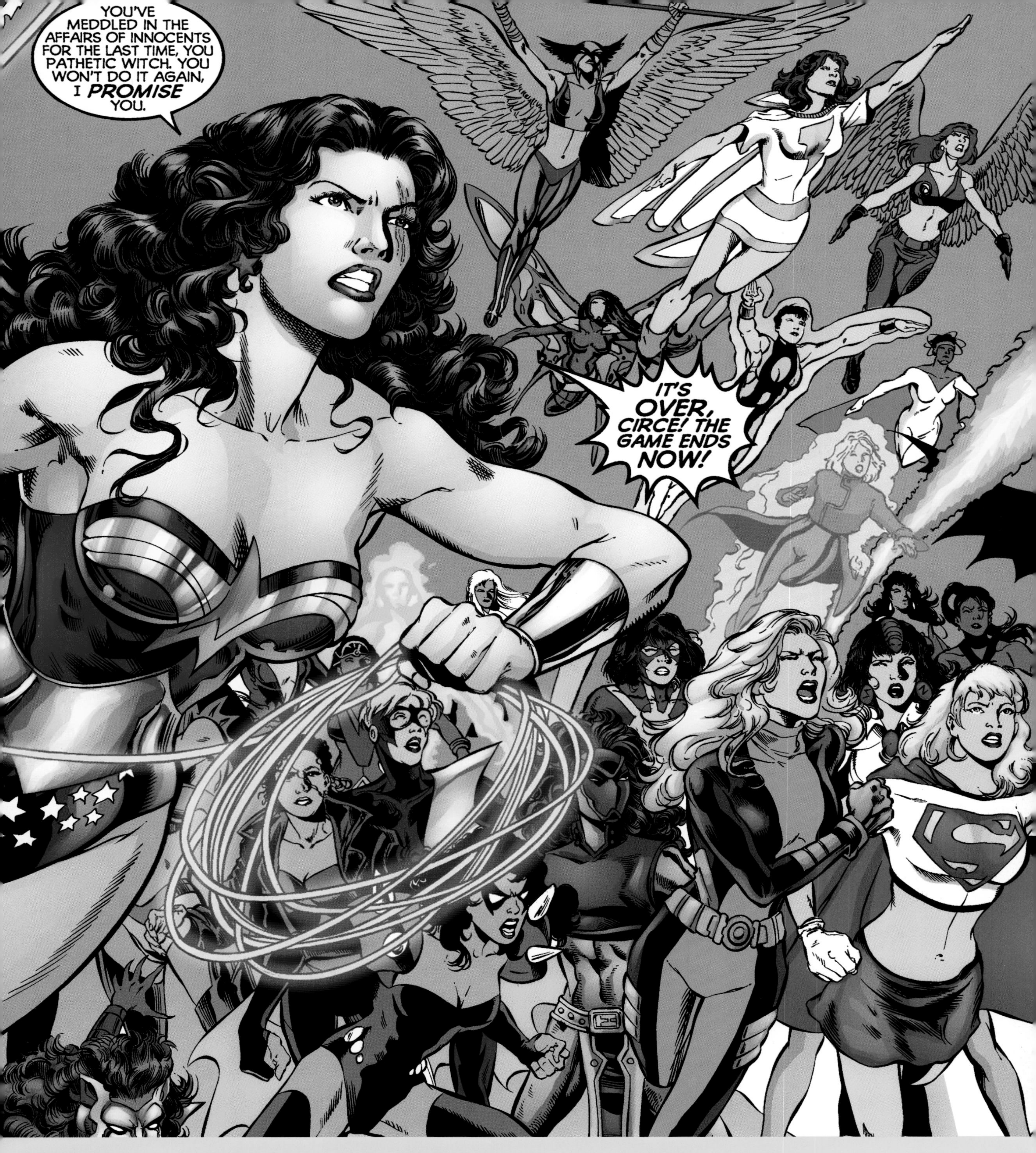
YOU'VE MEDDLED IN THE AFFAIRS OF INNOCENTS FOR THE LAST TIME, YOU PATHETIC WITCH. YOU WON'T DO IT AGAIN, I PROMISE YOU.
IT'S OVER, CIRCE! THE GAME ENDS NOW!

★ Friends and Allies

Diana's training on Paradise Island made her the best skilled crime fighter during the Golden Age of super heroes. Most others were either gifted their powers, gained them due to exposure to natural or created elements, or learned their skills on the job, but Wonder Woman was seemingly made for the role. It made perfect sense, then, when she joined the Justice Society of America after her debut in *All Star Comics*, which was home to comics' first super-team.

What made little sense, despite her unique and remarkable abilities, was that she was relegated to the stereotypical role of secretary, which only called on her skills as Diana Prince. She joined the JSA in *All Star Comics* #11, the same month her self-titled comic appeared in the summer of 1942. With Marston and Peter busy with her appearances in *Sensation Comics*, *Comics Cavalcade*, and now her own bimonthly title, they were not able to produce one chapter per month for the JSA title. After all, *All Star Comics* was designed to showcase those heroes who had not yet graduated to their own books, as had Superman, Batman, the Flash, Green Lantern, and now Wonder Woman.

It was only after Marston died that Wonder Woman finally had an active role in the Justice League, until the team and its title vanished in 1952. When a new generation of heroes banded together to form the Justice League of America, there was no question that Wonder Woman would become an equal player. For years the JLA's series was the only place readers would find the Amazon adventuring with other heroes in what was rapidly becoming a complex and shared universe of stories and adventures.

Above: When threatened, Wonder Woman and Batman can count on support from their allies. From left: The Huntress, Robin, Batman, Wonder Woman, Donna Troy, Nightwing, and Wonder Girl. Art by Phil Jimenez and Andy Lanning.

Right: Jim Lee pencils for the cover to *Infinite Crisis* #1 (December 2005). It's a good example of the trinity of heroic role models banding together against evil.

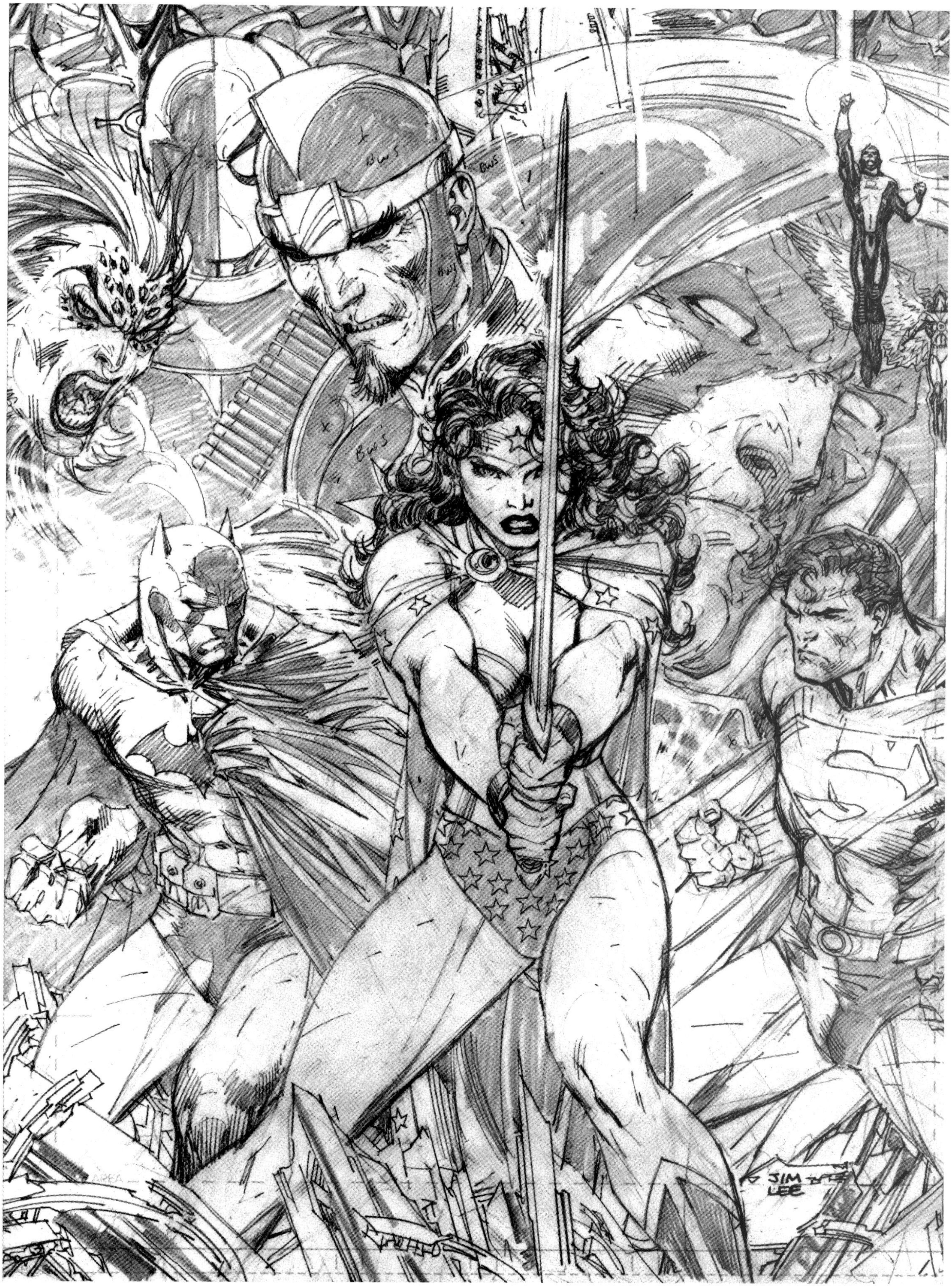
JIM LEE

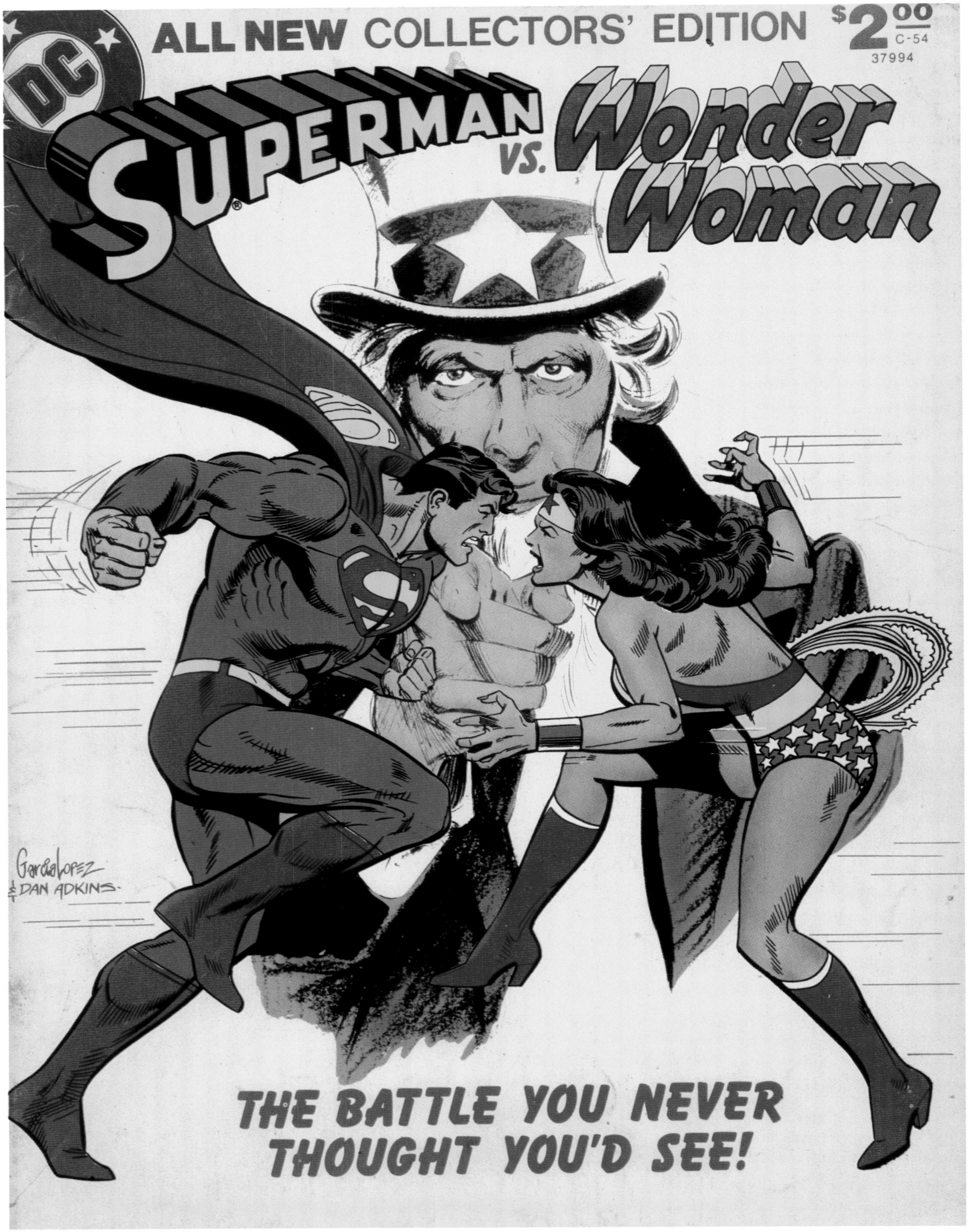
ALL NEW COLLECTORS' EDITION
$2.00
C-54
37994
DC
SUPERMAN VS. Wonder Woman
Garcia Lopez & DAN ADKINS
THE BATTLE YOU NEVER THOUGHT YOU'D SEE!

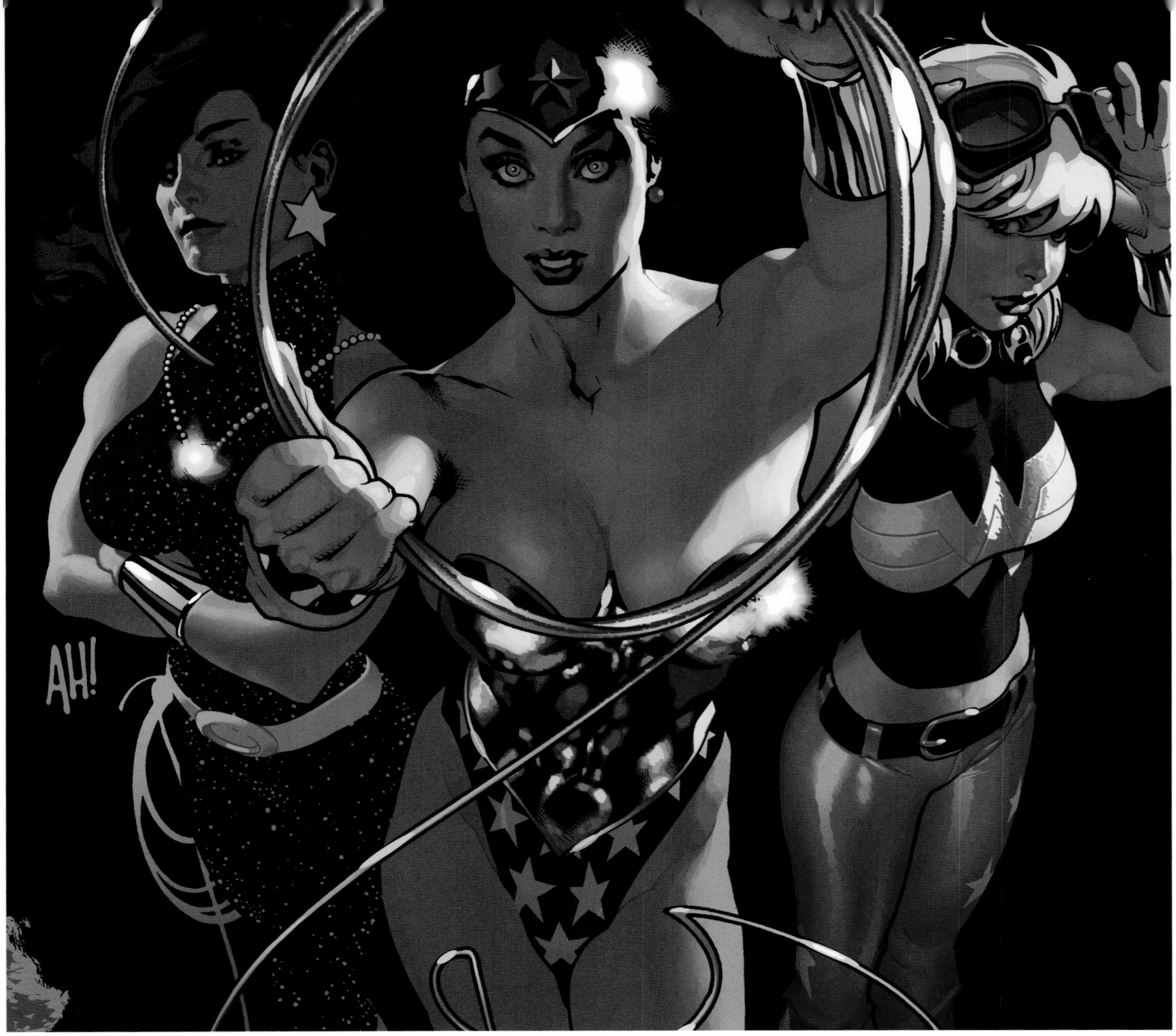
AH!

Left: In the 1970s, DC Comics released a series of tabloid-sized tales, including this World War II adventure that included the Man of Steel and Amazon Princess at odds. Cover by José Luis Garcia-Lopez and Dan Adkins.

Above: Wonder Woman, flanked by Donna Troy and Wonder Girl, in a cover detail from *Wonder Woman* [second series] #186 by artist Adam Hughes.

Interestingly, in the last decade or so, she has been increasingly seen as part of the DC Comics trinity, along with Superman and Batman. Their unique dynamic was explored in Matt Wagner's 2003 miniseries *Batman/Superman/Wonder Woman: Trinity*. Every other hero looked to these three for leadership and guidance. When Earth's heroes were targeted by the insane Maxwell Lord, the trinity found themselves at odds, and the tight bonds they had formed began to fray. In the aftermath of the event known as the Infinite Crisis, the trinity spent a year apart before the time seemed right to gather once more and rebuild their heroic bond, beginning with the Justice League.

The theme became the focal point of a yearlong weekly comic called *Trinity*, which lasted from 2008–09. The complex story revealed a "dark trinity" attempt to replace the heroic trio. When the heroes were removed from Earth's reality, a dire new world was formed. Eventually the trinity reappears—this time as gods without any humanity—and had to be convinced to aid Earth's inhabitants. It took the combined efforts of their loved ones to bring the trinity back to the correct reality—but only by forsaking their godhood. The Amazon Princess was depicted as the messenger of hope, love, and inspiration, while the Dark Knight was the epitome of human accomplishment and the Man of Steel was the supreme fighter.

Initially, there was no Wonder Girl in *Wonder Woman*, although a few Marston tales flashed back to his heroine's childhood. However, in 1959, not long before Superman editor Mort Weisinger began devising what were called "Imaginary Stories" filled with "what if" possibilities, Kanigher turned back the clock in his inimitable way and explored

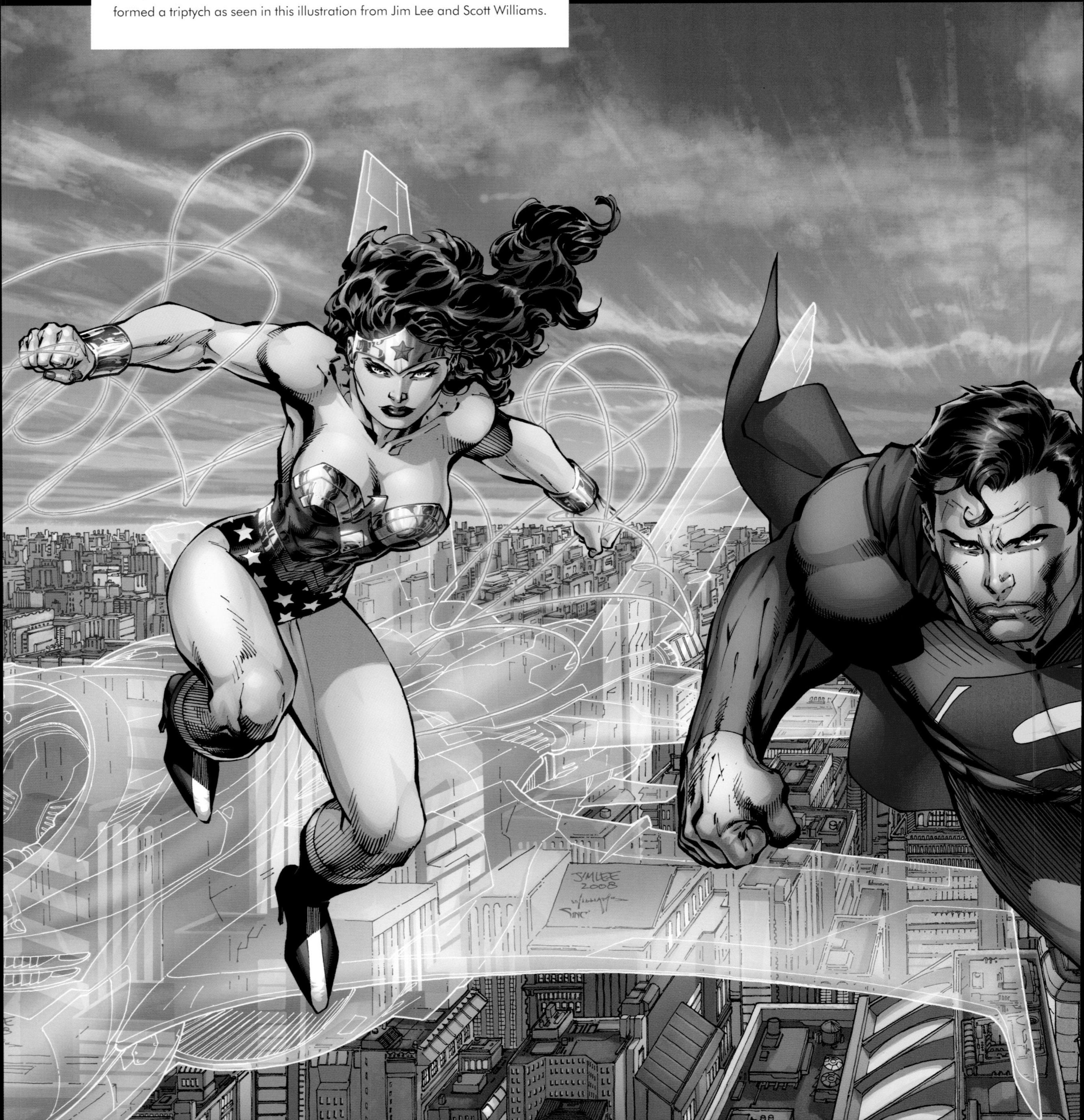
JIMLEE
2008

A fifty-two-week long series, *Trinity* explored the relationships between Wonder Woman, Superman, and Batman that placed them in a harrowing reality wherein the heroes did not exist. The covers for every three issues formed a triptych as seen in this illustration from Jim Lee and Scott Williams.

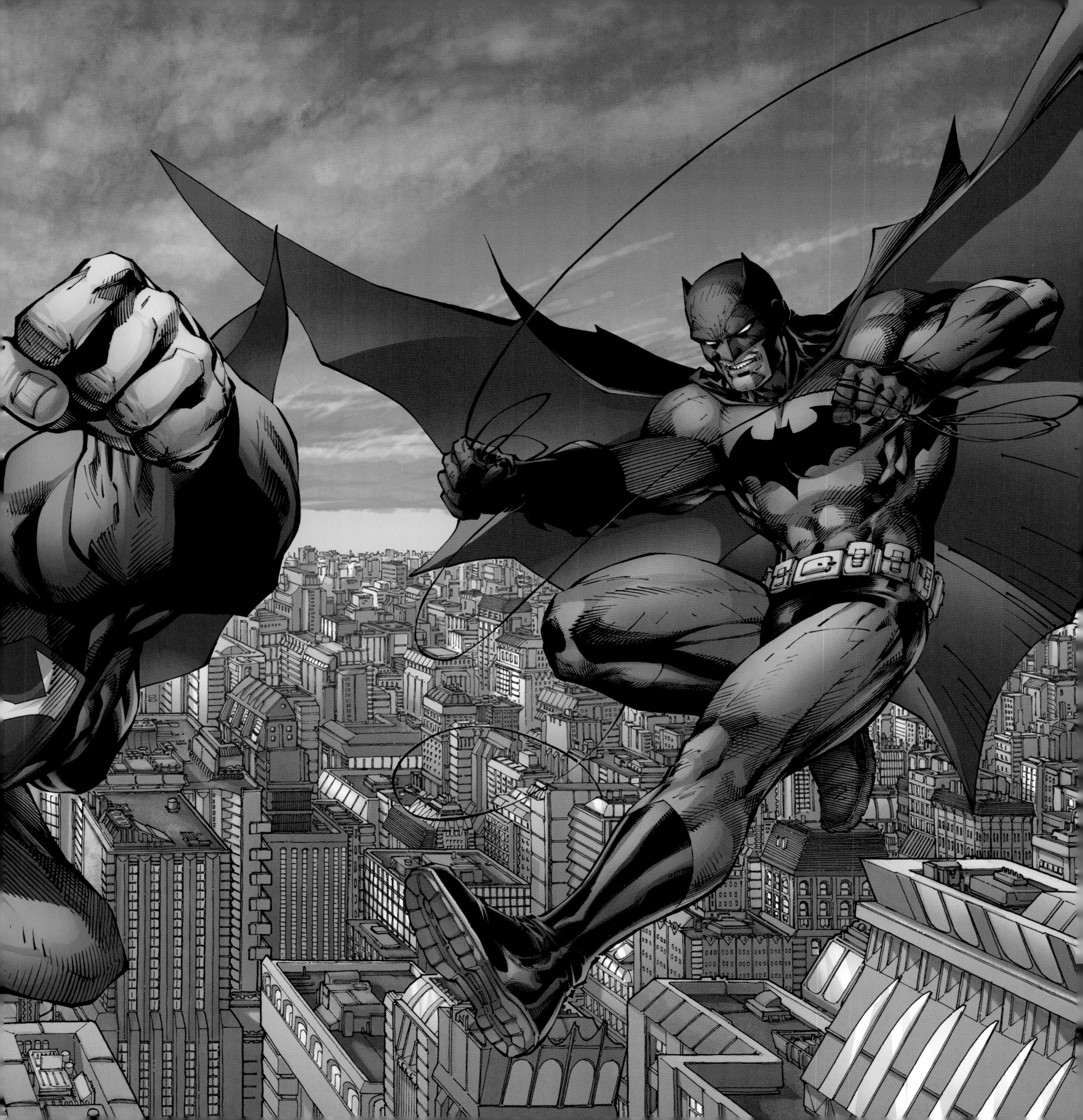

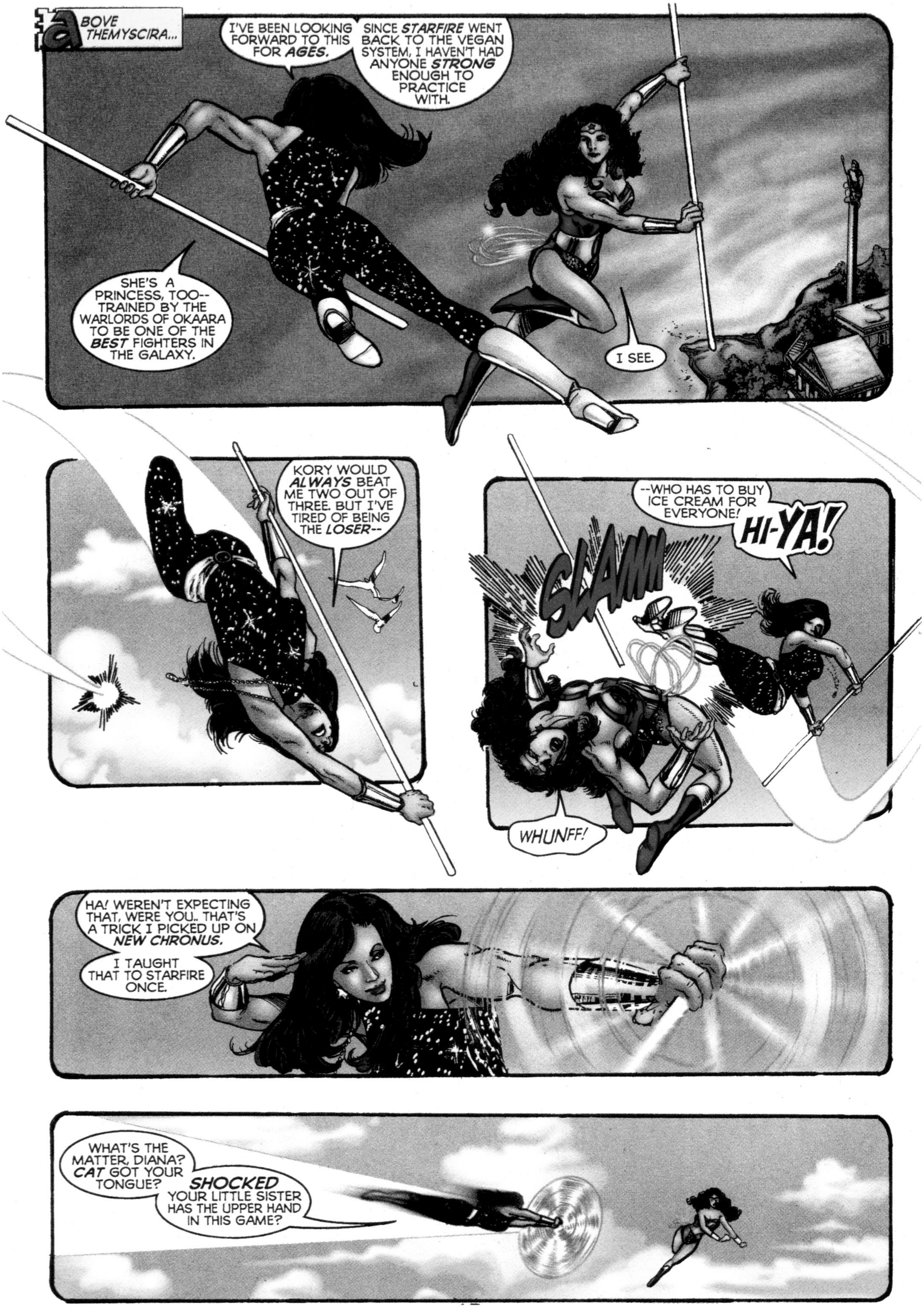
ABOVE THEMYSCIRA...
I'VE BEEN LOOKING FORWARD TO THIS FOR AGES.
SINCE STARFIRE WENT BACK TO THE VEGAN SYSTEM, I HAVEN'T HAD ANYONE STRONG ENOUGH TO PRACTICE WITH.
SHE'S A PRINCESS, TOO-- TRAINED BY THE WARLORDS OF OKAARA TO BE ONE OF THE BEST FIGHTERS IN THE GALAXY.
I SEE.
KORY WOULD ALWAYS BEAT ME TWO OUT OF THREE. BUT I'VE TIRED OF BEING THE LOSER--
--WHO HAS TO BUY ICE CREAM FOR EVERYONE!
HI-YA!
SLAMM
WHUNFF!
HA! WEREN'T EXPECTING THAT, WERE YOU.. THAT'S A TRICK I PICKED UP ON NEW CHRONUS.
I TAUGHT THAT TO STARFIRE ONCE.
WHAT'S THE MATTER, DIANA? CAT GOT YOUR TONGUE?
SHOCKED YOUR LITTLE SISTER HAS THE UPPER HAND IN THIS GAME?

Above: Despite their sisterly relationship, Wonder Woman and Donna Troy pull no punches while sparring to stay sharp. Art by Phil Jimenez.

Right: Chris Moeller's *JLA: A League of One* saw Wonder Woman subdue her fellow teammates in order to take on this dragon by herself.

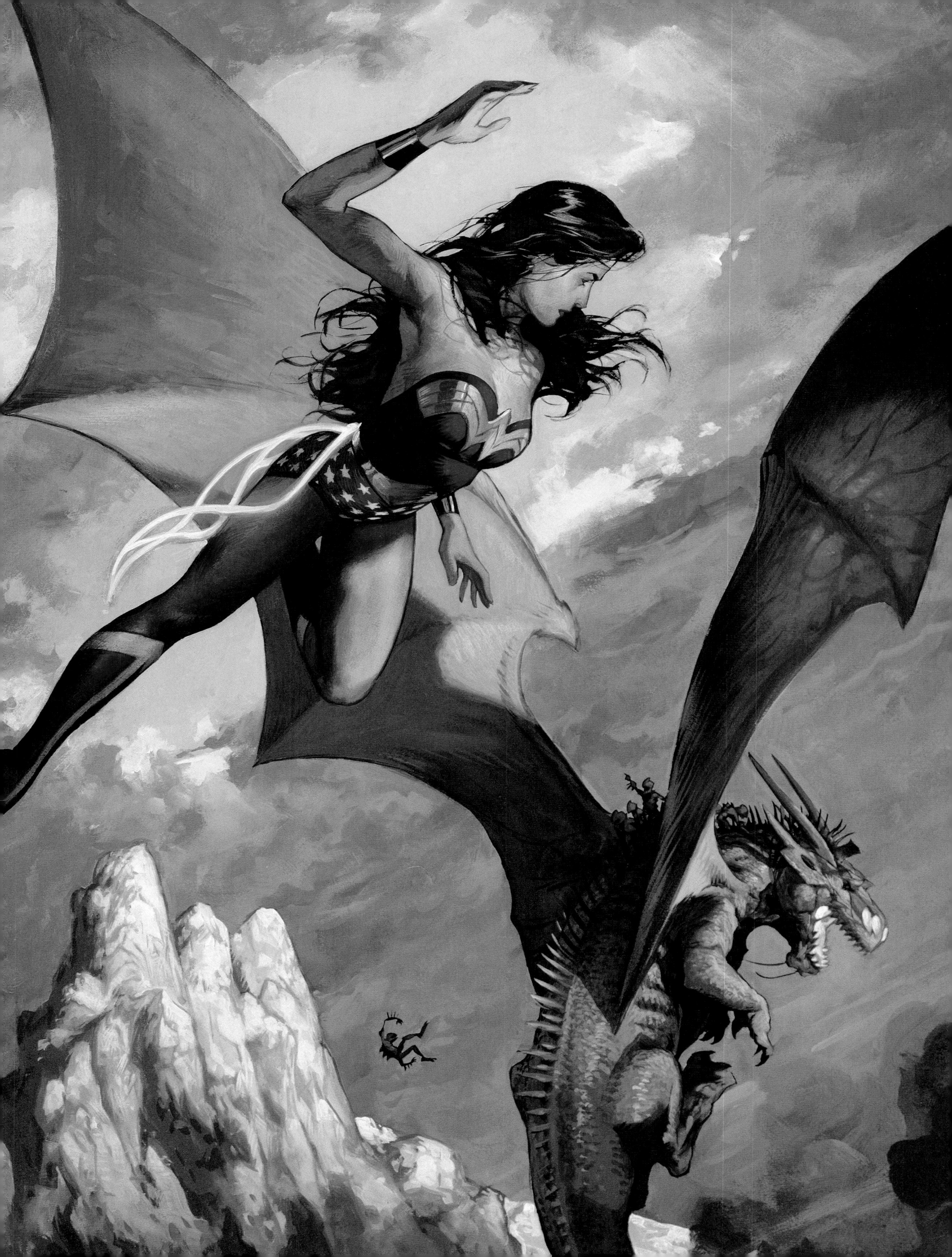

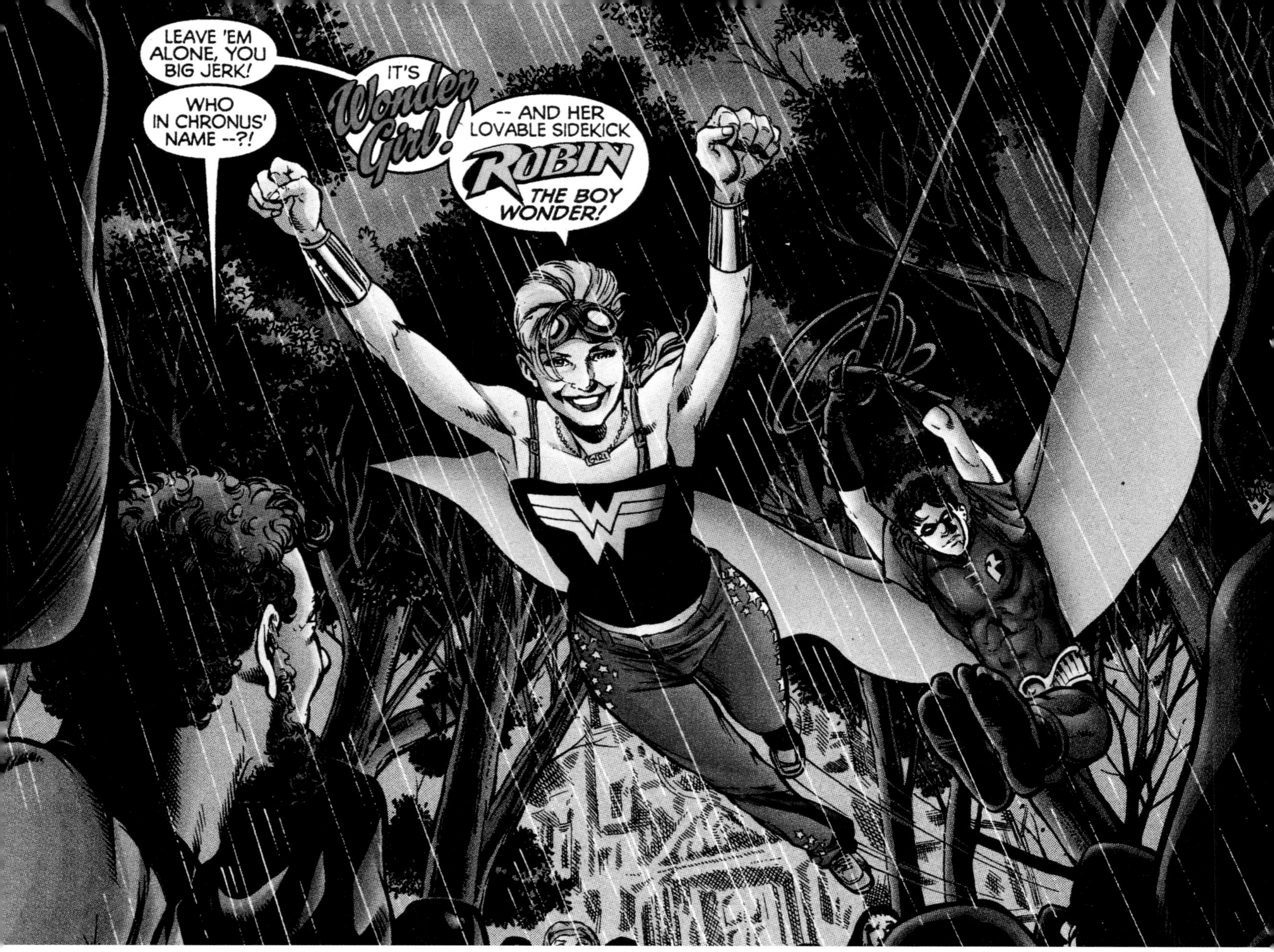
LEAVE 'EM ALONE, YOU BIG JERK!
WHO IN CHRONUS' NAME --?!
IT'S Wonder Girl!
-- AND HER LOVABLE SIDEKICK ROBIN THE BOY WONDER!

the story of Diana as a youngster. When these tales proved popular, he went even further back and told tales of a child who he called Wonder Tot. Fatefully, he began using all three incarnations of the heroine together in a series of stories called *Impossible Tales*.

However, when a different editorial office began casting around for a new team called the Teen Titans, writer Bob Haney mistakenly thought Wonder Girl was a separate character from Wonder Woman and used her as part of the team when it debuted in 1965. Readers were left confused by this until DC Comics newcomer editor and writer Marv Wolfman sought to give this new character a background and a name: Donna Troy. Since that fateful comic, *Teen Titans* #22 (August 1969), poor Donna has seen her origin twisted time and again as writers attempted to retrofit her backstory to accommodate whatever Wonder Woman's mythos was at the time. Diana was one of the more popular DC Comics heroines, and had gone by numerous names and lives. She even served as Wonder Woman for a year while Diana started a new chapter in her life. Through this all, Diana and Donna remained close sisters-in-arms.

Once Donna stopped using the name Wonder Girl, writer/artist John Byrne revived it for the supporting character Cassie Sandsmark, a friend of Diana's who was first seen in *Wonder Woman* #105 (February 1996). Originally depicted as an ordinary teen, Byrne made sure Cassie had matured and gone blonde, as befits the illegitimate daughter of the god Zeus. She led a newer incarnation of the Teen Titans, enjoyed a passionate romance with Superboy, and came to the Amazon's aid on numerous occasions.

Above: Cassie Sandsmark grew from shy and awkward teen into the self-assured heroine Wonder Girl, eventually succeeding Robin the Teen Wonder as leader of the Teen Titans. Art by Phil Jimenez and Andy Lanning.

Right: Cassie had no idea at first that she was actual a demigod, daughter to Zeus. In time, however, she pieced together enough information to confront the head of the Olympic Pantheon. Art by Gabriel Pearce, Ray Snyder and Marlo Alquiza.

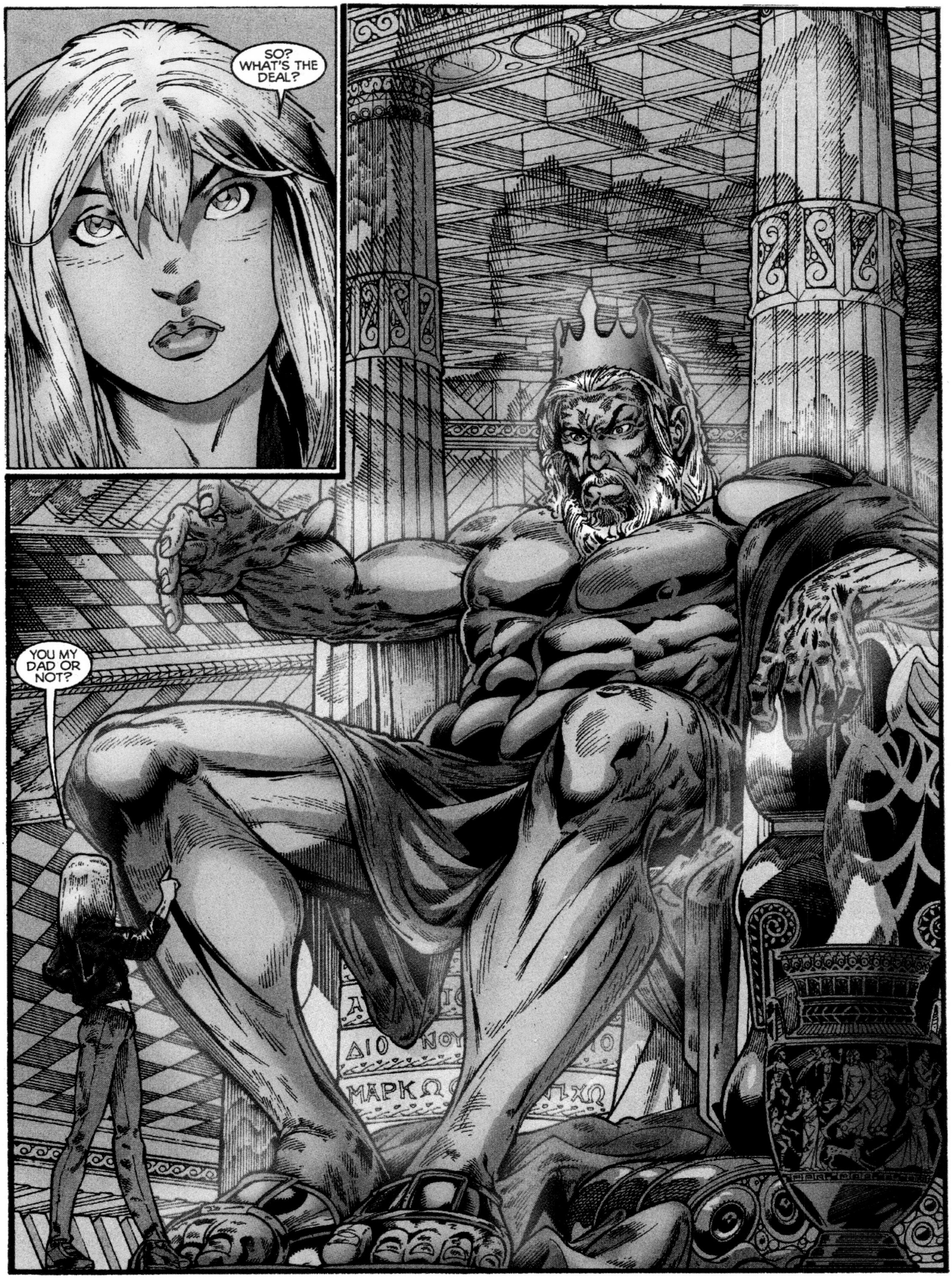
SO? WHAT'S THE DEAL?
YOU MY DAD OR NOT?
ΔΙΟ ΝΟΥ
ΜΑΡΚΩ

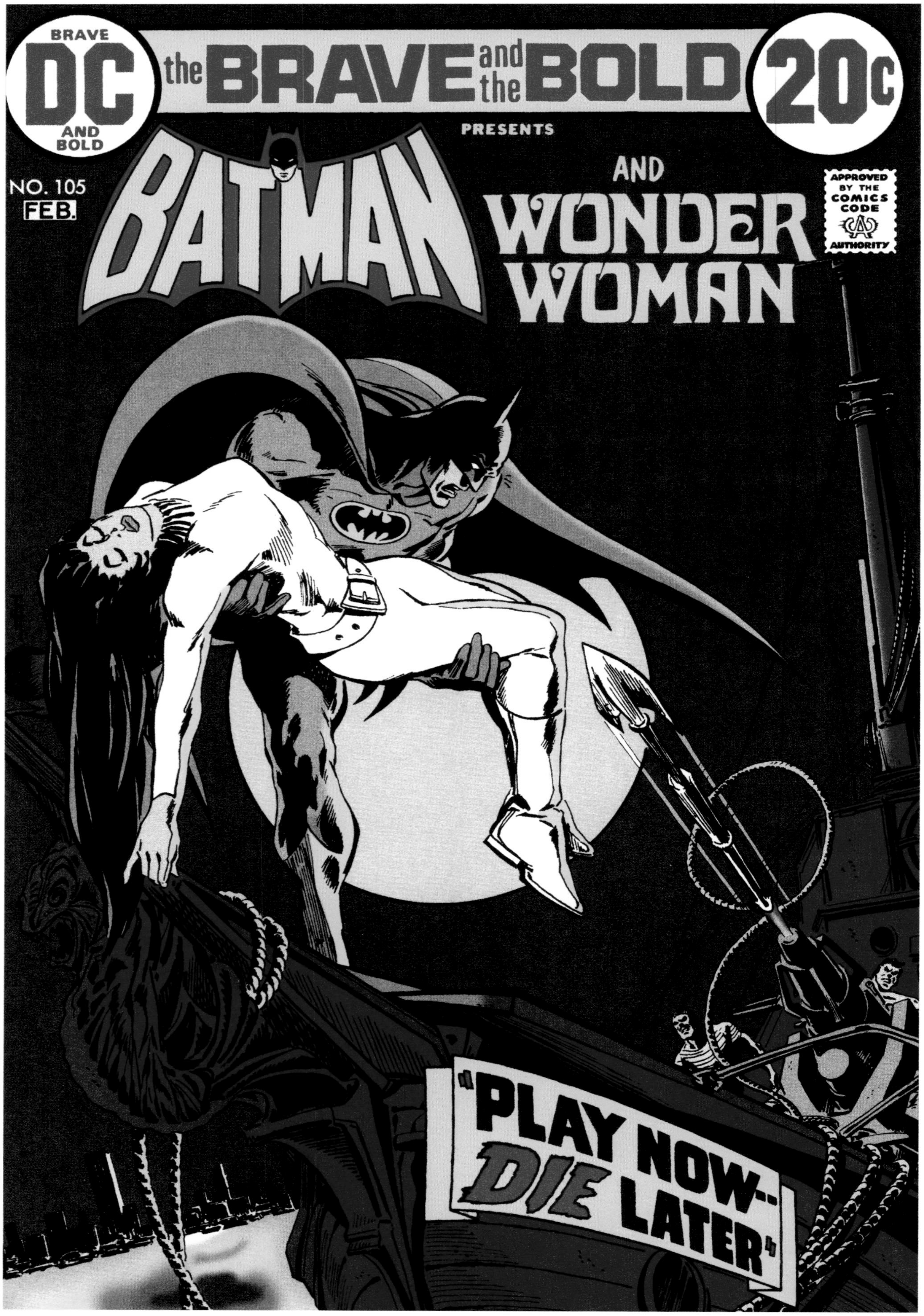
BRAVE
DC
AND
BOLD
the BRAVE and the BOLD
20c
PRESENTS
NO. 105
FEB.
BATMAN
AND
WONDER WOMAN
APPROVED BY THE COMICS CODE AUTHORITY
"PLAY NOW--
DIE LATER"

Above: Batman and Wonder Woman teamed up many times over the years but Wonder Woman as a damsel in distress was a very rare occurrence.

Right: In an alternate reality where Superman and Batman were villians bent on conquering the world, Wonder Woman learns just how tough it is to stop them. Art by Carlos Pacheco and Jesús Merino.

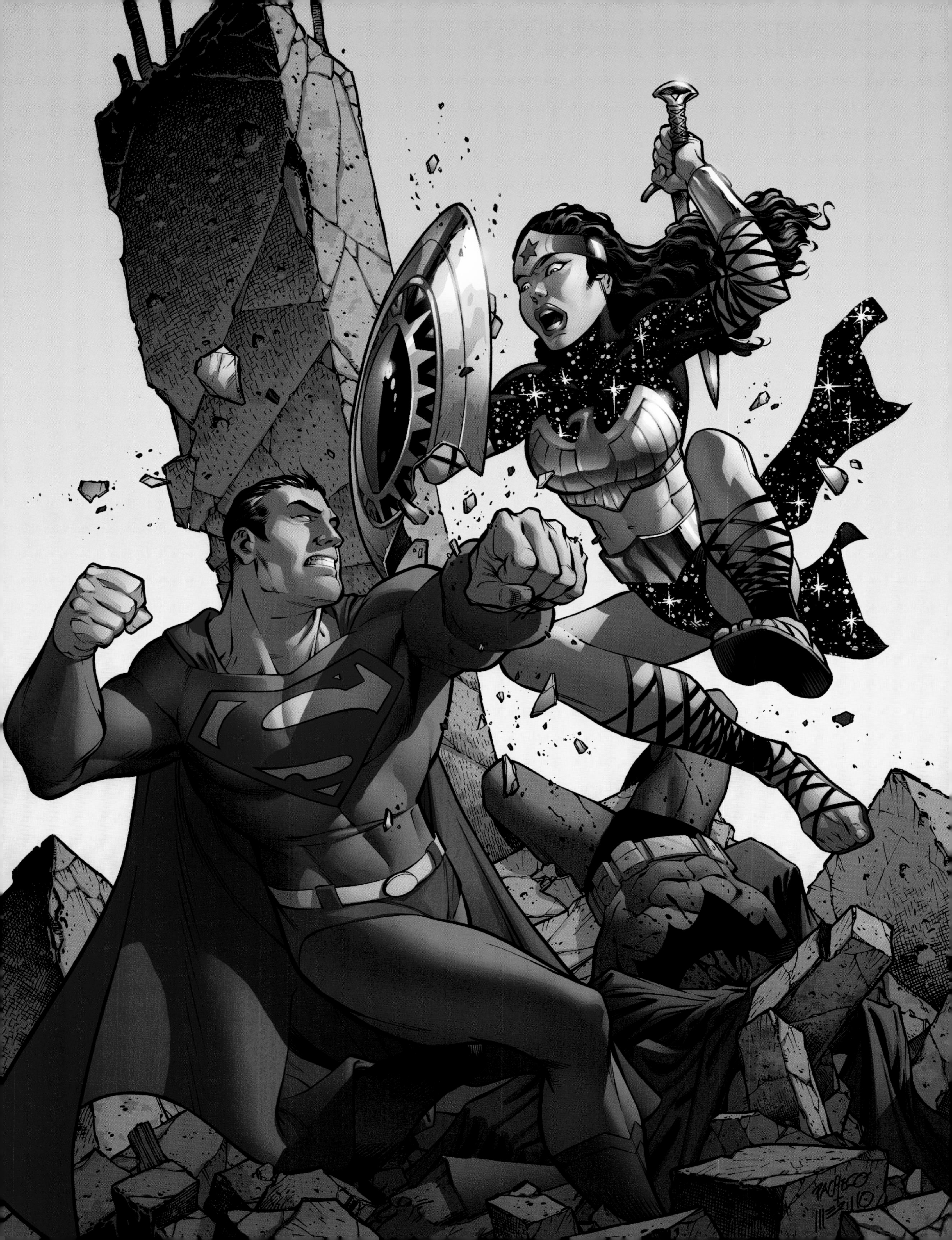

Wonder Woman and Donna Troy sketches by artists including Dustin Nguyen and Adam Hushes for various DC Direct action figures, busts, and sculptures.

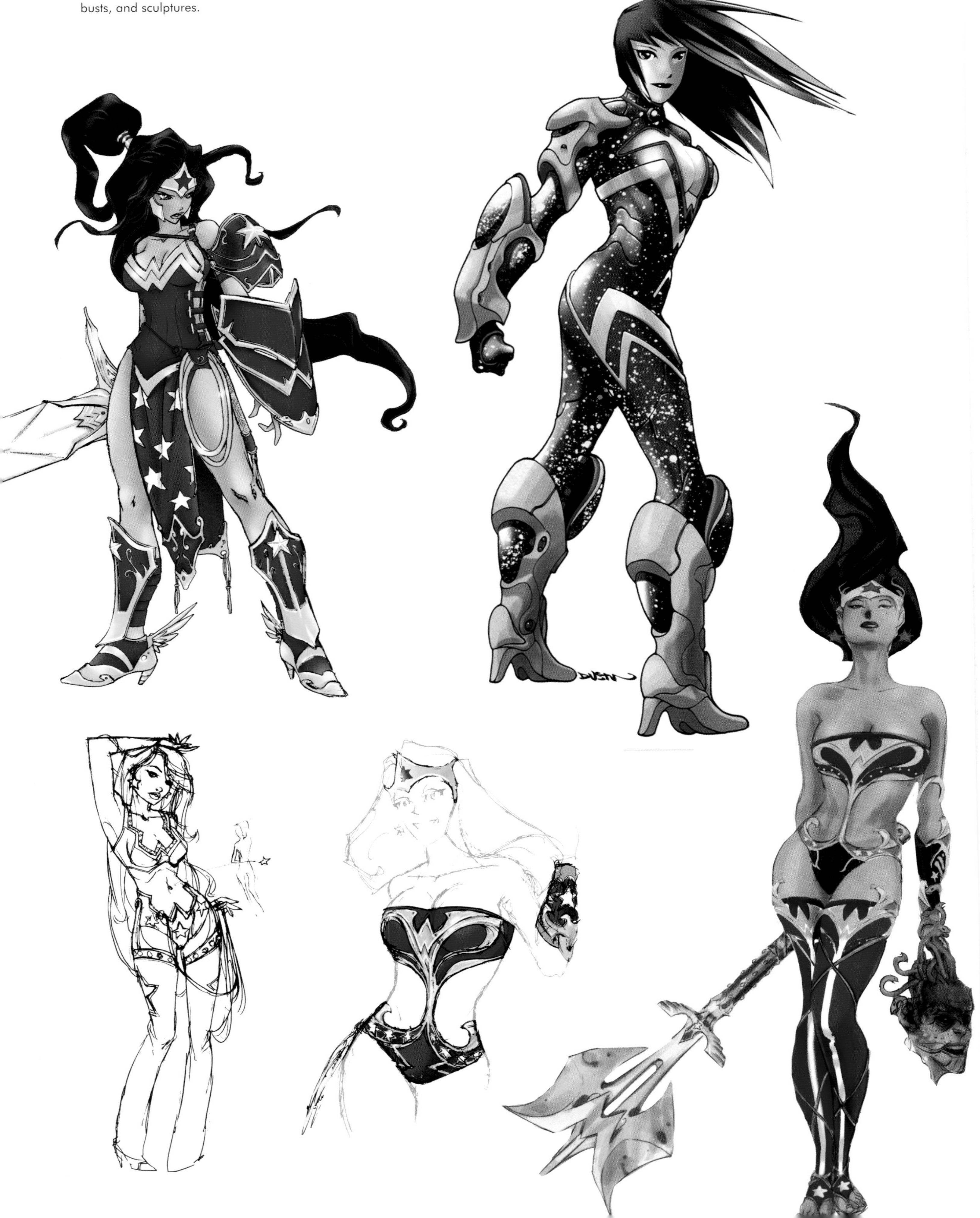

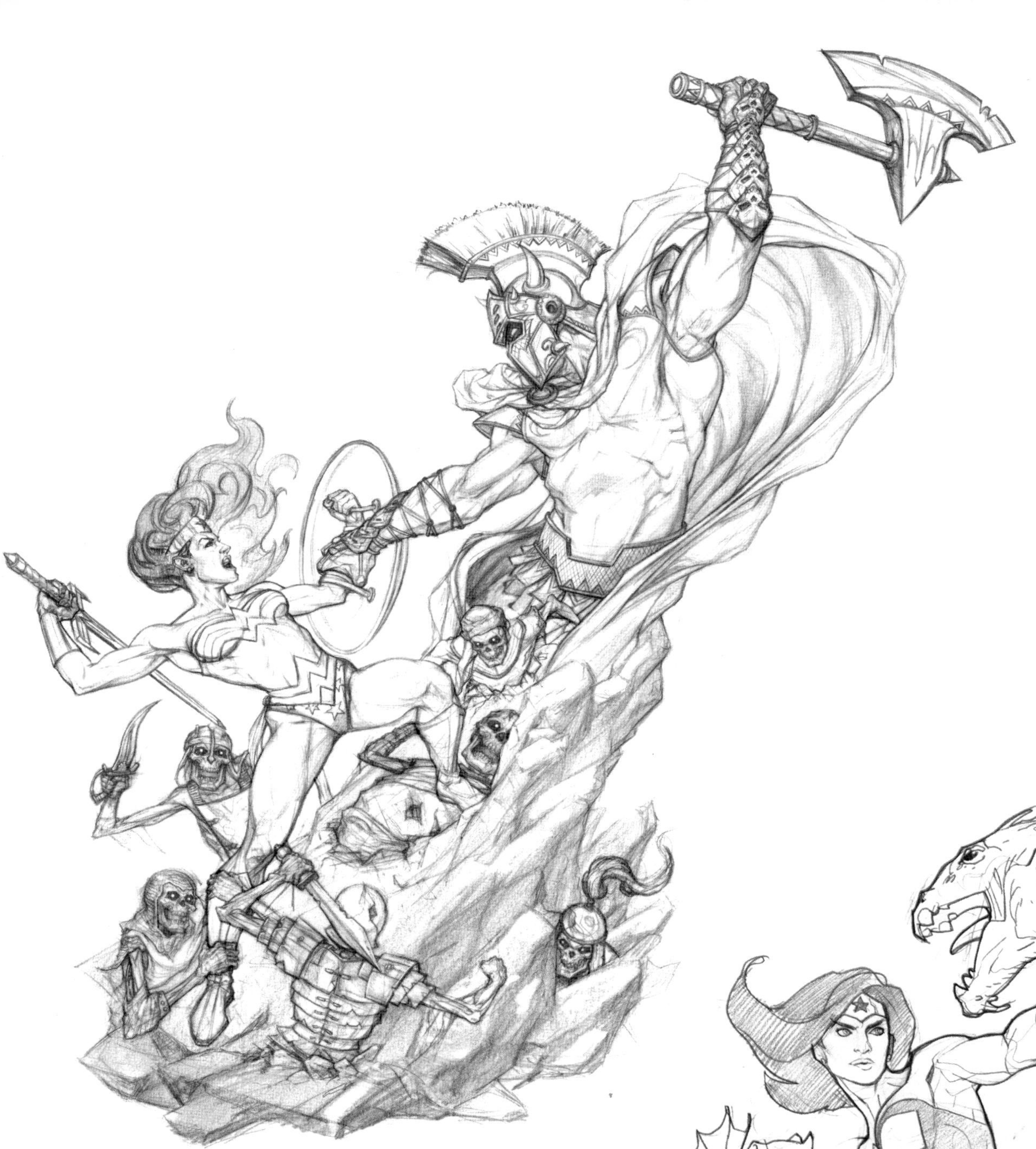

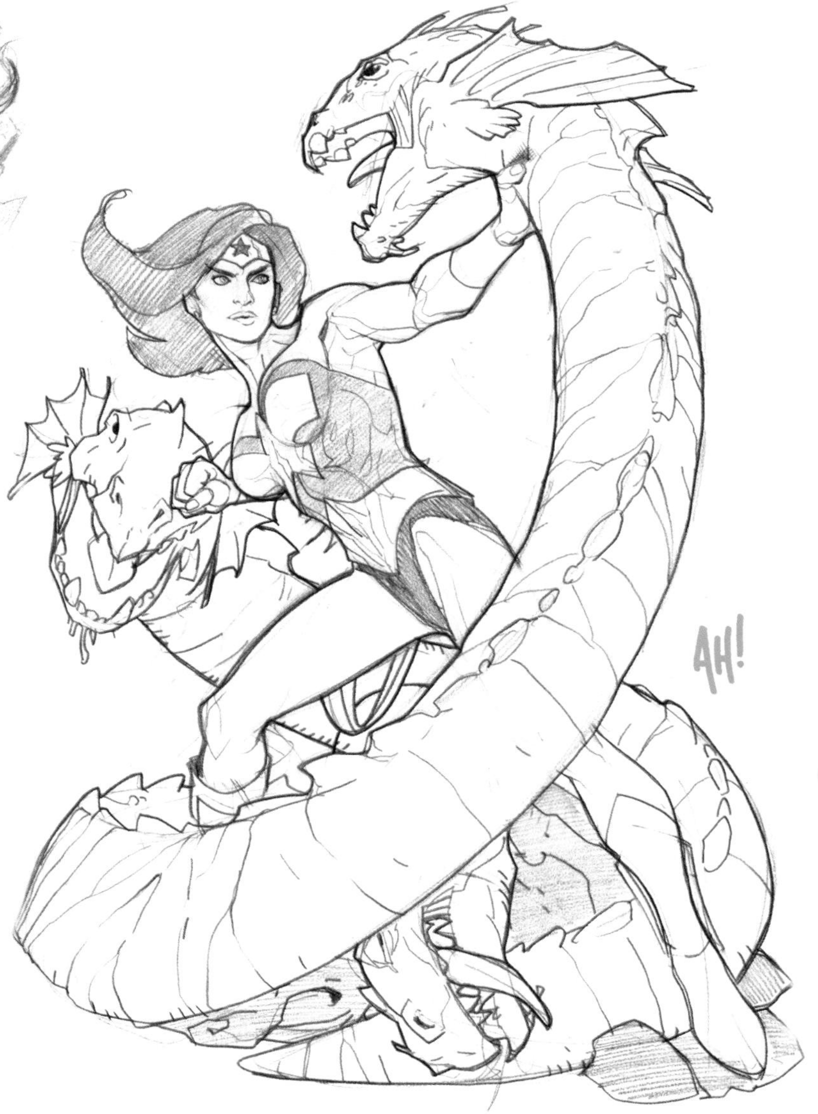
AH!

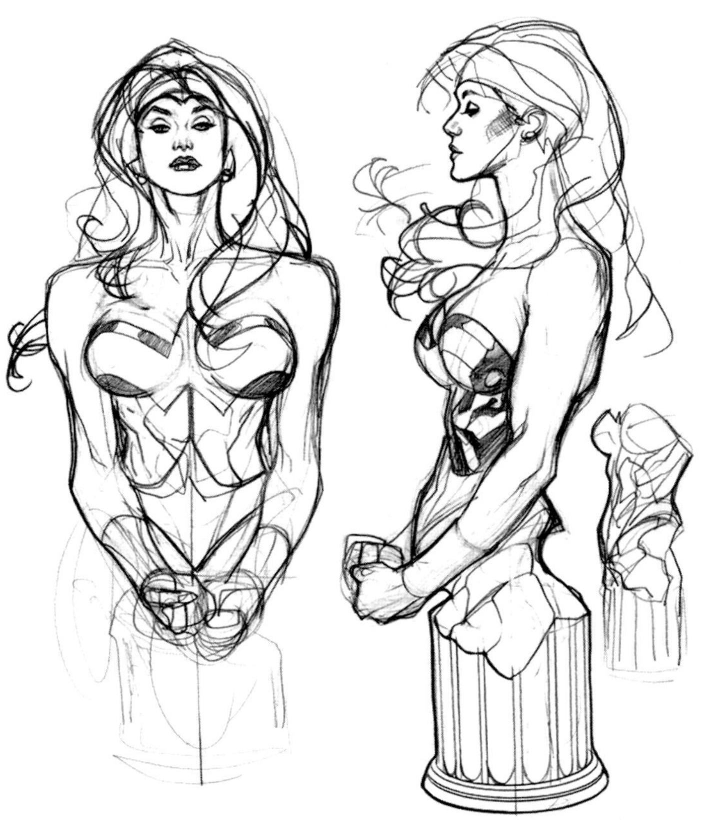

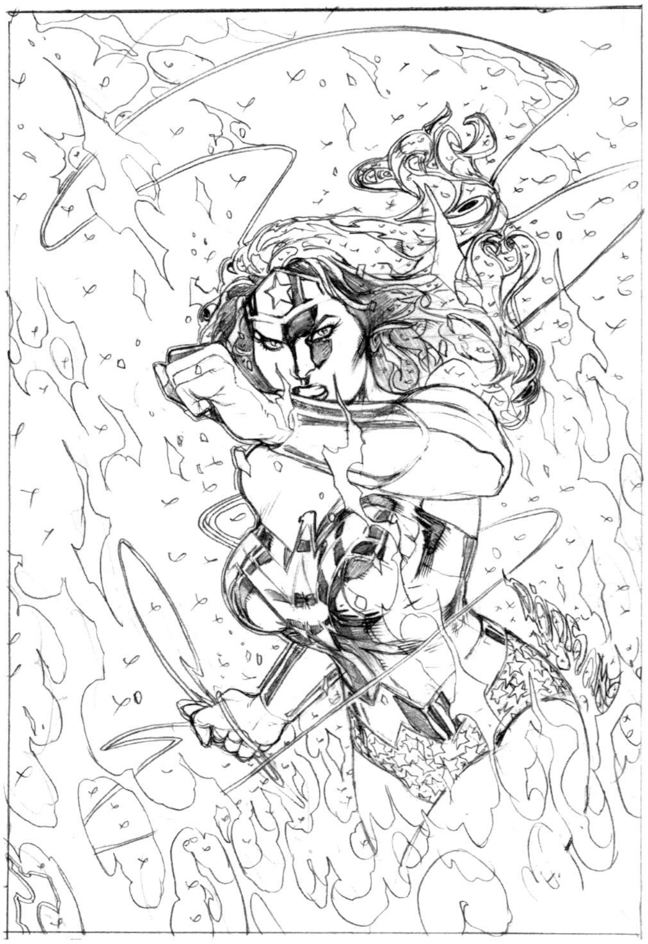

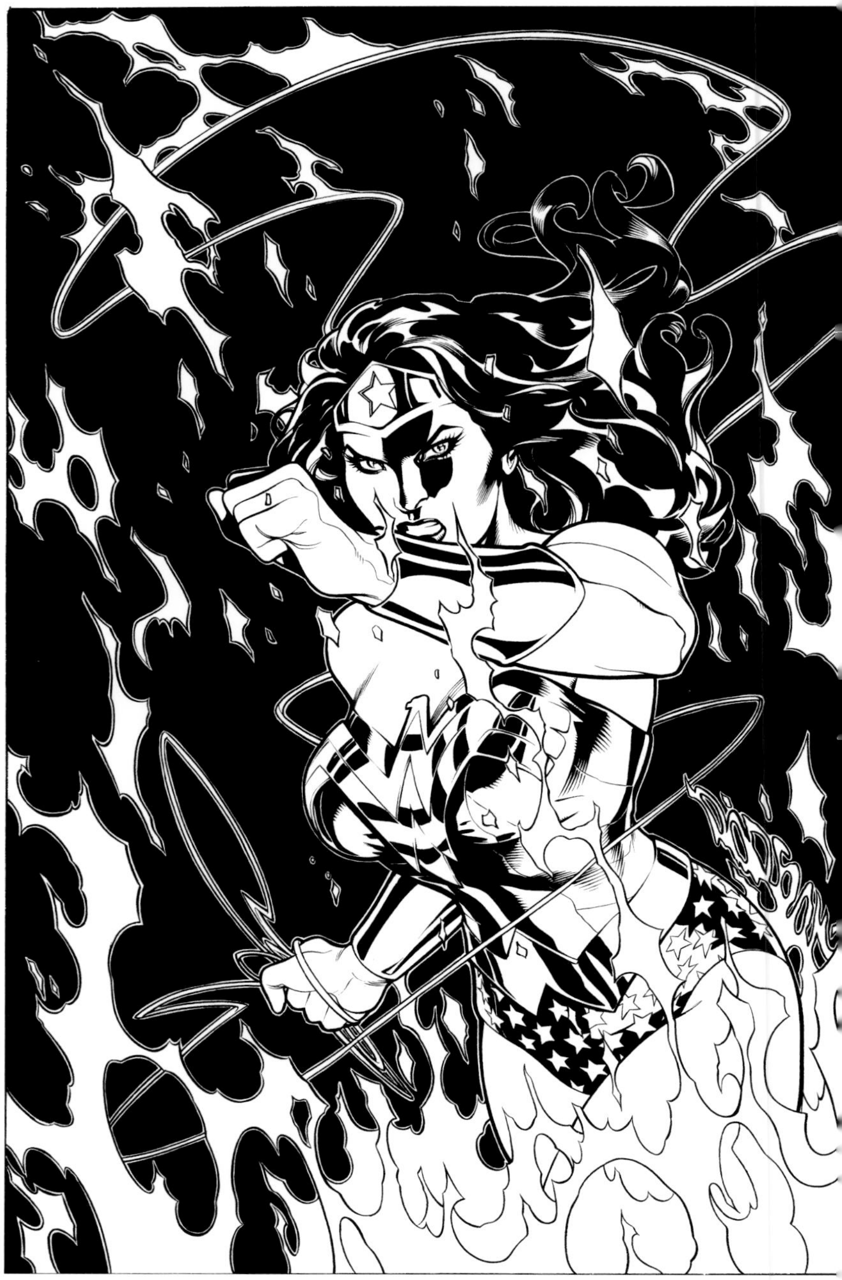

This page: The evolution of a cover: sketch (right); color rough (below right); pencils (above left). Art by Terry and Rachel Dodson.

Far right: Another Dodson and Dodson cover, this time for *Wonder Woman* [third series] #14 (January 2008), for writer Gail Simone's first issue. The Amazon Princess battles an army of intelligent gorilla commandos.

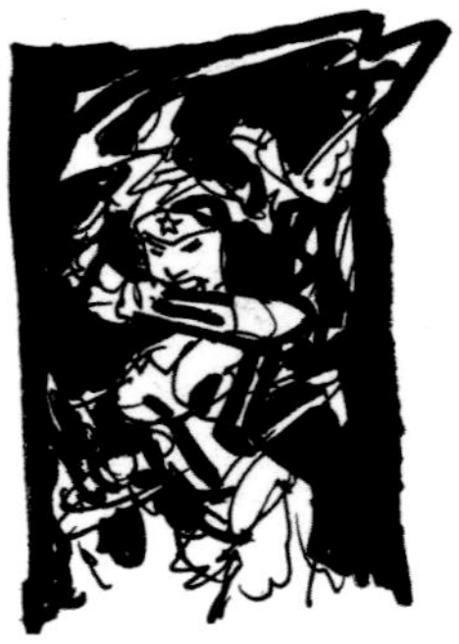

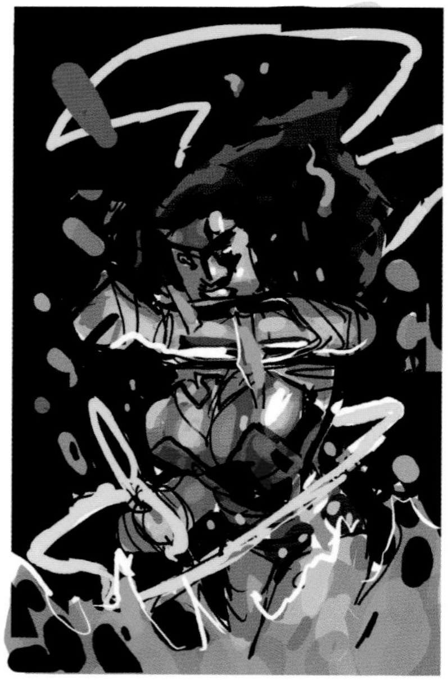

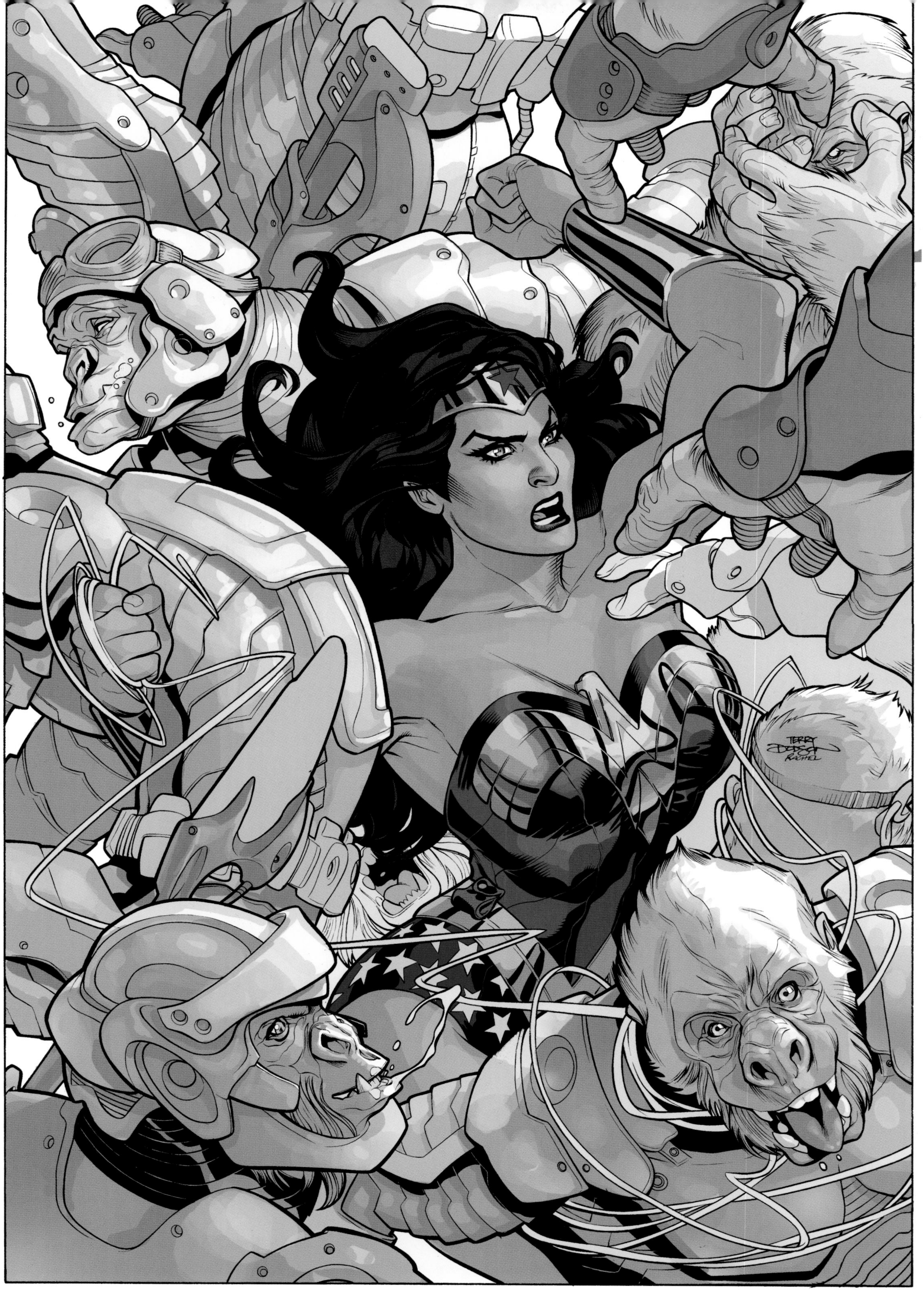
TERRY
DODSON
RACHEL

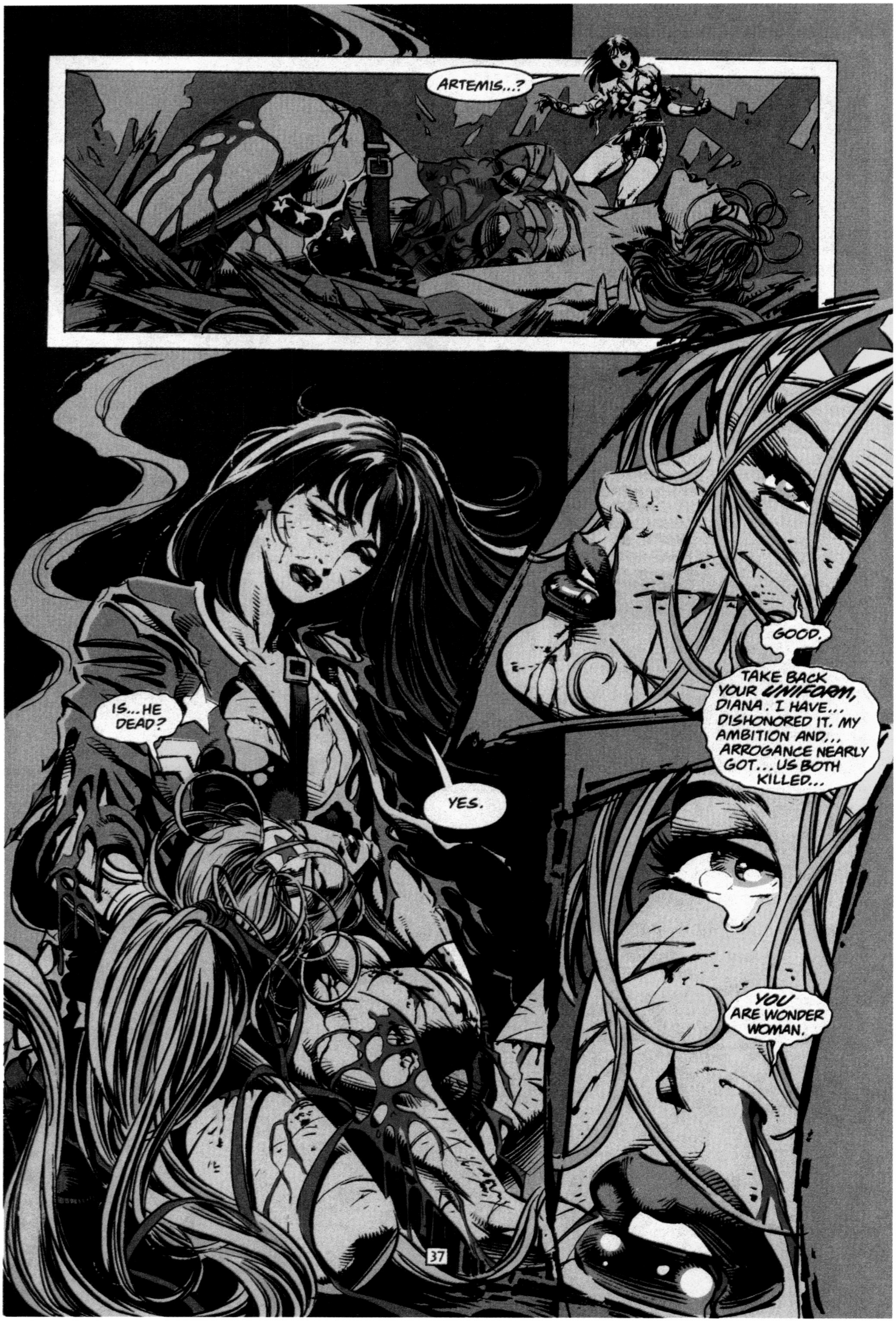
ARTEMIS...?
IS...HE DEAD?
YES.
GOOD.
TAKE BACK YOUR UNIFORM, DIANA. I HAVE... DISHONORED IT. MY AMBITION AND... ARROGANCE NEARLY GOT... US BOTH KILLED...
YOU ARE WONDER WOMAN.
37

Above and right: Artemis won the right to be Wonder Woman but learned that being a hero meant confronting dangerous and deadly opponents. At the story's end, she sacrificed her life to save others and returned the mantle of Wonder Woman to Diana in this sorrowful scene from writer William Messner-Loebs and artist Mike Deodato, Jr.

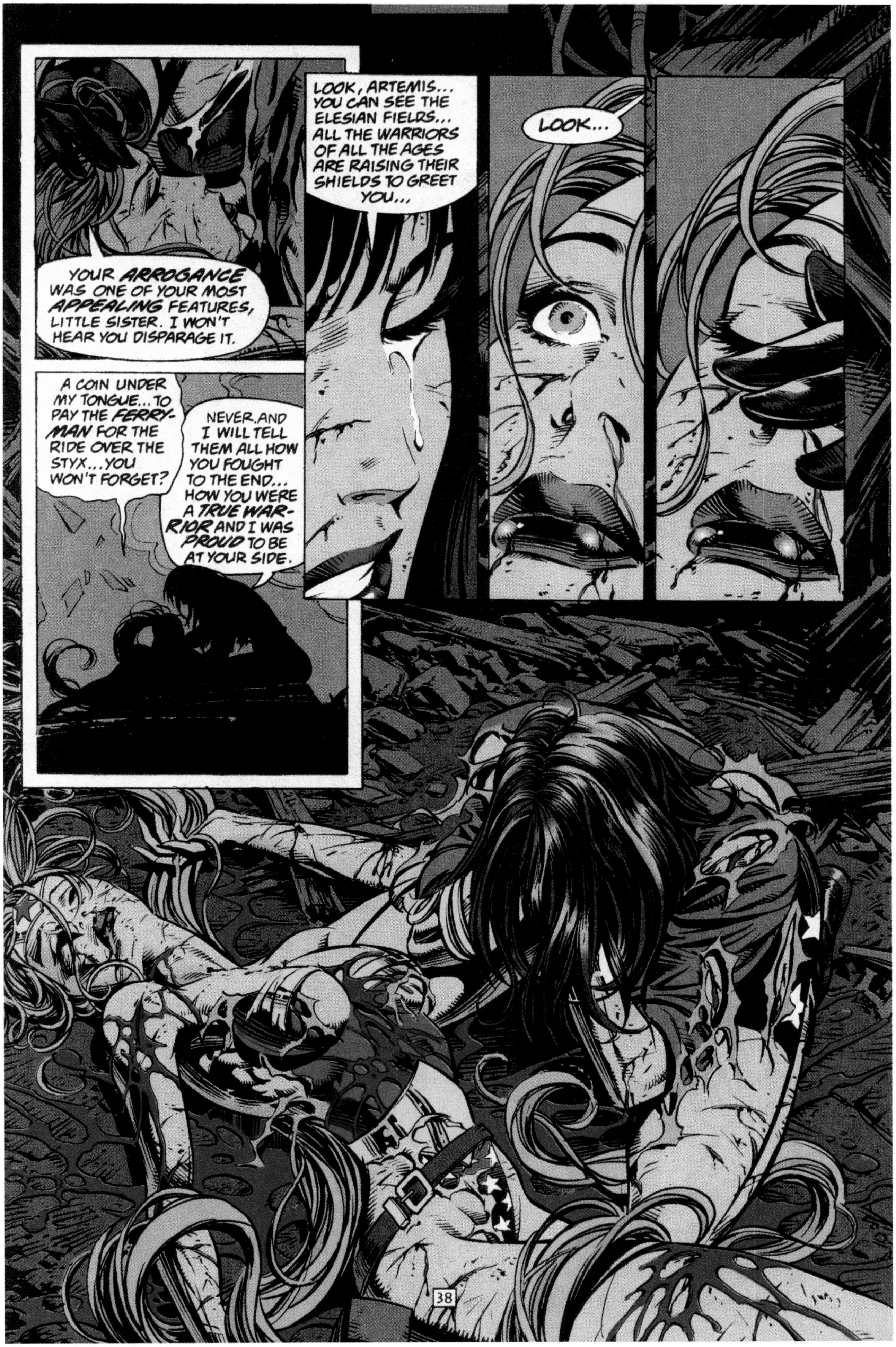
YOUR ARROGANCE WAS ONE OF YOUR MOST APPEALING FEATURES, LITTLE SISTER. I WON'T HEAR YOU DISPARAGE IT.
A COIN UNDER MY TONGUE... TO PAY THE FERRY-MAN FOR THE RIDE OVER THE STYX... YOU WON'T FORGET?
NEVER. AND I WILL TELL THEM ALL HOW YOU FOUGHT TO THE END... HOW YOU WERE A TRUE WAR-RIOR AND I WAS PROUD TO BE AT YOUR SIDE.
LOOK, ARTEMIS... YOU CAN SEE THE ELESIAN FIELDS... ALL THE WARRIORS OF ALL THE AGES ARE RAISING THEIR SHIELDS TO GREET YOU...
LOOK...
38

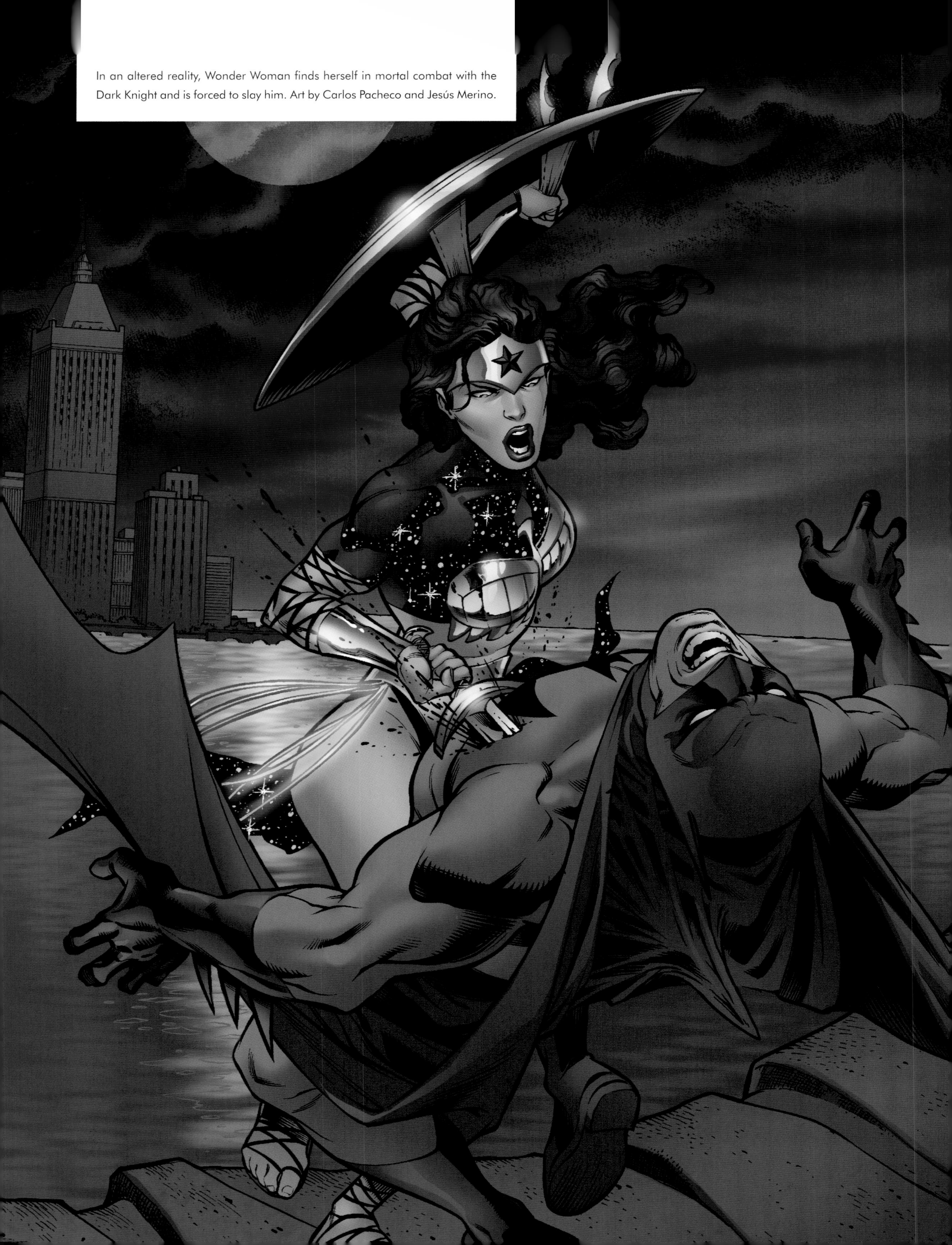

In an altered reality, Wonder Woman finds herself in mortal combat with the Dark Knight and is forced to slay him. Art by Carlos Pacheco and Jesús Merino.

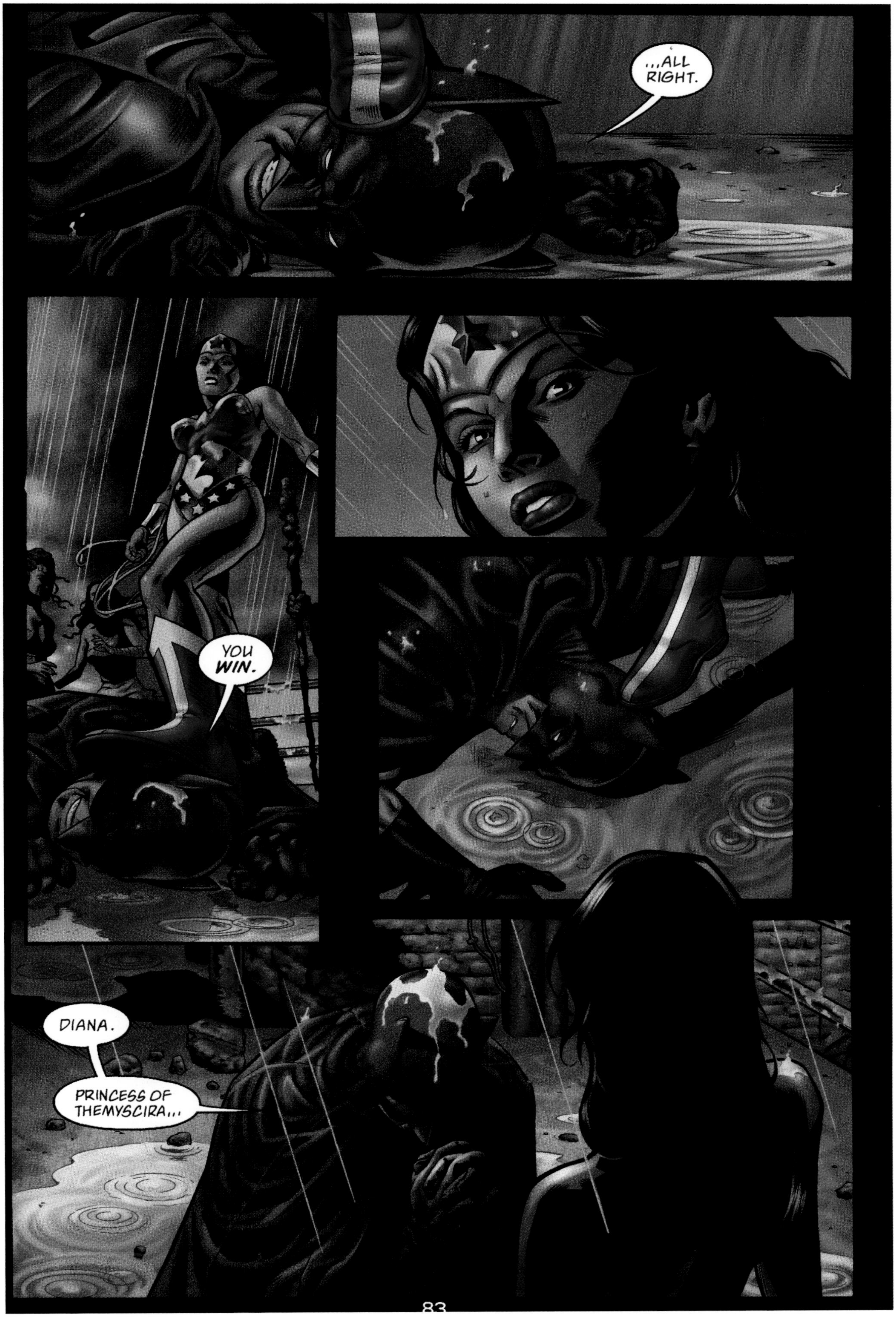
...ALL RIGHT.
YOU WIN.
DIANA.
PRINCESS OF THEMYSCIRA...
83

A different look at the allies when Batman approached the Themysciran Embassy for a case and had to enlist Princess Diana's assistance. Drawn by J. G. Jones and Wade von Grawbadger.

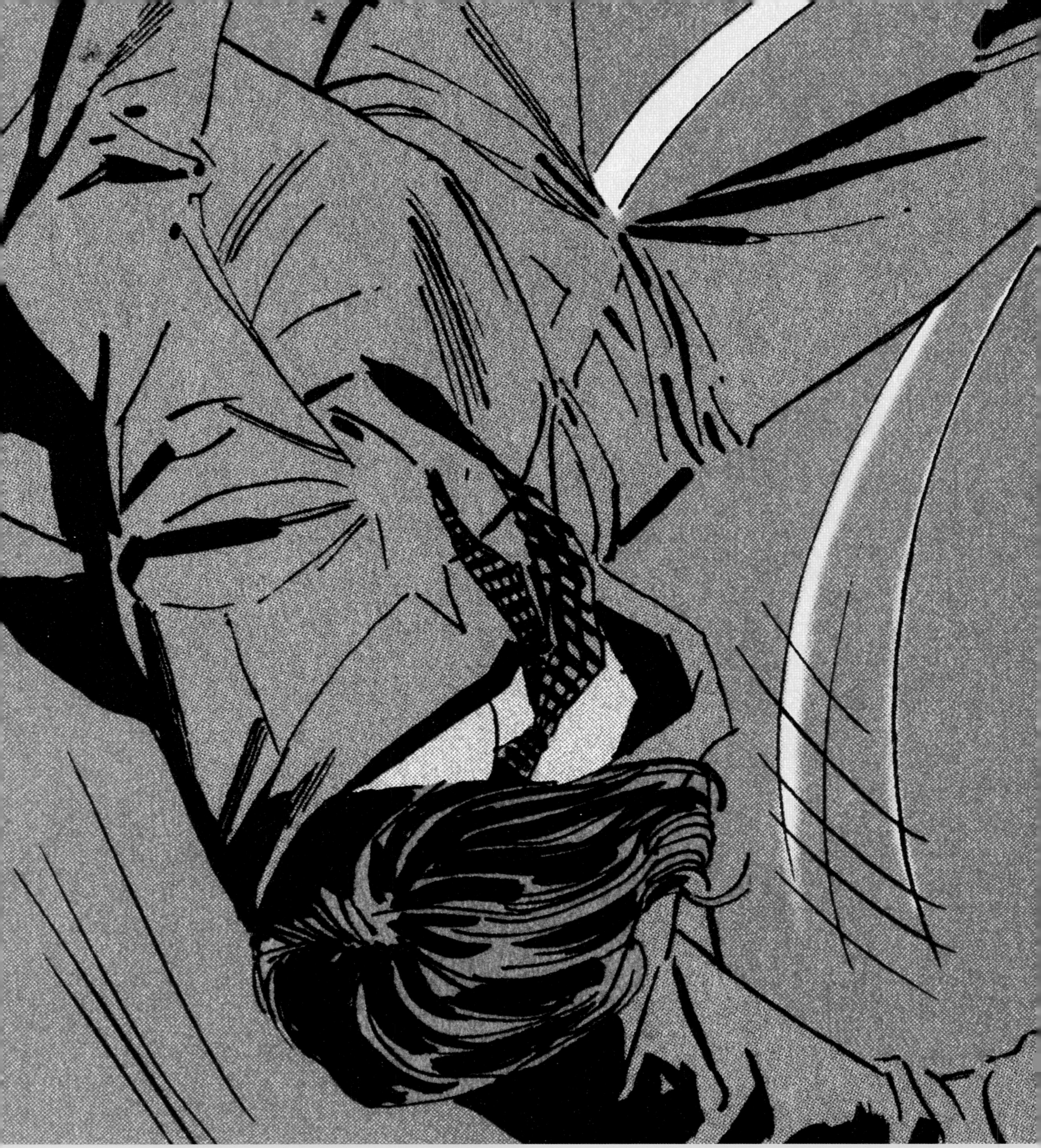

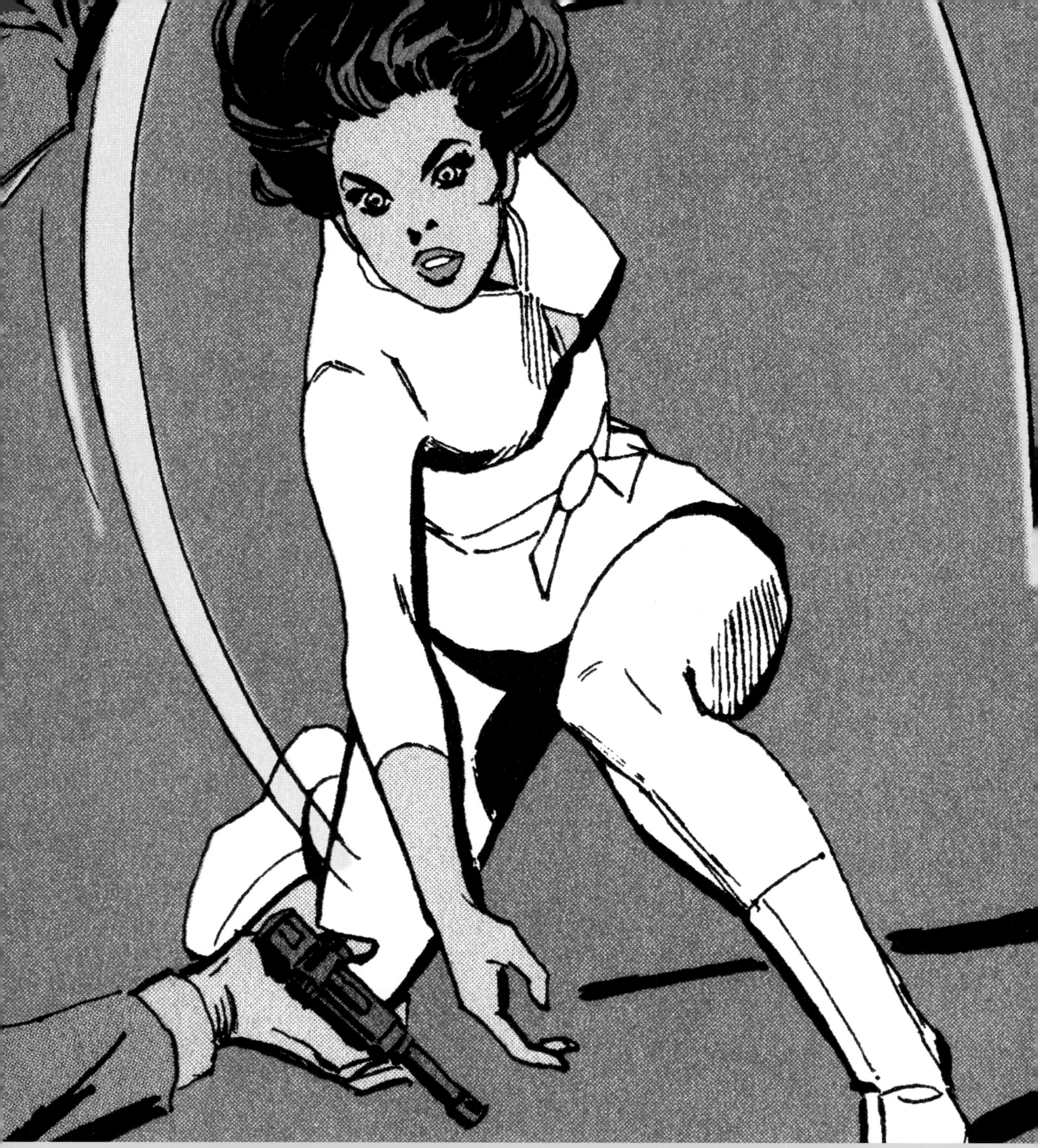

★ The Mod

The NEW WONDER WOMAN
HOW DIFFERENT IS SHE GOING TO BE?
YOU SAW THE GREAT CHANGE IN Diana Prince!
NOW WATCH WHAT HAPPENS TO Wonder Woman-- IN FUTURE ISSUES!
23

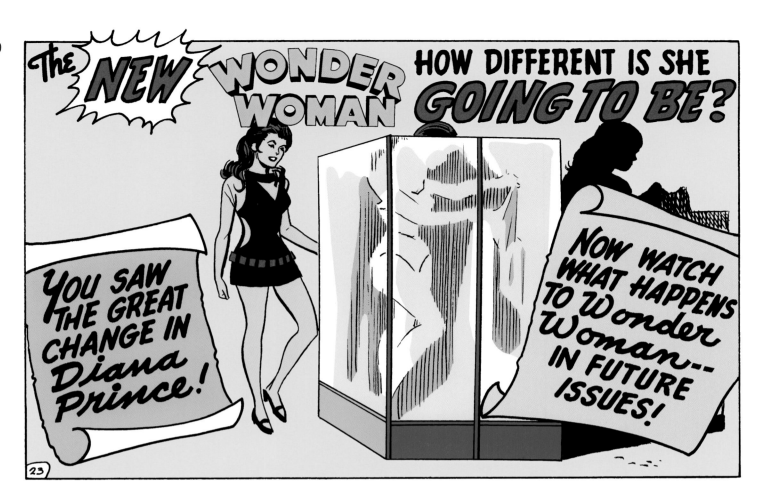

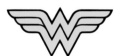

Change was in the air by 1968. Betty Friedan's 1963 shocker, *The Feminine Mystique*, had, by then, been read by enough women to alter the way they saw their careers, their marriages, and themselves. The term "women's liberation" was coined in 1964, and the demands for equal rights were renewed with a fervor and a voice that grew louder by the day. That year, issues of race and gender equality led to many changes across the political spectrum. Those issues were reflected in popular culture from the first prime-time show to feature a nonstereotypical single black woman, *Julia*, to America's premier comic book heroine renouncing her powers.

Wonder Woman had essentially remained the same since her inception, but comic books and its readership was changing dramatically in the 1960s. With artist Carmine Infantino now DC Comics' Editorial Director, the ailing Kanigher was replaced with Jack Miller as the *Wonder Woman* editor, who in turn tapped newcomer Dennis O'Neil to revamp the character. Veteran artist Mike Sekowsky, who had previously drawn the Amazon Princess as a member of the Justice League, stepped behind the drawing board. A bold new direction was established and with the September/October 1968 issue of *Wonder Woman*, readers were given a decidedly different heroine. For the first time in years, she actually seemed relevant.

The changes came fairly rapidly in those beginning issues, starting with Diana going undercover to rescue her beloved Steve Trevor, sans costume, in issue #178 (September/October 1968). In the following issues, Paradise Island and its immortal inhabitants had to leave for another dimension, having somehow expended their significant magical powers. Diana chose to stay behind on Earth, renouncing her Amazonian heritage

Above: The house advertisement that warned readers major changes were coming to Wonder Woman. No one could imagine just how dramatic things were going to get.

Right: Mike Sekowsky and Dick Giordano brought their romance comics skills to play as they added a Pop Art look to Wonder Woman's fashion makeover. In 1968, the series shed its staid look, which was no longer in style with readers.

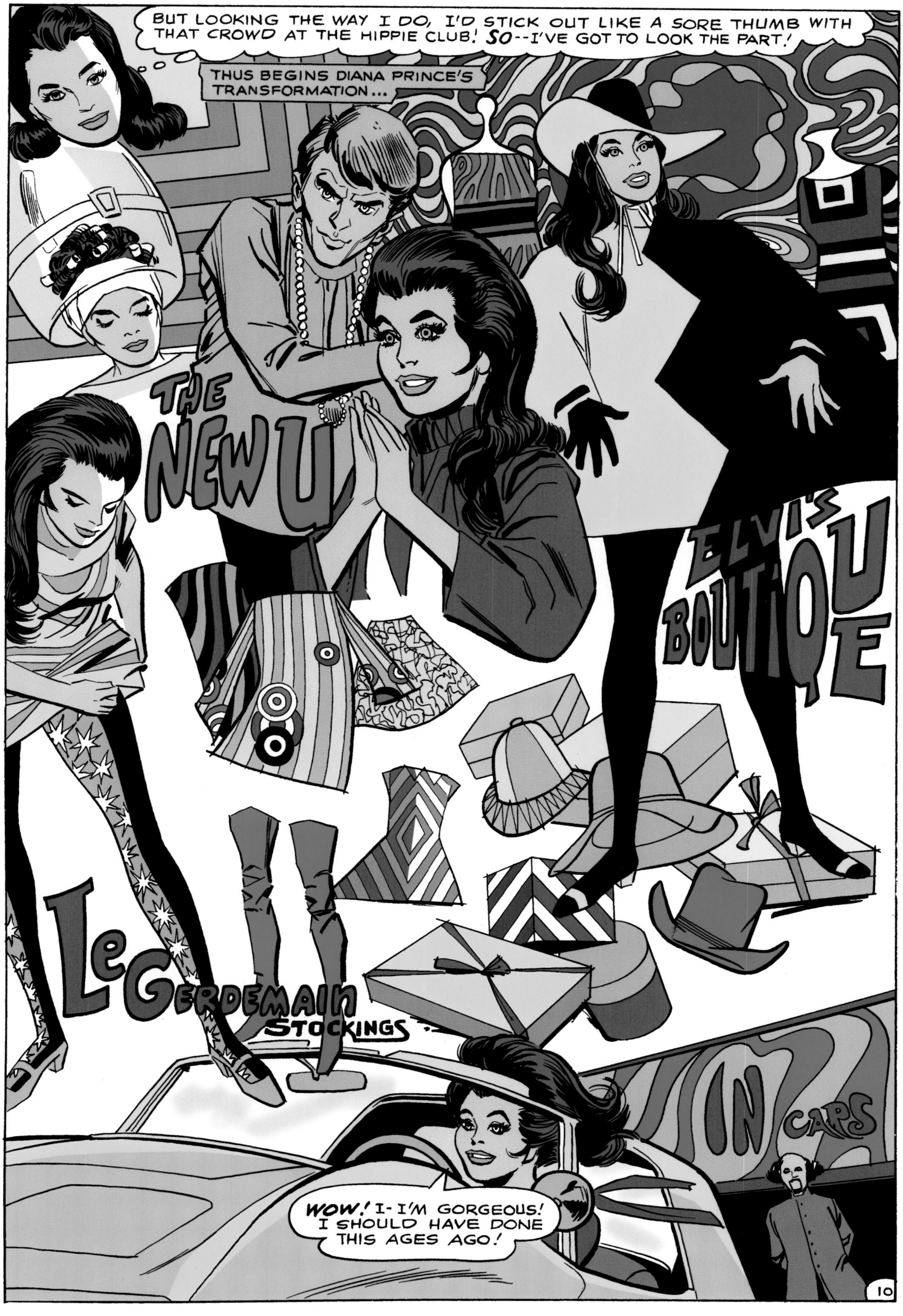

BUT LOOKING THE WAY I DO, I'D STICK OUT LIKE A SORE THUMB WITH THAT CROWD AT THE HIPPIE CLUB! SO--I'VE GOT TO LOOK THE PART!
THUS BEGINS DIANA PRINCE'S TRANSFORMATION...
THE NEW U
ELVI'S BOUTIQUE
LE GERDEMAIN STOCKINGS
IN CAPS
WOW! I- I'M GORGEOUS! I SHOULD HAVE DONE THIS AGES AGO!
10

IT IS MY DUTY TO DEMAND A DECISION OF YOU, DIANA!
OUR TIME ON EARTH GROWS SHORT! FOR TEN THOUSAND YEARS, WE HAVE LIVED HERE, PERFORMING THE MISSION ASSIGNED TO US...
...HELPING MAN-KIND FIND MATURITY! BUT NOW, OUR MAGIC IS EXHAUSTED!
WE MUST JOURNEY TO ANOTHER DIMENSION, TO REST AND RENEW OUR POWERS! WE ARE TIRED, DIANA... THE AGES WEIGH HEAVILY UPON US!
WILL YOU COME--?
BUT YOU HESITATE, DAUGHTER...?
I LOVE YOU, MOTHER...
...YOU AND MY SISTER AMAZONS! BUT STEVE TREVOR DESPERATELY NEEDS ME...
I MUST STAY!
SO BE IT!
8

Above and right: The transformation from Princess Diana, representative to Man's World, to Diana Prince, mortal. Note that she explains she's staying because Steve Trevor needs her; but he dies shortly after this sequence. Illustrated by Mike Sekowksy and Dick Giordano.

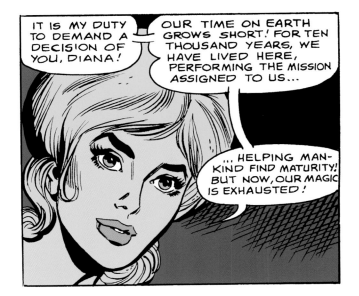

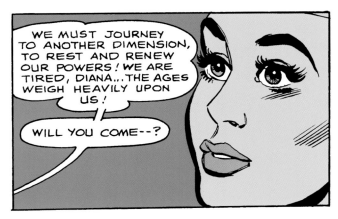

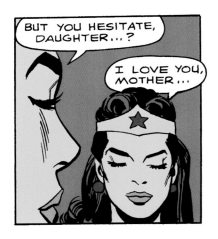

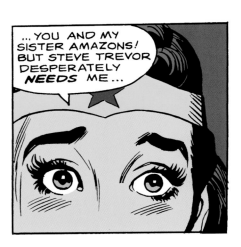

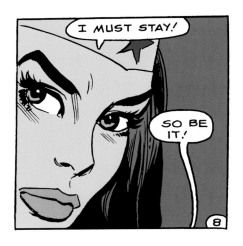

and forgoing her powers. She also resigned from the Justice League of America. The wizened and unfortunately named I-Ching was introduced as her new mentor. I-Ching was an enigmatic figure of indeterminate age and background, who taught her to fight without her powers and trained her in martial arts and Eastern philosophy. Of course, she gave up her Wonder Woman identity to remain with Steve Trevor, who suddenly died in issue #180 (January/February 1969). It was a move O'Neil made because he couldn't figure out what to do with what was essentially a dull character.

The staid book suddenly looked new and vibrant, thanks to a new color scheme and mod designs from Sekowsky. He was heavily influenced by then-popular British television series *The Avengers*, which had aired in America during this time. "In the late Forties, Big Mike had been Stan Lee's main man for teenage girl humor comics, with a nice touch for fashion and femme fluff," wrote Gerard Jones and Will Jacobs in *The Comic Book Heroes*. "Now he was just another DC guy who was going to find out how much the world had really changed in twenty years. This was like a super hero version of *That Girl* with a twist of Emma Peel, and although it had a goofy charm all its own, it sent male fans screaming for the hills and failed to captivate many girls."

The changes actually seemed to have worked at first, since average issue sales in 1969 rose to 171,197 copies, at a time when sales of the rest of the line were declining. That same year, Jack Miller was fired from the company and Mike Sekowksy became a staff editor. He replaced Denny O'Neil as the title's writer, thereby allowing him free reign over the whole series.

Under Sekowsky's control, *Wonder Woman* began to reflect society's interest in women's rights, although through somewhat clunky dialogue. From her new midtown Manhattan fashion boutique, Diana Prince battled street crime and Dr. Cyber's villainy, taking an extended break from the super hero fraternity, and made infrequent appearances

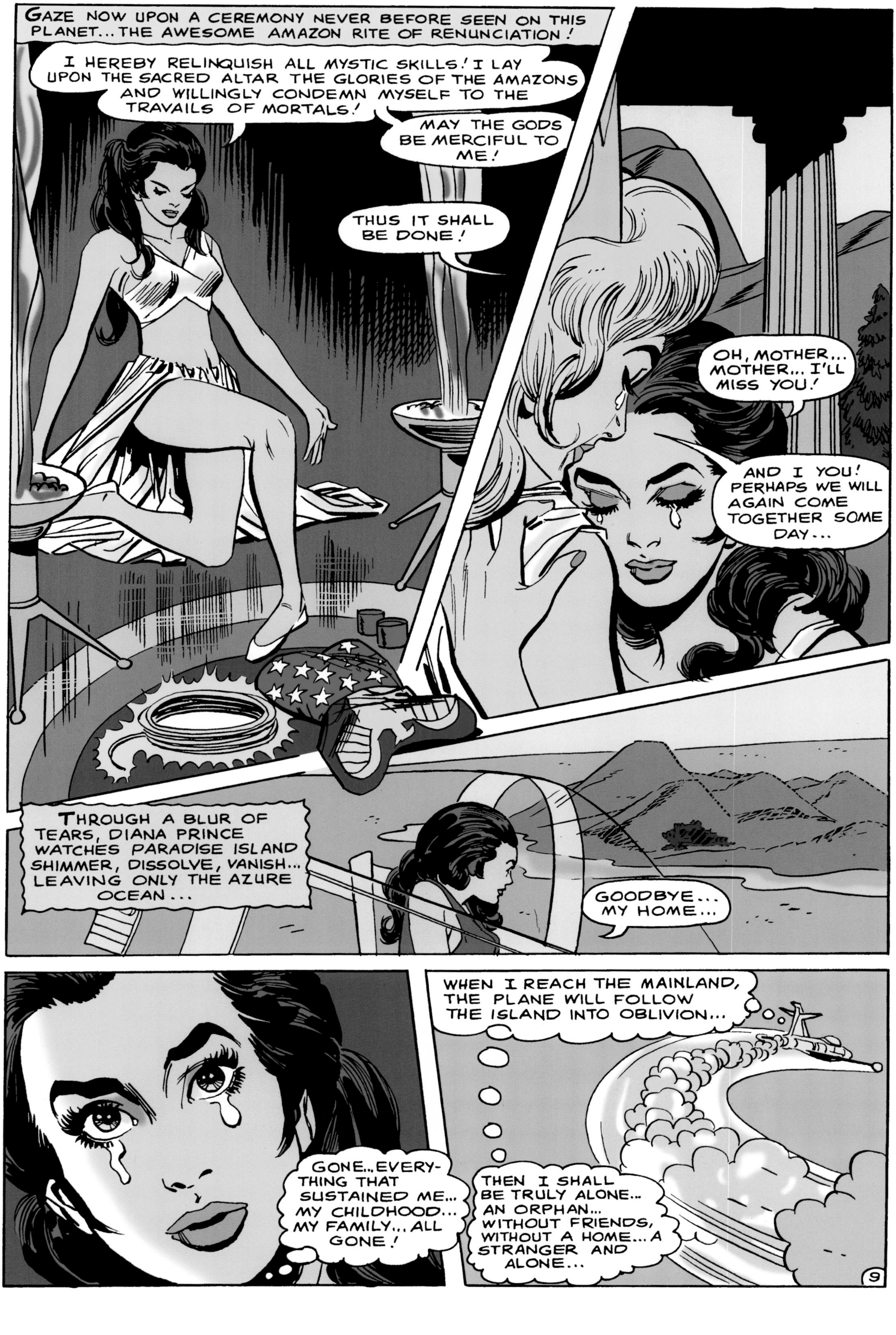
GAZE NOW UPON A CEREMONY NEVER BEFORE SEEN ON THIS PLANET... THE AWESOME AMAZON RITE OF RENUNCIATION!
I HEREBY RELINQUISH ALL MYSTIC SKILLS! I LAY UPON THE SACRED ALTAR THE GLORIES OF THE AMAZONS AND WILLINGLY CONDEMN MYSELF TO THE TRAVAILS OF MORTALS!
MAY THE GODS BE MERCIFUL TO ME!
THUS IT SHALL BE DONE!
OH, MOTHER... MOTHER... I'LL MISS YOU!
AND I YOU! PERHAPS WE WILL AGAIN COME TOGETHER SOME DAY...
THROUGH A BLUR OF TEARS, DIANA PRINCE WATCHES PARADISE ISLAND SHIMMER, DISSOLVE, VANISH... LEAVING ONLY THE AZURE OCEAN...
GOODBYE... MY HOME...
GONE... EVERY-THING THAT SUSTAINED ME... MY CHILDHOOD... MY FAMILY... ALL GONE!
WHEN I REACH THE MAINLAND, THE PLANE WILL FOLLOW THE ISLAND INTO OBLIVION...
THEN I SHALL BE TRULY ALONE... AN ORPHAN... WITHOUT FRIENDS, WITHOUT A HOME... A STRANGER AND ALONE...
9

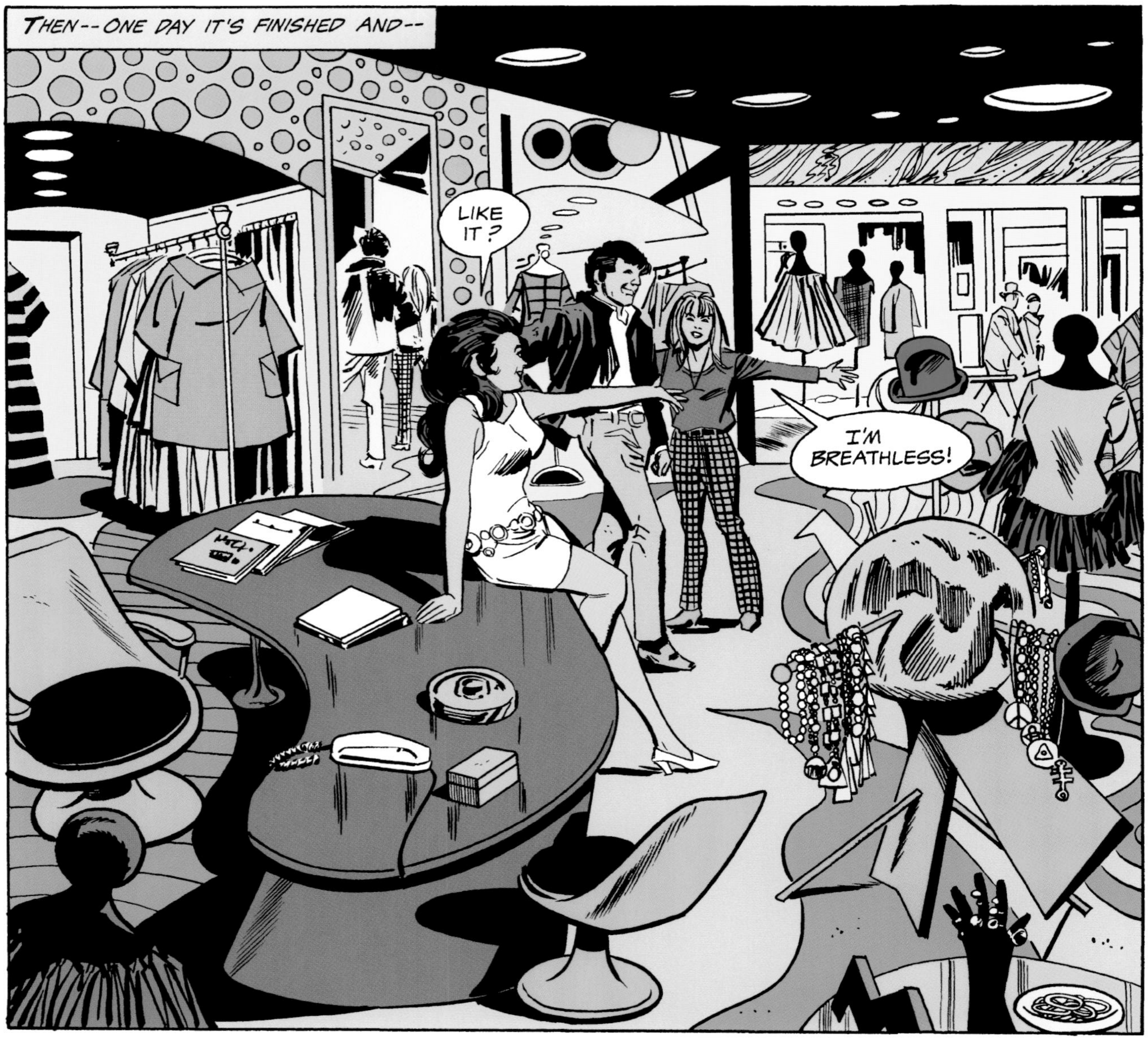
THEN--ONE DAY IT'S FINISHED AND--
LIKE IT?
I'M BREATHLESS!

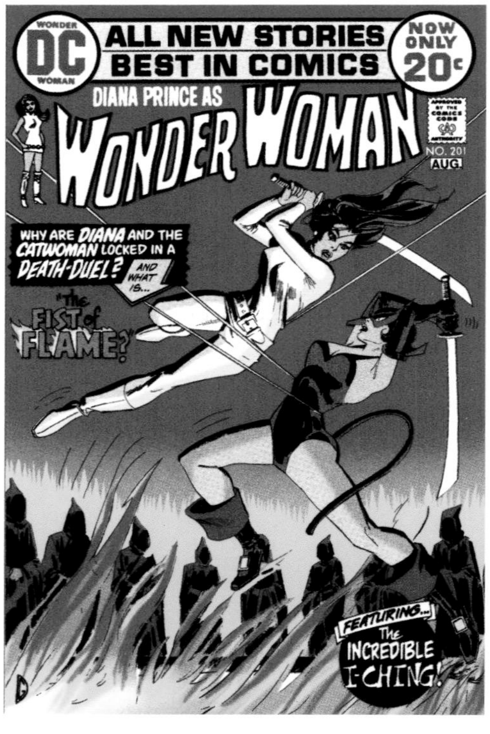
DC
ALL NEW STORIES BEST IN COMICS
NOW ONLY 20¢
DIANA PRINCE AS
WONDER WOMAN
NO. 201 AUG
WHY ARE DIANA AND THE CATWOMAN LOCKED IN A DEATH-DUEL? AND WHAT IS... "THE FIST OF FLAME"?
FEATURING... THE INCREDIBLE I-CHING!

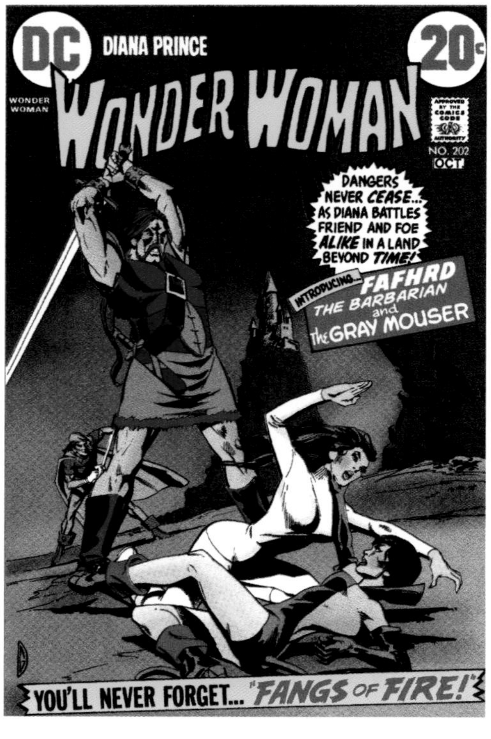
DC
DIANA PRINCE
20¢
WONDER WOMAN
NO. 202 OCT
DANGERS NEVER CEASE... AS DIANA BATTLES FRIEND AND FOE ALIKE IN A LAND BEYOND TIME!
INTRODUCING... FAFHRD THE BARBARIAN and THE GRAY MOUSER
YOU'LL NEVER FORGET... "FANGS OF FIRE!"

Above: A look at Diana's Manhattan fashion boutique, a place where she rarely spent time; writer/ penciller/ editor Mike Sekowsky sent Diana around the world on adrenaline-fueled adventures.

Far left: Writer Denny O'Neil and Dick Giordano went for more traditional super-heroics as Diana faced off against Catwoman. The second part of the cat-fight was also used to tease readers about DC's forthcoming adaptation of Fritz Leiber's *Fafhrd and the Grey Mouser*, who is threatening the women (near left).

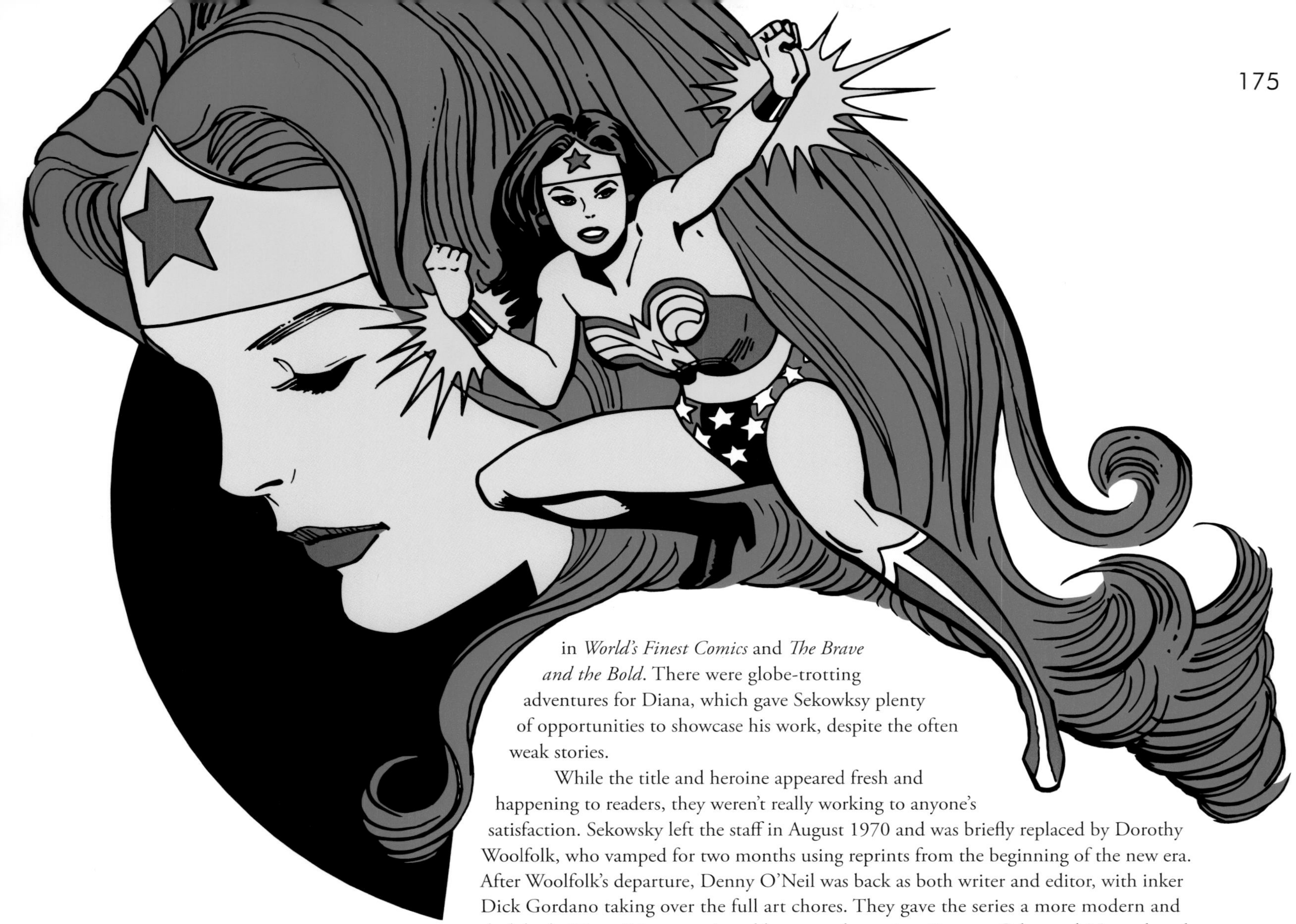

in *World's Finest Comics* and *The Brave and the Bold*. There were globe-trotting adventures for Diana, which gave Sekowksy plenty of opportunities to showcase his work, despite the often weak stories.

While the title and heroine appeared fresh and happening to readers, they weren't really working to anyone's satisfaction. Sekowsky left the staff in August 1970 and was briefly replaced by Dorothy Woolfolk, who vamped for two months using reprints from the beginning of the new era. After Woolfolk's departure, Denny O'Neil was back as both writer and editor, with inker Dick Gordano taking over the full art chores. They gave the series a more modern and sleek look. Diana Prince continued her struggles against Doctors Cyber and Moon, but she also tangled with older established foes including Catwoman.

Above: The imagery created for the DC Comics style guides was intended for use on merchandised properties from coloring books to apparel.

Pages 176-77: Wonder Woman is trained by the enigmatic I-Ching, introduced by writer Denny O'Neil and artists Mike Sekowsky and Dick Giordano in the early issues of the new status quo for the series. I-Ching was also seen counseling Superman in his own title before dying in a hail of bullets once a new creative team took over.

The women's liberation movement continued to captivate society through demonstrations, bra burnings, and demand for improved opportunities. Journalist and feminist Gloria Steinem, who had been covering women's rights even before Friedan, was tapped in 1970 to write the introduction to *Wonder Woman*, a hardcover collection of older stories. Steinem later went on to edit *Ms. Magazine*, with the first issue published in 1972, featuring the Amazon Princess on its cover. In both publications, the heroine's powerless condition during the 1970s was pilloried. A feminist backlash began to grow, demanding that Wonder Woman regain the powers and costume that put her on a par with the Man of Steel.

O'Neil tried to address feminist concerns with a story penned by science fiction great Samuel R. Delaney in *Wonder Woman* #203 (November/December 1972), but it was seen as being too little, too late. By 1972, Diana's adventuring caused her to lose the fashion boutique and her apartment. She moved in with her former employee, Cathy Perkins, and took a job at Grandee's Department Store. There, Cathy and her women's liberation group learned that Grandee was paying the all-female staff below minimum wage. When they staged a protest, Grandee countered by hiring thugs to break up the demonstration. Diana sallied forth and broke up the fight, resulting in the closing of Grandee's. No deed goes unpunished, though, and the liberation group was excoriated for forcing two hundred and fifty women out of work.

Shortly after issue #203, a healthy Kanigher was back on staff and was assigned to fix *Wonder Woman*, which he did in the following issue by killing I-Ching and others in the first few pages. By issue's end, it was as if the previous two dozen issues had never happened.

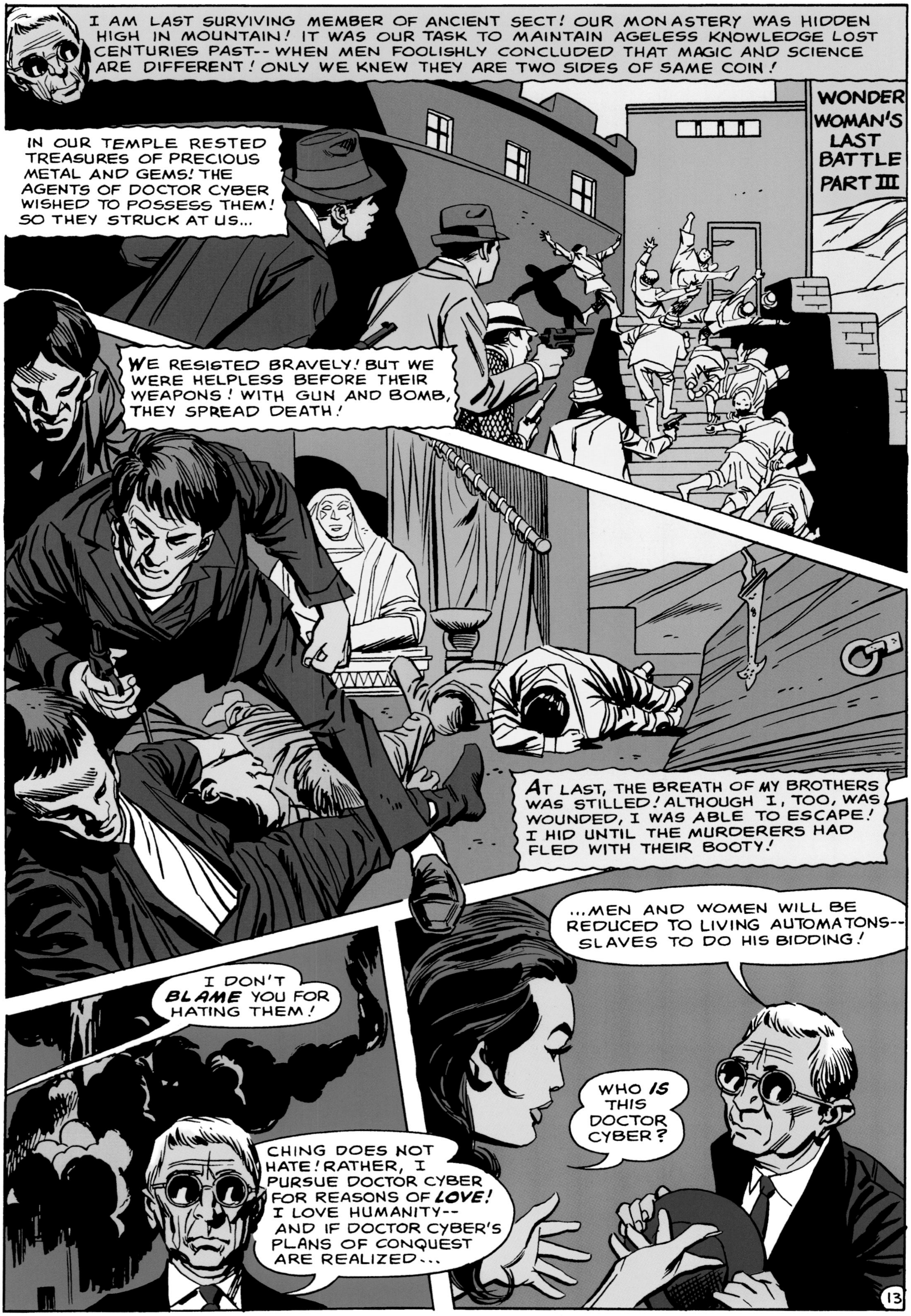
I AM LAST SURVIVING MEMBER OF ANCIENT SECT! OUR MONASTERY WAS HIDDEN HIGH IN MOUNTAIN! IT WAS OUR TASK TO MAINTAIN AGELESS KNOWLEDGE LOST CENTURIES PAST-- WHEN MEN FOOLISHLY CONCLUDED THAT MAGIC AND SCIENCE ARE DIFFERENT! ONLY WE KNEW THEY ARE TWO SIDES OF SAME COIN!
WONDER WOMAN'S LAST BATTLE PART III
IN OUR TEMPLE RESTED TREASURES OF PRECIOUS METAL AND GEMS! THE AGENTS OF DOCTOR CYBER WISHED TO POSSESS THEM! SO THEY STRUCK AT US...
WE RESISTED BRAVELY! BUT WE WERE HELPLESS BEFORE THEIR WEAPONS! WITH GUN AND BOMB, THEY SPREAD DEATH!
AT LAST, THE BREATH OF MY BROTHERS WAS STILLED! ALTHOUGH I, TOO, WAS WOUNDED, I WAS ABLE TO ESCAPE! I HID UNTIL THE MURDERERS HAD FLED WITH THEIR BOOTY!
I DON'T BLAME YOU FOR HATING THEM!
CHING DOES NOT HATE! RATHER, I PURSUE DOCTOR CYBER FOR REASONS OF LOVE! I LOVE HUMANITY-- AND IF DOCTOR CYBER'S PLANS OF CONQUEST ARE REALIZED...
...MEN AND WOMEN WILL BE REDUCED TO LIVING AUTOMATONS-- SLAVES TO DO HIS BIDDING!
WHO IS THIS DOCTOR CYBER?
13

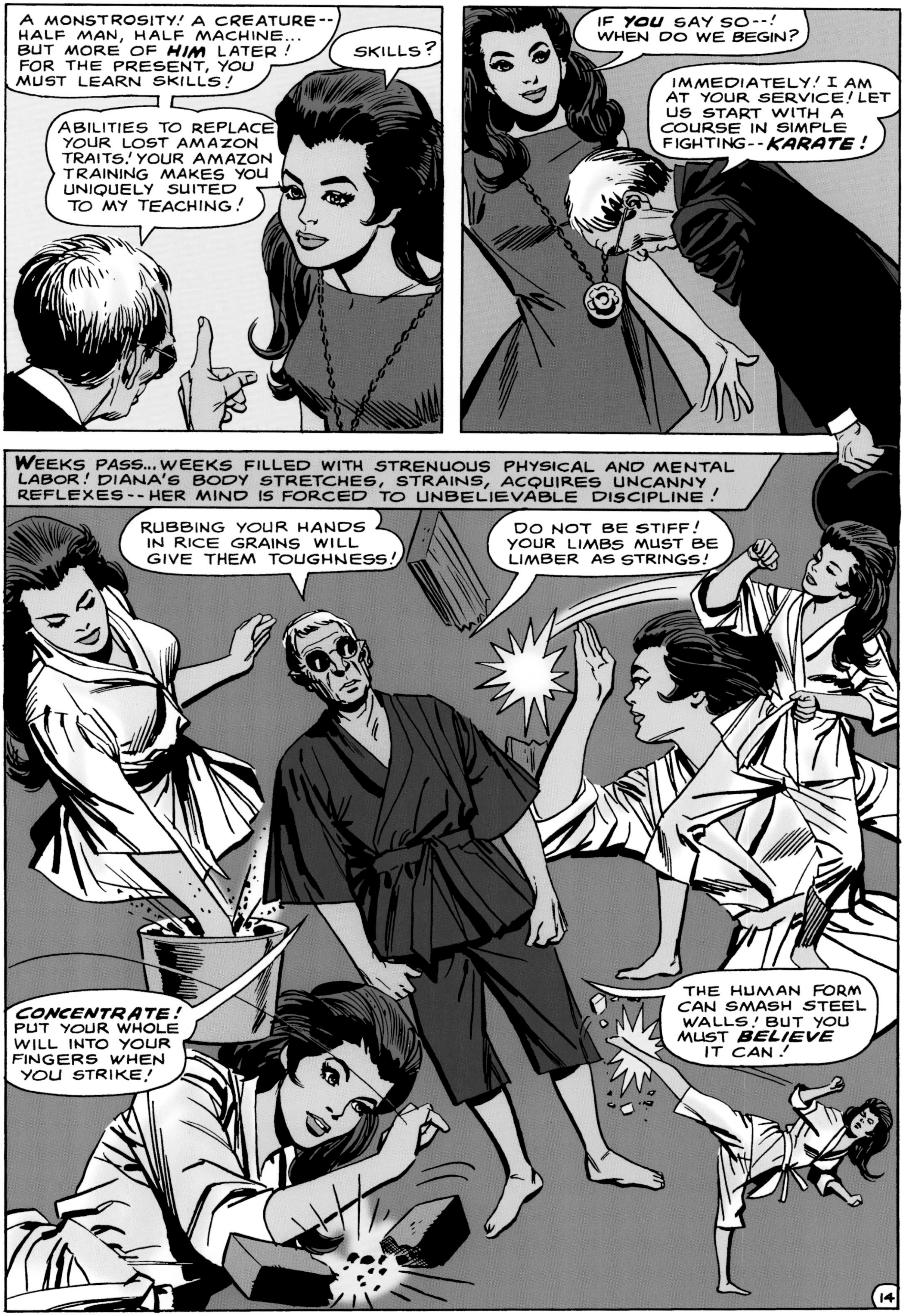
A MONSTROSITY! A CREATURE-- HALF MAN, HALF MACHINE... BUT MORE OF HIM LATER! FOR THE PRESENT, YOU MUST LEARN SKILLS!
SKILLS?
ABILITIES TO REPLACE YOUR LOST AMAZON TRAITS! YOUR AMAZON TRAINING MAKES YOU UNIQUELY SUITED TO MY TEACHING!
IF YOU SAY SO--! WHEN DO WE BEGIN?
IMMEDIATELY! I AM AT YOUR SERVICE! LET US START WITH A COURSE IN SIMPLE FIGHTING--KARATE!
WEEKS PASS...WEEKS FILLED WITH STRENUOUS PHYSICAL AND MENTAL LABOR! DIANA'S BODY STRETCHES, STRAINS, ACQUIRES UNCANNY REFLEXES--HER MIND IS FORCED TO UNBELIEVABLE DISCIPLINE!
RUBBING YOUR HANDS IN RICE GRAINS WILL GIVE THEM TOUGHNESS!
DO NOT BE STIFF! YOUR LIMBS MUST BE LIMBER AS STRINGS!
CONCENTRATE! PUT YOUR WHOLE WILL INTO YOUR FINGERS WHEN YOU STRIKE!
THE HUMAN FORM CAN SMASH STEEL WALLS! BUT YOU MUST BELIEVE IT CAN!
14

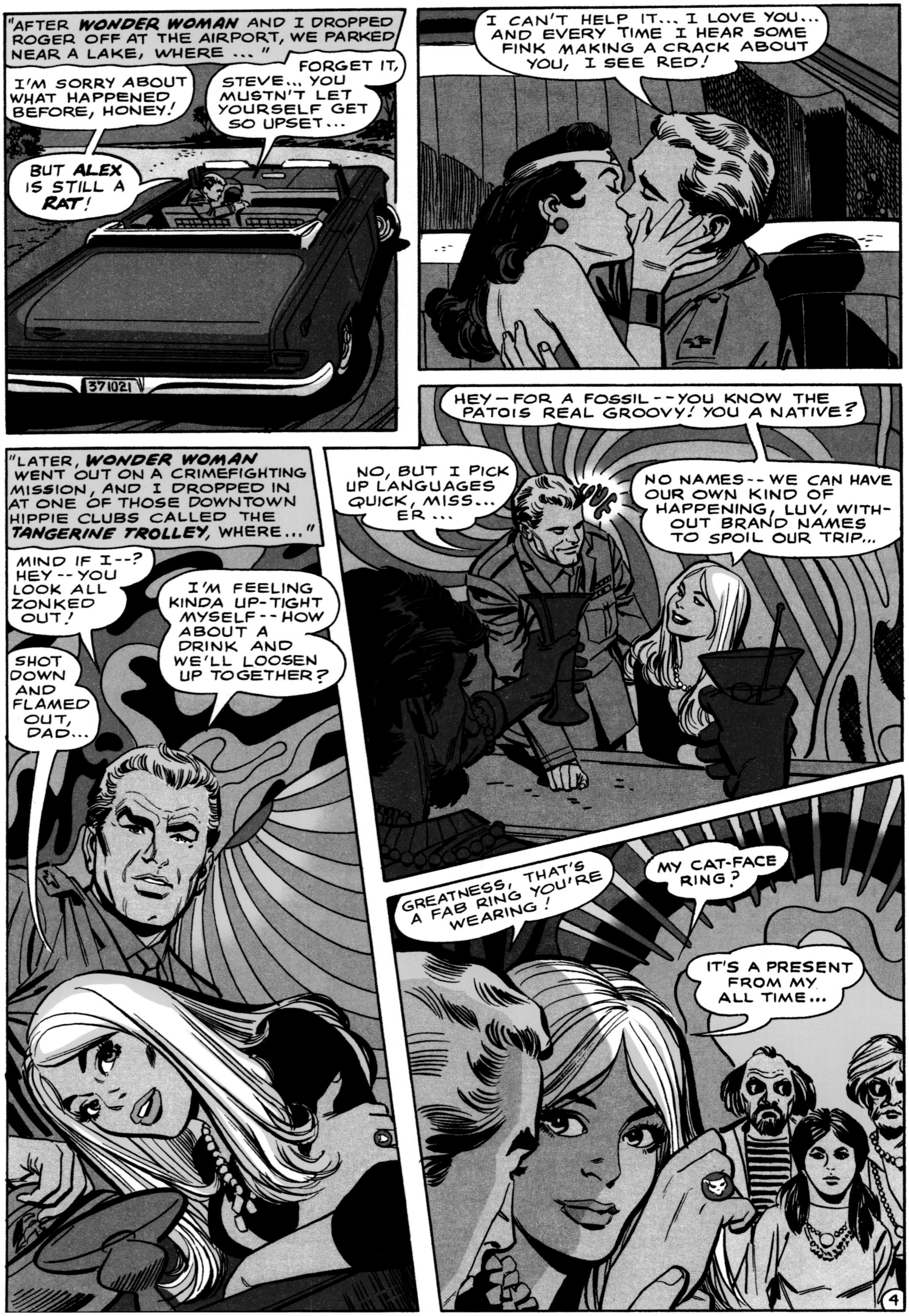
"AFTER WONDER WOMAN AND I DROPPED ROGER OFF AT THE AIRPORT, WE PARKED NEAR A LAKE, WHERE ..."
I'M SORRY ABOUT WHAT HAPPENED BEFORE, HONEY!
FORGET IT, STEVE... YOU MUSTN'T LET YOURSELF GET SO UPSET...
BUT ALEX IS STILL A RAT!
37 1021
I CAN'T HELP IT... I LOVE YOU... AND EVERY TIME I HEAR SOME FINK MAKING A CRACK ABOUT YOU, I SEE RED!
"LATER, WONDER WOMAN WENT OUT ON A CRIMEFIGHTING MISSION, AND I DROPPED IN AT ONE OF THOSE DOWNTOWN HIPPIE CLUBS CALLED THE TANGERINE TROLLEY, WHERE..."
MIND IF I--? HEY--YOU LOOK ALL ZONKED OUT!
I'M FEELING KINDA UP-TIGHT MYSELF--HOW ABOUT A DRINK AND WE'LL LOOSEN UP TOGETHER?
SHOT DOWN AND FLAMED OUT, DAD...
HEY—FOR A FOSSIL--YOU KNOW THE PATOIS REAL GROOVY! YOU A NATIVE?
NO, BUT I PICK UP LANGUAGES QUICK, MISS... ER ...
NO NAMES--WE CAN HAVE OUR OWN KIND OF HAPPENING, LUV, WITH-OUT BRAND NAMES TO SPOIL OUR TRIP...
GREATNESS, THAT'S A FAB RING YOU'RE WEARING!
MY CAT-FACE RING?
IT'S A PRESENT FROM MY ALL TIME...
4

Above and right: Before Princess Diana gave up her powers to remain on Earth, she and Steve Trevor continued their romance. Writer Denny O'Neil killed him off shortly after this scene. Illustrated by Mike Sekowksy and Dick Giordano.

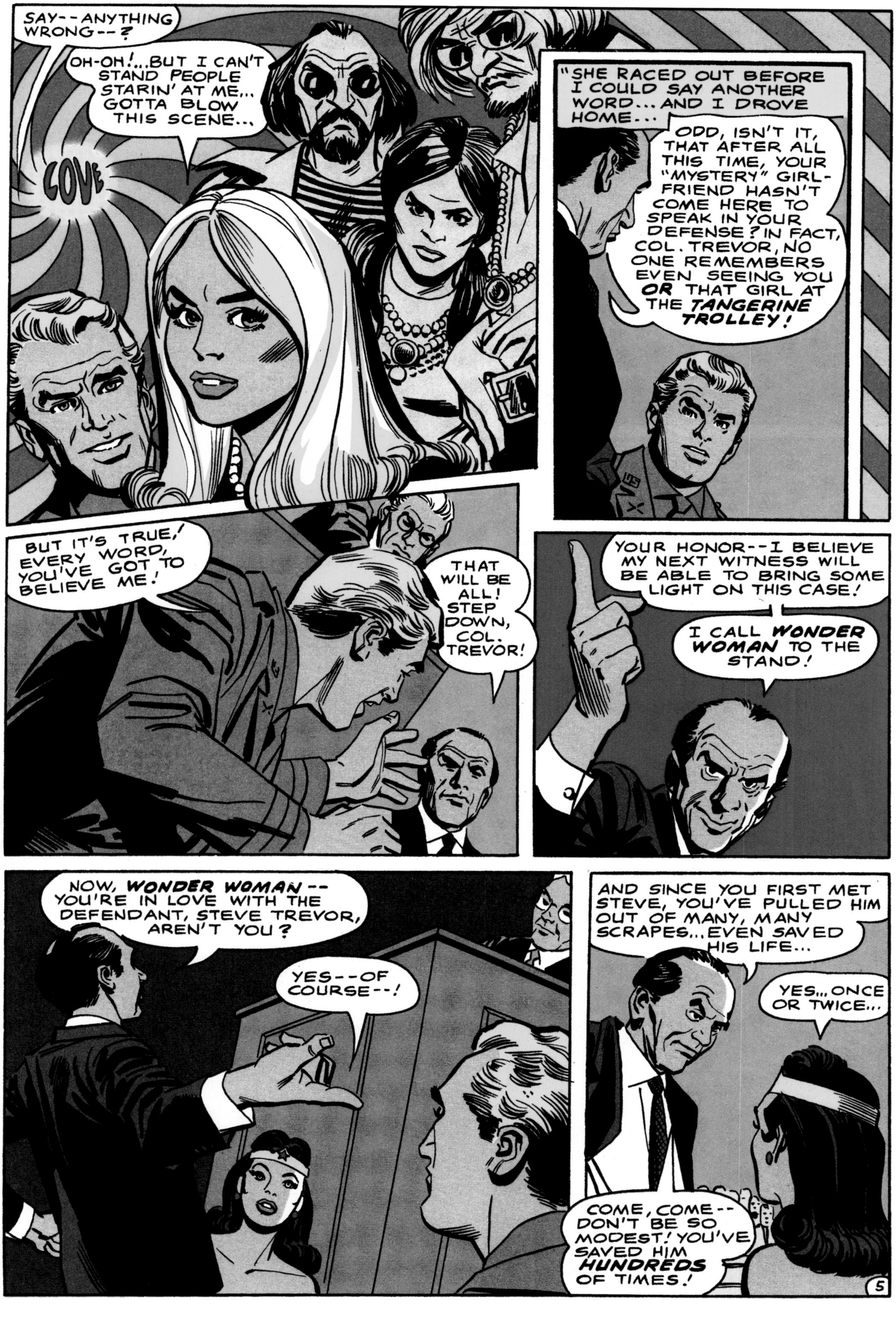
SAY--ANYTHING WRONG--?
OH-OH!...BUT I CAN'T STAND PEOPLE STARIN' AT ME... GOTTA BLOW THIS SCENE...
LOVE
"SHE RACED OUT BEFORE I COULD SAY ANOTHER WORD... AND I DROVE HOME...
ODD, ISN'T IT, THAT AFTER ALL THIS TIME, YOUR "MYSTERY" GIRL-FRIEND HASN'T COME HERE TO SPEAK IN YOUR DEFENSE? IN FACT, COL. TREVOR, NO ONE REMEMBERS EVEN SEEING YOU OR THAT GIRL AT THE TANGERINE TROLLEY!
BUT IT'S TRUE! EVERY WORD, YOU'VE GOT TO BELIEVE ME!
THAT WILL BE ALL! STEP DOWN, COL. TREVOR!
YOUR HONOR--I BELIEVE MY NEXT WITNESS WILL BE ABLE TO BRING SOME LIGHT ON THIS CASE!
I CALL WONDER WOMAN TO THE STAND!
NOW, WONDER WOMAN-- YOU'RE IN LOVE WITH THE DEFENDANT, STEVE TREVOR, AREN'T YOU?
YES--OF COURSE--!
AND SINCE YOU FIRST MET STEVE, YOU'VE PULLED HIM OUT OF MANY, MANY SCRAPES... EVEN SAVED HIS LIFE...
YES... ONCE OR TWICE...
COME, COME-- DON'T BE SO MODEST! YOU'VE SAVED HIM HUNDREDS OF TIMES!
5

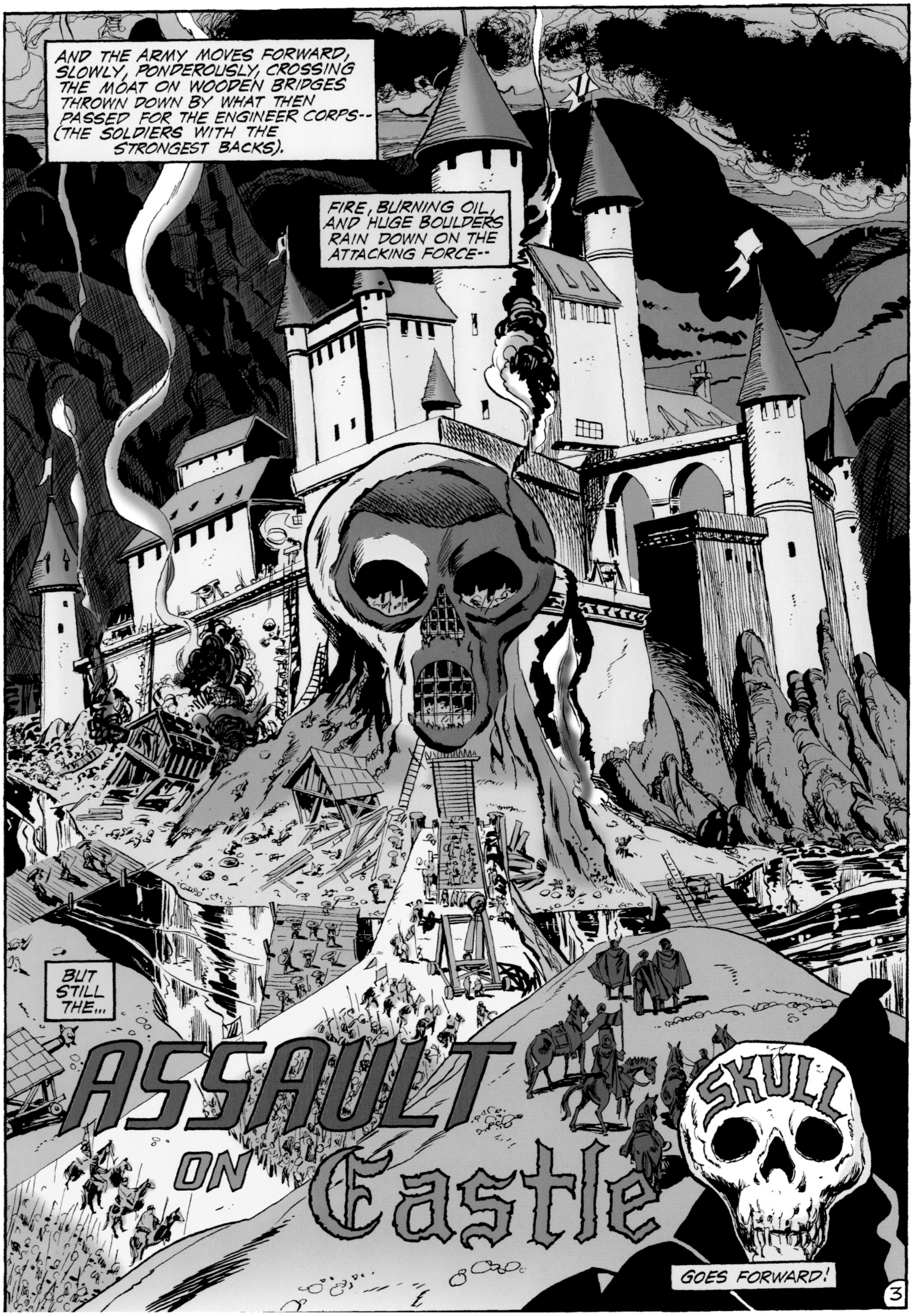
AND THE ARMY MOVES FORWARD, SLOWLY, PONDEROUSLY, CROSSING THE MOAT ON WOODEN BRIDGES THROWN DOWN BY WHAT THEN PASSED FOR THE ENGINEER CORPS-- (THE SOLDIERS WITH THE STRONGEST BACKS).
FIRE, BURNING OIL, AND HUGE BOULDERS RAIN DOWN ON THE ATTACKING FORCE--
BUT STILL THE...
ASSAULT ON Castle SKULL
GOES FORWARD!
3

Above: Sales increased for Wonder Woman due to creative new adventures and foes such as Dr. Cyber. The artwork of Mike Sekowsky and Dick Giordano imaginatively illustrated new dangers and environments, including Castle Skull and the Queen of Chalandor.

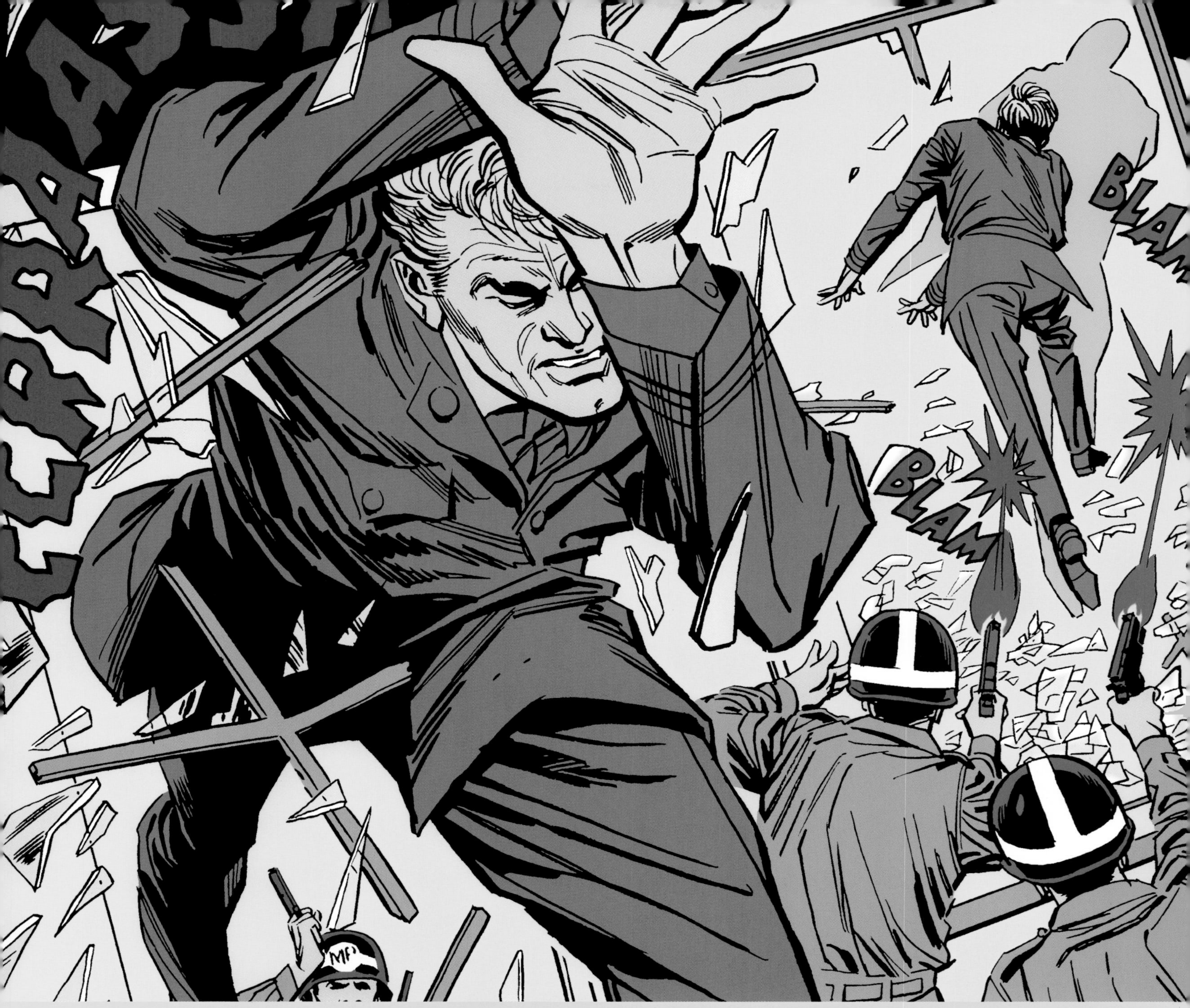
BLAM
BLAM

Mike Sekowsky

Mike Sekowksy started his comic illustration career at Marvel Comics in 1941, ranging from funny animals to Captain America. He later expanded to romance, Western, and horror stories. He migrated to DC Comics in the 1950s, where he drew science fiction and romance tales before being assigned the *Justice League of America* in 1960. He drew sixty-six consecutive issues, in addition to features for Tower Comics. When he left the comics world, he completed his career by working in television animation until his death in 1989.

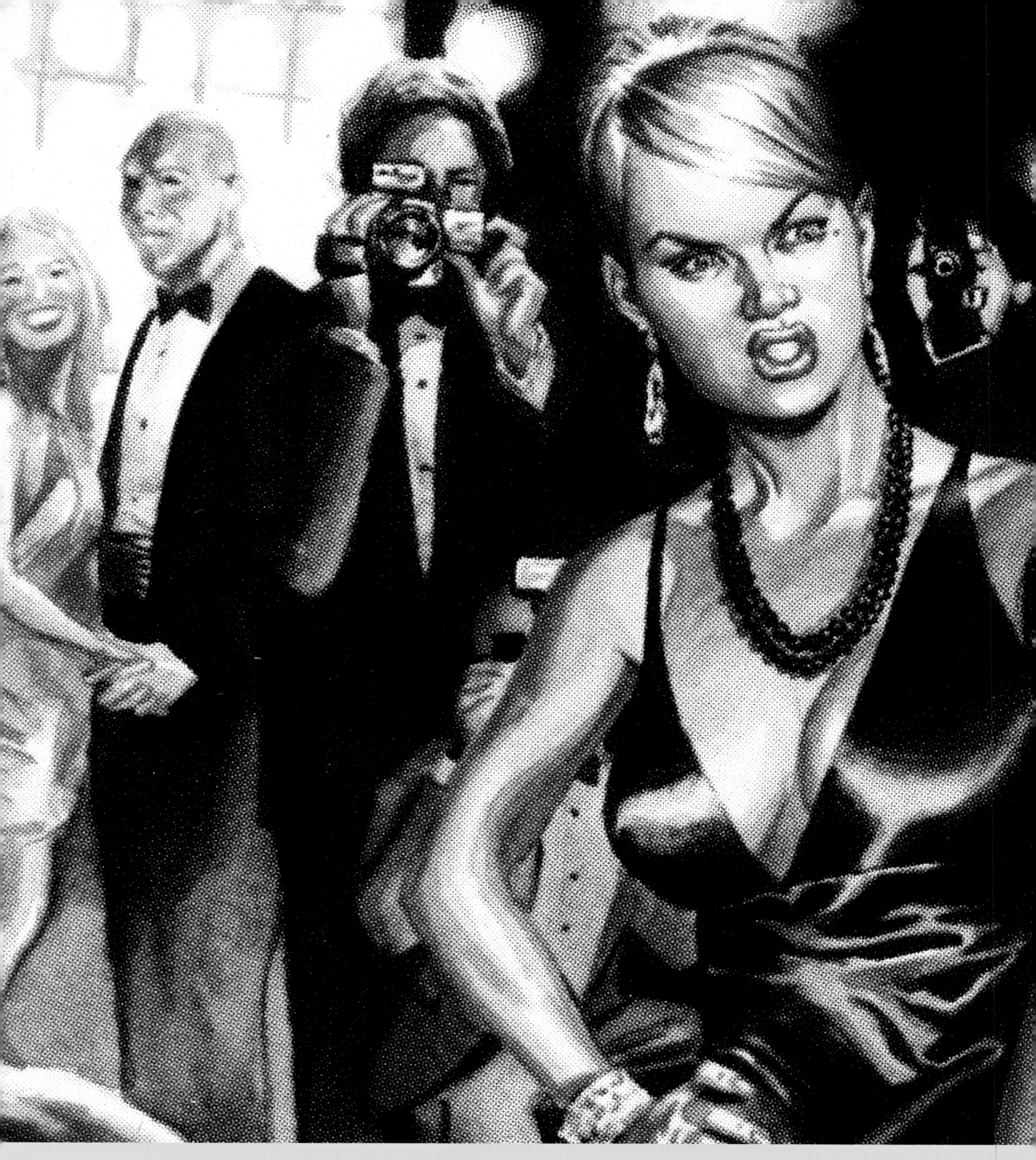

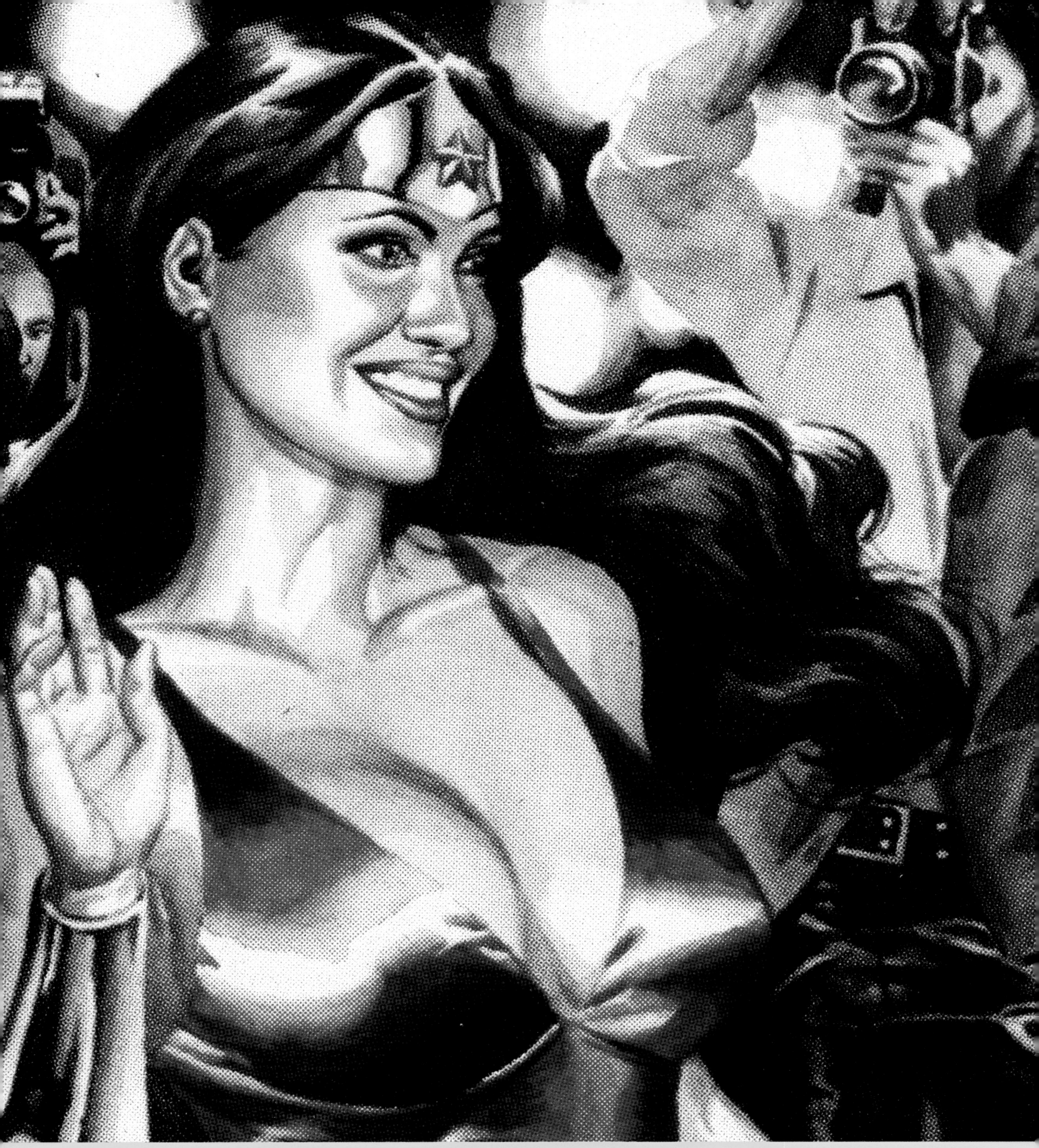

★ The Diplomat

Left: Princess Diana of Themyscira in formal attire. When making diplomatic appearances, Diana was certainly more eye-catching than those decked out in traditional diplomatic suits and dresses.

Right: The return of writer/editor Robert Kanigher restored Diana Prince to a mere secret identity for Wonder Woman. He also gave her a new assignment: working for the United Nations. Art by Don Heck and Dick Giordano.

Below: A character study by Matt Wagner.

Since her first appearance Diana was seen as an ambassador from Paradise Island to Man's World. In the early years she was also plunged right into World War II, fighting with the Allies and preaching universal messages of truth and justice, even as she espoused the equality of women in every aspect of society.

After the war ended, Marston and his successor Kanigher largely ignored this diplomatic aspect of her mission and chose to tell stories that focused more on her role as a super hero. The ambassadorial slant wasn't really touched on again until her reboot in 1987, and by then the neophyte visitor to Man's World needed a road map. This was provided to her by publicist Myndi Mayer, who managed the Amazon's public appearances and spun her message of peace to the mass media. In the wake of Mayer's sudden and tragic death, Diana found her own way, eventually bringing delegations and reporters to visit Themyscira in an effort to demystify her people and their ways.

And just like that, the theme of diplomacy and ambassadorhood was dropped for years in favor or other adventures and changes in status quo. However that changed in the early 2000s when writer/artist Phil Jimenez revisited elements that George Pérez had set up in the 1980s. Novelist Greg Rucka took over the title with issue #195 and introduced a Themysciran Embassy and its colorful staff. His initial storyline focused on Diana's role as a diplomat and ambassador. She even collected her essays and poems into a book entitled *Reflections: A Collection of Essays and Speeches*. Although a bestseller, many took offense at Wonder Woman's point of view. It sparked an unexpected controversy, led with vigor by businesswoman Veronica Cale, that preoccupied Diana from more pressing threats.

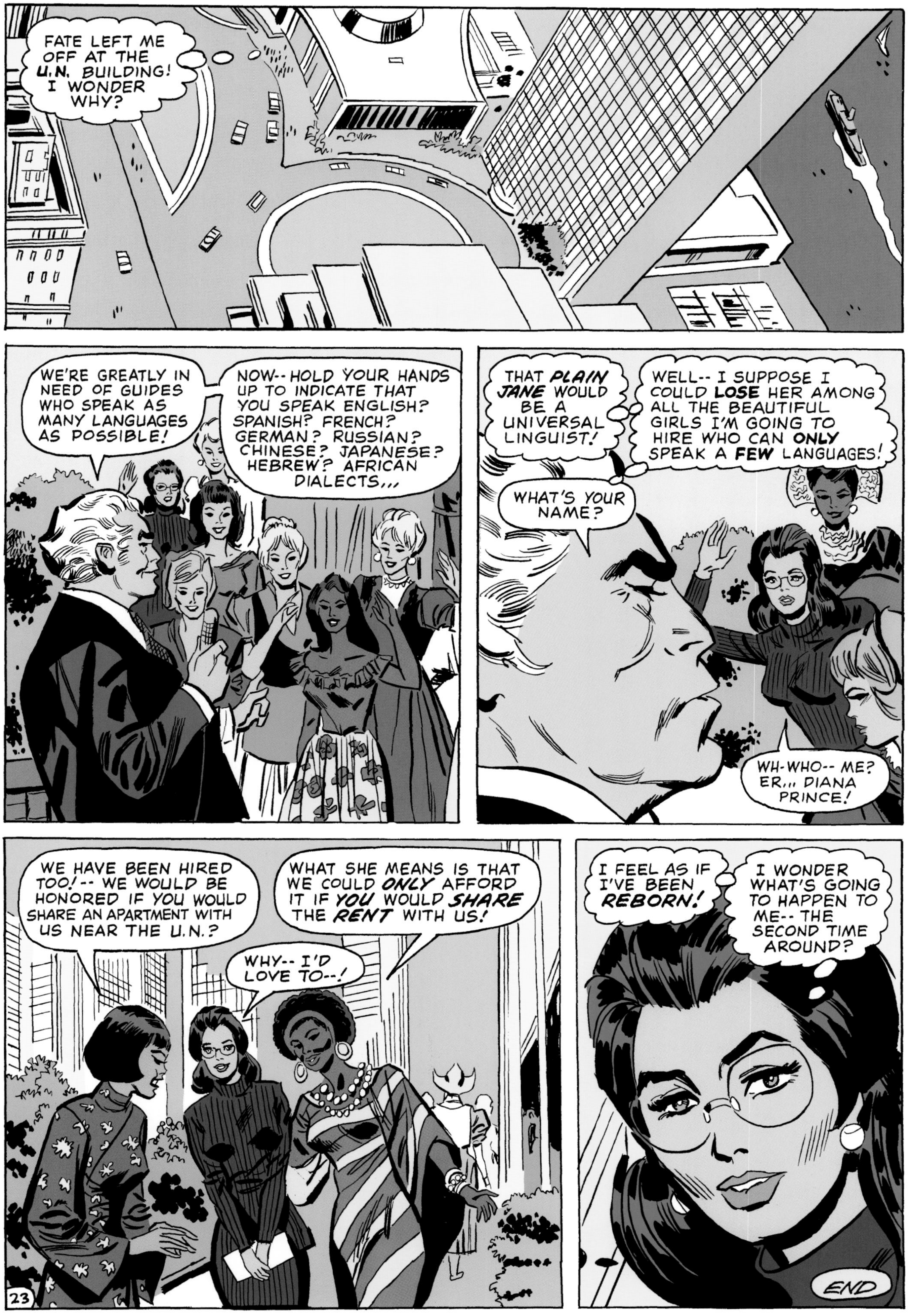
FATE LEFT ME OFF AT THE U.N. BUILDING! I WONDER WHY?
WE'RE GREATLY IN NEED OF GUIDES WHO SPEAK AS MANY LANGUAGES AS POSSIBLE!
NOW-- HOLD YOUR HANDS UP TO INDICATE THAT YOU SPEAK ENGLISH? SPANISH? FRENCH? GERMAN? RUSSIAN? CHINESE? JAPANESE? HEBREW? AFRICAN DIALECTS...
THAT PLAIN JANE WOULD BE A UNIVERSAL LINGUIST!
WELL-- I SUPPOSE I COULD LOSE HER AMONG ALL THE BEAUTIFUL GIRLS I'M GOING TO HIRE WHO CAN ONLY SPEAK A FEW LANGUAGES!
WHAT'S YOUR NAME?
WH-WHO-- ME? ER... DIANA PRINCE!
WE HAVE BEEN HIRED TOO! -- WE WOULD BE HONORED IF YOU WOULD SHARE AN APARTMENT WITH US NEAR THE U.N.?
WHAT SHE MEANS IS THAT WE COULD ONLY AFFORD IT IF YOU WOULD SHARE THE RENT WITH US!
WHY-- I'D LOVE TO--!
23
I FEEL AS IF I'VE BEEN REBORN!
I WONDER WHAT'S GOING TO HAPPEN TO ME-- THE SECOND TIME AROUND?
END

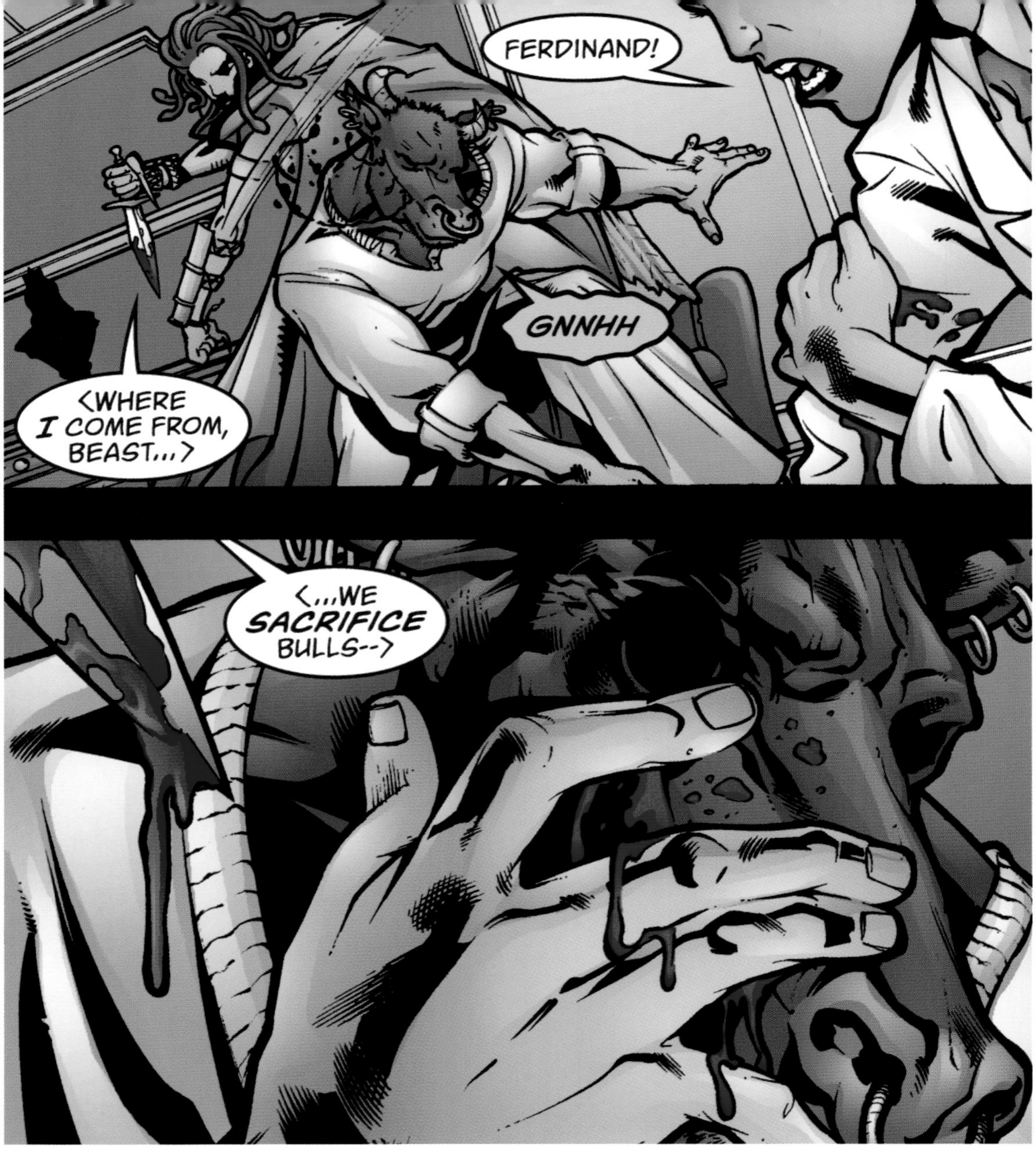
FERDINAND!
GNNHH
<WHERE I COME FROM, BEAST...>
<...WE SACRIFICE BULLS-->

Left: The evil Medousa attacked Ferdinand, the Themyscira Embassy's beloved chef, from artists Drew Johnson and Ray Snyder.

Right: In the wake of her book's release, Wonder Woman made numerous bookstore visits and dealt with awkward questions from her admirers. Art by Drew Johnson and Ray Snyder.

Below: Johnson's character sketch for Ferdinand before beginning his run on *Wonder Woman*.

"As we imagined it, *Reflections* wasn't anything but a book of ideas, a new way for Diana to promote her mission in the Patriarch's World," Rucka told website Comics Bulletin. "But looking at it at all realistically, there was no way to justify not having a polarizing response. Wonder Woman published a book? It was guaranteed that she'd piss someone off, someplace."

Rucka also addressed his critics about the action quotient, which had been dramatically dialed down. "There's plenty of action, there's just not a lot of violence. And considering who Wonder Woman is—the Themysciran ambassador to the UN, an Amazon trained for war but bred for peace, a near-goddess blessed with the wisdom of Athena—violence is never going to be an ill-considered response. It's against everything in her character. When Diana goes to the sword, she goes to the sword understanding precisely what that means, understanding just how unpredictable and dangerous violence is.

"It's decisive, and precise, never undertaken in haste, nor without care."

Fans of Rucka's run on the series also enjoyed the employees at Themyscira House, the Central Park–based embassy. As Rucka explained to news website Comic Book Resources, "[I wanted] to make sure there's a support group of characters there for [Diana] to interact with and a cast of characters through whose eyes we can see Diana. The second purpose is that they enforce the differences between Diana and all these different heroes. I did some research into what it means to be an ambassador to the United Nations, and it's a twenty-hour-a-day job if you're lucky, and if you're not, it's a twenty-six-hour-a-day

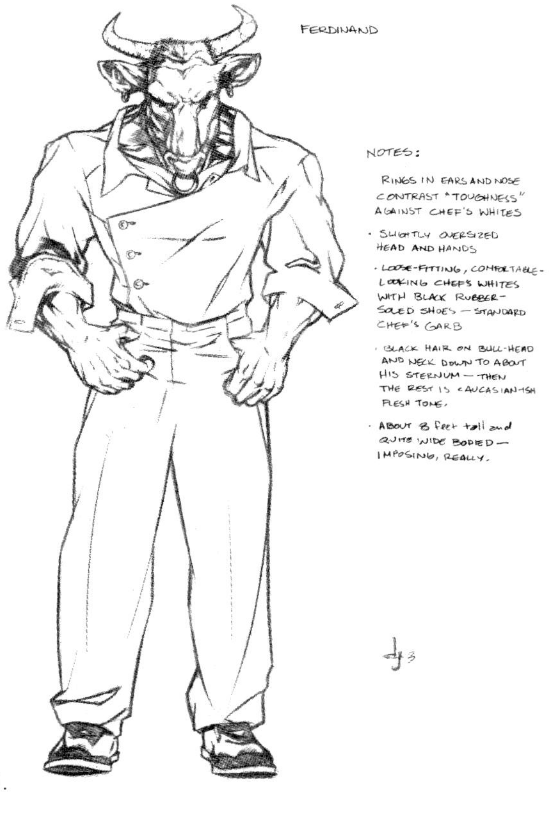
FERDINAND
NOTES:
RINGS IN EARS AND NOSE CONTRAST "TOUGHNESS" AGAINST CHEF'S WHITES
· SLIGHTLY OVERSIZED HEAD AND HANDS
· LOOSE-FITTING, COMFORTABLE-LOOKING CHEF'S WHITES WITH BLACK RUBBER-SOLED SHOES — STANDARD CHEF'S GARB
· BLACK HAIR ON BULL-HEAD AND NECK DOWN TO ABOUT HIS STERNUM — THEN THE REST IS CAUCASIAN-ISH FLESH TONE.
· ABOUT 8 feet tall and QUITE WIDE BODIED — IMPOSING, REALLY.

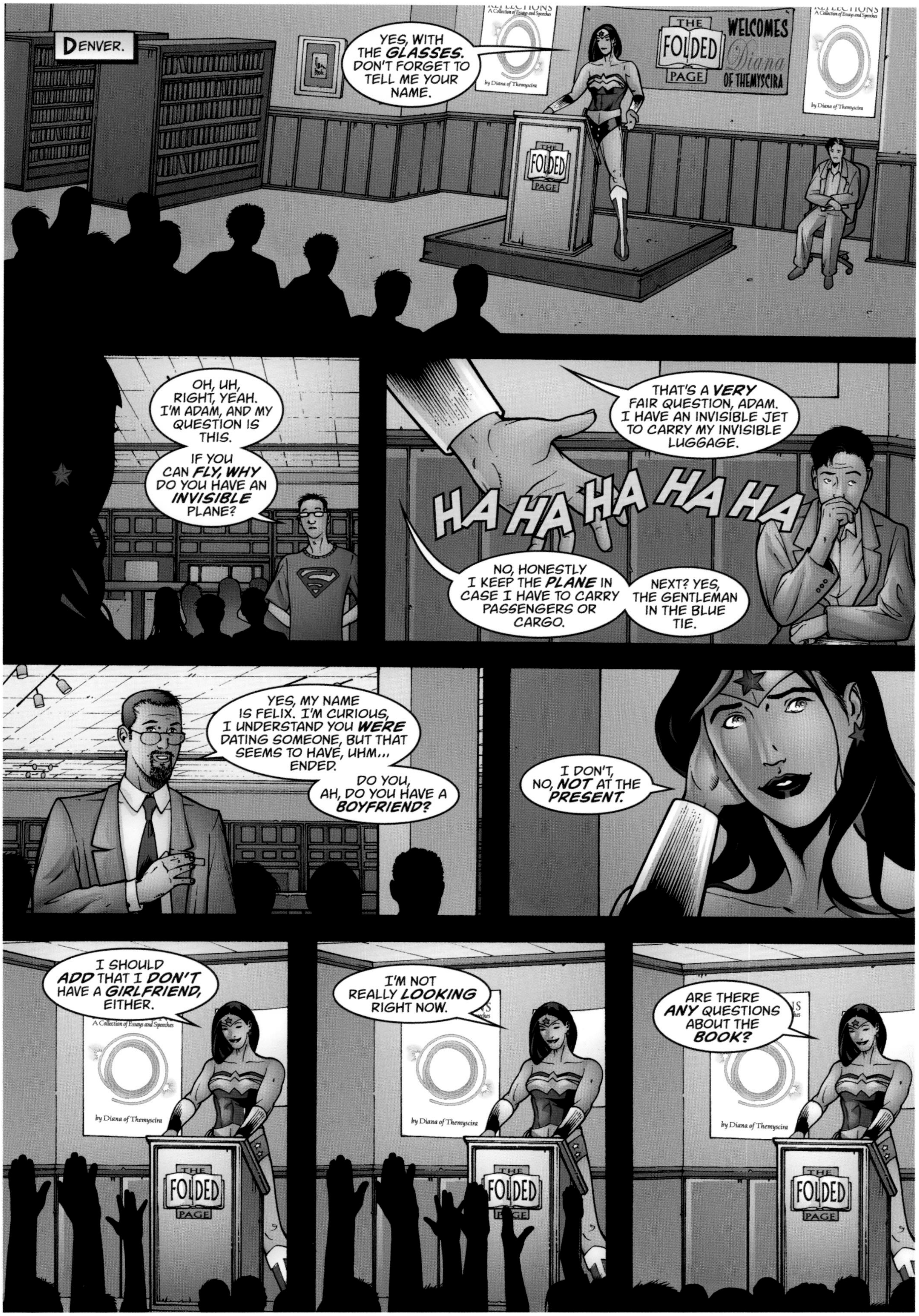
DENVER.
REFLECTIONS A Collection of Essays and Speeches by Diana of Themyscira
THE FOLDED PAGE WELCOMES Diana OF THEMYSCIRA
YES, WITH THE GLASSES. DON'T FORGET TO TELL ME YOUR NAME.
THE FOLDED PAGE
OH, UH, RIGHT, YEAH. I'M ADAM, AND MY QUESTION IS THIS.
IF YOU CAN FLY, WHY DO YOU HAVE AN INVISIBLE PLANE?
THAT'S A VERY FAIR QUESTION, ADAM. I HAVE AN INVISIBLE JET TO CARRY MY INVISIBLE LUGGAGE.
HA HA HA HA HA
NO, HONESTLY I KEEP THE PLANE IN CASE I HAVE TO CARRY PASSENGERS OR CARGO.
NEXT? YES, THE GENTLEMAN IN THE BLUE TIE.
YES, MY NAME IS FELIX. I'M CURIOUS, I UNDERSTAND YOU WERE DATING SOMEONE, BUT THAT SEEMS TO HAVE, UHM... ENDED.
DO YOU, AH, DO YOU HAVE A BOYFRIEND?
I DON'T, NO, NOT AT THE PRESENT.
I SHOULD ADD THAT I DON'T HAVE A GIRLFRIEND, EITHER.
I'M NOT REALLY LOOKING RIGHT NOW.
ARE THERE ANY QUESTIONS ABOUT THE BOOK?

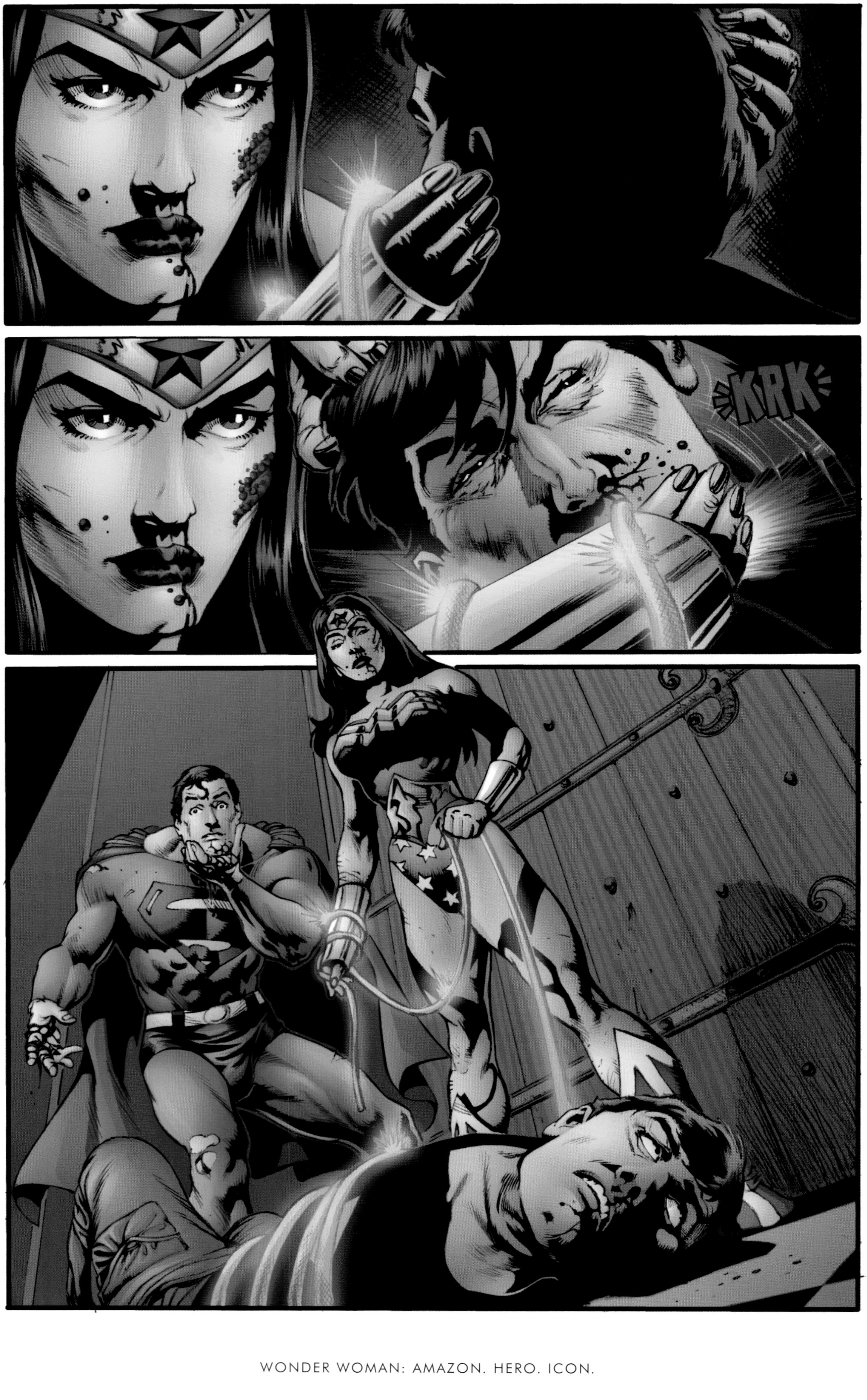
KRK

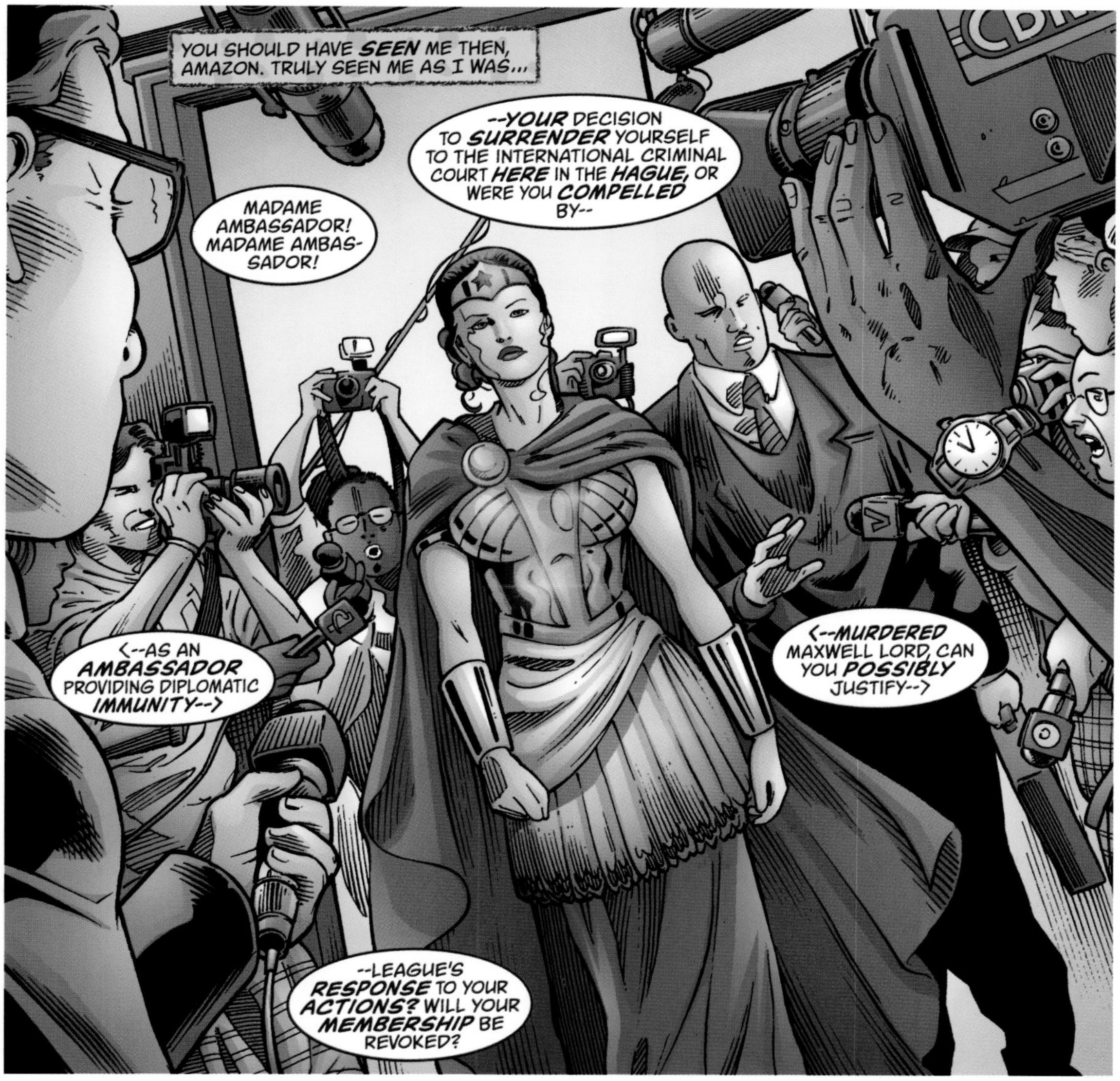
YOU SHOULD HAVE SEEN ME THEN, AMAZON. TRULY SEEN ME AS I WAS...
MADAME AMBASSADOR! MADAME AMBAS-SADOR!
--YOUR DECISION TO SURRENDER YOURSELF TO THE INTERNATIONAL CRIMINAL COURT HERE IN THE HAGUE, OR WERE YOU COMPELLED BY--
<--AS AN AMBASSADOR PROVIDING DIPLOMATIC IMMUNITY-->
<--MURDERED MAXWELL LORD, CAN YOU POSSIBLY JUSTIFY-->
--LEAGUE'S RESPONSE TO YOUR ACTIONS? WILL YOUR MEMBERSHIP BE REVOKED?

Left: Diana's warrior instinct resulted in her decision to kill Maxwell Lord to end his psychic attack. Snapping his neck freed Superman from Lord's mental thrall, but not before he nearly beat Batman to death. This sequence, drawn by Rags Morales and Michael Bair, proved to be pivotal in how the world at large perceived the Amazon Princess.

Above: After Lord's death, Princess Diana surrendered herself and became the subject of a media circus that preoccupied the world after its heroes ended a global threat—one orchestrated by Maxwell Lord. Art by Cliff Richards and Ray Snyder.

job. The . . . politics involved are fascinating, but not super appropriate to the series. UN procedure [would make] a pretty boring book."

Rucka acknowledged that the unique character Ferdinand, the Minotaur who served as the embassy chef, was a breakout hit with readers. It was also during this time Diana was established as being a vegetarian.

"One of the really cool things about Diana," Rucka added, "is that she straddles these two worlds, one very realistic—as much as a DCU super hero book can have a realistic world—and this world that is established out of mythology. It's just so cool that she can be on the street, after talking to Superman, after addressing the UN general assembly, and [then] on the next page be on Olympus arguing with Zeus, for example."

Given her exploits with the JLA and on her own, she was certainly the best-known ambassador to the United Nations. The public perception of her changed when she had to battle Medousa in a televised duel during a time when Diana had been briefly blinded. Soon after that battle, audiences around the world gasped as they watched her snap Maxwell Lord's neck, the recording deprived of the audio that explained she had little choice given Lord's mental enslavement of Superman.

At the end of the extended storyline, Themyscira was no more (so it seemed), and Diana's role as an ambassador came to an end. She still appeared before the World Court to answer charges of murder, which were subsequently dropped. The United States, however, convened a grand jury to consider similar charges, so Wonder Woman employed attorney Kate Spencer, whose alter ego was the costumed Manhunter. As expected, the grand jury refused to indict Wonder Woman in light of all her selfless and heroic deeds throughout the years.

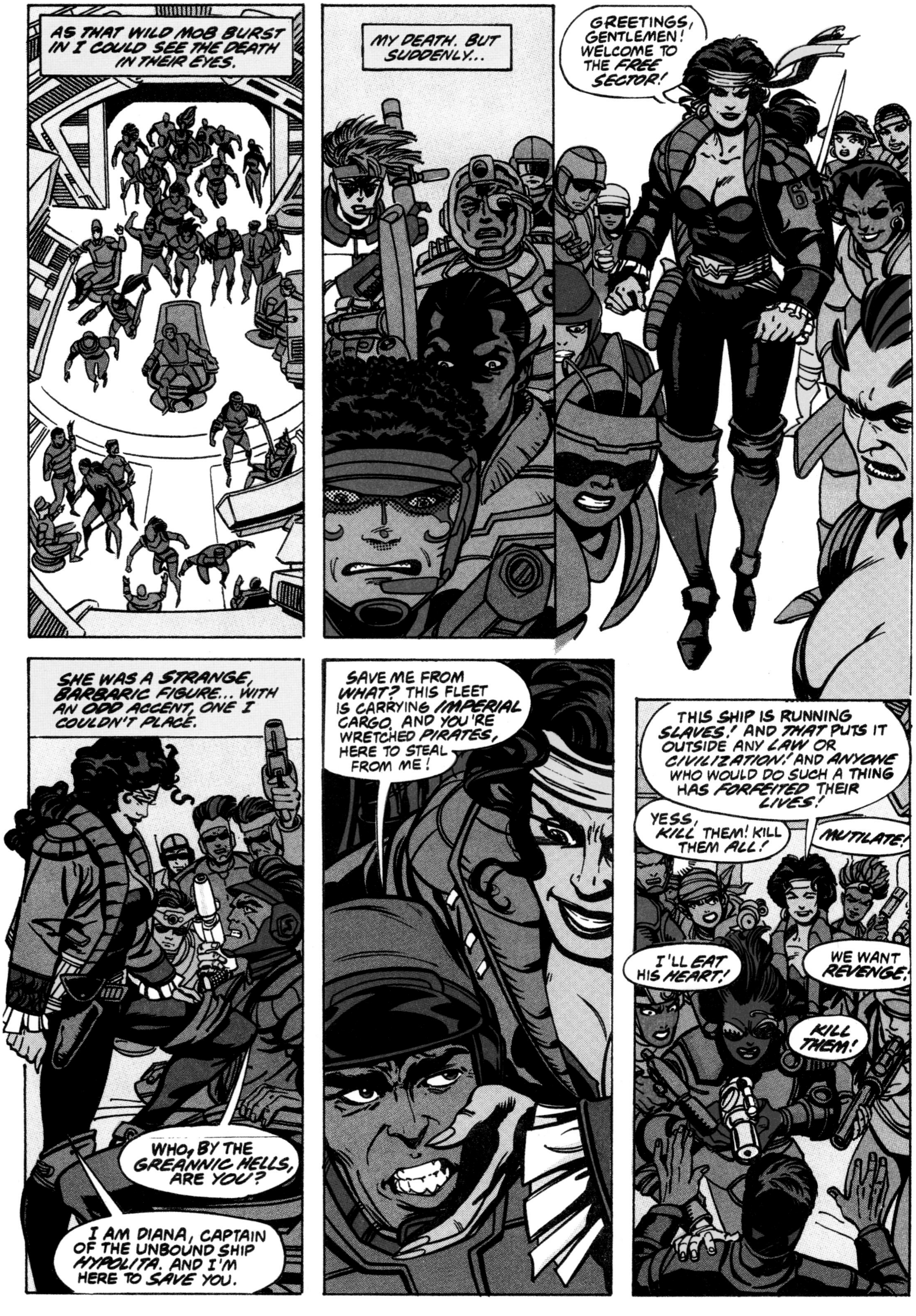

AS THAT WILD MOB BURST IN I COULD SEE THE DEATH IN THEIR EYES.
MY DEATH. BUT SUDDENLY...
GREETINGS, GENTLEMEN! WELCOME TO THE FREE SECTOR!
SHE WAS A STRANGE, BARBARIC FIGURE... WITH AN ODD ACCENT, ONE I COULDN'T PLACE.
WHO, BY THE GREANNIC HELLS, ARE YOU?
I AM DIANA, CAPTAIN OF THE UNBOUND SHIP HYPOLITA. AND I'M HERE TO SAVE YOU.
SAVE ME FROM WHAT? THIS FLEET IS CARRYING IMPERIAL CARGO, AND YOU'RE WRETCHED PIRATES, HERE TO STEAL FROM ME!
THIS SHIP IS RUNNING SLAVES! AND THAT PUTS IT OUTSIDE ANY LAW OR CIVILIZATION! AND ANYONE WHO WOULD DO SUCH A THING HAS FORFEITED THEIR LIVES!
YESS, KILL THEM! KILL THEM ALL!
MUTILATE!
I'LL EAT HIS HEART!
WE WANT REVENGE!
KILL THEM!

Above and right: While Wonder Woman spent a year in space, she aided numerous races, including leading a rag-tag team of freedom fighters to end the evil reign of a conqueror, as seen in this sequence from artists Paris Cullins and Robert Campanella.

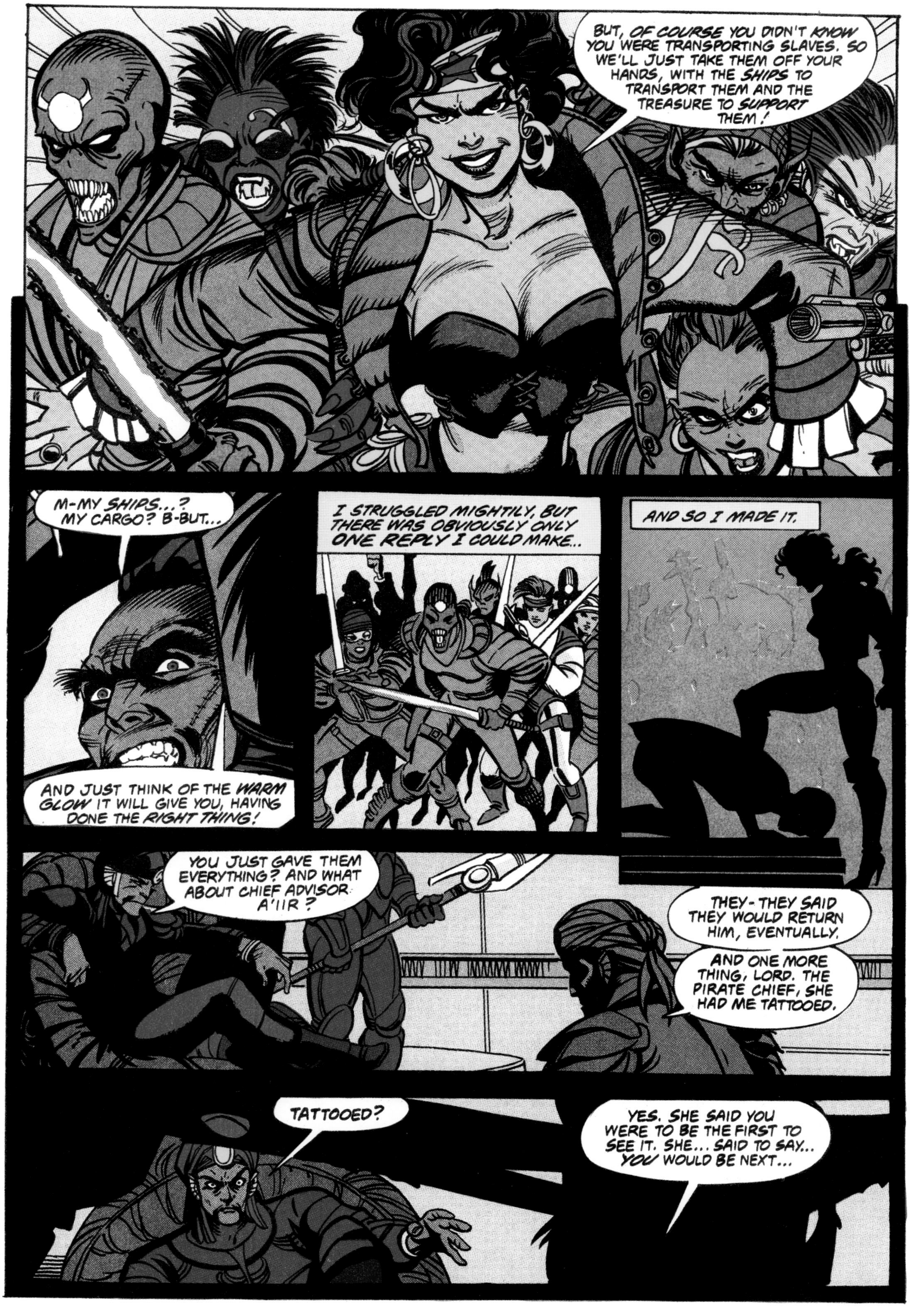
BUT, OF COURSE YOU DIDN'T KNOW YOU WERE TRANSPORTING SLAVES. SO WE'LL JUST TAKE THEM OFF YOUR HANDS, WITH THE SHIPS TO TRANSPORT THEM AND THE TREASURE TO SUPPORT THEM!
M-MY SHIPS...? MY CARGO? B-BUT...
AND JUST THINK OF THE WARM GLOW IT WILL GIVE YOU, HAVING DONE THE RIGHT THING!
I STRUGGLED MIGHTILY, BUT THERE WAS OBVIOUSLY ONLY ONE REPLY I COULD MAKE...
AND SO I MADE IT.
YOU JUST GAVE THEM EVERYTHING? AND WHAT ABOUT CHIEF ADVISOR A'IIR?
THEY- THEY SAID THEY WOULD RETURN HIM, EVENTUALLY.
AND ONE MORE THING, LORD. THE PIRATE CHIEF, SHE HAD ME TATTOOED.
TATTOOED?
YES. SHE SAID YOU WERE TO BE THE FIRST TO SEE IT. SHE... SAID TO SAY... YOU WOULD BE NEXT...

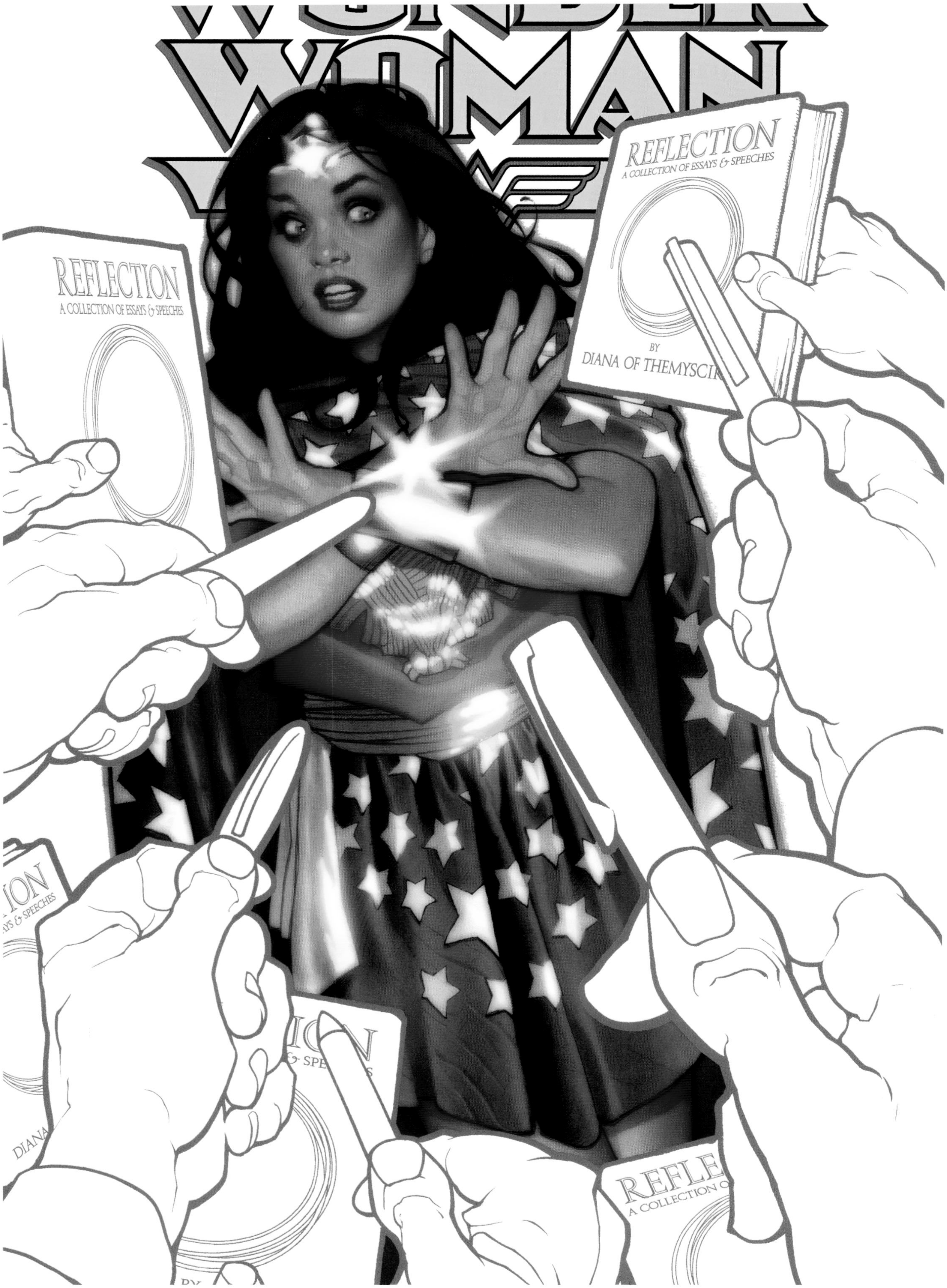
WOMAN
REFLECTION
A COLLECTION OF ESSAYS & SPEECHES
REFLECTION
A COLLECTION OF ESSAYS & SPEECHES
BY
DIANA OF

Above: To spread her message, Wonder Woman collected her various essays, speeches, and poems into *Reflections*, which became a controversial best seller. Adam Hughes's cover shows the response was not at all what Diana of Themyscira expected.

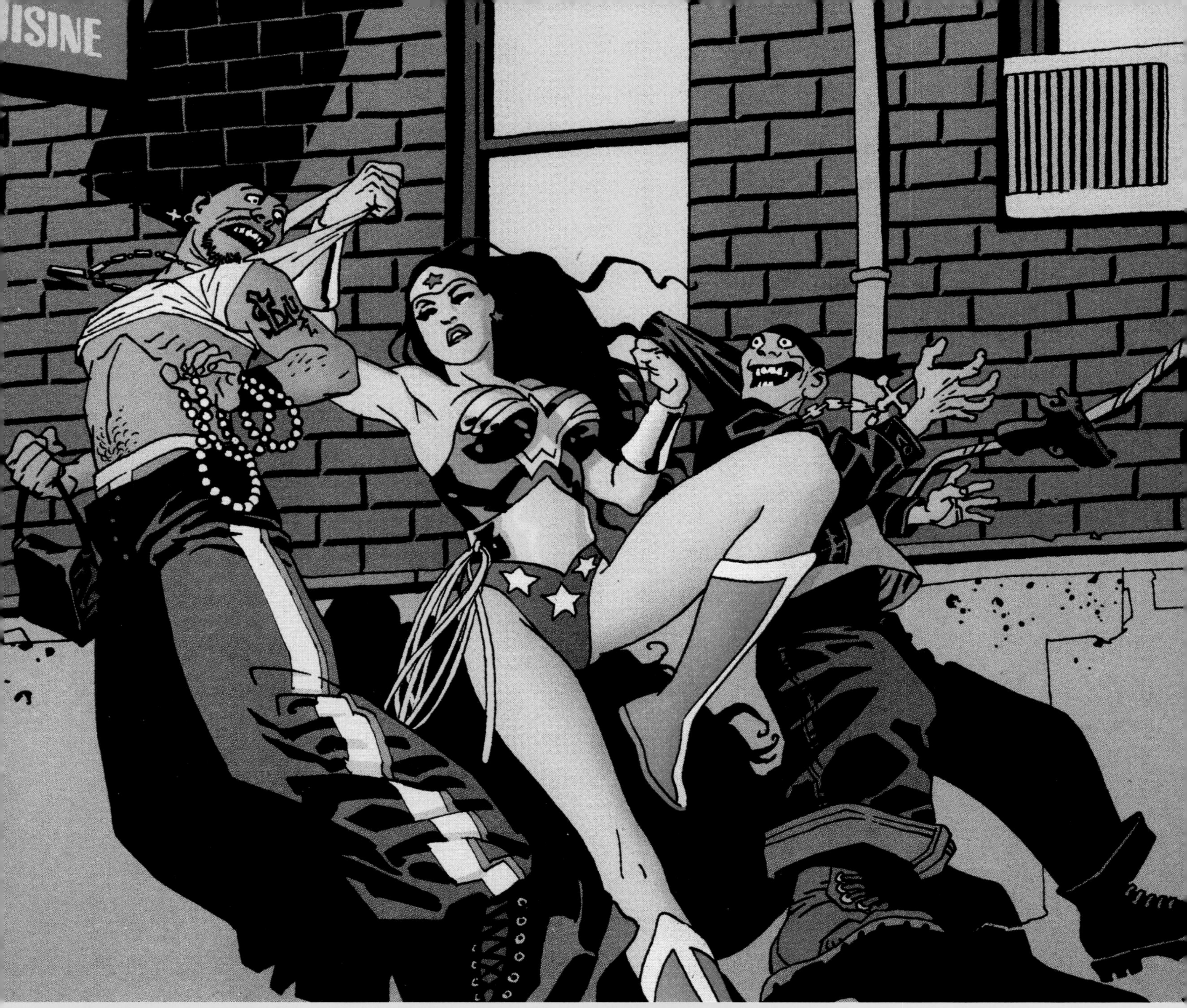

Greg Rucka

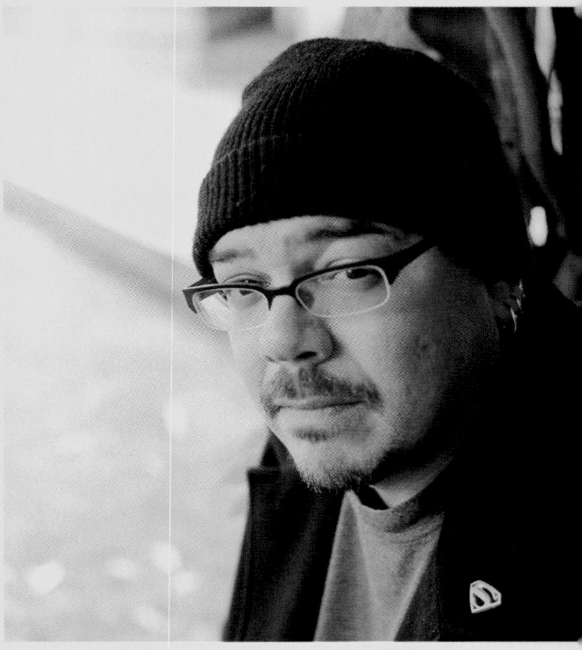

Novelist Greg Rucka created the private investigator Atticus Kodiak and received critical acclaim for his bestselling mysteries. Editor Denny O'Neil picked up one of the books at random, liked the writing, and hired Rucka to come write Batman for DC Comics. Since then, Rucka has split his time between comics and prose. At one point, he was simultaneously writing the adventures of Superman, Batman, and Wonder Woman (#195, October 2003–#226, April 2006), a feat not accomplished since O'Neil himself did the same in the 1970s. Recently, his graphic novel, *Whiteout*, with artist Steven Lieber, became a 2009 feature film.

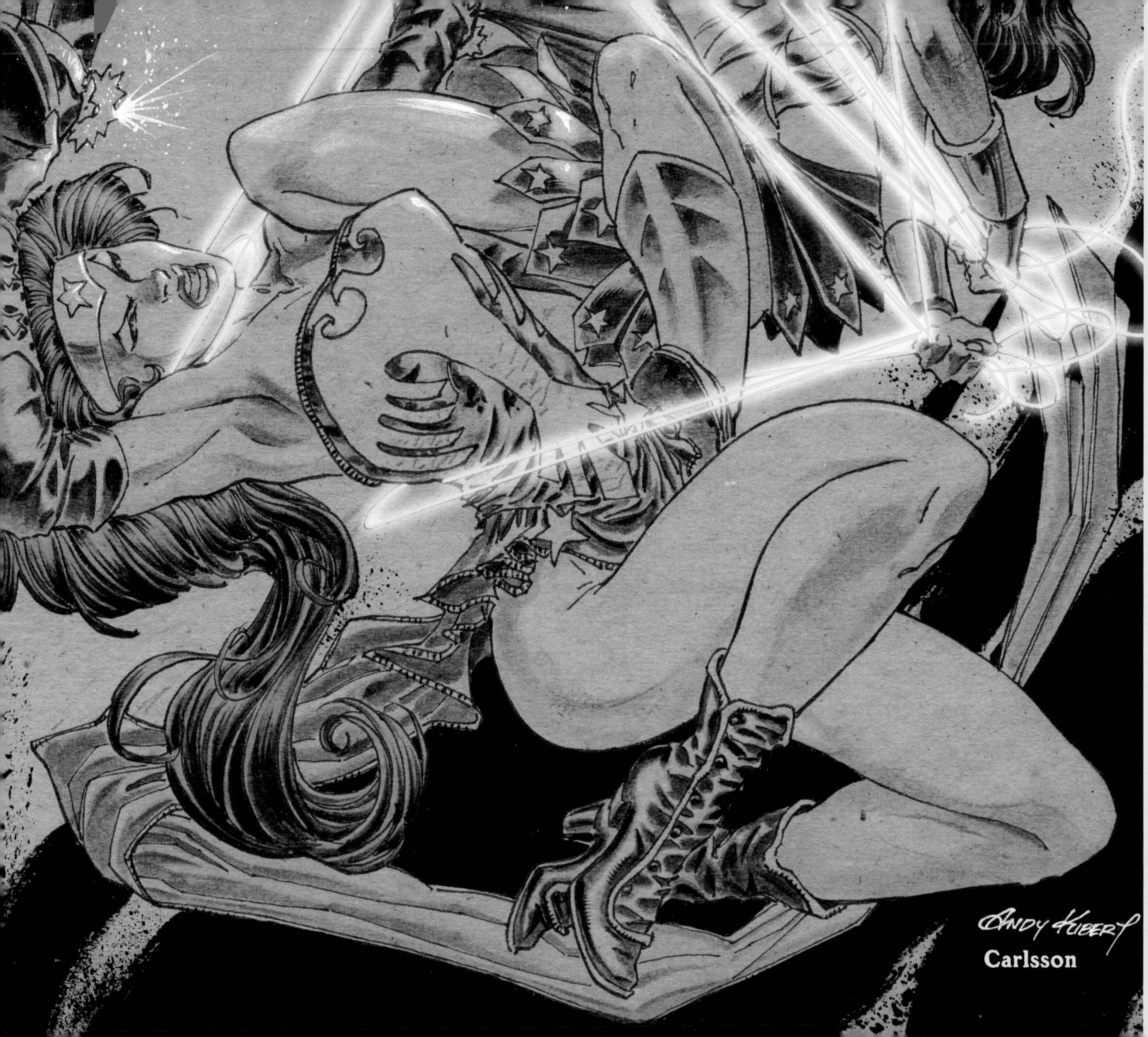
Andy Kubert
Carlsson

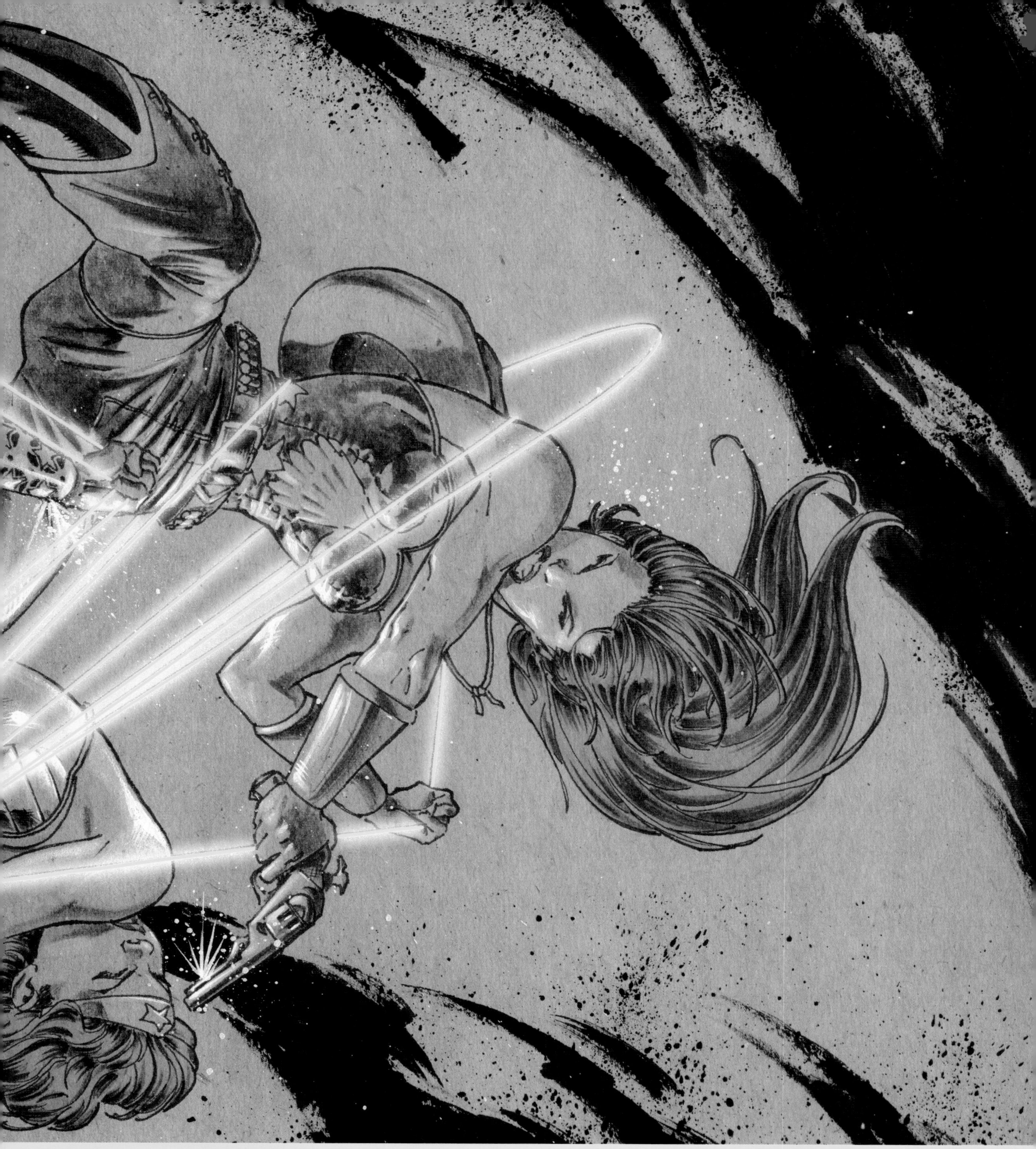

★ The Other Realities

Accept for a moment that all comic book adventures are imaginary; works of fiction to entertain and occasionally enlighten.

Now accept that an internal continuity develops for each character, a sustained status quo that may evolve with time, but remains constant. Much like your favorite prime-time television series, Wonder Woman and the larger DC Universe has a continuity that forms the framework for writers and artists.

In comics, though, this continuity was a gradual evolution and as a result, most story elements contradicted previously told tales, whether intentionally or otherwise. Such attempts at streamlining the comic book reality began in 1985, with *Crisis on Infinite Earths*. The book took the countless parallel Earths and condensed them into one, with the hopes that future storylines would be simplified for new and old readers alike.

For the Amazon Princess, this major event allowed her a fresh start, taking the best of Marston's concepts and reworking them, moving them toward a modern context.

In the decades prior to *Crisis*, though, Marston and company told many delightful stories, sending his creation to other worlds and other time periods, including one memorable visit with Julius Caesar. One of his earliest tales involved Wonder Woman running for president—and winning—in 3004.

Kanigher did much of the same when he inherited the series, but by 1959, he also began telling impossible tales of Diana's younger days, first as Wonder Girl, and then in 1961, as Wonder Tot.

Above: Under writer/editor Robert Kanigher, Wonder Woman appeared in numerous "Impossible Tales" which let the adult team up with her junior self, joining Queen Hippolyta in adventures through time and space.

Right: When stories about Diana as Wonder Girl proved to be popular, Kanigher went further into Wonder Woman's past and introduced Wonder Tot, who fought another of Kanigher's recurring themes: a robot duplicate of the super heroine. Art by Ross Andru and Mike Esposito.

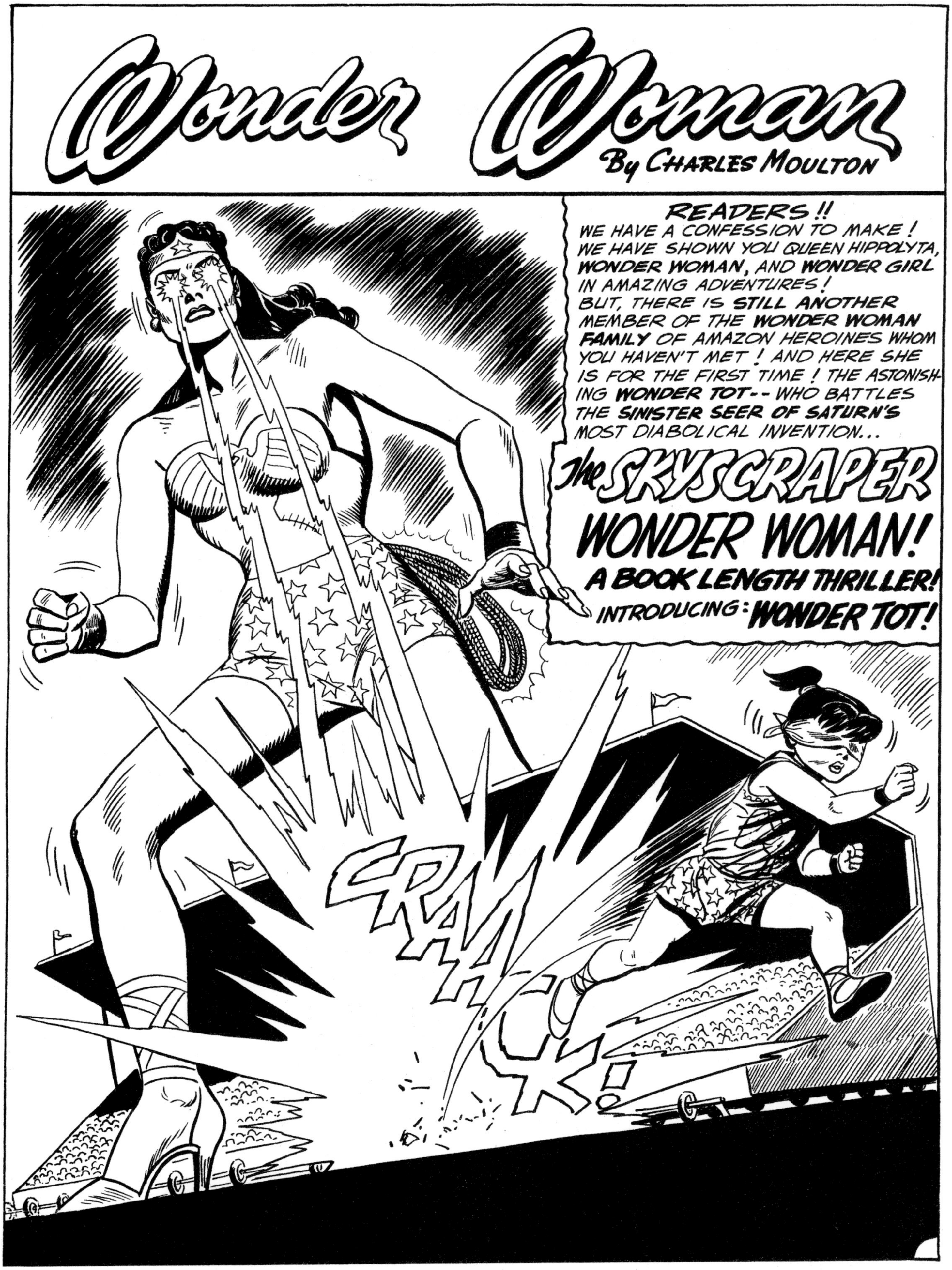
Wonder Woman
By CHARLES MOULTON
READERS!!
WE HAVE A CONFESSION TO MAKE! WE HAVE SHOWN YOU QUEEN HIPPOLYTA, WONDER WOMAN, AND WONDER GIRL IN AMAZING ADVENTURES! BUT, THERE IS STILL ANOTHER MEMBER OF THE WONDER WOMAN FAMILY OF AMAZON HEROINES WHOM YOU HAVEN'T MET! AND HERE SHE IS FOR THE FIRST TIME! THE ASTONISHING WONDER TOT-- WHO BATTLES THE SINISTER SEER OF SATURN'S MOST DIABOLICAL INVENTION...
The SKYSCRAPER WONDER WOMAN!
A BOOK LENGTH THRILLER!
INTRODUCING: WONDER TOT!
CRAAACK!

...SOME ARE DEAD!

At one point, with sales flagging and tastes changing, Kanigher wrote a story inserting himself as a character. In the tale, he was a writer and he called the entire cast into his office and fired everyone but Diana, Hippolyta, and Steve Trevor. So much for those imaginary tales. In 1982, Roy Thomas explored other roads not taken in the landmark *Wonder Woman* #300 (February 1983). Something called the Shadow-Thing plagued Diana's dreams and the Sandman came to her aid, but not before she saw flashes of potential futures, such as a promotion to major, ruling Paradise Island in the wake of Hippolyta's death, falling in love with a man who turned out to be a criminal, marrying Superman, and becoming a power-hungry world-conquering despot. She even traveled to Earth-2, where she met her counterpart, who had been married to Steve Trevor for twenty years and was parent to Lyta Trevor, a heroine named Fury. In the end, Diana discovered the Shadow-Thing was a physical manifestation of her own fears. After recognizing the truth, thanks to her magic lasso, the creature vanished for good.

However, there still remained a desire to explore "what if" scenarios, and with just one universe now, DC's writers and artists began crafting tales under a separate imprint called Elseworlds. One of the most beautiful of these projects was *Amazonia*, an oversized publication that imagined Diana as arriving in Man's World during nineteenth-century Victorian England. Written by William Messner-Loebs and illustrated by Phil Winslade, the 1997 book dealt with the subjugation of women and the lurking threat from —who else?—Jack the Ripper.

Inspired by the German silent vampire film *Nosferatu*, writers Jean-Marc and Randy Lofficier and artist Ted McKeever produced a trilogy of related one-shots, including 2003's *Wonder Woman: Blue Amazon*, which also borrowed elements from *The Blue Angel* and *Dr. Mabuse, the Gambler*.

Wonder Woman also played a role in numerous other Elseworlds that involved the DC Universe's super heroes, none more influential than *Kingdom Come*. The publication saw her as a noble warrior in a world that rejected its champions, as well as allowing Superman and Diana finally to come to terms with their feelings for one another.

Similarly, *Whom Gods Destroy*—a 1997 miniseries from Chris Claremont, Dusty Abell, and Drew Geraci—also looked at the relationship between the two heroes. The story began in the near-future, with an aging Lois Lane living in a world where the Nazi Party still ruled Germany. Lois was flying over Germany when her plane was forced to crash-land after being attacked by Harpies. Crawling away from the wreckage, she discovered that the Greek gods were the real power in Europe, complete with Diana acting as a Nazi warrior. It's Lois who eventually becomes Wonder Woman and fights to free humankind from the gods. In the end, Diana is defeated and Lois, as Wonder Woman, wins Superman's heart.

Realworlds, a variation on the Elseworlds series, imagined the heroes in our world. The Wonder Woman volume depicted a Hollywood actress Brenda Kelly, star of the *Wonder Woman* serials, caught up in the post–WW II Communist witch hunts.

Above: Ted McKeever reimagined Wonder Woman in the Elseworlds take *Wonder Woman: Blue Amazon*, which was inspired by the great German silent films of the early twentieth century.

Right: Phil Winslade illustrated *Amazonia*, which imagined Wonder Woman in Victorian England. His art style attempted to replicate the woodcut style popular during the era.

Pages 200-1: The following two pages depict Wonder Woman in an alternate reality leading the charge with freedom fighters against the thirtieth century's Legion of Super-Heroes. Art by Carlos Pacheco and Jesús Merino.

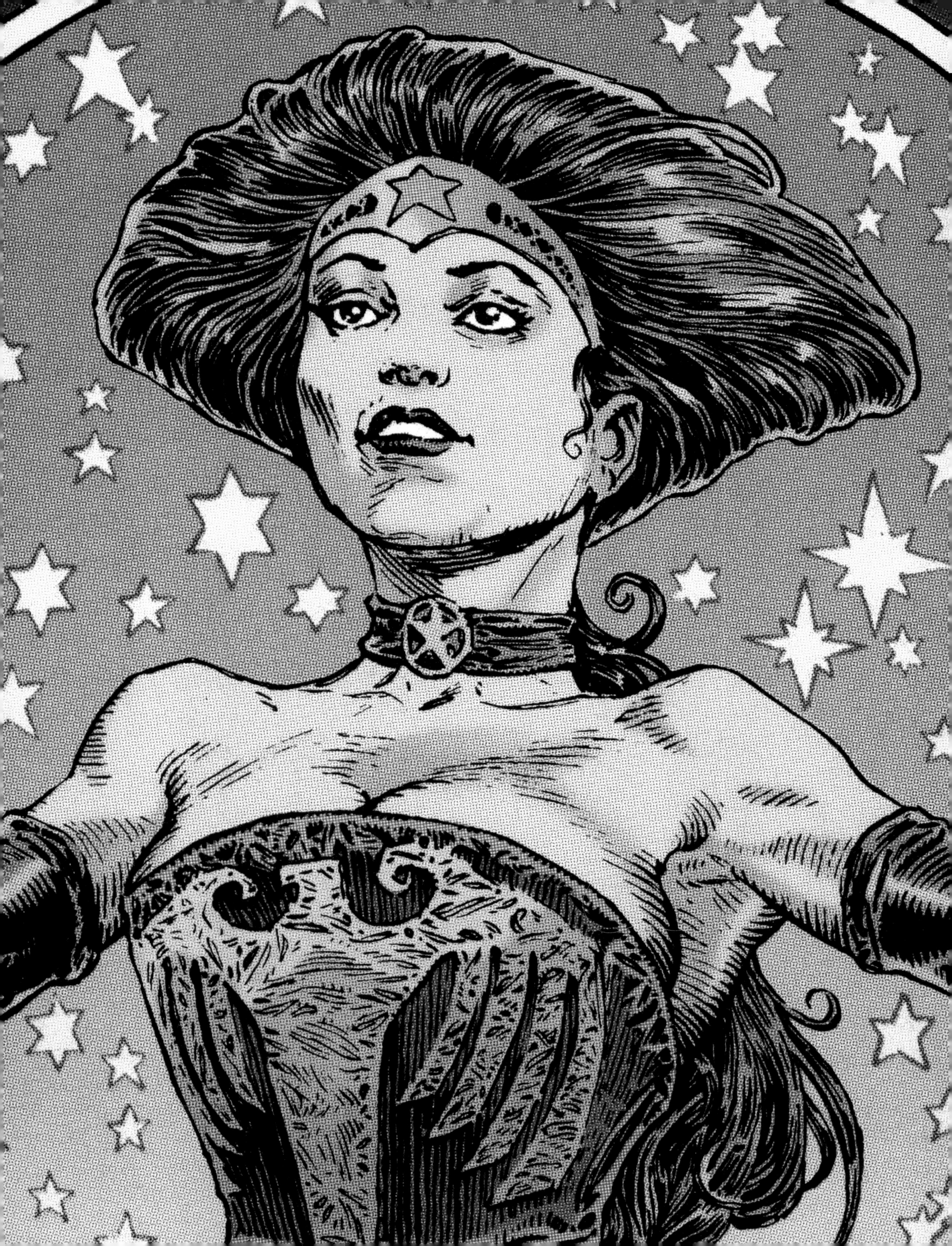

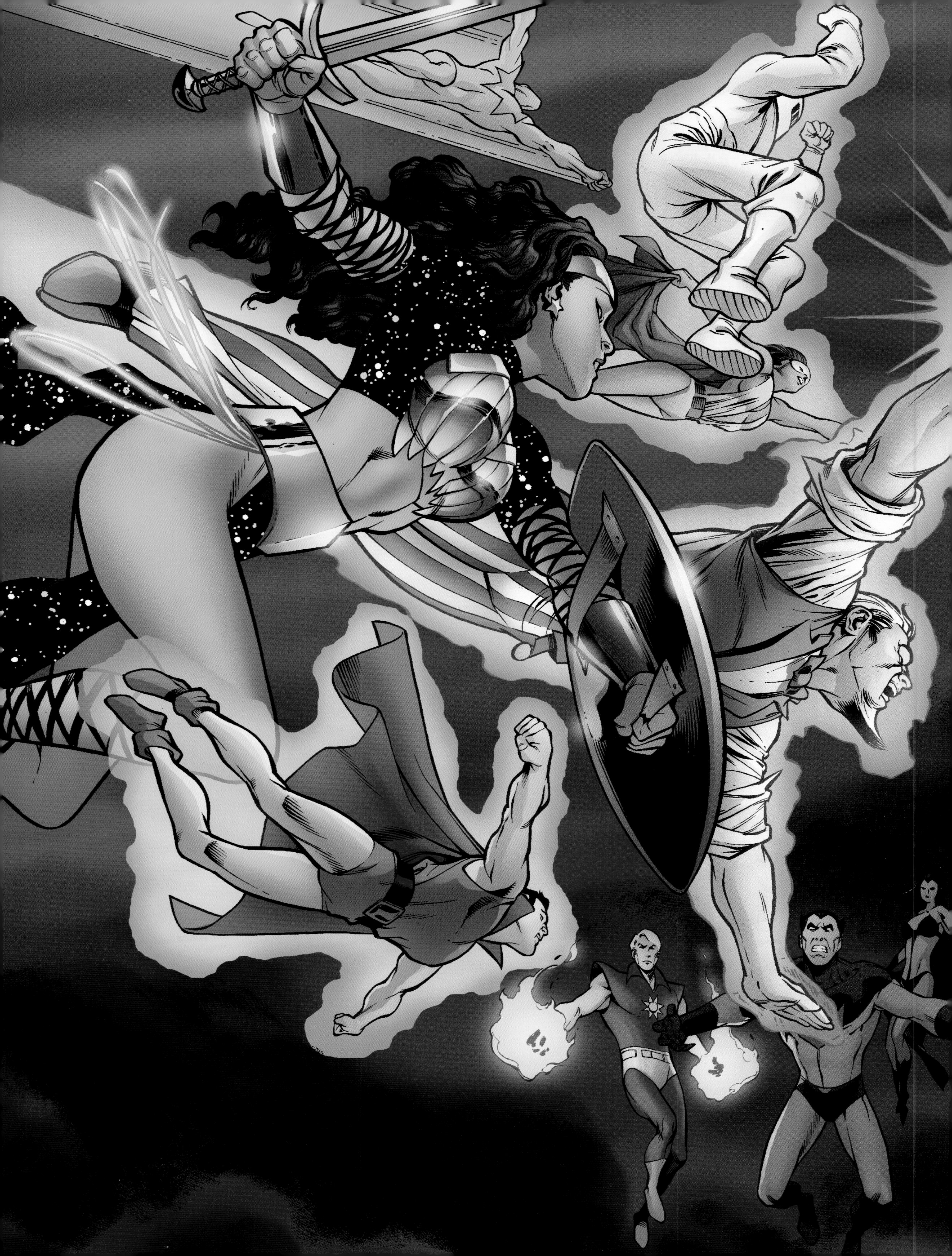

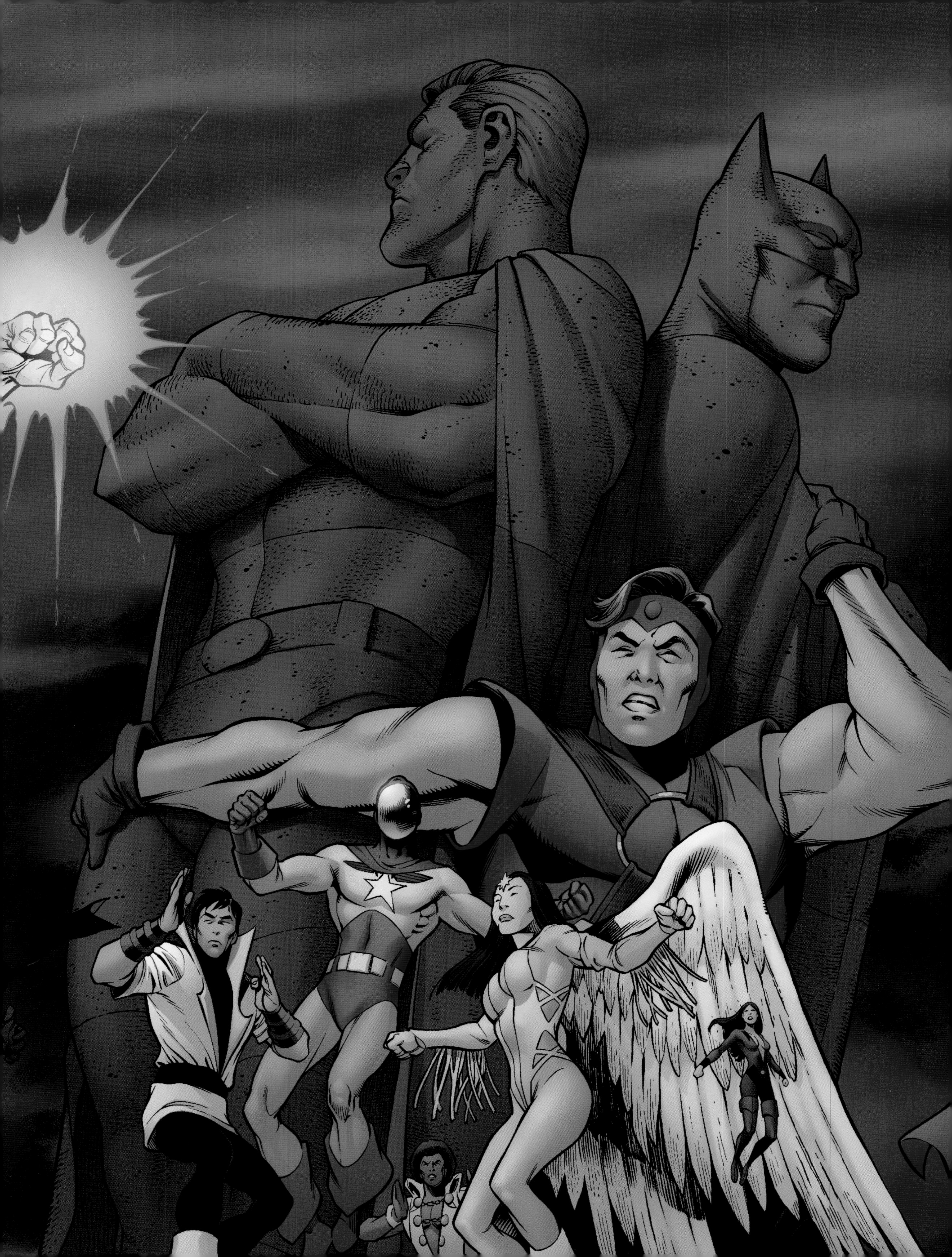

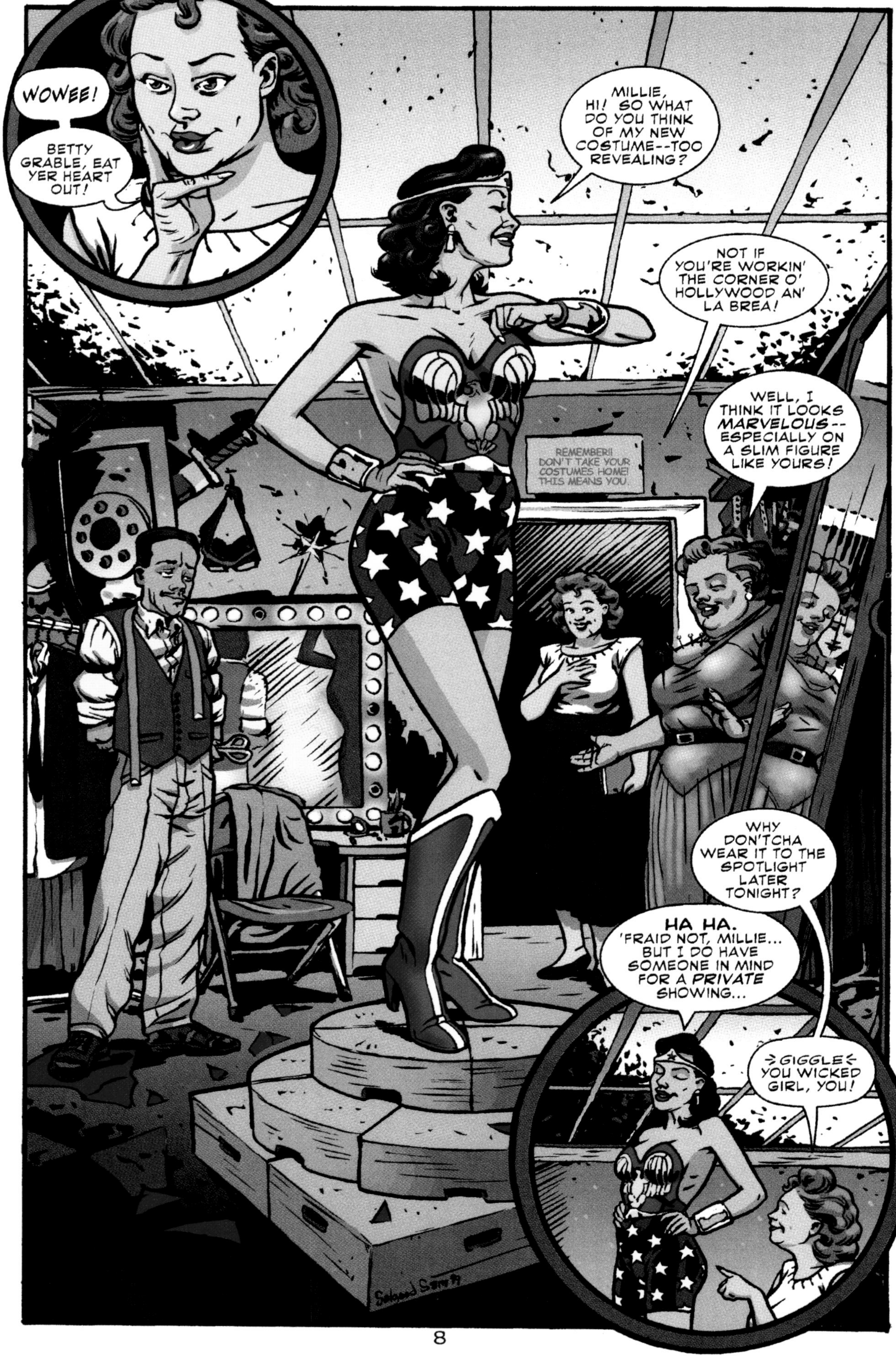
WOWEE!
BETTY GRABLE, EAT YER HEART OUT!
MILLIE, HI! SO WHAT DO YOU THINK OF MY NEW COSTUME--TOO REVEALING?
NOT IF YOU'RE WORKIN' THE CORNER O' HOLLYWOOD AN' LA BREA!
WELL, I THINK IT LOOKS MARVELOUS-- ESPECIALLY ON A SLIM FIGURE LIKE YOURS!
REMEMBER!! DON'T TAKE YOUR COSTUMES HOME! THIS MEANS YOU.
WHY DON'TCHA WEAR IT TO THE SPOTLIGHT LATER TONIGHT?
HA HA. 'FRAID NOT, MILLIE... BUT I DO HAVE SOMEONE IN MIND FOR A PRIVATE SHOWING...
GIGGLE YOU WICKED GIRL, YOU!
Salgood Sam
8

Above: *Realworlds: Wonder Woman* showed what our world's heroine might be: a 1940s movie serial star and not a super hero. Art by Salgood Sam.

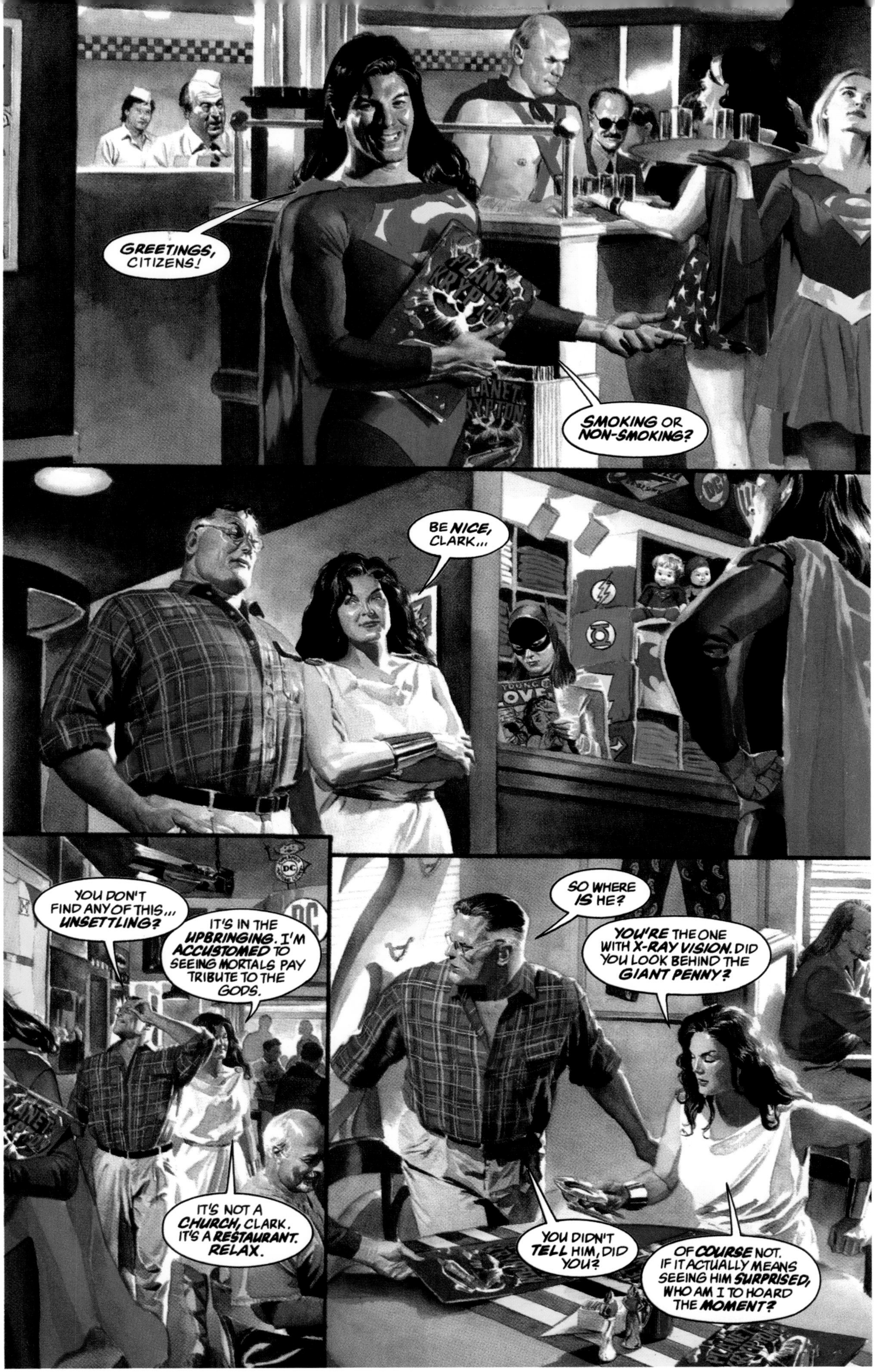
GREETINGS, CITIZENS!
SMOKING OR NON-SMOKING?
BE NICE, CLARK...
YOU DON'T FIND ANY OF THIS... UNSETTLING?
IT'S IN THE UPBRINGING. I'M ACCUSTOMED TO SEEING MORTALS PAY TRIBUTE TO THE GODS.
IT'S NOT A CHURCH, CLARK. IT'S A RESTAURANT. RELAX.
SO WHERE IS HE?
YOU'RE THE ONE WITH X-RAY VISION. DID YOU LOOK BEHIND THE GIANT PENNY?
YOU DIDN'T TELL HIM, DID YOU?
OF COURSE NOT. IF IT ACTUALLY MEANS SEEING HIM SURPRISED, WHO AM I TO HOARD THE MOMENT?

Above: Writer Mark Waid and artist Alex Ross conceived of a more mature Superman and Wonder Woman in the classic graphic novel, *Kingdom Come*. Here, they arrive at the Planet Krypton restaurant, where the servers dressed as super heroes.

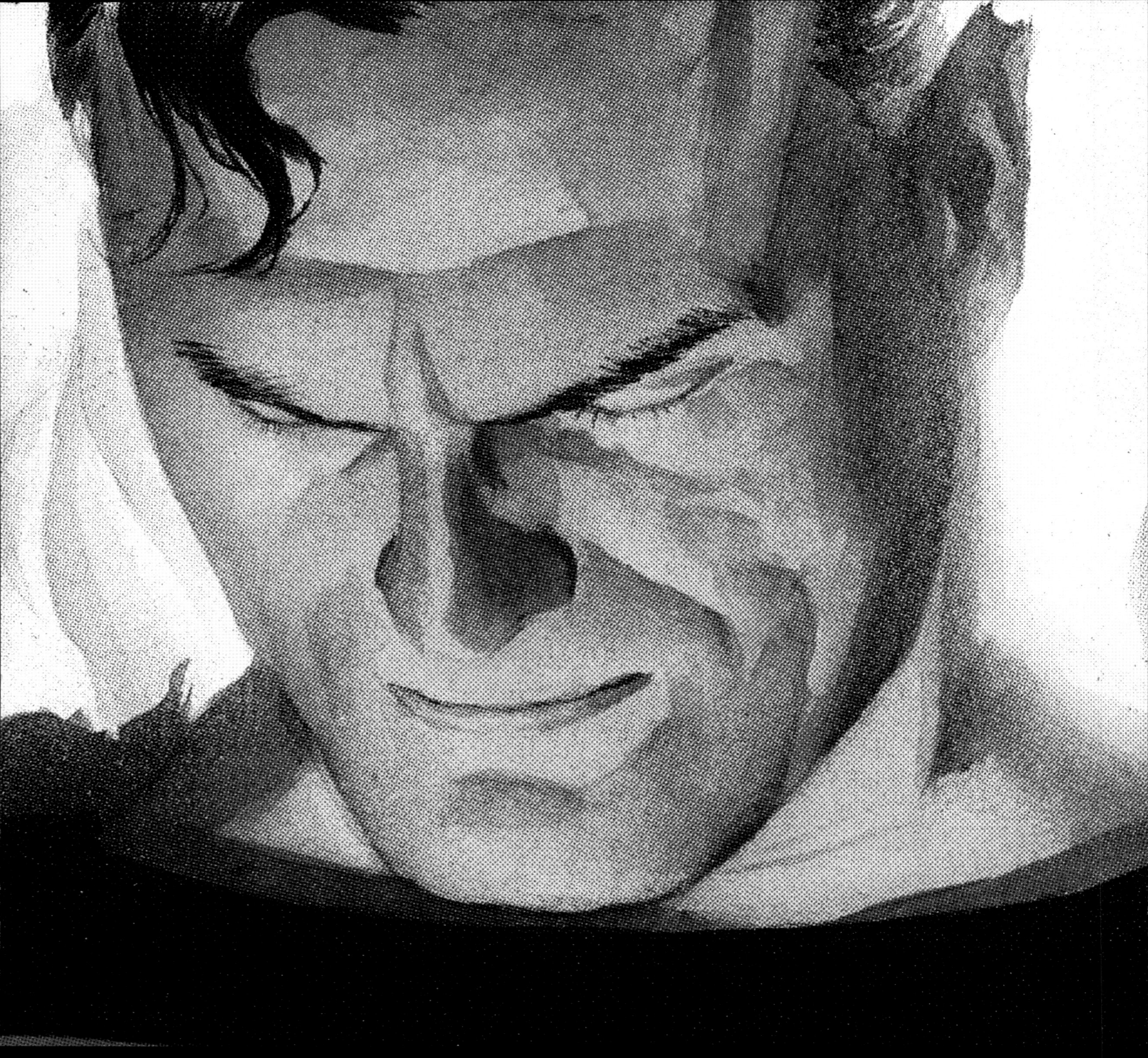

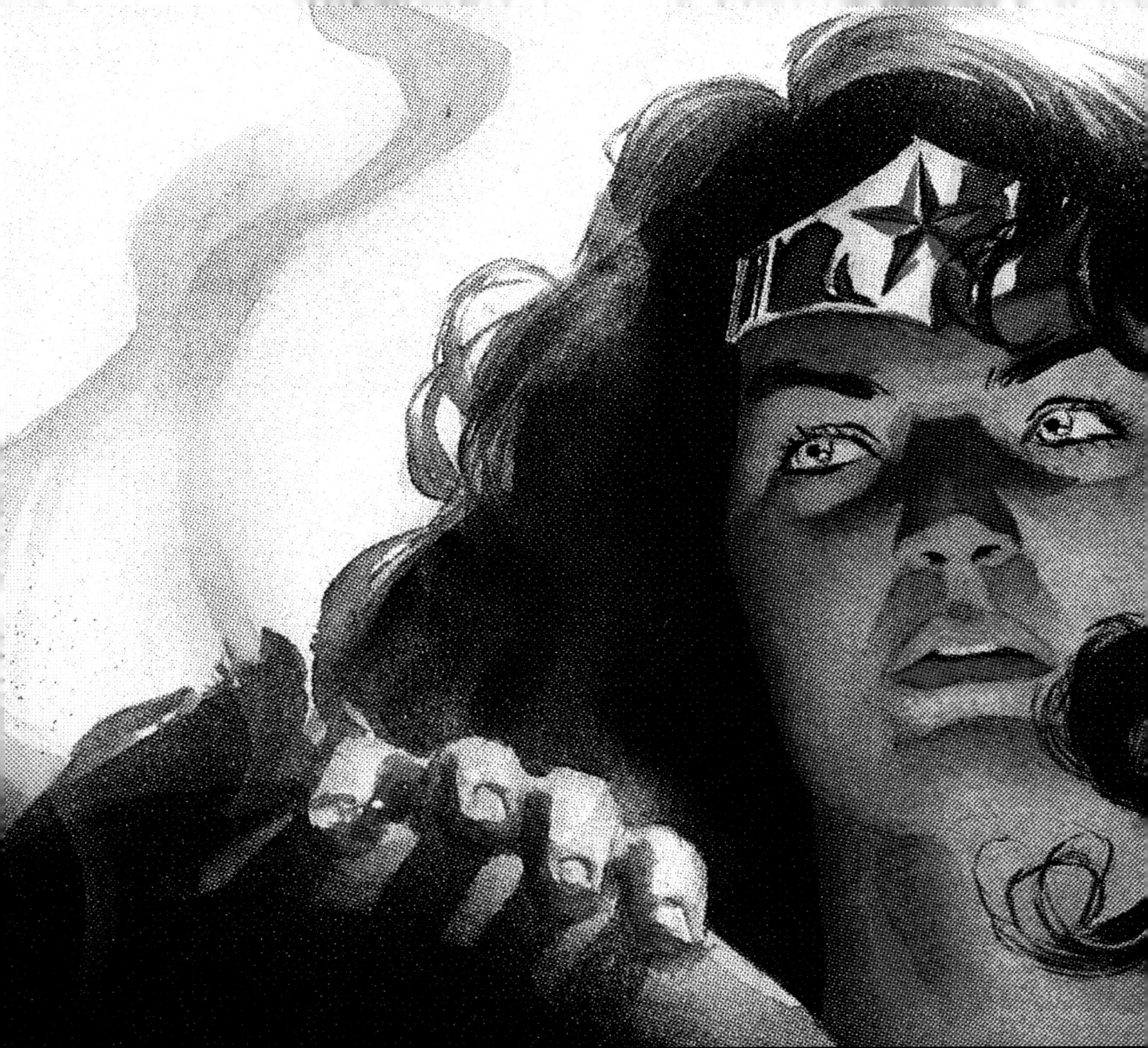

Above: A detail from *Kingdom Come*. Wonder Woman tries to comfort her friend and ally, Superman, after coaxing him to return and rejoin the fight for truth, justice, and the American way.

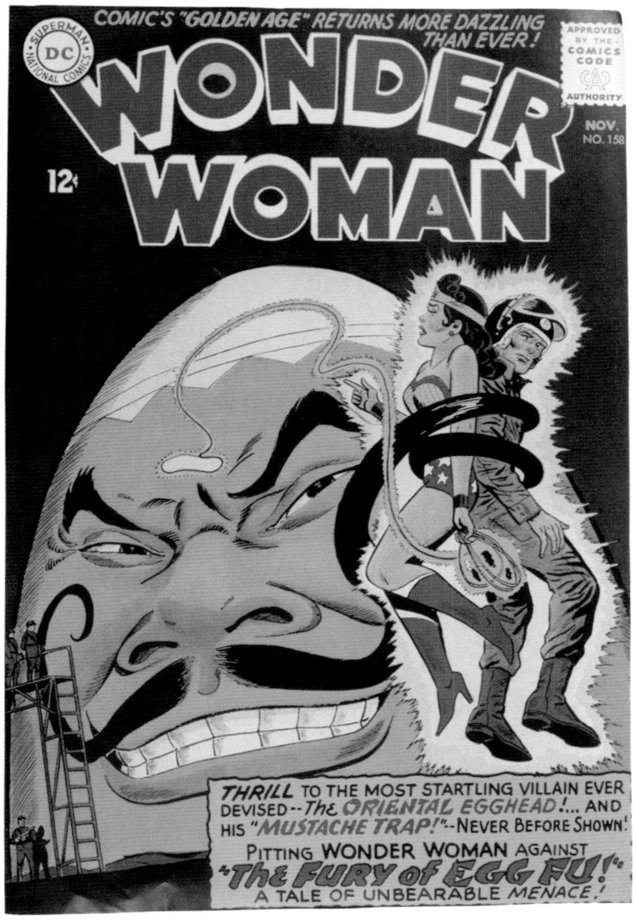
COMIC'S "GOLDEN AGE" RETURNS MORE DAZZLING THAN EVER!
SUPERMAN DC NATIONAL COMICS
APPROVED BY THE COMICS CODE AUTHORITY
WONDER WOMAN
NOV. NO. 158
12¢
THRILL TO THE MOST STARTLING VILLAIN EVER DEVISED--The ORIENTAL EGGHEAD!... AND HIS "MUSTACHE TRAP!"--NEVER BEFORE SHOWN!
PITTING WONDER WOMAN AGAINST
"The FURY of EGG FU!"
A TALE OF UNBEARABLE MENACE!

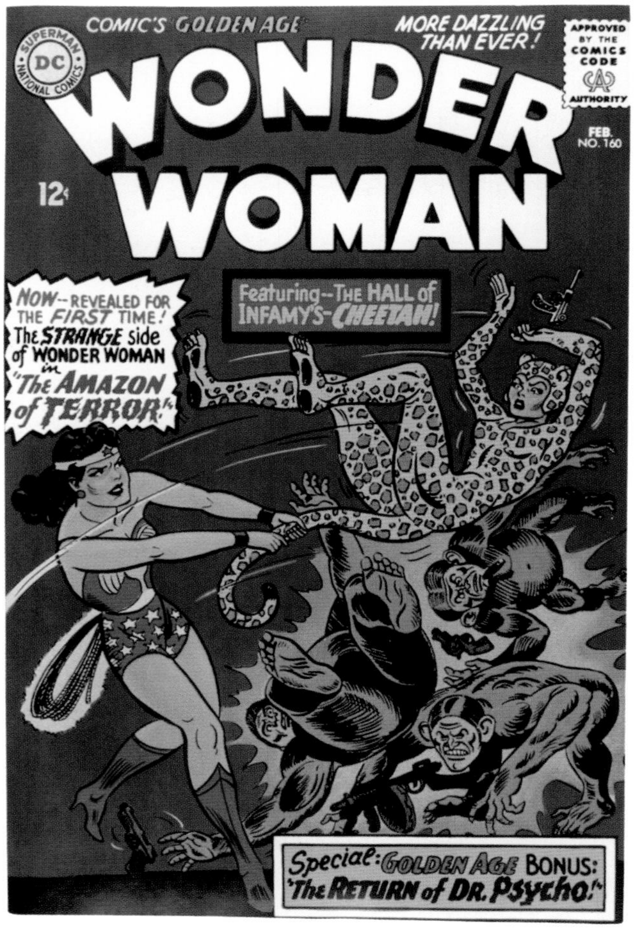
COMIC'S GOLDEN AGE
MORE DAZZLING THAN EVER!
SUPERMAN DC NATIONAL COMICS
APPROVED BY THE COMICS CODE AUTHORITY
WONDER WOMAN
FEB. NO. 160
12¢
NOW--REVEALED FOR THE FIRST TIME! The STRANGE side of WONDER WOMAN in "The AMAZON of TERROR"
Featuring--The HALL of INFAMY'S--CHEETAH!
Special: GOLDEN AGE BONUS: "The RETURN of DR. PSYCHO!"

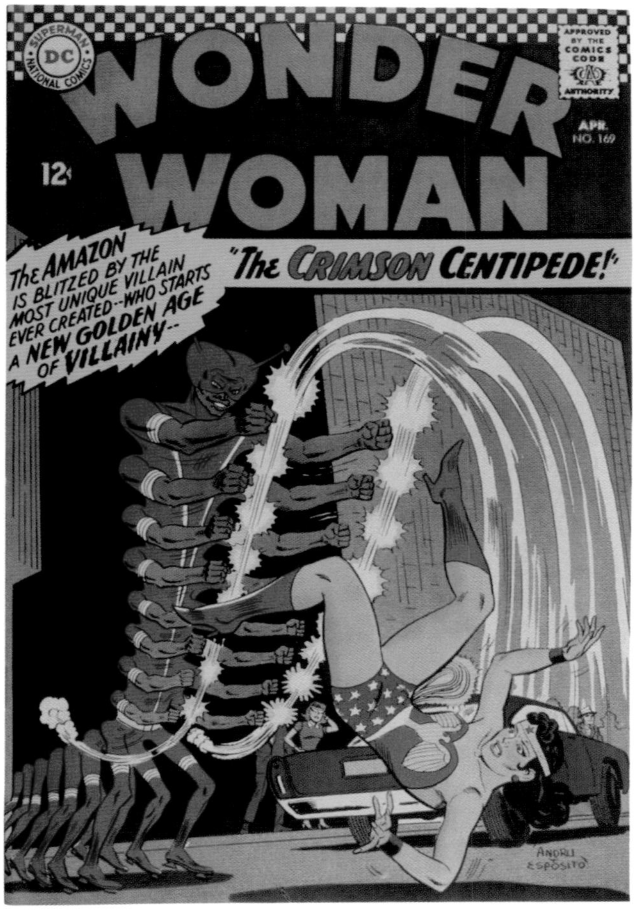
SUPERMAN DC NATIONAL COMICS
APPROVED BY THE COMICS CODE AUTHORITY
WONDER WOMAN
APR. NO. 169
12¢
The AMAZON IS BLITZED BY THE MOST UNIQUE VILLAIN EVER CREATED--WHO STARTS A NEW GOLDEN AGE OF VILLAINY--
"The CRIMSON CENTIPEDE!"
ANDRU ESPOSITO

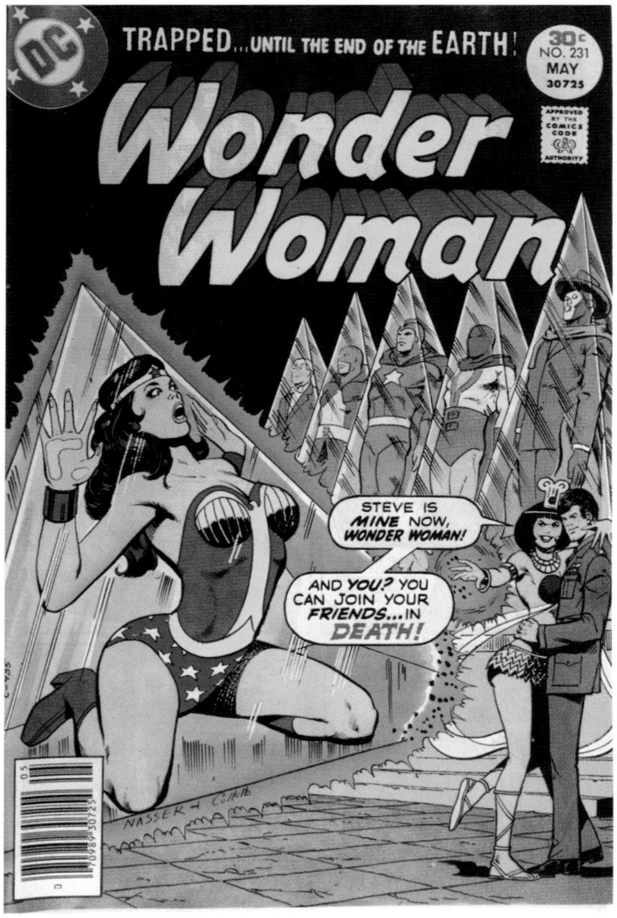
DC
TRAPPED...UNTIL THE END OF THE EARTH!
30¢ NO. 231 MAY 30725
APPROVED BY THE COMICS CODE AUTHORITY
Wonder Woman
STEVE IS MINE NOW, WONDER WOMAN!
AND YOU? YOU CAN JOIN YOUR FRIENDS...IN DEATH!
NASSER + COLAN

Wonder Woman's enemies came from other places, other realities and were often seemingly outlandish, from the threat of Egg Fu to a reincarnated Egyptian goddess on a parallel world. Above left, above right, and below left: Cover art by Ross Andru and Mike Esposito. Below right: Cover art by Michael Nasser and Vince Colletta.

URLS STEVE OVER ONE SHOULDER AND...
LOOK OUT, ANGEL! BEFORE SHE CRUSHES YOU!
FEMALE! SHE CA
LOVE AND HAT
WITH THE SAM
BREATH!
TH A CAST OF HER GLITTERING
AGIC LASSO...
HOW CAN I
GHT ANYONE WHO'S SO INFATU-
TED WITH STEVE—THAT SHE
ANTS TO KILL ME? I'LL JUST
ASSO HER SO SHE CAN BE
UT BACK IN HER CAGE AGAIN!
AT THAT MOMENT...
I AM PROF. ZOOL, WONDER WOMAN! THIS GORILLA IS THE PERFECT SUBJECT FOR MY EVOLUTION MACHINE--SINCE SHE SHOWS SUCH REMARKABLE HUMAN TRAITS THAT SHE MUST BE ONE STEP AWAY FROM A COMPLETE EVOLUTION!
HOW OFTEN, PROF. ZOOL-- MUST WE TELL YOU WE DON'T ALLOW EXPERIMENTATION ON OUR ANIMALS?
AN UNOBSERVED WITNESS TO
THIS DRAMA IS THE EVIL GEN
THAT GORILLA IS THE INSTRUMENT WITH WHICH I WILL DESTROY WONDER WOMAN!

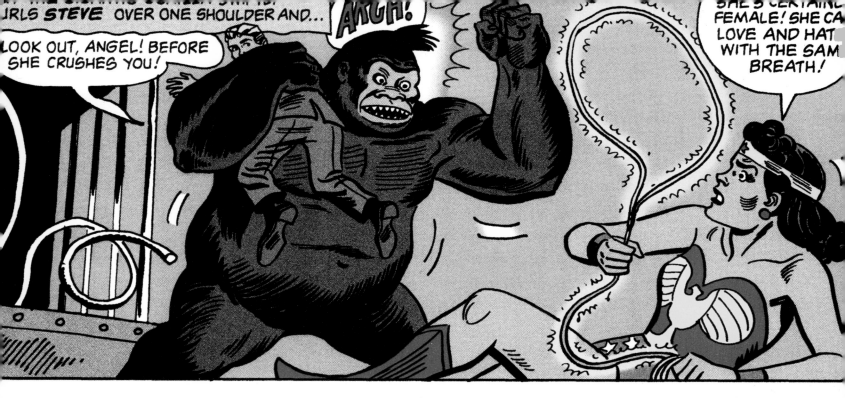

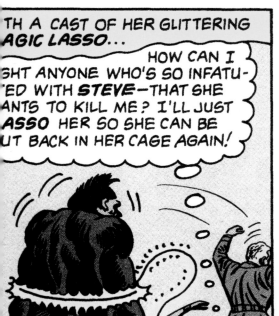

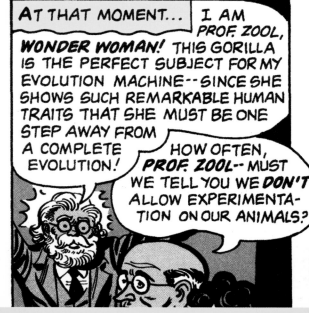

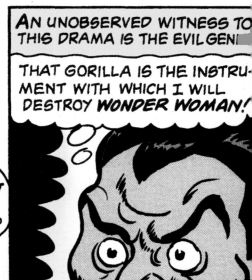

Robert Kanigher

Considered one of DC Comics' most prolific writers, Robert Kanigher (1915–2002) proved adaptable to any character or genre. After writing for other publishers, he arrived at DC Comics in 1945 and was quickly added to its editorial staff. There he remained until 1968, only to return for a brief stint from 1973–5. He pounded out stories every morning and night, and during his lunch hour, filling the gaps in everyone's schedule. In addition to his twenty-year tenure with Wonder Woman, following Marston's death, Kanigher developed DC's war line, writing Sgt. Rock stories and scripting a revival of the Flash, thereby signaling the birth of comics' Silver Age.

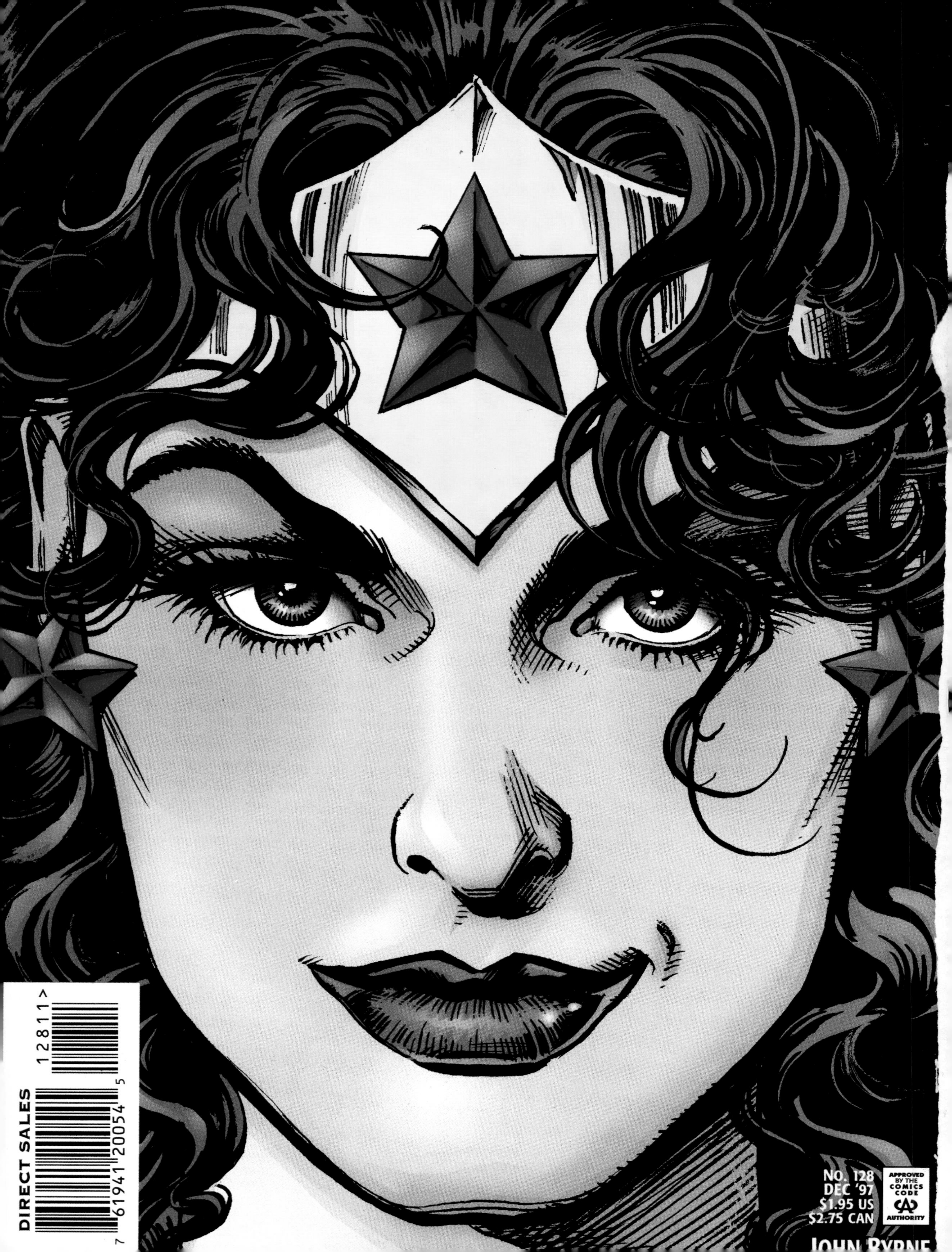

DIRECT SALES
NO. 128
DEC '97
$1.95 US
$2.75 CAN
APPROVED BY THE COMICS CODE AUTHORITY